RETHINKING SOCIAL ACTION THROUGH MUSIC

Rethinking Social Action through Music

The Search for Coexistence and Citizenship in Medellín's Music Schools

Geoffrey Baker

https://www.openbookpublishers.com

© 2021 Geoffrey Baker

This work is licensed under a Creative Commons Attribution 4.0 International license (CC BY 4.0). This license allows you to share, copy, distribute and transmit the text; to adapt the text and to make commercial use of the text providing attribution is made to the authors (but not in any way that suggests that they endorse you or your use of the work). Attribution should include the following information:

Geoffrey Baker, *Rethinking Social Action through Music: The Search for Coexistence and Citizenship in Medellín's Music Schools*. Cambridge, UK: Open Book Publishers, 2021, https://doi.org/10.11647/OBP.0243

In order to access detailed and updated information on the license please visit https://doi.org/10.11647/OBP.0243#copyright

Further details about CC BY licenses are available at https://creativecommons.org/licenses/by/4.0/

All external links were active at the time of publication unless otherwise stated and have been archived via the Internet Archive Wayback Machine at https://archive.org/web

Updated digital material and resources associated with this volume are available at https://doi.org/10.11647/OBP.0243#resources

Every effort has been made to identify and contact copyright holders and any omission or error will be corrected if notification is made to the publisher.

ISBN Paperback: 9781800641266
ISBN Hardback: 9781800641273
ISBN Digital (PDF): 9781800641280
ISBN Digital ebook (epub): 9781800641297
ISBN Digital ebook (mobi): 9781800641303
ISBN XML: 9781800641310
DOI: 10.11647/OBP.0243

Cover image: Medellin, Colombia. Photo by Kobby Mendez on Unsplash at https://unsplash.com/photos/emtQBNCrU3Q. Cover design by Anna Gatti.

The dominant systems of education are based on three principles—or assumptions at least—that are exactly opposite to how human lives are actually lived. [...] First, they promote standardization and a narrow view of intelligence when human talents are diverse and personal. Second, they promote compliance when cultural progress and achievement depend on the cultivation of imagination and creativity. Third, they are linear and rigid when the course of each human life, including yours, is organic and largely unpredictable. As the rate of change continues to accelerate, building new forms of education on these alternative principles is not a romantic whimsy: it's essential to personal fulfillment and to the sustainability of the world we are now creating.

Sir Ken Robinson

—Pero una cosa es creer en la música como un oficio, y otra prometer que salvaremos a un país o a la humanidad con ella —contestó Sánchez.

Pablo Montoya, *La escuela de música*

For Miranda

Table of Contents

List of Acronyms	xi
Acknowledgements	xiii
Introduction	1
PART I	
1. Creating, Redirecting, and Reforming the Red	39
2. The Red Pushes Back: Tensions, Debates, and Resistance	99
3. The Red through a Social Lens	153
4. The New Image of Medellín to the World	209
PART II	
5. Change	265
6. Challenges	315
7. Possibilities of Transformation	351
Afterword	383
Bibliography	411
List of Figures	443
Index	447

List of Acronyms

ACI	Agency for Cooperation and Investment
ASA	Art as Social Action
BIPOC	Black, Indigenous, and People of Colour
BLM	Black Lives Matter
CLCS	Conservatory Lab Charter School
CM	Community Music
ESI	El Sistema-inspired
IDB	Inter-American Development Bank
ISME	International Society for Music Education
LAO	League of American Orchestras
MVLM	Medellín Vive La Música
NEOJIBA	Núcleos Estaduais de Orquestras Juvenis e Infantis da Bahia
OG	Orquestra Geração
PBL	Project-Based Learning
SATM	Social Action Through Music
SBYO	Simón Bolívar Youth Orchestra
SIG	Special Interest Group
SIMM	Social Impact of Making Music
SJME	Social Justice in Music Education
TED	Technology, Entertainment, Design

Geoffrey Baker is Professor of Music at Royal Holloway, University of London, and Director of Research at the music charity Agrigento. He is the author of three previous books and numerous essays and documentary films on music in Latin America. For his blog and further information, please visit https://geoffbakermusic.co.uk.

Acknowledgments

A book such as this, founded on fieldwork, is a collective construction. So much of it is based on conversations and interviews, reading and listening to others' ideas, and watching others at work, that the employees and students of the Red (the Network of Music Schools of Medellín) are really co-creators. I am extremely grateful to all of them for their warmth, openness, and patience. I particularly thank everyone who agreed to be interviewed or who conversed with me at greater length. The list would be too long to name everyone, but in the process of writing this book I have relistened to every interview and reread every field note, so nothing and no one has been forgotten. While it is inevitable that my perspective will not reflect the views of everyone in such a large organization and will contradict the opinions of some, I learnt from every encounter, conversation, and observation, and I applaud all those who have played a part in the Red's search for coexistence and citizenship through music education.

I am indebted to the general directors who opened the doors of the Red to me and kept them open at different times over a period of eight years: Marta Eugenia Arango, Ana Cecilia Restrepo, Juan Fernando Giraldo, and Vania Abello. I was also fortunate to receive the support of Mábel Herrera at the Ministry of Civic Culture. I am hugely grateful to Aníbal Parra and Luis Fernando Franco, who were vital pieces of the puzzle and left a significant mark on this book. Their professional and personal support was invaluable.

A number of people with expertise in Social Action Through Music or closely related fields agreed to read and comment on my draft manuscript. My warmest thanks to them for undertaking such a major task. In alphabetical order: Dr Christine D'Alexander, Northern Illinois University, Co-Chair of the ISME Music Education for Social Change SIG, Teaching Artist and Program Director at YOLA (2011–17); Dr Anna

Bull, Portsmouth University, author of *Class, Control, and Classical Music* (OUP, 2019); Dr Louise Godwin, musician, researcher, and arts manager, formerly with an El Sistema-inspired program in Australia; Dr Graça Mota, Porto Polytechnic, former chair of the ISME El Sistema SIG; Dr Ludim Pedroza, Texas State University, Venezuelan author of academic articles on El Sistema; Dr Andrea Rodríguez, researcher and National Psychosocial Lead at the Colombian program Batuta; and Professor John Sloboda, OBE, FBA, Guildhall School of Music & Drama, President of SIMM (Social Impact of Making Music). Additionally, Ana Cecelia Restrepo (former general director of the Red) read and responded to Chapters 1 and 2. I am very grateful to all of these readers for their time, effort, and comments. Nevertheless, any errors, misunderstandings, and flaws are entirely my responsibility.

There are many others—musicians, scholars, and educators from around the world—who have played a less direct but no less important role in my research over the last decade: sharing their ideas and experiences; inviting me to share my own perspectives in a variety of academic and non-academic spaces; and, above all, offering moral support, giving me vital sustenance to continue with the fascinating but not always popular work of thinking critically about Social Action Through Music. I cannot name everyone here, but they know who they are and I gratefully recognize and remember their input. Nevertheless, I would like to make special mention of Lukas Pairon, John Sloboda, and many others at SIMM (both board members and event participants) for creating an invaluable space for critical thinking about the social impact of making music in recent years. I must also recognize the numerous Venezuelan musicians who have supported me, whether behind the scenes or, like Gabriela Montero, Gustavo Medina, and Luigi Mazzocchi, in public. I know both the value and the potential cost of such support.

A special note of thanks to Louise Godwin for many stimulating conversations about music and social action, for continually drawing important ideas to my attention, and for putting up with a year of "once the book is out of the way..."; Natalia Puerta, who made some important introductions in Medellín; and D., whose direct help with the fieldwork was invaluable and whose indirect help with this book has been immeasurable.

I gratefully acknowledge support from the Arts and Humanities Research Council, whose Leadership Fellowship (grant reference AH/P011683/1) enabled the fieldwork; Royal Holloway University of London, which assisted throughout the process and provided research leave to allow the drafting of the book manuscript; and Agrigento, whose trustees were patient and understanding during the final stages of writing and publication, permitting me to finish the project calmly. The Music & Letters Trust and Royal Holloway generously contributed towards the publication costs, and the Red kindly provided some of the photos.

My thanks to all at Open Book Publishers, particularly Alessandra Tosi, Lucy Barnes, Anna Gatti, and Luca Baffa. I am thrilled to have the opportunity to publish this book in open access so that it can be freely available to readers in Latin America and around the world.

Fig. 1. Archive of Red de Escuelas de Música. CC BY.

Introduction

> Music education is far more ambiguous morally than might be thought.
>
> Richard Matthews, "Beyond Toleration—Facing the Others"

> Everything I do in the Red, I do because I love this program…
> that's why I'm always so agitated
>
> Music school director

> In less than three years Medellín will see something almost unimaginable: some two thousand children and youths from popular neighbourhoods will be members of a huge band. But a symphonic one. […] In the hands of the young people, the flutes, saxophones, violins, trumpets, clarinets, violoncellos, trombones, euphoniums, snares, bass drums, and cymbals will sound in unison to tell Medellín that a new era of music has begun in the city, their musical vocation has awoken, and their instruments have managed to unite what weapons tore apart.

Thus began a 1997 article entitled "Music schools: more civility and culture" ("Escuelas de Música" 1997, 6).[1] Did music education manage "to unite what weapons tore apart" and bring civility and peace to Medellín, the most dangerous city on Earth?

From the 1970s to the early 1990s, Colombia's second city was home to Pablo Escobar's Medellín Cartel, and it sat in the midst of a national conflict that had been bubbling for decades. It gained notoriety as the murder capital of the world. In the 1990s, aiming to reverse the city's fortunes, the municipal and regional governments produced several strategic development plans that led to some striking urban policies, the best known of which, implemented by Mayors Sergio Fajardo (2004–07)

---

1   All translations by the author.

and Alonso Salazar (2008–11), was labelled "social urbanism." Many of the city's iconic features date from this period. Library parks, designed by leading architects, were constructed in some of the city's most disadvantaged neighbourhoods, and cable cars appeared to carry people up the steep hillsides that led to them. Another novel transport solution, an outdoor escalator, put the violence-ravaged barrio of Comuna 13 on the tourist map.

Alongside such attention-grabbing architectural and infrastructural projects, successive city governments invested in education and culture, which were seen as central pillars of urban transformation ("Medellín" n.d.). The year 1997 saw the opening of the first six schools of the Red de Escuelas de Música de Medellín—the Network of Music Schools of Medellín—after the signing of two Municipal Accords the previous year. A third agreement in 1998 established citywide youth music ensembles, most notably a youth symphony orchestra. The Red grew quickly and came to encompass twenty-seven music schools, focusing primarily on classical music, funded by the city government, and serving around 5000 students. Most of the schools were located in *barrios populares*, or "popular neighbourhoods," as low-to-middle income sectors are known. The Red was presented as a response to the acute problem of violent crime that such neighbourhoods faced; it defined itself as a social program, its goal to promote peaceful coexistence.[2]

During this period of intensive urban development, Medellín's murder rate fell dramatically—from 381 per 100,000 in 1991 to 20 in 2015. The city was also garlanded with many international awards, such as the World's Most Innovative City, the World's Smartest City, and the Lee Kuan Yew World City Prize. Medellín became a global showpiece of urban renewal. Journalists and policy-makers from around the world began speaking of "the Medellín Miracle."

The Red, too, garnered international acclaim. From 2000, its ensembles began a series of overseas tours, the second of which culminated in a performance for the Pope at the Vatican. Foreign conductors and coaches visited the program regularly to work with the students. The Red enjoyed a boost in visibility a few years later as the

---

[2] The Spanish term *convivencia* has more positive connotations than the English "coexistence." It suggests more than just tolerating others. There are hints of the English "conviviality."

international boom of Venezuela's El Sistema, with its slogan of "social action through music" (SATM), led to global interest in Latin American youth orchestras. The Red became widely known as another SATM success story and an integral part of the Medellín Miracle.

In 2012, I made my first visit to Medellín. I met up with figures in the city's cultural scene and explored several neighbourhoods. I was impressed by the friendliness and dynamism of those whom I met, whose projects included not just the Red but also hip-hop schools, a record label and production company, and a "free culture" enterprise.

I was in the midst of writing a book about El Sistema (Baker 2014). This program had gained global renown, attracting labels like "the Venezuelan musical miracle"; yet, over several years of research, I had discovered significant gaps between its public image and internal realities and a striking disjuncture with contemporary thinking on music education and social development. I was fascinated by Medellín after my brief visit to the city, but I also saw the Red and other cultural programs as addressing some of my concerns about the Venezuelan paradigm. Medellín and the Red found their way into the final part of the book, where I discussed advances in and alternatives to the Venezuelan model.

The current book picks up from that point. It is a "post-El Sistema" project—not just in terms of my own trajectory, but also because it focuses on a program that has tried to move beyond the Venezuelan model, and it is based on research conducted during a period when El Sistema's fortunes have waned significantly. Venezuela's prolonged political and economic crisis has led to an exodus of students, performers, teachers, and conductors; the international tours have ceased; and the program's weaknesses have been underscored by copious recent research (e.g. Logan 2015a; Pedroza 2015; Scripp 2016a, 2016b; Fink 2016; Logan 2016; Baker and Frega 2016; Baker and Frega 2018; Baker, Bull, and Taylor 2018; Baker 2018). However, as with other such "posts-," this does not mean that the original term is buried and forgotten. On the contrary, El Sistema hangs over this book as it hangs over the field of SATM. For all its recent travails, it continues to be the dominant model and main reference point for SATM internationally. It has been copied in dozens of countries around the world, and many of the issues in the wider field can be traced back to Venezuela. Any serious conversation about SATM needs to include El Sistema.

While this book was always intended as a sequel to my previous one, it turned out to be more closely connected than I had initially imagined. I learnt that El Sistema was not only an inspiration for but also a direct formative influence on the Red: their founders worked closely together, and teachers from the Venezuelan program travelled regularly to Medellín during the first half-dozen years. The Red was profoundly shaped by El Sistema, giving the latter a more prominent role in this book than I had originally anticipated.

I formulated a research project focusing on three issues. Firstly, I wanted to continue thinking about social development through music education. My research in Venezuela had revealed a program with serious flaws, but were the problems specific to that institution or were they inherent in the model? Could SATM work better elsewhere? I had seen Medellín as a ray of hope after all the problems that I had discovered in Venezuela, but would my initial impressions hold up under closer inspection?

Secondly, I wanted to devote more attention to SATM and citizenship education. I had previously argued that, despite the frequent linking of El Sistema with this term, the program generally produced loyal subjects, trained to obey authority, rather than citizens, educated to participate in democratic processes (Baker 2016a). Since the Red is managed by Medellín's Ministry of Civic Culture and emphasizes citizenly values in its official vision, exploring more deeply the possibilities of SATM as citizenship education seemed a logical focus for my new research.

Thirdly, I wondered what part music education might have played in Medellín's process of urban renewal. Social urbanism included significant investment in education and culture, and journalistic and popular accounts of a city transformed often highlighted artistic projects. What might research reveal about the role of the Red in the Medellín Miracle and about the effectiveness of SATM? And what might critical debates around social urbanism tell us about socially oriented music education?

Social Action through Music

I define SATM as a field centred in Latin America, where the largest and best-known examples are located, but with strong cultural and ideological ties to Europe and with a global reach, since El Sistema has served as an inspiration around the world. SATM consists of music education programs with a number of characteristics. They identify social action (or a related term, such as social inclusion) as the primary or at least an important goal. They place large ensembles at the centre of learning—often but not always the orchestra. Classical music originally took pride of place and, while there has been some diversification in terms of repertoire, in many instances it still does. SATM is usually more intensive than most extra-curricular music programs (El Sistema's intermediate and advanced students often attend daily for several hours or more), and participation is free (or more rarely, at low cost). In Latin America, programs are often intermediate to large in size, reaching thousands of participants, rather than the millions who might (in theory) be exposed to school music or the dozens or hundreds in a community music program; but SATM programs in the global North are frequently smaller.

The origins of the label SATM are obscure, but it appears to date from the mid-1990s. It was popularized by El Sistema but may have been borrowed from a smaller Brazilian program of the same name (Baker 2014). It is also associated with El Sistema's funding by the Inter-American Development Bank (IDB): it adorns the program's Caracas headquarters, built with an IDB loan. The term was not widely used in Medellín, but it is an appropriate one for a program that was shaped by El Sistema, was created around the time the label emerged, and prioritized a social objective. Also, the Red, like El Sistema, was supported by the IDB in its first phase.

Musically and pedagogically speaking, SATM owes considerable allegiance to older practices and philosophies of music education of European origin (including ones that date back to the Spanish Conquest), and it shows parallels with the Suzuki method. It therefore sits somewhere between conventional collective music education and newer fields such as community music (CM) and music education for social change. Its practices are closer to the former, while its aims or claims are similar to the latter.

As such, SATM can be approached from a variety of points of view. Since its model is similar to that of youth orchestras and bands around the globe, music education research can shed considerable light on its strengths and limitations. I took this approach in my previous book, and as many of the issues are broadly the same across the SATM field, I will not repeat those arguments or the literature on which they are based here. Research on social justice in music education (SJME), which has seen considerable growth in recent years, would seem another logical vantage point. However, SATM occupies an ambiguous, liminal position with respect to this area of research, as with its practice. In terms of social aims, there are apparent points of contact, yet SATM also embodies many conventional practices and aspirations that this field critiques, above all a focus on large ensembles and classical music performance, and so it is far from a favoured model in SJME research. *The Oxford Handbook of Social Justice in Music Education* (Benedict et al. 2015) devotes just one of its forty-two chapters to El Sistema, and the perspective therein is distinctly ambivalent (Shieh 2015). There are occasional references to the approach and practices that it incarnates in other chapters, but they are strikingly critical (e.g. McCarthy 2015; Kelly-McHale and Abril 2015; Matthews 2015). Gaztambide-Fernández and Rose (2015) critique the Venezuelan model directly, and their analysis lays bare just how far it lies from contemporary thinking on SJME. This disjuncture is also evident in the terminology: El Sistema does not refer to social justice but rather to social action and social inclusion, which are ideologically distinct.

Both the overlap and the tensions may be illuminated by considering the twin aims of the handbook. The blurb on its dust jacket begins:

> Music education has historically had a tense relationship with social justice. On the one hand, educators concerned with music practices have long preoccupied themselves with ideas of open participation and the potentially transformative capacity that musical interaction fosters. On the other hand, they have often done so while promoting and privileging a particular set of musical practices, traditions, and forms of musical knowledge, which has in turn alienated and even excluded many children from music education opportunities.

The book examines both sides of the equation: it echoes SATM in exploring "social justice in action," but whereas SATM has historically focused on the end result (social action *through* music), this handbook is equally concerned with the means (social justice *in* music), so it also explores "cycles of injustice that might be perpetuated by music pedagogy." (Indeed, a central implication of the book is that there can be no social justice *through* music education without social justice *in* music education.) This twin aim not only distinguishes SJME from SATM, but it also highlights the latter as an ambiguous model: simultaneously a potential route to justice and site of injustice. El Sistema and its practices feature in both sections of the book, evoked as both an example of social justice in action and an object of criticism; Shieh's chapter alone, even though it appears in the section "Social justice in practice," raises critical questions about El Sistema's social justice credentials, going so far as to describe the program's conception of poverty as "grotesque" (2015, 574). So while one might look at the book's title and logically conclude that SATM fell either inside or outside this field of study, neither is entirely true: it straddles the boundary, somewhat uncomfortably.

Similarly, there have been some efforts to draw together SATM with the field of community music (CM), but *The Oxford Handbook of Community Music* (Bartleet and Higgins 2018a) barely mentions El Sistema, and many of the values that CM embodies and upholds run directly contrary to the Venezuelan program. While El Sistema was founded by the conservative politician and economist José Antonio Abreu, a minister of state who was a right-hand man of several presidents, Bartleet and Higgins (2018b) see the roots of CM in the UK counter-culture era of the late 1960s and 1970s, and Price (2018, x) writes of the field's "punk ethic" in the 1980s. While Abreu consorted with the architects of neoliberalism in Venezuela, CM emerged from the socialist-leaning community arts scene. Boeskov (2019, 114) characterizes CM as non-hierarchical, anti-authoritarian, and "operating from outside or on the margins of the established, the authorized, the legitimate and dominant culture"—a description that could hardly be further from El Sistema, which came to operate out of the Office of the President. If CM upholds cultural democracy, SATM embodies the opposing notion of democratization of culture. SATM looks less like CM's sibling than its neoliberal alter-ego.[3]

The picture from the research field is thus somewhat paradoxical. El Sistema is probably the best-known example of socially oriented music education among the general public, and it is the most widely reported in the media, which has frequently presented it as a miracle story; yet it plays only a minor role in cornerstone texts in the academic field and analyses of its approach are often unflattering. More positive accounts of socially oriented music education in such sources are generally focused on practices and values (such as bottom-up, non-formal, or creative) that are strikingly different from SATM.

SATM has spawned its own sub-field of research, running in parallel to—and sometimes blissful ignorance of—the fields cited above. The problematic nature of this sub-field is evident in a literature review (Creech et al. 2016) that is both a valuable resource and a potential minefield: professional, peer-reviewed research is mixed with student dissertations and non-academic advocacy without any sort of quality control, which makes it an excellent starting point for further research in responsible hands but has enabled others to present a distorted vision of relevant scholarship. Nevertheless, there are two broad points that can be derived from this literature review and from surveying more recent publications: firstly, writing on SATM is extremely varied, some would say polarized, embracing positions ranging from fervent advocacy to trenchant criticism; and secondly, there is an increasing amount of peer-reviewed scholarship at the critical end of the spectrum (in addition to the sources above, see e.g. Allan et al. 2010; Baker 2015a; Bull 2016; Dobson 2016; Rosabal-Coto 2016; Kuuse, Lindgren, and Skåreus 2016; Baker 2016b; Baker 2016c; Hopkins, Provenzano, and Spencer 2017; Rimmer 2018; Rimmer 2020). SATM has generally been presented to the world as a stunning success, worthy of extensive emulation; but from the perspective of research, matters look considerably more complicated.

---

3 See, however, Krönig (2019) for a complicating view of CM.

Ambiguity and Ambivalence

There is a major current of research that focuses on the positive potential of music, exemplified by Susan Hallam's (2010) landmark article "The power of music." I align myself with a different current, one centred on ambivalence about music and the ambiguity of its effects. This is not to question the value of the former but rather to suggest that it only tells part of the story and there is nothing inherently beneficent about music. The words "ambiguous" and "ambivalent" point to contradictory characteristics, feelings, and interpretations. When applied to music, they evoke conflicting aspects, contrasting effects, and mixed views.

Belfiore and Bennett (2008) demonstrate that for most of the history of Western civilization, music and the arts have been subjected to contradictory interpretations; there are both positive and negative traditions, going back nearly 2500 years. The negative tradition, beginning with Plato, saw the arts as a source of corruption and distraction and as having potentially damaging effects on individuals and society. Belfiore (2012) argues that historically this perspective carried significant weight, and the positive stance arose mainly as a reaction against the influence and popularity of the negative view. For example, Aristotle's attempt to salvage the mimetic arts was a response to Plato's condemnation. However, as Belfiore and Bennett note, the negative tradition has been almost entirely displaced by the positive one since the 1980s as the need to argue for arts subsidy in terms of social and economic benefits has taken hold. Invoking the negative tradition today is near heresy. Nevertheless, for most of the last 2500 years, human beings have not regarded the arts as necessarily a positive social force.

There is a growing academic literature that focuses on such ambiguity in music, including in "musical-social work" (Ansdell 2014, 193) like SATM. Hesmondhalgh (2013) centres ambivalence to the extent that his book *Why Music Matters* is labelled a "manifesto for a more ambivalent music sociology" by Bull (2019, xviii), whose research on class and control in classical music education is another exemplar of this genre. In CM, Boeskov's (2019) PhD thesis is subtitled "Exploring ambiguous musical practice in a Palestinian refugee camp," while Kertz-Welzel (2016, 116) notes: "The ambiguity of community music is a well-known problem." Matthews (2015, 238) opens his essay on SJME with the statement: "Music education is far more ambiguous morally than might be thought." Boia and Boal-Palheiros (2017) highlight ambivalence, complexity, and contradiction in their study of the Portuguese El Sistema-inspired program Orquestra Geração.

If there is a body of work that addresses this topic directly, there is much more that sheds indirect light on it, revealing contradictory processes and effects and illustrating the complexity of practice and research in fields such as SATM (e.g. Sarazin 2017; Rimmer 2018; Fairbanks 2019), CM (e.g. Krönig 2019; Ansdell et al. 2020), music education (e.g. Bradley 2009; Bull 2019), participatory arts (e.g. Thompson 2009; Daykin et al. 2020), and cultural policy and planning (e.g. Belfiore 2002, 2009; Belfiore and Bennett 2010; Lees and Melhuish 2015; Stevenson 2017).[4] As Bowman (2009a, 11) argues: "Music and music education are not unconditional goods. They can harm as well as heal.... [I]ntended results on one level may be undesirable on another." Elsewhere, he writes (2009b, 125–26): "Music's performative and participatory power has both a potentially dark side and a progressive one."

Gaztambide-Fernández (2013, 214) argues that "claims about the power of the arts to inspire, to liberate, or to transform tend to obscure both the complexities and the possibilities that lurk within experiences with the arts in education." Cultural practices

> are constituted through that very complexity: the ballet is beautiful not despite but because many young dancers starve themselves to look the part; the orchestra sounds magnificent not despite but because of the militaristic regimes that rule how many musicians are trained; we need to embrace such complexity and foment an understanding of the arts in education through a more robust language that does not require that all worthy experiences involving symbolic creativity be defined a priori as both good and predictable.

If the El Sistema boom has seen classical music touted as a tool for social inclusion, Gioia (2018) explores its exclusionary uses as a deterrent aimed at stigmatized social groups, or

---

4 A special issue of *Music and Arts in Action* on contradiction, ambivalence, and complexity in El Sistema and youth orchestras is also in preparation at the time of writing.

a sonic border fence protecting privileged areas from common crowds. [...] So our metaphor for music's power must change from panacea to punishment, from unifying to separating force, as its purpose slips from aesthetic or spiritual ennoblement into economic relocation. Mozart has traded in a career as doctor for the soul to become an eviction agent for the poor.

In the same vein, Cheng (2019, 47) notes that classical music is used in public spaces to repel "the homeless, the would-be criminals, black and brown youths, and other people who are presumably up to no good"—ironically, the same social constituency that SATM is supposed to redeem, according to its official narrative.

The "power of music" ideology has been critiqued from various angles. Clarke (2018) highlights music's relational character, which sheds doubt on the appropriateness of speaking about music as though it were a thing that possessed power and underlines that its effects can never be taken for granted. In his critique of the "rhetoric of effects," Gaztambide-Fernández (2013) argues that "the arts don't do anything"; rather, artistic forms are something that people do. Cobo Dorado (2015) and Henley (2018) suggest that in the field of music education, it is pedagogy rather than music that potentially—though not necessarily—generates desirable social effects. Odendaal et al. (2019) argue that the findings of neuroscientific studies of music's impact are often exaggerated in their "translation" to mainstream and social media, while Sala and Gobet (2020) roundly refute the dominant argument about the cognitive effects of music education.

Other academic fields provide further reasons not to assume the efficacy of any social intervention. Ambivalence over the theories, practices, and effects of development have long been standard fare among scholars (e.g. Ferguson 1994; Escobar 1995). Easterly (2006) critiques utopianism in development, while Cornwall and Eade (2010) display a healthy scepticism towards the field's "buzzwords and fuzzwords." Ramalingam's (2013) milestone book on development and complexity theory, *Aid on the Edge of Chaos*, serves as a valuable example, particularly since much music-making, too, exists "on the edge of chaos" and might be thought of as a complex adaptive system. As such, it can have varied effects and produce unintended consequences, which makes either predicting or proving its social impact very difficult. As Ramalingam argues, blueprints and "best practices" may work at some times and places but not others. "Obvious" solutions can turn out to be counter-productive in practice. The question of whether foreign aid really works has proven unanswerable, but, in some cases, it has made matters worse for the poor and vulnerable. Ramalingam describes it as "less a global welfare system and more a global postcode lottery with few handpicked winners and many, many more losers" (8). His insistence on complexity serves as a warning against the over-simplification of music's social effects.

Scholarship on public art and cultural policy, too, reveals scepticism and fully-fledged debates about the potential of artistic interventions—even the best intentioned—to have mixed or downright negative impacts and problematic unintended consequences. There has been much discussion of "artwashing"—projects that may have laudable elements, but which are conceived as cover for other (usually economic) objectives and may contribute to problematic dynamics such as gentrification. Some argue that culture has become a favoured area for sticking-plaster solutions to the damaging social and economic effects of neoliberal policies (e.g. Logan 2016).

Of particular relevance to SATM, scholarship on after-school programs reveals an equally ambiguous picture. It might be assumed that such programs have a positive impact on youth outcomes, but many studies have found no or even negative effects (e.g. Gottfredson et al. 2010; Taheri and Welsh 2015; Bernatzky and Cid 2018). Urban cultural planning generates feel-good language and there is widespread belief in its value, but the evidence for its efficacy is mixed and it rarely achieves the ambitions set for it (Stevenson 2017). In short, many experts in a range of fields adjacent to SATM take nothing for granted and approach common assumptions about the impact of social and artistic interventions with some scepticism.

An ambivalent approach to music may derive from any number of sources, including scholarship and personal experience. In my case, it comes primarily from my own historical and ethnographic research. I spent many years studying Latin American musicians (past and present) as liminal figures, embroiled in complex negotiations over power (Baker 2008; 2011). I have also undertaken two years of fieldwork on SATM, as well as a decade of complementary and online research, giving me ample opportunity to witness its complexity first-hand. In Medellín, many people expressed a mixture of fondness and concern about the Red. I witnessed elation and arguments, tears of joy and tears of sadness. In El Sistema and among the first generation of Red students (who were overseen by Venezuelans), I repeatedly encountered a love-hate relationship with music education: as Cheng (2019) puts it, quite a few loved music till it hurt. The intensity of these programs led to intense experiences for participants at a formative and impressionable age. Yet alongside the stories of socializing and enjoyment were others about excessively long hours, authoritarian conductors, and abrasive teachers. For some, SATM was both magical and abusive at the same time. As Gaztambide-Fernández writes, joy and suffering were bound up together in a mutually constitutive relationship.

However, one does not need to do fieldwork or pore over archives or scholarly tomes to question the positive narrative about music. There is plenty of evidence closer to hand. While there is an impressive body of research on music's beneficial effects on health and wellbeing, the music profession is also associated with a high incidence of mental and physical health problems.[5] Precarity, low pay, and overwork are commonplace in the performing arts professions.[6] Classical music is often the focus of exalted claims about its ennobling powers, and SATM rests on a narrative about classical music education as a route to personal salvation, yet such stories elide pervasive allegations of endemic sexual harassment and abuse in specialist music schools and conservatoires (e.g. Pace 2015; Krafeld 2017; Newey 2020) and revelations about the misdeeds of some of the field's most illustrious figures. Teraud (2018) notes that "classical music has always enabled bad behaviour," while Lebrecht's (2018) article on "sex, lies and conductors" examines "the sordid underbelly of conducting where sex is considered a perk of the job." As such articles imply, contradiction is nothing new: Reverend Haweis extolled the uplifting effects of great music in his enormously popular 1871 book *Music and Morals*; he also had an illegitimate daughter by one of his parishioners (Bull 2019). As Geir Johansen asked at the

---

5   On the music profession and poor mental and physical health, see "HMUK" (2017) and Lebrecht (2017); on the orchestral profession and performance-related injuries, see "Los músicos salen" (2019).
6   On poor pay and precarity, see "ArtsPay" (2019); Loar (2019).

Social Impact of Making Music conference in London in 2017, tongue only partly in cheek: if music is so transformative, how come musicians aren't better people?

Over-Simplification

If recognition of music's ambiguity has led to considerable ambivalence on the part of scholars, the same is not true of the music sector, or at least of its public face. As Belfiore and Bennett (2008, 192–93) note, "understanding the claims for the power of the arts involves the engagement with some highly complex intellectual issues. However, public pronouncements about the value or impact of the arts rarely reflect this complexity and tend to fall back instead on a somewhat ritualistic use of the 'rhetoric of transformation.'" Cheng's (2019) study offers one explanation: the "musical mystique," as he calls it, which has an enduring hold, even over those who should know better. We should be tired of correlations between a love of classical music and ethical personhood, he suggests, but the regularity with which the trump card of classical-music-loving Nazis has to be brought out underlines the pervasiveness and persistence of the fantasy of music as an ennobling force. Cheng argues that this is not a simple matter of knowledge or ignorance: rather, the musical mystique is enticing—a siren song.

SATM illustrates Belfiore and Bennett's point, and its rhetoric of transformation undoubtedly reflects Cheng's "musical mystique," but it also has more expedient roots. The concept of SATM was seized upon in Venezuela in the mid-1990s because of its utility as a funding lever; it was the key to El Sistema's expansion. As Spruce (2017, 721) notes, "discourses are not always as they seem—self-evident and neutral—but function as the means by which hegemonic groups sustain their influence and interests." El Sistema's international diffusion at least partly reflects these origins. If it has attracted idealists, it has also become—in some hands—a business, a professional lifeline, or a marketing strategy. Fairbanks (2019, 13), former director of a US Sistema program, has written about his growing doubts over "whether Sistema programmes were truly about empowering marginalised youth, or whether they might be more accurately described as ventures in musical entrepreneurship, with 'social justice' being exploited as means for obtaining vast amounts of funding."⁷ An artist management agency run by former El Sistema employees promises: "WE WILL MAKE A SOCIAL IMPACT ON EVERY PLACE OUR ARTISTS PERFORM."⁸ Such a statement is an absurdity from the perspective of research on the social impact of the arts, but it makes sense from the point of view of distinguishing one's product in a crowded marketplace. The rhetoric of transformation is a currency, and the stronger and simpler its message, the more it is worth.

There are other pressures and incentives that lead away from complex questions and towards over-simplification. In the UK, at least, arts practitioners—like academics—are increasingly ruled by a social impact agenda when it comes to securing funding, which hardly favours modesty. Many of us are obliged to play a game that rewards over-claiming with respect to impact, and many of us need a simplified sales pitch to explain to others the value of what we do.

Then there is the "ideas industry" (Drezner 2017), in which public intellectuals have been displaced by "thought leaders" with an evangelical desire to proselytize their views and change the world. Simple "big ideas" are the most valuable commodity in this "marketplace of ideas," while criticism and complexity—the bedrocks of academic research—are a lesser currency. What sells are often ideas that *appear* true because they cohere with the way people expect the world to be—simple, predictable, linear. SATM rests on the idea that the orchestra is, in Gustavo Dudamel's words, "a model for an ideal global society" (Lee 2012). In reality the professional orchestral world is no bed of roses. Were collective music-making as powerful and beneficial as is sometimes claimed, one would expect orchestral musicians to be some of the happiest and healthiest people on earth, but there is a body of academic research and anecdotal evidence to suggest otherwise (see Baker 2014; Dickenson 2019). Nevertheless, the youth orchestra as a model of social harmony and inclusion is one of these "big ideas" that *feels* right, and it was consolidated by the heart of the ideas industry: TED (Technology, Entertainment, Design). Abreu was awarded a TED prize

---

7   Spruce (2017, 720) also raises concerns that the term social justice "is reached for by groups and organisations as a means of justifying and promoting their approaches to music education and to gain political approbation and consequently privileged access to funding."
8   Quatre Klammer, "About Us", https://www.quatreklammer.com/aboutus.

in 2009; his talk on El Sistema was watched by over a million viewers; and he spent his prize on El Sistema advocacy in the US, founding the Abreu Fellows Program at the New England Conservatory.[9]

Celebrities, journalists, and documentary makers, too, have brought SATM to a wide and avid audience. El Sistema has been promoted by the likes of Simon Rattle, Plácido Domingo, and Claudio Abbado, and eulogized in widely disseminated films such as *Tocar y Luchar* (2006) and *El Sistema: Music to Change Life* (2009). But such parties are usually more interested in dramatic stories of salvation and redemption through the power of music than in digging into more complex realities. The simplified "rhetoric of transformation" provides much better copy for books, articles, films, liner notes, and concert programs than the practical and philosophical challenges of music and social change that many researchers know so well.

However, research is not immune to such tendencies. Bartleet and Higgins (2018, 11) allude to "overly sentimentalized notions of community music in the literature [as well as] in broader public advocacy campaigns for musical participation." Some quantitative evaluations of SATM have relied on future projections of social impact based on simplistic models of human behaviour and optimistic financial calculations (Logan 2015b; Scruggs 2015), or have used questionable methodologies to analyse existing achievements (Baker, Bull, and Taylor 2018), and most avoid more than the most fleeting reference to the growing critical literature on SATM; they appear to be designed more for securing funding than for identifying critical issues. Qualitative research, meanwhile, can easily go astray if the researcher is insufficiently experienced, fails to ask the right questions or look in the right places, or is not attuned to music's ambiguity. A particular strength of Cheng's study is his acknowledgment of "a battle between the sucker and skeptic who dance within each of us" (2019, 39)—scholars such as himself included. He admits, "without shame or guilt, my susceptibility to the musical mystique. I can verbalize [...] why this mystique can be problematic and even dangerous. But it hardly means my mind and body are now impenetrable by lines of dangerous thinking" (232). Some research on SATM bears out these words.

---

9   José Antonio Abreu, "The El Sistema music revolution", TED 2009, https://www.ted.com/talks/jose_antonio_abreu_the_el_sistema_music_revolution.

Over-simplified and exaggerated stories about SATM thus come at us from all sides. Advocacy, marketing, big ideas, media narratives, celebrity endorsements, and program evaluations all have their value and their place in the world, but none of them are a simple mirror of SATM's realities. Some accounts are shaped to maximize appeal to readers and viewers, while others aim to promote a program, a sector, or an art form. Most well-known narratives of SATM have their origins in efforts to mobilize support from funders, politicians, institutions, the public, and participants themselves. They project "aspirations, justifications, and claims that help to build external interest and visibility, in particular among potential supporters some distance from the project" (Howell 2017, 240).

Critique

Critical research is important in order to counteract this tendency towards over-simplification and exaggeration and to reveal music's ambiguity and complexity. This step is necessary for SATM for two reasons: gaining a more realistic perspective, understanding how SATM actually operates rather than what it aspires to do, will improve *knowledge about* the field; and highlighting complexity may provoke more discussion, debate, and experimentation, and thus improve *practice within* the field. Critical research enables us to understand the past and present of SATM more deeply and to look towards a better future.

Jorgensen (2001) likens the philosopher of music education to a building inspector who evaluates a construction. In other words, critical scrutiny—while it may not always be welcomed or valued by the builders—is a necessary task, and it may also be generative and even emancipatory. Recognizing problems is an essential first step towards searching for solutions in music education (Bates 2018), while critique may support "the larger project of aligning paradigms of cultural activism with their utopic potential" (Ndaliko 2016, 12). The UK's FailSpace research project focuses on the productive potential of studying failure in the cultural sector, arguing that honesty is important for improvement and "learning from failure should be an integral part of the process of making and implementing cultural projects and policies."[10] (It also notes that such honesty about failure "is not always welcome in formal evaluation processes, which tend to focus on celebratory facts and figures about a project's success and conceal or brush-off negative outcomes or issues.") There may be good reasons to focus on positives (raising the stock of music education, securing funding, boosting self-esteem), but idealistic, sentimental, or kitsch (Kertz-Welzel 2016) portrayals of SATM that exaggerate benefits, elide ambiguities, and minimize problems increase the probability of an education shaped by illusory beliefs rather than rigorous thinking on socially oriented music education. In this sense, utopian perspectives may actually be counterproductive, by obscuring rather than illuminating the complex issues that SATM raises and thereby slowing down necessary reform. The history of El Sistema illustrates the deleterious effect of excessive adulation and banishment of criticism.

The value of critique has been grasped more widely in CM than SATM. Bartleet and Higgins (2018b, 7), for example, "recognize the need for deeper and more critical reflection on the underlying processes and assumptions of community music initiatives," stating that "it is inadequate to simply say 'something miraculous happens' in community music." Dave Camlin concurs: "it's important that all of us working in the cultural sector are able to look really critically at our practices" (Camlin et al. 2020, 166).

The community musician and scholar Gillian Howell has emphasized that, within the field of music and peace-building, the order of good intentions is usually an illusion that gives way in practice to disjunctures and unexpected complexities.[11] For example, she examines (together with Solveig Korum) a long-term Norwegian project for peace and reconciliation in Sri Lanka in which a large investment in music produced a disappointing return, since idealistic intentions and optimistic rhetoric were underpinned by vague, uncritical ideas about the inherent power of music to transform society rather than a detailed, articulated, evidenced theory of change (Korum and Howell 2020). The gaps between official accounts of the cultural sector and what really

---

10 FailSpace, "About", https://failspaceproject.co.uk/about/.
11 Keynote address, 4th SIMM-posium on the Social Impact of Making Music, Bogotá, 26 July 2019.

takes place is also a central focus of FailSpace, which emphasizes the value of acknowledging such gaps in order to foster improvement. Public portrayals of SATM, however, are unduly shaped by the illusory narrative of order and tend to avoid the disjunctures. The gaps are not hidden: take the example of Jonathan Govias, who has documented his journey from guru of the El Sistema-inspired field to arch-critic ("apostle to apostate," as he puts it) in great detail on his widely-read blog.[12] Or the Venezuelan violinist Luigi Mazzocchi, whose somewhat similar trajectory and painstaking critique of El Sistema, his alma mater, were documented by the music education researcher Lawrence Scripp (2016a, 2016b). Yet the public defection of such prominent figures has failed to shift the dominant narrative of SATM in North America. Ambiguity, ambivalence, and complexity are widespread in this sector, but they are rarely countenanced in public discourse.

Indeed, an ambivalent stance often raises hackles in the mission-driven SATM field. In development studies, in which there is a much longer and wider tradition of critical thinking, ambivalence is more of a mainstream position. Ndaliko's (2016, 10) statement that "beneath the utopic idealism of charity as a selfless act of service, doing good is in fact an industry [...] in dire need of scrutiny" would raise few eyebrows in the fields of development or aid. The arts, however, often form an exception, as Ndaliko goes on to argue:

> the universalist humanist appeal of art and creativity allows otherwise rational organizations and individuals to endorse [...] projects whose equivalents would be ludicrous if proposed in the fields of economics, governance, or medicine. But because it is about creativity rather than more quantifiable matters, the whistleblowers join the cheerleaders in celebrating "art" as a set of inherently positive practices and products. (15)

Ndaliko notes that it is particularly hard to acknowledge the value of critical thinking on culture in challenging contexts because art "often becomes a kind of moral oasis that shifts focus away from critical scrutiny of the conditions of its production to sentimental celebration of its very existence" (12). But if we truly believe that music is a potential driver of social change and deserves to be taken seriously as such, then we

---

12 Jonathan Andrew Govias, https://jonathangovias.com/.

need to be willing to apply "the same level of rigor to studying cultural activities as is routinely applied to issues of economics, government, development, and structural aid" (15). As decades of research on development have shown, it is not enough for one's heart to be in the right place.

This does not just mean evaluating policies in order to determine their effectiveness; it also means broader and deeper critique. It is not enough to know whether a program achieves certain goals; it is also necessary to interrogate the validity of those goals and consider cultural, political, philosophical, and ethical questions that they raise (see Belfiore and Bennett 2010; Baker, Bull, and Taylor 2018). As Bartleet and Higgins (2018, 7) argue, we need a "more nuanced approach [that] focuses on *understanding* the changes that are taking place rather than simply *proving* them; the latter can so often happen in advocacy-driven research or in evaluative research undertaken to respond to funding-body requirements."

The urgency of critical thinking in the SATM field is in part a reflection of the zeal with which it has been avoided by El Sistema. SATM's figurehead program has always been action-focused and had little time for reflection, self-criticism, or debate. Its founder's catchphrases—"rest comes with eternal rest"; "double rehearsal today"—illustrate his driven character. Foreign visitors to Venezuela who tried to probe more deeply met evasiveness (Agrech 2018) or a brick wall. As Marco Frei (2011) noted, "anyone who asks critical questions of El Sistema in Venezuela will make no friends. If you ask the creative director and founder Abreu to talk about problems in El Sistema, he looks irritated. 'Problems?' he asked with a questioning glance through thick glasses. 'We grow, grow, grow.'"

Self-Critique, Change, and Conflict

After I made a short reconnaissance trip to Medellín in 2016, the Red went through a change of leadership. When I arrived in 2017 to begin my fieldwork, the program had a new general director, and it was in a slightly tense state of transition and anticipation. At our first meeting, program leaders articulated a self-critique of the Red's history and a vision of change. It immediately became clear that there were interesting movements under way. Crucially, as my research unfolded, I found that some of the most critical opinions about the Red came from past and present figures at management level. Leading figures were not afraid to reflect critically and at length in meetings and written reports on the program's shortcomings. In some respects, the Red's management was closer to the ambivalence of music scholars than to the relentless optimism so commonplace in the SATM field's public face.

On the one hand, this meant that my critical perspective on SATM found a natural home. As I began my research, I slotted into an institution in which analysis and ambivalence were relatively normal. On the other hand, I soon became less interested in critique than self-critique. My own critical perspective, which had been so necessary when faced with El Sistema's self-congratulation, could take a back seat when the Red's employees (and students) offered so many trenchant views of their own.

Boeskov (2019, 9) identifies his research as "part of a burgeoning self-critical movement within the field of community music," and he suggests that "one of its central tasks is to contribute to moving the field beyond simplistic and romantic views of music's transformative powers, to deal with the complex, contradictory, and ambiguous outcomes of participatory music making." When such a self-critical movement is articulated in print, it becomes more visible. But when it is not, as in the case of the Red, then it remains largely unknown to the outside world and does not register in public discussion or even academic research. I see my role here primarily as bringing the Red's self-critiques out into the open and thereby contributing to a self-critical movement within SATM more broadly.

SATM as a potential catalyst of social change is a major topic of this book, but even more central is change *within* SATM. Continuity is a hallmark of El Sistema, which was led by José Antonio Abreu for its first forty-three years and retained a remarkable consistency of practice over that time. In contrast, the Red has been through five changes of leader in twenty-three years, with accompanying shifts in practice and philosophy, making it an excellent case study of the multiplicity of approaches that may be covered by the label of SATM. Its changes make for much to explore: their nature, their causes, their effects, and the responses they provoked. These changes distanced the Red from El

Sistema, inviting a relational perspective: how did it diverge from the Venezuelan model? What can we learn from this process?

Change is an important yet under-researched topic within SATM. Studies of SATM have tended to be synchronic and thus to present SATM programs as relatively static and consistent. Evolution over time has not been analysed in any depth. The present book takes a diachronic approach and places the emphasis on transformations and their effects.

In my previous book I argued that El Sistema was riddled with problems and in urgent need of rethinking. A number of years later, there have been signs of movement from some corners of the SATM field. The shift from discussions about adoption versus adaptation to the widespread usage of the label "El Sistema-inspired" (ESI) gestures (if subtly) to a certain distancing from Venezuelan practices. Anecdotally, approaches within this field appear to have diversified; if some programs still venerate the Venezuelan model, others seem to borrow little beyond its name today. El Sistema was created in 1975 and looked back, both practically and ideologically, to earlier centuries. It became internationally fashionable in 2007, but educational thinking had changed significantly in the meantime and its approach has been much questioned since. It was only a matter of time before SATM engaged with more contemporary ideas.

Yet the explicit alignment of so many programs with El Sistema has limited the space for full, open, critical discussion of the fault lines in the Venezuelan model that necessitate change. Many have been willing to discuss how El Sistema might be adapted to other national contexts; but few have dared to suggest publicly that El Sistema needs to be transformed because it is flawed and out of alignment with current ideas about music education and social change. Institutional alliances and political sensitivities mean that public discussion of change, when it occurs, generally takes the form of offering a solution without naming the problem.

The field thus shows a paradoxical mixture of change and coyness about it, with some programs simultaneously praising El Sistema as a miraculous success and, with rather less fanfare, altering its formula. If positive transformation of SATM is to flow unimpeded, there is a pressing need for more information, analysis, and open debate around where, how, and why it has changed to date; what the achievements, challenges, and failures of such processes have been; and how it might change further in future.

This book is predicated on the idea that change is taking place in some quarters of SATM, but information is limited; processes of reform have been insufficiently documented, analysed, and discussed in public. Its contribution is firstly to examine a specific case study of change in detail (in Part I), and secondly to consider the question of change in SATM more broadly (in Part II). I am not suggesting that the Red is the most advanced example of SATM; processes of reform have gone further in some places, though they have barely begun in others. I thus treat the Red as neither unique nor a model to simply follow (or avoid), but rather as a case study that illuminates the past and present of the SATM field and points to possible directions for its future. I believe its journey offers lessons—positive, negative, and everything in between—for others. In other words, I hold up the Red not as an example of the "right" way to do SATM, but rather as an example of *rethinking* SATM, of a constant search for renewal—and there is much we can learn from observing this process, whatever the results. This book is intended to serve as a catalyst for thinking and talking publicly about change and thereby to contribute to growth in SATM. The field's shifts, however large or small they may be, need to be made more visible, audible, and comprehensible. At present public discourse revolves much less around new developments than around the triumph and supposed success of the old model, and this does not help the process or pace of change.

The Red repays close attention as an example of a SATM organization that has rethought and renewed its practices repeatedly in order to give greater priority to its social objective and adapt to a changing context. It is also an example of a "middle-aged" program in Latin America: younger than the venerable El Sistema, but older than its offshoots in the global North. It has been running for long enough to have had to confront the issue of change, and it may be instructive for more recent ESI programs around the world to learn in detail about an older example of SATM's development outside of Venezuela. During my time in Medellín, the Red pursued a sufficiently distinct line that it might be considered an alternative to El Sistema, or at least an alternative-in-progress. The problems and limitations of the Venezuelan model are now well known within the research field, so while this book adds to this critical literature, it is more focused on advances and transformations. I finished my previous book turning outwards from El Sistema's problems to consider wider lessons and possible solutions, and that search lies at the heart of this book.

When I was in the later stages of writing, COVID-19 struck, followed shortly afterwards by the resurgence of Black Lives Matter. Since my fieldwork was completed and the book's outline already in place, I decided not to scatter references to these major developments throughout the text but rather to return to them in the Afterword, which brings the book up to date at the end of 2020. Yet 2020 moved change towards the top of the agenda in many areas of human life, including music education and SATM, and so it added a new degree of urgency to much of what is described and analyzed in these pages. I believe that fewer people will need convincing of the need for a serious discussion of change today than when I sat down to write in 2019.

Self-critique and change, two central themes of this book, are bound up together. Changes in personnel since 2005 have led to internal critiques of the Red, to changes in (or attempts to change) the program, and to critiques of the (attempted) changes. This cyclical process has led, perhaps inevitably, to internal frictions and conflict. Indeed, it was only a matter of days after my arrival in Medellín to begin my fieldwork before the first clouds began to intrude on my sunny picture of the program. By the time I returned for a post-fieldwork follow-up visit two years later, the Red was in full crisis mode. Over this period, the processes of critical reflection and change that the program was undergoing provoked escalating tensions, debates, and disputes, and my focus on these processes led me also to explore their complex effects.

Like change, internal critique and conflict have not been a focus of academic research on SATM. There are illuminating studies by former employees of ESI programs who have gone on to write critically about their experiences after they left (e.g. Dobson 2016; Godwin 2020). Fairbanks (2019), the former Sistema director, offers an in-depth account of his journey from enthusiasm and advocacy to significant doubts about his own work and the field more broadly. However, open critiques and self-critiques by current employees, and the tensions and debates they occasion within a program, are terra incognita in SATM scholarship. Yet they can be very revealing. Close scrutiny of these dynamics within the

Red sees a somewhat monolithic, romantic view of SATM programs as harmonious and unified break down. The Red reveals itself as a multi-faceted, internally differentiated field, in which contrasting philosophies and practices coexist but also compete, and as a set of different and, at times, opposing constituencies (management, school directors, ensemble conductors, teachers, students, parents, administrators, researchers), which articulated different and sometimes opposing views. The picture that emerges is more complex than the standard narrative of SATM and it illuminates some of the choices available to such programs and the possible consequences of those choices.

Representing the Red

Such tensions and debates were of considerable importance to the program's actors and ought to be of considerable importance to anyone interested in understanding SATM more deeply. As Ndaliko (2016, 19) argues, taking cultural development work seriously means being willing "to preserve some of the more uncomfortable conversations and negotiations that take place behind the scenes of the polished press releases and websites competing for support." However, these uncomfortable debates do not define the Red or represent the whole of the program. I offer a realist take on SATM that contrasts with the idealist take of institutional publicity, advocacy, and the music industry, but I do not try to convey everything. My focus is not the Red of routine musical activities and everyday pleasures, but rather the Red of meetings and conversations in the corridors and coffee breaks. There is much else that could be studied and written, but that must be a task for others.

The result is a fieldwork-based critical analysis of key issues rather than a standard descriptive ethnography. It is not an evaluation either; rather, it focuses on a long-term process of *self*-evaluation. The question driving it is not "is the Red a good thing?" but rather the one that preoccupied many of my interlocutors: "how could it work better?" My primary intention is to share the Red's experiences with others around the world and shed light on central questions in SATM research and practice. Nevertheless, during my fieldwork, a number of current and former employees expressed interest in my perceptions of the Red. They were keen to know how a foreigner with experience of studying music and SATM elsewhere perceived their program. Senior figures responded positively to my invitation to read a draft of this text, welcoming an external critical perspective. Consequently, as well as conveying insiders' views of the Red to the outside world, I also offer an outsider's perspective on the Red for the consideration of the program itself and the cultural sector in Medellín more broadly, placing the Red's key issues in the context of academic fields and studies that were not well-known within the program.

Like many of my interlocutors, I could see that all was not rosy with the Red, and I believe that critical discussion is necessary; but, also like them, I feel an emotional attachment to the program and wish it success. Researching SATM properly requires a healthy dose of scepticism, yet I am not a sceptic in my everyday interactions with the Red, but rather something more like a critical friend. One school director told me: "Everything I do in the Red is because I love this program… that's why I'm always so agitated." He was one of the most critical voices in meetings, yet, as he explained in our interview, he criticized because he cared deeply about the program. I can identify with his mixture of attachment and critique and his desire to build the Red up, not pull it down.

The Red was full of pleasures and sociability; the program's staff undertook important and sometimes challenging work; and there were many moments when I was moved and inspired by the results. If such points take a back seat in this book, it is for two main reasons. Firstly, the training provided by the Red is quite conventional for music education in the Euro-American world, and therefore its positives need no explaining to anyone with even a cursory knowledge of this field. Such positives are widely discussed in the public sphere; the issues and debates, much less so. Secondly, I believe that an examination of the issues that preoccupied the employees and participants of the Red is ultimately more productive (if less comfortable) for the field than the celebration that has dominated public discourse. I am inspired by Ang's (2011, 790) characterization of "intelligent knowledge" as "bound to be highly selective" if it is to lead to constructive action. My underpinning belief is that debate about SATM's issues is more fruitful than a Panglossian vision.

Bartleet and Higgins (2018, 8) argue that discomfort and tensions in CM "are quite possibly a sign of health and growth." Much of what

I analyse in this book might be thought of as *growing pains*, with all the contradictions that this term captures. If I am interested in the pains—the discomfort and the tensions—it is because I am interested in the growth.

Some writers on SATM have advocated for a balanced, neutral, or objective approach. Rather than making such claims (which have been endlessly problematized by scholars), I take inspiration from currents such as emancipatory social science (Erik Olin Wright, cited in Wright 2019) and decolonial music education (Shifres and Rosabal-Coto 2018), in which researchers are not afraid to take a position—indeed, they regard it as positive. As Terry Eagleton (2004) argues, "intellectuals take sides," because "in all the most pressing political conflicts which confront us, someone is going to have to win and someone to lose." I also subscribe to musicologist Björn Heile's (2020, 176) view:

> I doubt that we can ever be value-free, neutral, and objective. More importantly, I haven't got the slightest intention or inclination to be, and the very idea seems to me to misconstrue the nature of scholarship and the public function of musicology. I entered this profession out of my passion for music; renouncing that would amount to a betrayal of what I believe in. [...] I also believe that the greatest scholarship and criticism is ultimately driven by passion for its subject—usually love, although sometimes scorn.

The subtitle of Griffiths's (1998) book on educational research for social justice is indicative: "getting off the fence." She offers a vision of action-oriented educational research that "is not necessarily research *about* education or its processes. Rather, it is research which has an *effect on* education" (67). Accordingly, educational research for social justice is not balanced or neutral, but rather ethically and politically committed and clear about what it aims to achieve: improving the practices of education. Such an approach is commonplace among researchers in fields such as CM and SJME, who frequently "get off the fence."

Embracing ambiguity, ambivalence, and complexity should therefore not be confused with neutrality or sitting on the fence. It may in fact suggest a more disruptive approach, aimed at dominant but flawed ways of thinking and acting. Ramalingam (2013) provides a good example: complexity is his central theme, yet he is scathing of the conventional ways of the aid establishment.

In short, this book is intended as a critical contribution to debates that I witnessed and participated in from 2017–19, and I do take sides. I am concerned by stasis and stagnation in orthodox SATM; I believe in progressive educational change; and I admired those figures in the Red who were willing to ask difficult questions and disrupt established ways of thinking and acting. I was encouraged to see movement around some of SATM's deep-seated issues, and while, as someone who had taught music or music studies in education institutions for much of my adult life, I could sympathize with those who were unsettled by the process, I broadly supported the shifts that were proposed and attempted. This is a book about change in SATM, and it is a book that is committed to such change.

What follows is therefore a perspective on SATM. It is constructed out of the perspectives of many others—musicians and researchers, in Medellín and around the world—but a central point of this book is that opinions varied considerably even within a single program at a particular moment in time. Thus I am not suggesting that this is the one and only way to view the subject, nor do I expect it to appeal to everyone. Viewing SATM through a critical lens is not to everyone's taste. Nevertheless, I hope that this perspective speaks to readers interested in critical thinking about SATM and positive change within the field.

Researching the Red

I spent a year carrying out fieldwork in Medellín (2017–18), with a two-week reconnaissance trip in 2016 and a two-week follow-up in 2019. For several months, I was assisted by my wife, D.[13] As a native Spanish speaker who both trained and taught in a Latin American SATM program, D. is an insider to this culture. This allowed her to make an instant connection with staff and students in the Red. Her participation greatly enriched the research, providing a distinctive perspective that allowed for triangulation with my own and frequently enabling observation in two places at once. During this time, I focused on the decision-making processes and responses among leaders and senior staff, while D. spent more time with students and teachers. The

---

13   The decision to remain anonymous is hers.

students' voices are cited less frequently in this book, because of its focus on adult-led processes of change, but they were very much part of our observations and conversations.

Long-term ethnographic fieldwork is an appropriate method for exploring the complexities and tensions of SATM in real life, beyond idealistic visions and mission statements. Fieldwork may serve as a reality check, slowly revealing the practice behind the theory, warts and all. Anderson (2011) and Mosse (2004) argue for the importance of ethnography for testing taken-for-granted assumptions and assertions in educational and development contexts respectively. The American Buddhist teacher Charlotte Joko Beck (1995, 175) writes about what she calls "Zen bullshit," or a tendency "to toss around many fancy concepts." She goes on: "It's not that the statements are false. [...] But if we stop there, we have turned our practice into an exercise of concepts, and we've lost awareness of what's going on." Critical ethnography, too, might be thought of as an attempt to go beyond an exercise of concepts and beliefs, beyond "buzzwords and fuzzwords" (Cornwall and Eade 2010), and be aware of what is actually going on. Constant critical attention is required lest one fall into "music bullshit"—repeating slogans and fine-sounding claims that miss the complexities of what is taking place in front of one's eyes.

Constant attention is also required because SATM programs and their contexts change over time. Consequently, their effects may also change. As Ramalingam (2013) points out, the fact that a particular action is effective in one place and time is no guarantee that it will work later or elsewhere. What worked in SATM in 1975 may no longer work in the 2020s; what worked in Venezuela may not work in the UK; in fact, what worked in one of the Red's schools might not work in another.

At first sight, SATM may present an entirely rosy aspect, and in a brief conversation with a stranger, employees and students will generally focus on the positives. Idealistic discourses are deeply embedded in the field. Students grow up surrounded by particular conceptions of music—literally, in the case of the Red, where posters announced the official vision of the program on the walls of every school. When the two parties do not know each other, interviews and formal conversations may therefore simply reveal the extent to which dominant discourses have been imbibed. But in long-term fieldwork, as trust builds and the researcher starts to understand key issues and probe more deeply, interlocutors often begin to reveal other sides to the story and contradictory opinions. Many eventually show a mix of enthusiasm and reservations that is quite normal within large institutions. Ambiguity and ambivalence emerge, then, from building relationships and conversations over time.

Fieldwork also uncovers complexity and messiness. Some great ideas are realised partially or not at all. Some projects are artistic successes but social failures and vice versa. For external consumption, much of this detail vanishes as a cleaned-up, upbeat vision is conveyed. But if the ethnographer does their job properly, they will come to see other sides to the story.

However, ethnography has its limitations, which are particularly apparent when it is applied to a voluntary project, since it carries a strong risk of survivorship bias. Those who join a program like the Red or El Sistema are a self-selecting population to begin with, and with many students dropping out within the first couple of years and a steady attrition rate after that, concentrating on observations and interviews with current participants, particularly more proficient and articulate ones, means considering only a narrow group that is well-suited and adapted to the program. Those who are less enthusiastic normally leave and their voices disappear. The greater visibility of successes than failures can lead to excessive optimism on the part of the researcher—something apparent when comparing some interview- or observation-based writing on El Sistema with the almost imperceptible social effects identified by quantitative studies (e.g. Alemán et al. 2017; Ilari et al. 2018). Without care, qualitative research on SATM can end up resembling a medical research trial that assesses the effectiveness of a cancer drug by interviewing the patients who are still alive five years after treatment. Unsurprisingly, it seems to work every time.

It is important to take the opinions of current participants and staff seriously, while at the same time remembering that they represent only the survivors. Fieldwork thus needs to be combined with other methods if it is not to present an overly restricted vision of a program and overstate its potential as a motor of social development. If ethnography usually focuses on those who survive, organizations that want to improve need to focus on those who do not. Researchers should bear in mind that the game of SATM has losers as well as winners, and many never even get the chance to play; research that focuses on the positive experiences of the winners could hardly be described as balanced or neutral, and it may offer little to the other two groups.

I adopted several strategies. Bell and Raffe (1991) argue that educational research on a specific project should also be comparative and historical, considering its relation to similar endeavours in the present and the past. (This is another area in which ethnographic studies of SATM have sometimes been weak.) I followed this route, drawing on my earlier research on El Sistema and Latin American music history. Another was simply to be conscious of and interested in the problem. Remembering that voices were missing made it easier to hear them. All current staff and students knew that participants dropped out, and they often knew why. It did not take much probing to see that the Red was not a program for everyone, raising questions about SATM's central discourse of social inclusion.

I also spent a lot of time in meetings. Long meetings—up to eight hours long. Management meetings, staff meetings, school meetings, social team meetings. Academics usually regard research leave as a precious opportunity to escape from such activities, but I saw myself as very fortunate to be given permission to attend them, and they provided an invaluable space for understanding the internal dynamics of the program. My research revolved around change, so I seized the opportunity to observe the generation of new ideas and discussion of old problems in real time, rather than having to rely on interpretations filtered for my consumption in interviews. In meetings, some of the Red's "ghosts"—figures and issues from the past—emerged from the shadows. A final strategy was to read a number of internal documents, provided to me by senior employees (past and present). These written sources brought into clearer focus the principal issues that had occupied the Red for many years, allowed absent voices to sound, and added another dimension to my observations.

The openness of the Red's leaders was a research finding in its own right. I was somewhat astonished to find that general directors (past and present) not only spoke openly with me about problems and the need for change, but also gave me access to so many activities and materials. I am not so naïve as to think that I heard and saw everything, but the contrast with the opacity of El Sistema's higher reaches was striking, and it pointed to a fundamental difference of ethos between the programs.

Thanks to the Red's openness, I spent much of my fieldwork year behind the scenes, witnessing the frictions and frank discussions beneath the surface of official positions and public statements. I often attended the weekly meeting of the management board, and I spent a lot of time with the social team, sometimes accompanying them on trips to schools and ensembles. As my fieldwork progressed, it took on an increasing element of participation and collaboration as well as observation. In meetings, I was regularly asked my opinion or drawn into collective discussions, and I made comments or suggestions when it seemed appropriate; many private conversations had an element of exchange rather than simply a one-way flow of information. As a foreign professor of music with extensive research experience, I was of interest to some staff, and they often bounced ideas off me or solicited my views. This continual dialogue led the Red to offer me a consultancy position in 2018 (one that I was unfortunately unable to take up for contractual reasons). I also dusted off my clarinet and joined in workshops for teachers and students, and I took part in professional development seminars for staff. In short, I became a participant observer.

I interviewed the Red's first four general directors, in some cases more than once, and interacted extensively with the fifth, who was in charge during my fieldwork. I also had a conversation with the sixth, appointed in 2020, shortly before I finished this book. I carried out a large number of interviews with managers, staff, and students, but I also witnessed and took part in many discussions as I hung out with staff over lunch and in coffee breaks between meetings, and I had many informal, private conversations. Most interviews were undertaken under conditions of anonymity, and I will extend anonymization or pseudonymization to all actors, as is standard practice in academic studies of education, unless identifying the subject is unavoidable for the narrative to make sense (for example, in the case of the general directors) and their view is relatively uncontroversial, or their view or action was made publicly. Quotations that are referenced derive from internal reports; those that are not come from my own interviews and observations.

Structure of the Book

Part I is organized in terms of four broad critical perspectives on the Red. The first chapter offers a brief history of the program through the lens of self-critique and change, followed by a closer description of the developments that took place during my fieldwork. Here, the dominant perspective is that of the Red's management, and the focus is on their assessments of the program and the modifications they implemented as a result. In the second chapter, these developments are viewed primarily through the eyes of the Red's music teachers and advanced students. Chapter 2 captures their critical responses to the changes outlined in Chapter 1 and the most prominent tensions and debates in the program. It explores a prominent dynamic of the Red for much of its history: resistance. Chapter 3 focuses on debates that were no less important but less conspicuous or urgent, and more conceptual. The emphasis shifts to centre the critical perspective of the Red's social team. Finally, Chapter 4 is where I explore overarching issues that I considered important but were not much discussed in the Red—above all, the effectiveness of SATM and its relationship to urban renewal.

Since open debate has historically been a foreign concept to El Sistema and some of its closest followers, the most substantial critical conversations on SATM have taken place *outside* programs: initiated by external researchers or commentators, and responded to (or not) by SATM representatives, spokespeople, and advocates.[14] Critiques of SATM have thus centred on the researcher or observer's perspective, if regularly drawing on the voices of participants and ex-participants (as in the case of my previous book). In the case of the Red, however, multiple changes of leadership have led to the juxtaposition and confrontation of different approaches, and thence to open and sometimes heated debate *within* the program. Accordingly, this book is structured in such a way as to prioritize the internal critiques by the management, staff, students, and social team. The central questions of the first three chapters were posed by the Red's actors. I place my own questions last because I believe that the most interesting aspects of the Red's history concern its

---

14 This assertion derives from personal communications from employees of ESI programs in several countries, as well as my research in Venezuela. For published examples, see Dobson 2016 and García Bermejo 2020.

self-questioning. My initial research questions guided my research and feature prominently in these pages, but I opted to structure the text less around them than around the Red's own concerns.

In reality, however, matters are less clear-cut. Much as I prioritize the views of others, my perspective inevitably shapes the first two chapters and I offer my own analysis in places. Also, drawing a clear line between viewpoints is impossible. The Red's internal debates overlapped with my own prior research and opinions. It is especially challenging to separate my views from those of the social team, as there were many parallels to start with and we discussed key issues regularly over the course of the year. As a result, Chapter 3 intertwines the concerns of my interlocutors and my own, reflecting our interaction in Medellín. The outline above should thus be regarded as a broad intention and approach rather than a strict framework, with the objective being to convey a polyphonic critical debate within and around the Red that challenges a dichotomy of inside/advocacy versus outside/critique.

The primary purpose of this book is to contribute to efforts to understand the challenges and possibilities of SATM. As such, it is more philosophical than practical, focused more on understanding than fixing. The practical contribution of such research is largely indirect; it aims to provide a conceptual foundation for changing practice rather than a set of instructions. I am inspired, again, by Ramalingam and his call for the aid sector to grapple with new ways of thinking rather than tweaking conventional practices. He portrays aid as a sphere of altruistic activity that has been compromised by a mixture of bold action and limited reflection—a critique that is highly pertinent to SATM's history. His vision reverses the equation: it is marked by bolder thinking and more cautious action. It focuses on asking the right questions rather than providing the right answers. That said, I am also inspired by the vision of action-oriented educational research articulated by Griffiths and others. In Part II, I attempt to balance these two approaches. I heed both Ang's (2011, 790) wariness of definitive or one-size-fits-all solutions and her aim to "provide pointers for action [...], framing complex situations and messy problems in ways that will empower us to find pathways through them." Consequently, Part II offers an overarching analysis of SATM with an eye on future reforms or revolutions—a sort of manifesto for rethinking and remaking SATM. But my aim is not to tell music educators, program leaders, and policy-makers what to do, but rather to provide questions and pointers that they can use to construct their own solutions.

The organization of this book also takes inspiration from Ruth Wright's (2019, 217) gloss on Erik Olin Wright's vision of social justice oriented sociological research, or emancipatory social science, as focused on three essential tasks: "first, to elaborate a systematic diagnosis and critique of the world as it exists; second, to envision viable alternatives; and third, to understand the obstacles, possibilities and dilemmas of transformation." Part I is devoted to the first task, while Part II tackles the second and third. The book ends with an Afterword that considers the Red's most recent changes and the implications of 2020's upheavals for SATM.

There has been an explosion of musical-social work around the world in recent years, and while activities have taken a multiplicity of forms, common threads often emerge. As such, this book may appeal to readers interested in topics such as music education for social change/justice/inclusion, CM, and classical music education and culture. It also connects to fields such as ethnomusicology, the sociology of music, and urban studies, since many of the issues that arise are broad ones concerning music, society, politics, and the city. Above all, this book is directed at those who want to think more deeply about SATM, from whichever scholarly or professional perspective. It is built on the belief that many involved or interested in SATM may find value in exploring a specific case study in depth, probing the field's possibilities and limitations, and considering how it might evolve in future.

PART I

1. Creating, Redirecting, and Reforming the Red

Miraflores, 20 November 2017

On a sunny Monday morning in November, the Red's school directors and teachers gathered in the sparse, functional hall of the Miraflores music school. The exposed concrete is characteristic of Medellín's recent public buildings, and I came to think of it as the architectural style of social urbanism. Today's meeting was a special one. The social team welcomed the attendees and explained that they were going to lead an exercise of critical reflection on the Red's past, with the aim of constructing proposals for the future.

The Red's historical imaginary revolved around its five general directors over the previous twenty years. Consequently, the staff were divided up into five groups according to the leadership period in which they had joined. I accompanied the group representing the first phase. There were more than two-dozen employees from this period, which had ended thirteen years earlier. I listened to them reminisce about this formative time in the Red and in their own lives; most had been students at that point and went on to join the program as teachers later on. Eventually a representative of each group was invited to stand up, summarize their account of their period, and outline their proposals.

This timeline exercise illustrated the importance of history telling in the Red. Its history was a constant if background presence: the program was conceptualized as consisting of five periods, and staff and advanced students regularly referred back, whether nostalgically or critically, to earlier ones. In conversations, features of the program were regularly

© Geoffrey Baker, CC BY 4.0   https://doi.org/10.11647/OBP.0243.01

associated with the five general directors. The social team's exercise was designed to bring this subtext to the surface and make it a topic of open discussion, with the hope of turning private nostalgia and criticisms into a public process of collective construction.

This chapter constructs a similar timeline, if one with a slightly different emphasis and purpose. The Red's exercise was designed to bring the program's "ghosts" out into the light of day, to shed light on the past and the staff's feelings about it, and thence to look towards the future. My intention is to take one step back and consider the history of the Red through the lens of internal processes of self-critique and change, of which this exercise was just one example. Like the timeline exercise, this chapter constructs and analyses a history in several parts, with the ultimate objective of fostering positive change; but here, the focus remains on the Red's management. It is not *the* history of the Red but rather *a* history, one that narrates the Red as a series of changes of leadership. It emphasizes the critical reflections on and transformations in the program that occurred at each stage, told from the perspective of the leaders and managers who made them. There are many other stories to tell, but I will leave alternative perspectives and the balance they provide for later chapters.[1]

After outlining the processes from the 1990s until 2017, I focus in more detail on the period from 2017–19, during which I undertook my fieldwork. Here I will provide a more ethnographic account of management-led critique and change. A new leadership team was appointed between my initial reconnaissance trip in 2016 and the start of my fieldwork in 2017, and my fieldwork consequently coincided with one of the more intensified periods of reflection and transformation in the Red's history, reinforcing my initial intention to focus on these issues.

---

1   This chapter is one-sided in the sense that it only presents successive managements looking backwards and critiquing what went before. The former general directors did not always take a benevolent view of what came after them, but exploring those "reverse" critiques is beyond the scope of this study. The first general director draws the short straw here, with four successors looking back on his tenure without him having a right of reply. So I should underline that he had many devoted admirers among the first generation of Red students.

1. Creating, Redirecting, and Reforming the Red 41

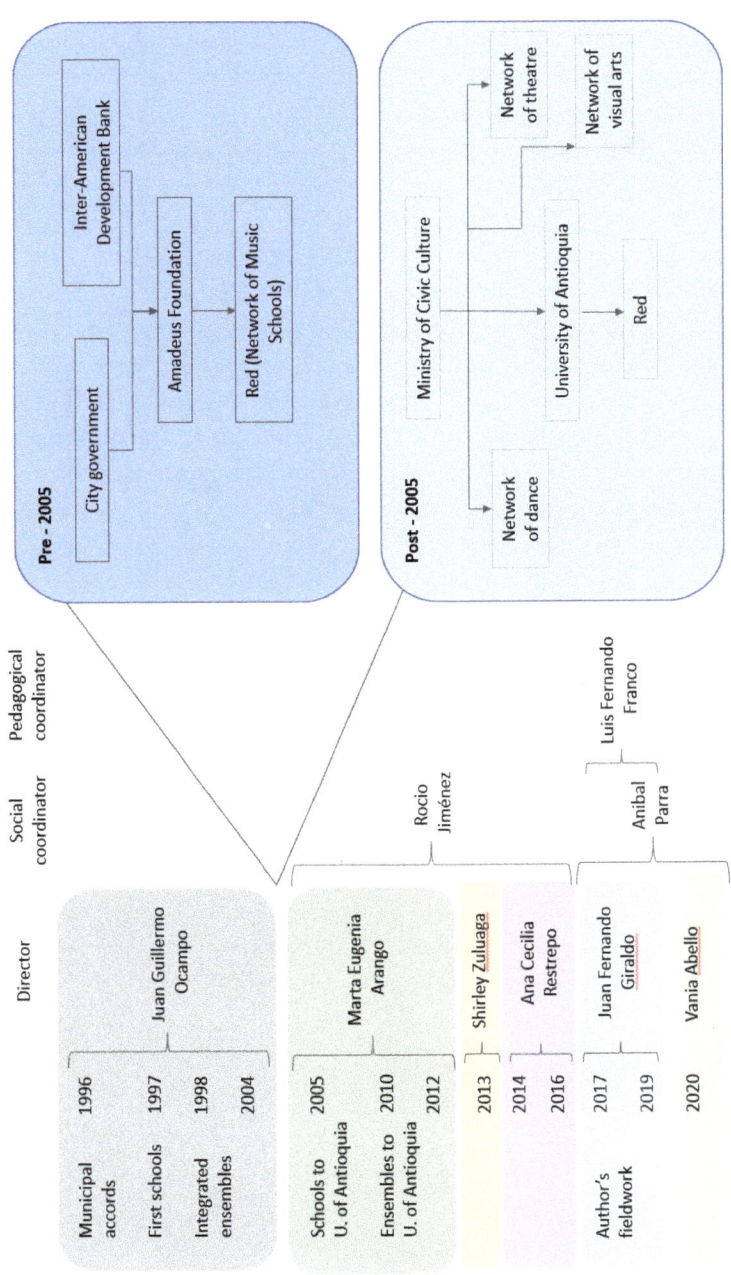

Fig. 2. Timeline and institutional affiliations of the Red. Diagram by the author. CC BY. For a larger version of this diagram, please visit https://geoffbakermusic.co.uk/timeline-of-the-red/.

The Red in Brief

The Red that I came to know had much in common with the Red of the early days. It was divided into thirteen schools for orchestral stringed instruments and thirteen for symphonic winds. A more recent addition was the Colombian music school at Pedregal, which focused on traditional stringed instruments. Each school had its own ensembles, most prominently chamber orchestras or symphonic bands of different levels. From 1998, the Red also had "integrated ensembles" that brought together students from across the program. The crown jewel was the youth symphony orchestra, but the number of ensembles had steadily increased to include two training orchestras (beginner and intermediate), three choirs, two popular music ensembles, two tango ensembles, and a symphonic band. The number of students had also risen steadily over time to around 5000, with an age range of 7 to 25. Many of the older participants also studied at university, in some cases pursuing a music degree.

Students could take lessons in either the morning or the afternoon, depending on the schedule of their primary or secondary school. While the program had begun with a somewhat informal approach, it eventually developed quite a detailed curriculum of multiple cycles and levels. Students might learn their instrument individually or in small groups, and in the second cycle they also took classes such as theory, choir, and corporal expression (movement exercises derived from dance and theatre). They also took part in the school ensembles. These groups tended to rehearse in the early evenings, while the integrated ensembles gathered on Saturdays. The program was committed to regular showcase performances; both school and integrated ensembles performed in theatres, parks, and squares across the city.

Fig. 3. Corporal expression. Photo by the author (2018). CC BY.

Two of the schools were located in high-income neighbourhoods, and the rest in middle- or low-income barrios. A few were situated in areas of heightened violence and, at moments during my fieldwork, either had to close briefly or included some students who were unable to reach the school for classes. Others had been moved from such areas over the course of the Red's history and were now sited in more tranquil (though not affluent) zones.

The Red's physical aspect had changed over time because many schools operated out of rented buildings and a number had moved at least once. In some cases they had moved quite far from their original site. Some schools were eventually housed in library parks or other new constructions and thus boasted enviable facilities. Others continued to function out of rented buildings, even houses, and suffered from problems including a lack of space, soundproofing, or ventilation. During my fieldwork the Red had no headquarters, meaning that managers and meetings were peripatetic and often gathered in ordinary classrooms—a sign of a program with few delusions of grandeur.

Creating the Red: Juan Guillermo Ocampo

According to the Red's founder, Juan Guillermo Ocampo, the pre-history of the program began in 1988, when he started a company called Amadeus Foundation to serve the city's classical music sector, selling scores, books, instruments, and strings. This was a response to "the city's cultural shortcomings, above all in the area of music." Ocampo also began offering music appreciation classes in some of the city's popular neighbourhoods, using both musicians and videos. This was the first time that classical music went up to those barrios, he said, and despite negative preconceptions of the genre, there was considerable interest. In 1990, he organized a concert, Merry Christmas Antioquia, involving hundreds of musicians, as part of an attempt to broker a truce between rival gangs in the barrios of Aranjuez and Castilla. (Antioquia is the province of which Medellín is the capital.) Ocampo recalled one gang leader saying: "I want the first sound my children hear to be a violin and not a machine gun." This is also the time when the famous slogan, "a child who takes up an instrument will never take up a weapon," first emerged, and when Ocampo decided that children in these barrios should have their own schools providing music education for free. He was struck by the contrast between the moribund state of classical music in the city centre and these barrio events, where there was such receptivity to the music. He felt the urge to invert the standard dynamic: rather than expecting the public to go to an orchestra, to take the orchestra to the public.

However, Medellín's shortcomings only worsened when the city's main professional orchestra, the Antioquia Symphony, closed in 1991. The city barely had a classical music scene at this point: it was producing few musicians, there was little funding, and the audience was small. There was virtually no market, meaning that Ocampo's company, Amadeus, struggled. Yet for Ocampo, the death of the orchestra simply underlined the need for a revolution: to take classical music to the people. In 1993, he bought a special projector at a music fair in Germany, as well as a screen and a public address system, and he set up "El momento de la música," a free, outdoor event every Friday in a park, where he projected a video of classical music and explained it to the audience.[2] Families would go and eat a picnic as they watched the show. For Ocampo, the popularity of this event disproved the commonplace idea that classical music was not appealing to the Medellín public.

The Red emerged from these various strands: Ocampo's music appreciation efforts, his interest and work in the barrios, and the

---

2   Amadeus Fundación (amadeusfund), "El momento de la música", Instagram, 7 March 2019, https://www.instagram.com/p/Butjimih6TH/.

cultural vacuum left by the collapse of the Antioquia Symphony. He wanted to give children in poorer neighbourhoods the chance not just to listen to music but also to make it. His goal was social, he said: he was not interested in producing professional musicians. The Red was about transforming lives and values; music was the tool for this work. He believed that music education should be demanding and have high artistic aspirations, since this was the key to seducing young people into a love of music that opened up the possibility of transformation. He was interested in changing their conceptions of what was possible for them in life and wanted to see them put their lives on the line for music, in a big concert, rather than for a criminal gang.

Ocampo stated that he did not know about El Sistema when he dreamt up the Red. Indeed, the 1997 article with which this book began made no mention of it, citing instead an agreement with an organization and a conductor from Madrid. However, Ocampo made contact with José Antonio Abreu around the time that the Red was starting up, and he then travelled to Venezuela and met with El Sistema's founder repeatedly. He remembered thinking, why reinvent the wheel? Abreu agreed to provide help, and during the first phase of the Red, El Sistema teachers led by Rubén Cova—whom Ocampo described as his "soul brother"—travelled regularly to Medellín to provide *seminarios* (intensive workshops) for the Colombian students, even using the same repertoire as in Venezuela. Cova was present at the first rehearsal of the Red's symphony orchestra, and Ocampo appears in a 2000 photo with his arm around Abreu.[3] In practice, then, the Red and El Sistema were joined at the hip almost from the start.

The first phase of the Red was one of rapid construction and growth. 1996 saw the first municipal accords, 1997 the opening of the first six schools, 1998 the further municipal accord that established the choirs and orchestras, and 2000 the first international tour (to Ecuador). By that point, another fourteen schools had opened. The program also established itself at the heart of Medellín's urban ceremony, for example performing at the opening of the new Museum of Antioquia in 2000 in the presence of Fernando Botero. The world-famous painter and

---

3 Amadeus Fundación (amadeusfund), Instagram, 8 March 2019, https://www.instagram.com/p/BuwLYwsBc-_/ (first rehearsal); https://www.instagram.com/p/BuwzPAxBovO/ (Ocampo and Abreu).

Medellín native was so impressed that he made a significant donation of instruments to the Red. By 2004, seven years after the first schools opened, the program had undertaken five international tours and was only one short of its eventual full house of twenty-seven schools.

This period was remembered by many alumni as the golden years of the program. They constructed something new and unexpected out of nothing, with high levels of discipline, commitment, and hard work. The experience of performing on major stages overseas was one that they could never have imagined and would never forget. This boom period was made possible by Ocampo's charisma and oratorical skill (which I experienced first-hand during our four-hour interview), which enabled him to convince the authorities, the young musicians, and their families to believe in his utopian project. His magnetic personality only served to augment the considerable media interest in this "rags to musical riches" story.[4]

However, not everyone was convinced by Ocampo. He described himself as an outsider engaged in a titanic struggle with the city's cultural establishment, which first saw him as a threat and then went after him and his resources. He aroused suspicions and distrust in some quarters. In 2003, as the Red experienced its greatest triumph in the presence of the Pope at the Vatican, the Inter-American Development Bank (IDB) opened an investigation into the contract between the city government and the Red, 60% of which was funded by the bank, after it received complaints about alleged irregularities ("El BID" 2003). Eventually the contract was resumed, but on 21 January 2005, the newspaper *El Tiempo* published an article entitled "Apostle of Medellín's child musicians imprisoned in the US" ("Preso" 2005). After being arrested on arrival at Miami airport on 25 November 2004, Ocampo was charged and convicted of membership of a money-laundering ring known as The Organization, which had "washed" more than $19 million for the Cali Cartel. According to his brother, Ocampo's arrest was part of a campaign against him and his project. Whatever the truth, Ocampo spent the next few years in jail.

---

4   For evidence of media interest, see *El libro* (2015) and Amadeus Fundación's Instagram page, amadeusfund (https://www.instagram.com/amadeusfund/).

Changing Direction: Marta Eugenia Arango

2005 thus saw a major upheaval in the Red. After Ocampo's arrest, the IDB withdrew its support, and the municipal government handed over the administration and operation of the music schools to the University of Antioquia. The university appointed a new general director, Marta Eugenia Arango, a sociologist and educationalist who had been the head of its continuing education division and had run a program to train and certify directors of municipal bands. However, the government left the management of the integrated ensembles in the hands of Amadeus. (They too were taken over by the university in 2010.) The following year, Arango produced a comprehensive diagnosis entitled "Present and future of the Red: Foundations for a change of direction" (Arango 2006). This report was the summary of a year of observation and reflection, and it combined critical analysis of the existing program with proposals for future changes. It was the first concrete example of a process that has continued ever since.

There are a number of important themes that emerge from Arango's report and our two interviews. She regarded the Red's parallels with El Sistema with suspicion. She criticized the personalization of both organizations, in which the leader used public money to finance a personal mission, and took most decisions and plaudits himself. Photos of Ocampo (some even spoke of "altars") were said to be more in evidence in the music schools than symbols of the city government that funded the program. Arango ordered the removal of the photos, a symbolic move that spoke of her principal desire: to forge a genuinely public program, *by* as well as *for* the citizenry. Regarding the prominent role of parents' associations in the first phase, she argued that she did not want students' families to make pastries, organize raffles, paint the schools, and generally sustain the Red when resources were lacking, thereby taking on what was really an obligation of the state; she wanted them to participate as citizens and exercise their civic rights by overseeing the Red, ensuring that resources were being used properly and employees were doing their job. The Red was not "free" but rather funded out of their taxes, and so it was their right and responsibility to supervise it. One of her principal aims was thus to change the parents' conception of and participation in the program in order to make it a truly public enterprise, and her report proposed "a massive campaign of citizenship education for the families and neighbours of the schools, in order to generate processes of empowerment and participation that are conducive to genuine co-management of the program" (32).

Revealing her sociological training, Arango criticized what she perceived as vertical and charitable dynamics in the Red, which projected an image of poor, hungry children from desperate barrios in need of alms. She perceived the Red's public face as showing the city and the students in the worst possible light, instrumentalizing the situation in the barrios to provoke pity and raise funds. In Arango's analysis, the Red had generated a tension: on paper, the program was supposed to generate peaceful coexistence and citizen empowerment, but in reality, its image-construction (colloquially termed "poverty porn" in the aid sector) undermined the Red's social aims. In contrast, she emphasized the strength and dignity of the participants, who were building something to share with the world, and she pursued a more horizontal model in the program's international agreements. Arango brought in foreign musicians to participate in an international band congress (from 2010) and a festival of chamber music (from 2011). The latter, Festicámara, was led by the US conductor Scott Yoo, who collaborated with the Red for several years.

Arango observed a generalized lack of reflection among staff about what it meant to construct coexistence through music. So her team began to look more closely at the curriculum and ask in which moments coexistence was strengthened. They tried to make both staff and students more conscious of the program's existing social processes; but they also critiqued the generalized belief that coexistence was an automatic consequence of collective music-making, and took an important step to reinforce the program's social impact. The Red had previously provided work experience for trainee psychologists, but Arango replaced them with professionals and introduced a psychosocial dimension. In this way, the Red's social action split into two branches: collective music-making and psychosocial accompaniment.

The emphasis thus shifted from attending to specific psychological issues among individual participants to organizing collective activities like workshops, aimed at constructing notions of peaceful coexistence and citizen participation among the student body and staff. For example, the program began to deal openly with issues of gender and sexuality, which had been largely left unspoken in the first phase. Parents were also included in such pedagogical processes. The Red began to teach them about participatory budgeting, which allowed them to apply for public funds to strengthen the Red's projection in the barrios.

In our interviews, Arango came across as a believer in the power of music, but one aware of gaps between theory and practice and room for improvement. She did not propose a radical rethink of the relationship between the musical and the social sides of the Red, but rather efforts to be more explicit about social processes and to fortify them via psychosocial support. However, the document that she authored in 2006 reveals a more ambivalent view. There is a brief but potent reference to "a big weakness in the program [...] that of over-encouraging individual musical achievements, producing arrogant behaviours in the adolescents" (13). This point is elaborated in a section on the social component of the curriculum, which centres on the Red's primary objective, promoting coexistence:

> in the everyday workings of the program one can observe a certain deviation from this social achievement and/or goal, since a high percentage of the advanced students who participate in the principal orchestra and/or choir, who have also had the opportunity to perform on national and international stages, develop arrogant attitudes as regards their knowledge, with displays of exclusion towards their peers and—more worrying still—disrespect towards the teaching and administrative staff of the program. (17)

Furthermore, after eight years of functioning, supervised by El Sistema, the Red had no activities or strategies for reflecting on and tackling such issues: nothing directed at building coexistence, conflict resolution, ethical reflection, democratic participation, or valuing difference. Arango proposed that the Red's various constituencies should construct guidelines for coexistence and collective agreements for dealing with internal conflicts, and that the program should offer talks and workshops on these topics.

Arango aimed a more consistent critique at the administrative side of the Red. A consequence of personalization, in her eyes, was limited attention to planning or strategy; Ocampo had simply kept everything in his head and told the employees what to do. She perceived the program as chaotic and uneven, and her priority was to bring administrative order and thereby construct a new organizational culture. A hands-on leader, she would visit schools without warning to see if the teachers turned up on time, and would phone them up if they did not (which was regularly the case). She was determined to identify those who failed to lead by example: those who talked about music inculcating values such as discipline and responsibility but did not act accordingly. Other changes included contracting teachers to the university, which meant a significant salary increase; providing proper training, equipment, and uniforms for the school secretaries; and improving the program's local and national communications strategy.

From an educational perspective, Arango noted that the Red did not have a unified, documented pedagogical model; instead, staff mixed elements from various approaches, often without a clear understanding of which method they were using or why. The first concrete proposal of her report was to create a pedagogical model for the Red, to document it, and to spread it to all the schools over the coming years. The second was to do the same with the curriculum. In 2007, the program launched an annual National Seminar of Music Pedagogies and Didactics, and in 2010 it began a comprehensive reconstruction of the curriculum into cycles and levels—important steps towards a formalization of the program.

On a cultural note, Arango started a process of reflection on why the Red placed such emphasis on symphonic music, given that Colombia is a country of municipal bands. She noted the absence of plucked strings—so prominent in Colombian music—and a general tendency to marginalize popular music. She was in no way averse to classical music, which she saw as providing an excellent base for musical training, but she felt that the Red could not ignore national traditions. Consequently, the Red created the Youth Symphonic Band in 2008, under the direction of the Belgian Frank De Vuyst, and the Popular Music Ensemble and

Tango Orchestra in 2009.[5] Arango was also surprised to find that the Red declared itself to be a symphonic project without any further explanation of its rationale in its documentary materials. Her report noted that the contribution of the symphonic format to the social and musical objectives of the program was unclear. She raised the question of whether the Red's schools should, in future, open up to music and music education in all their varieties, becoming centres of musical activity and personal development without qualification of genre or format.

Arango's view of her predecessor was ambivalent. She critiqued many aspects of the institution that she had inherited, yet she also recognized Ocampo's role in creating an important program for the city and the sense of loyalty he had engendered in students, staff, and families. She saw him as similar to Abreu, much influenced by the Venezuelan leader, and as having tried to do similar things in Medellín. She, in contrast, had no relationship with El Sistema. She made overtures at the start but was rebuffed (possibly because of Rubén Cova's close relationship with Ocampo and Amadeus).

In sum, the transition from Ocampo to Arango constituted a major shift in institutional culture. Ocampo was universally recognized as a charismatic leader and motivator whose obvious passion for the Red inspired others to believe and opened the way for the program. Arango was also perceived as a strong character, but much more of an administrator than the dreamer Ocampo. The social team summed up this shift: "It could be said that the first phase of the program was ruled more by passion and love, the second by institutional and economic factors (organization and systematization)" ("Informe" 2017a, 38).

The Social Turn: Rocío Jiménez

It is necessary to interrupt the story of the Red as a succession of general directors in order to make room for an individual who was just as influential in the trajectory of the program. Rocío Jiménez, a psychologist, was appointed by Arango in 2006 to take charge of

---

5   Although tango is of Argentinean origin, it has a long and prominent history in Medellín.

the social side of the Red, and she remained in post for a decade—throughout the tenure not just of Arango but also of her two successors. She began by providing psychological attention to individual students, but as she was joined by other team members, her approach shifted to a psychosocial one, which led her to work with all the Red's constituencies via workshops and training sessions. Rather than waiting for matters to go wrong before intervening, the idea was now to nip negative dynamics in the bud.

Jiménez first encountered the Red in 1997, when she did some consulting work in relation to the program's application for support from the IDB. She recalled two contrasting sides to this initial experience: the enchanting music-making, and the shouting of the conductor. From the outset, then, she saw that the coin had two sides: great potential, but also fierce discipline. When she began to work for the Red a decade later, she was struck that many elements ran counter to the original proposal that she had seen. She had no doubt about the positive potential of music education, but she also grasped that a program of this kind could be quite problematic. She set out to close the gap between theory and practice.

Jímenez was critical of the Red both as an institution and as an expression of classical music culture. She disliked the way that it became an all-consuming obsession for some students and staff, leading to unhealthy dynamics such as dependency, stasis, and trauma upon reaching the age limit and being obliged to leave. "There is life outside the Red!," she asserted. She fought to clear Sundays of rehearsals, insisting on the importance of leisure and family time. There were issues concerning gender, ranging from the assignment of instruments according to gender stereotypes, to unhealthy relationships between teachers and students. Competition was intense: the Red was supposed to focus on coexistence and collaboration, but she found rivalries everywhere (between directors, schools, ensembles, and students), as well as egotism and bullying. She was unconvinced by the Red's social claims: all that musicians care about is that the ensembles sound good, she said, the rest is secondary for them. Star students were allowed to behave however they wanted because conductors needed their services.

The hierarchical dynamics of classical music, the arbitrary power wielded by figures of authority, and the normalcy of conductors dominating the students all concerned Jiménez. She saw the pyramidal structure of the Red as both the source and the means of reproduction of the program's discontents. In response, she led the project of constructing collectively a "Manual for Coexistence." For Jiménez, the manual was key to giving students a greater voice and teaching them to defend their rights, including against infringements by staff. It was intended to create procedures and ensure that students knew about them; to make it easier for them to speak up and complain; to make directors and conductors more accountable; and to combat rule by whim. It was also aimed at maintaining the power of the collective without sacrificing the individual.

Jiménez described the Red as potentially the most powerful political program she had ever seen (in the sense of constructing political subjectivity among participants). For her, its transformational potential lay not in playing the violin or sitting in an orchestra rehearsal, but rather in the social and political processes that it could generate. But this meant giving students more of a voice. What she encountered in practice were students with no say, at the whim of adults, wheeled out by the city government to provide an attractive soundtrack to urban activities. She viewed the Red as a contradiction: how could it serve as a site for education in democracy when its dynamics were so autocratic? The Manual for Coexistence, according to Jiménez, was the foundation for realizing the political potential of the Red. Constructing and using the manual was supposed to be where students learnt to assume and use their voice—a prime example of and catalyst for SATM. "Empowerment" was the word that she kept returning to—and it was to be found (or not) primarily in the Red's organizational dynamics rather than its musical activities. By focusing too much on sounding good, she felt, the Red had limited students' empowerment and constrained their political voice in society.

The Social Team's Diagnosis

The need for a thorough overhaul of the Red's approach to its social mission become even clearer in internal diagnostic reports produced by

Jiménez's team.[6] The first one dates from 2008, a year after the team's constitution, and constitutes its opening gambit ("Informe" 2008). Drawing on group interviews with all the Red's constituencies, this document lays bare the complexities and tensions within the program, fleshing out Arango's critique two years earlier.

The responses of the students, made under conditions of anonymity, revealed considerable evidence of social problems within the Red. They acknowledged dynamics such as fights, gossiping, disrespect, insulting jokes, older students dominating younger ones, and "a lot of rivalry and jealousy between the woodwind/brass and strings and between instruments" (6). The social team identified a range of problems among the participants including poor communication, little acceptance of difference, the formation of cliques, symbolic violence (sarcasm, mockery, aggression, nicknames, exclusion), and stigmatization and discrimination on the basis of where a student lived or how they dressed or spoke. The report concluded:

> it is common to find imaginaries and rivalries that contradict the goal of the Red to "generate civic coexistence through music," exemplified by phrases such as "the thing is that the strings think they're the best, as though they were from another level, another class, they think that they play real music"; "the [wind] bands are like a pub band, a bunch of rowdy, excitable guys who just play popular music"; "the kids from Las Playas and El Poblado are untouchable, people say they're really arrogant"; "the kids from Moravia are delinquents, give them a snack and they're all over it; the kids from Miraflores or 12 de Octubre are kind of ruffians." (7)

The students also criticized the school directors and teachers, citing arbitrariness and lack of clarity in the exercising of rules and exclusion from decision-making processes. They urged the Red "to care about them as people and not just as musicians" (7).

If the students presented a strikingly negative portrait, the parents were overwhelmingly positive. They spoke of their pride in their children, their admiration for and gratitude to the staff, and the happiness and positive changes that they perceived in their offspring. Some called the Red a blessing and even a miracle. The fact that they

---

6   The social team had different names over the course of its history, but I will often use "social team" for the sake of simplicity.

drew polar opposite conclusions to their own children and the social team raises fascinating questions about any attempt to characterize or evaluate a program of this kind.

The teachers' views fell somewhere in the middle. They expressed considerable doubts about their capacity to deal with social problems. The opening paragraph of the report alludes to "the anxieties, worries, and frustrations" that the teachers experienced and "the impotence that stems from receiving multiple demands to solve social or family problems, to which, they state, they lack the means to give adequate responses" (3). Further on, summarizing teachers' responses, the report states: "The objective is very good and attractive, but rather ambitious and utopian. They could go some way towards achieving it [...] but they wonder, how far does the social responsibility of the Red go?" (14). Underpinning these doubts are others about their training and skills: "they feel overwhelmed and lacking important tools when it comes to working on issues relating to values and to helping achieve what they consider the program's 'ambitious' social objective" (17). Consequently, "some express concern about the gaps that they recognize in their education, for example in psychology, which would allow them to understand social phenomena better and to deal constructively with situations that arise with the students" (14). Responses to these gaps reveal contradictory views. Many teachers felt that they needed specialized training (for example, in pedagogy, psychology, and conflict resolution) in order to deal with the Red's social objectives and challenges. Yet there was also a widespread view that fulfilling the social aim was the job of the teachers of corporal expression, not music, and responses to a question about promoting non-violent attitudes were summarized as: "we musicians are trained specifically in that subject [i.e. music]; a psychological approach is a matter for a specialist in that area" (15).

There was a general perception that while the Red supposedly prioritized social goals, its practices were in reality geared around musical outcomes, even at the cost of social ones. Again summarizing teachers' responses, the report notes that "they perceive distance and inconsistency between the theory and the practice" (17), and it continues: "The objective of the program has gone off course, the social is supposed to be more important than the musical but it does not work in that way, since there has been more concern with demanding musical results; the social has been forgotten by the leadership of the Red and the demands have become purely musical" (14).

Many teachers expressed angst about the evaluations known as "pedagogical displays" (which they called "anti-pedagogical"), since they believed that the social focus was lost in these spaces: "a kid can play an instrument badly but socialize much better, but this isn't evaluated and it's not visible in the display" (14). Hence, ten of the fifteen focus groups stated that they focused on the musical aspect in their daily routine, since this is where the program expected to see results. In short, the music teachers did not portray their work as a miraculous social balm; on the contrary, their responses placed numerous question marks over SATM.

This picture was reaffirmed by the school directors. They too argued that the program's social objective was overly ambitious, and that their schools could offer options but could not be responsible for the behaviour of students. They recognized that their skills were predominantly musical rather than social, and they were wary of utopian aims, which they saw as going beyond their capacities and responsibilities and more of a cliché than a realistic goal. However, there was marked disagreement over the value of the program's official objective: for some it was the essence of the Red, while for others "the inclusion of the social in the objective is the way to obtain economic resources, as is the case when they focus on a particularly vulnerable population" (22). There was more agreement on the dissonance of a program that was supposedly social in emphasis and yet which only evaluated musical results, had no social indicators beyond size, and paid little attention to the issue of dropouts. They called on the leadership to take the social processes in the schools more seriously—for example, by evaluating social results as well—and to provide them with more relevant tools: "There is limited understanding of concepts such as discipline, respect, rigour, solidarity, which are part of the Red's objective; we should go more deeply into what each of these concepts implies and how they can be generated and strengthened" (23).

Some directors highlighted a contradiction between education shaped by the needs of the professional arts world and the Red's social goal. They suggested that such education generated unhealthy competition, tension, and pressure. They regarded its expectations of excellence and low tolerance of mistakes as an obstacle to realizing the program's social aims.

Later social team reports substantiated this picture. A 2010 PowerPoint provides a long list of problems in the Red as reported by students.[7] The first point on the first slide details "Problems of coexistence," which include disrespect, intolerance, arrogance, lack of unity and teamwork, personal conflicts and physical fights, cliques, divisions, bad atmosphere and behaviour, competition and rivalry, and dropping out as a result of mockery, rumours, and mistreatment. The students reported conflicts between their musical and school studies leading to poor academic performance; tensions with their families over the Red; and dissatisfaction with the program's pedagogy and relations between students and staff.

A subsequent report ("Informe" 2012) focused on the integrated ensembles. The social team reflected on the slippage between social objectives and realities:

> It is important to underline that the notion that has taken hold in the Red concerning the immediate, spontaneous effect and impact of music education on socio-affective development and the construction of social links and bonds, automatically producing education in values like respect for difference, solidarity, gratitude, equity, tolerance, etc. as the student population comes together in the schools and integrated ensembles, has given rise in recent years to a lack of purposefulness in the pursuit of the Red's objective of coexistence. However, it is obvious and acknowledged by coordinators, directors, assistants, and students, that there is a lack of knowledge and closeness among the students; the existence of cliques; arrogant and mocking attitudes among soloists; rivalries between schools, wind and string ensembles, and instrument groups; and distance, isolation, and difficulties in the socialization and integration of new arrivals in the schools and ensembles.

The issue of rivalry and competition—both between ensembles and within them—features prominently and repeatedly. The social team organized a workshop to try to heal the divisions between the string and wind sections in one ensemble.

---

7   "Taller sentido de pertenencia: bandas y orquestas."

A later report returned to this issue and gave further details of one example that emerged in a workshop with the main orchestras ("Intervención" 2013):

> it was clear that there was a kind of undervaluing or pejorative vision of the violas, and similarly with the wind instruments, which were regarded [...] as responsible for the mistakes and problems in rehearsals, which did not flow smoothly as a result. This revelation points to the need for deeper analysis of the real or imaginary hierarchies that may be at work and being reproduced in the ensembles, generating discontent, discrimination, and exclusion.

This report underlined that collective music-making did not necessarily produce social bonding: "Although the members of the ensemble have already spent more than five months coming together for rehearsals up to three times a week and for many hours, [the nature of] their interactions meant that they could barely tell each other apart and did not know each others' names." In the light of such reports, it is little wonder the leaders felt that the Red needed a change of direction.

The City Government Takes Charge: Shirley Zuluaga

Arango's successor, Shirley Zuluaga, had the shortest tenure of its leaders, spending just a year in post. She introduced some significant practical changes but was arguably most notable for what she represented: an appointment by the city government, meaning greater municipal control over the Red. If 2005 had seen the government take over the music schools from Amadeus, it had handed over decision-making and operative responsibilities to the University of Antioquia, which chose Arango as general director. But after Aníbal Gaviria was elected mayor in 2012, the city government decided to take a more hands-on approach, which included appointing the Red's leaders from then onwards. As one insider told me, the new government wanted to do more than just hand over funds to the university; it wanted control and recognition. The changes in this and subsequent phases of the Red are related to this closer connection between the program and the Ministry of Civic Culture.

Zuluaga had been involved in the design of Medellín's Cultural Development Plan 2011–20, and her appointment reflected the culture ministry's desire to bring the Red more into line with the city's cultural policy. Also, the ministry felt that the program was overly defined by its operator (the University of Antioquia) and the external alliances that it had formed. The government was keen to strengthen the Red as a public program of the city of Medellín.

Zuluaga's term, like Arango's, began with a critical assessment of the current state of the Red. I draw here on interviews with Zuluaga and a senior official in the culture ministry at the time, Sonia Pérez.[8] From here on, I continue with a personalization of the Red's history around the figure of the general director, reflecting both the way the history is told by most actors and the relative simplicity that this personalization brings to its retelling. But the leaders' opinions and actions should be understood as more of a collective construction, developed through dialogue both "upwards" (with ministry officials) and "downwards" (with the Red's management team). After 2013, the story becomes more about senior management and less about a single, dominant figure. For example, Zuluaga took over as leader but Arango's team remained in place, so the change of direction was neither abrupt nor absolute.

Like Arango before her, Zuluaga stressed the notions of publicness and of participants as citizens with rights but also responsibilities. They received a music education paid for by public money, but with it came the responsibility to behave as examples in their communities. The Red began to work on the latter aspect more: for example, participants had the right to use transport provided by the Red, but they also had a duty to do so responsibly. The new leadership aimed to fortify a general consciousness of the Red as a public service and of what this signified.

The culture ministry regarded psychosocial accompaniment as an important element of programs aimed at young people from popular barrios, hence it strengthened this side of the Red. The team had been reduced to just Jiménez by the time of transition, so two new members were added. The new leadership felt that there was still too much attention directed at individuals, so it renewed an emphasis on psychosocial rather than psychological support: on collective wellbeing, group exercises, social confluence and coexistence, and education in values and citizenship. Where individual treatment was required, there

---

8   Pseudonym.

was now a move to look to pathways and professional services offered by the government rather than the Red. For example, if a student had drug problems, it was no longer considered a responsibility of the Red to find a solution. Rather, this was viewed as specialized, time-consuming work that reduced the program's capacity to serve the student body as a whole and was therefore best carried out by relevant professionals employed by the government.

Changes were introduced to the pedagogical displays that each school put on annually for the management. These had taken on the character of collective examinations, but the new leadership decided to make them more educational and less judgmental. The psychosocial team was brought into the process to provide more focus on the human component. As Zuluaga noted, many staff had received training in which social skills were not valued as highly as musical ones. The leadership emphasized that the discipline that musical training demands should never contradict the social and human aspects of the program.

The renewed emphasis on the psychosocial component went hand in hand with a critique that the Red had increasingly become a pseudo-conservatoire rather than a program of citizen education through music. The leadership insisted that the Red needed to be clear that it was not intended to offer formal music education but rather a community program through music; there were other routes to becoming a professional musician in Medellín. As such, it needed to grant more importance to the social side. According to the culture ministry, the students saw themselves as proto-professional musicians and were treated as such by the university, contradicting the intention behind the Red. This critique was explained to staff and advanced students in the main ensembles, and also to international collaborators such as Scott Yoo. This adjustment of focus had a mixed reception; some were more interested in musical quality, and Yoo was one who stopped working with the Red at this point.

There was still concern over a certain charitable character to the Red. Pérez, the former ministry official, connected this aspect to the program's external links. She believed that when foreigners came from afar, holding out possibilities of a donated instrument or travel or study overseas, or simply offering their interest and concern, it encouraged participants to portray their life and circumstances in a dramatic way in order to capture attention and generate sympathy. In her eyes, this charitable dynamic perpetuated an unequal relationship. Part of the drive to incorporate the Red more fully into the city government was to move away from perceptions of its students as sad cases in need of aid, towards ones of citizens exercising their rights. The Red was supposed to dignify participants, said Pérez, not re-victimize them.

A number of changes were consistent with a period of greater government scrutiny and control of the program. More attention was paid to the training and qualifications of teachers, and while this made for more development opportunities, there was also a process of "normalization" (insisting that staff have a professional qualification), which meant unwelcome changes (such as salary reductions) for some and departure for others. Efficiency in the use of public resources was a priority for the new government at this time, so Zuluaga re-examined the program's major costs such as transport.

Musically speaking, this was a period of intensified performance activity. Zuluaga launched an initiative called "Jueves de nota," which saw Red ensembles taking over public buildings such as libraries one Thursday a month. The aim was to provide a focus for the schools, to give the Red more visibility in the city, and also to make connections with other public institutions and programs. Ensembles also performed in city parks at the weekends and took part in major events such as festivals. Some staff recalled this as the busiest moment in the Red's history, as well as the time when the program became tethered more tightly to the city's political machinery.

Humanizing the Red: Ana Cecilia Restrepo

With a background in dance, the next general director, Ana Cecilia Restrepo, was familiar with the broad cultural issues around a program such as the Red, if not with the details of musical training. She was appointed by the culture ministry in 2014 to replace Zuluaga and continue the work that the latter had begun, so this change of leadership displays more continuities than ruptures. Since Zuluaga only spent a year in the post, her reforms were still at a relatively early stage. Restrepo's tenure saw the extension of critiques and reforms that had originated in the ministry with the change of government in 2012.

Here I draw on interviews with Restrepo and three other individuals at the management level of the program. As with Zuluaga, directions and decisions were negotiated with the ministry and other managers, rather than reflecting simply an individual vision.

The new leadership insisted once again that the Red should fulfil its mission and put the social first. The program was funded by the Ministry of Civic Culture as a program to promote coexistence and citizenship, so music should be the means towards such ends. Yet behind the inspiring rhetoric, the program still followed a conventional approach of focusing on musical training and preparing the more skilled and committed students for a professional future; the social benefits were largely assumed and relegated to the background.

As one manager put it, Medellín could not provide a musical career for more than a fraction of those who were studying in the Red, so it made much more sense to focus on the social angle. That was the part that all participants were going to use long-term, hence the leadership wanted to take it more seriously. But another manager noted that many teachers in the arts preferred to focus on artistic matters and found discussion of social issues less interesting, and they would rather separate out the social, leaving it to specialists, so that they could get on with teaching children how to make art. The new leadership thus perceived a gap between theory (social action *through* music) and practice (the tendency towards separating the music and social sides in the Red), which it was determined to address. It argued that social action should be visible in the musical activities and not just corporal expression classes, psychological consultations, or psychosocial workshops. Now the aim was to infuse the social into the musical by bringing a socio-affective element into the music curriculum and examining the sociality of music learning.

The new leadership also looked critically at the integrated ensembles. Since they brought together students from across the city, they had considerable social potential. However, they tended to be led by conductors who were more interested in musical quality, and both students and teachers saw them as the musical pinnacle of the program, leaving the social relegated to the margins. These ensembles were thus where tensions between musical and social goals were particularly in evidence. There was a sense that these ensembles could be a much more interesting social laboratory if they allowed more time for integration rather than prioritizing musical outcomes, and if they were led by more individuals with broad skills, diverse musical interests, and commitment to social processes rather than to producing polished performances and/or developing their own conducting career.

The emphasis on musical results meant that the ensembles had historically rehearsed all weekend, but under Restrepo this was reduced to a single day. The new leadership was concerned that the Red might be damaging the students' social relationships with non-musicians, particularly with their families. They saw a contradiction between the program's social claims and its encouragement of parents and children to wash their hands of each other for the whole weekend. As one school director put it, this was a turning point, when "people began to think that music wasn't everything, that there was also family life to think about."

As part of this turn towards the social and the renewed efforts to realize the program's aims more fully, the management pushed back against costly events and activities such as high-profile concerts, international guest conductors, and foreign tours, arguing that they spent lots of precious money and did little to promote social action. How could such expenditure be justified at the top of pyramid when the Red struggled with resource problems at the base, such as the supply and maintenance of instruments and accessories?

Once again, there was criticism of a perceived confusion between social action and charity: a tendency to equate "social" with "the poor," and to assume that participants needed to be given everything in order for them to participate. As with leaders going back to Arango, there was an emphasis instead on the Red as a space for claiming and exercising rights, one in which commitment and co-responsibility were required and students were constructed as active participants rather than passive recipients. One manager argued that the Red's vision should be to offer an equitable music education across the city rather than a paternalistic salvation narrative.

During this period, a critique of the Red's classical emphasis was articulated more clearly. While the most obvious focus was on repertoire, and the response was a push towards more Colombian music, there was also a critical perspective on the conservatism of classical music education and its resistance to change. That this was a matter of a conceptual shift, rather than personal preference for one repertoire or another, was underlined to me by Pérez, the city cultural official, who criticized the atmosphere and dynamics of the Red and questioned the suitability of classical music education for such a social program. She felt that a spark of joy was missing: "in music, in the search for perfection, for technical skill, something very striking happens within the individual… like that loss of enjoyment in the search for perfection." She was shocked to find young musicians being made to do press-ups if they made a mistake, yet she saw this as congruent with the insistence of classical music training on technical perfection, which "generates certain rigidities that aren't what a project like the Red needs." She was not simply anti-classical music, acknowledging that "what symphonic music does is very beautiful, because what it does is make the kids sound together, in a society that struggles to sound together—the metaphor is very powerful." She saw it as "the search for harmony in a society that still can't find it," but she continued, "yet it can't be based on the perfection of the artist—it needs to be based on enjoyment."

At a more ideological level, she identified the Red as "a colonial phenomenon… it's perpetuating a colonial dynamic." She identified the higher status of orchestral musicians in relation to their popular counterparts in Medellín as evidence that "the colonial spirit is still strong" and that the city still had a lot of work to do to "embrace our own identity." This view was echoed by one of the Red's senior managers: "In these kinds of programs, in this city, we are sending a very colonialist message, about venerating a music that we don't make, that we don't appropriate." Pérez's critique also had a practical angle. She was concerned that the Red created false expectations: the more it resembled a conservatoire, the more it encouraged students to imagine classical music as their future. Yet this field was very limited in Medellín, which had only two professional orchestras and a modest audience. There were many more opportunities for salsa and rock musicians in the city.

Critiques of the focus on classical formats and repertoire by the Red's leadership were allied to broader arguments concerning curriculum, pedagogy, and the general ethos of conventional music education: "There are elements in musical training that really work against attempts to be inclusive, emancipatory, to grant rights rather than denying them, and not to incite abuses of power." The leadership felt that the Red needed more humanity and empathy, particularly in the integrated ensembles; the way that many of its teachers were trained removed the human aspect and focused on technique, and so music education became all about "playing, playing, playing." Creativity was another concern. It was prominent in the first-year music initiation program, but once the children received their instruments, it declined dramatically and the focus shifted squarely to performance. The leadership saw other arts education programs in the city teaching contemporary styles or taking a problem-based approach to learning. Despite the original intention of a non-formal program, the Red looked rigid, formal, and conventional in comparison.

The Colombian Turn: Juan Fernando Giraldo

El Poblado, 19 July 2019

As the Red's newly elected student representatives arrived at the music school in El Poblado for their first meeting, they were greeted by a small ensemble performing traditional, improvisatory pipe and drum music from the Colombian coast. This "ceremony" was performed by Juan Fernando Giraldo (the Red's general director), Luis Fernando Franco (the pedagogical director), the head of the Moravia school, and two teachers. For the meeting itself, they were joined by other senior figures in the program. The leaders began with some short, informal speeches to the students. The Red had historically regarded playing music as participation, said Giraldo, but the leadership now wanted to move participation to another level: as well as making pedagogical changes, they also intended to give students more of a role in decision-making, hence the creation of this committee of representatives. The Red had traditionally been adult-centric, he said, simply imparting knowledge from teachers to learners; but now it was going to take greater account of the students' voices, interests, and experiences.

A city official posed a political question to the students: who does the Red belong to? What does it mean to say that the Red is a public program? It meant that it belonged to them, not to the government. Franco spoke of their desire to engage more with open pedagogies, neurodiversity, and creativity, as part of a push to make the program more profoundly inclusive and innovative. The leaders finished by underlining that these new directions were not simply a matter of personal preference but rather connected to local cultural policy (the city's ten-year Cultural Development Plan) and international currents in music education (the program had recently received a visit from its Brazilian counterpart Projeto Guri and sent representatives to soak up ideas at the Latin American music education conference FLADEM).

After the meeting, the social team led the students in a variety of group bonding exercises in the school, starting discussions about their possible roles and responsibilities. The students summarized their views on posters that were then stuck up on the walls of the hall. The session ended with the students putting on comedic sketches about their perceptions of the discussions, complete with props, wigs, and costumes.

This meeting summarized many of the new directions of the Red from 2017 onwards, when Giraldo was appointed as general director. The musical ritual with which it began was no mere ornament: it articulated the leaders' cultural philosophy. The Red had professional musicians in charge for the first time, and they publicly performed the Red's new direction as well as describing it.

New Directions in 2017–18

Giraldo explained to me on my first day of fieldwork that his priority was identity and diversity. Giraldo and Franco, the pedagogical coordinator, are musicians with a strong interest in Colombian popular music. They critiqued the narrowness of the Red's offering, in comparison with the breadth of styles in the city, and the somewhat limited reflection of local or national identity, as evidenced by the program's historical preference for European classical music and the symphony orchestra. They argued that the diversity of the city's population demanded musical diversification by the Red, and they imagined a program that was tied less to a conservatoire-style curriculum and pedagogy and more to local musical realities. As Giraldo said in a media interview, "we've already explored and reflected on the violin, a European tradition, on the cello, the flute, so why not produce and research what we are, what we want to be?" (Vallejo Ramírez 2017).

As we listened to a rehearsal together on my first day, Giraldo criticized the ensemble sotto voce for lacking swing in the popular repertoire; the notes were there, he said, but the timing and feel were not. His response was to encourage a greater focus not just on Colombian repertoire but also on the technical and stylistic aspects of this music, promoting the study of traditional Colombian percussion, plucked strings, and clarinet. More conceptually, the leaders were concerned about a perpetuation of a colonialist, Eurocentric mindset and hierarchization of culture that had defined music education in Colombia for centuries. Consequently, they advocated for a horizontal relationship between Colombian music, other popular musics, and the European symphonic tradition, imagining an intercultural Red built on dialogue and mutual learning between genres and styles.

A second critique focused on the Red's historical focus on performance and its relative neglect of creation and reflection. The leaders were concerned by the narrowing of activities after the ludic first-year musical initiation program. Older students tended to be more confident with melodies, while their rhythmic and harmonic knowledge was usually weaker. The leadership's response was to create a rhythmic-harmonic laboratory, initially as a pilot program in three schools, to strengthen these aspects of the curriculum. One benefit of studying harmony is that it opens a door to musical creation. Many students, and even many of their teachers, were afraid to play without written music in front of them. The leaders believed it was essential for the program to confront this fear of spontaneous invention and self-expression. Giraldo is a jazz saxophonist, while Franco is a composer. Unsurprisingly, then, boosting creativity was a central focus of their vision. They organized intensive workshops on improvisation with both teachers and students, and pushed teachers to incorporate more creative activities in their lessons. Franco also linked the new emphasis on creativity with the social objective of the Red: as well as diversifying the artistic side, it equipped students with a key skill for the fast-changing modern world.

Fig. 4. Archive of Red de Escuelas de Música. CC BY.

When the city government announced that it would fund a tour to the US in 2018, the leadership decided not to send one of the existing integrated ensembles (as had happened in the past) but rather to create a new hybrid ensemble of instruments and musicians from different genres. Cellos and oboes lined up alongside bandoneón, electric guitar, and Andean plucked strings. They rejected the standard model for tours by Latin American youth orchestras, which typically perform canonic European repertoire followed by some lighter, stylized Latin American pieces. The Red's tour was designed as a pedagogical experience, with the focus mainly on the preparation process rather than the final product. For example, the rules and protocols for the tour were constructed during a collective exercise involving the social team and all participants, rather than simply handed down by adult leaders. The students had to think about the consequences of their actions and behaviours, rather than just being told what they could and could not do. The repertoire was all newly composed and the students played a major role, participating in creative workshops over a period of months under the supervision of adult composers and, in the later stages, Giraldo himself. The participants were split into two laboratories, one focusing on alternative media of sound production, the other on intercultural approaches to music. These laboratories involved many participatory exercises but also critical listening, making field recordings, and undertaking field trips (to a famous tango café and a salsa recording studio and radio station). The end result was a forty-five-minute sonic portrait of Medellín, seen through the eyes of the Red's students and capturing the musical and auditory diversity of the city.

Fig. 5. Creating music for the US tour. Photo by the author (2018). CC BY.

Fig. 6. Creating music for the US tour. Photo by the author (2018). CC BY.

70 Rethinking Social Action through Music

Fig. 7. Student-composed lyrics for the US tour. Photo by the author (2018). CC BY.

Fig. 8. Field trip to Salón Málaga tango café. Photo by the author (2018). CC BY.

1. Creating, Redirecting, and Reforming the Red

Fig. 9. Field trip to Latina Stereo salsa recording studio and radio station. Photo by the author (2018). CC BY.

In 2018, the social team was reconfigured as a territorial team, based on the diagnosis that the music schools were quite insular. Historically, they had provided spaces to retreat from the city's violence. Many had little or no connection to other cultural groups or organizations in their neighbourhoods; they were like islands or bubbles in the city. The establishment of a territorial team was designed to help them connect to their surrounding area and collaborate with other musicians and cultural actors. The leaders wanted to reframe the Red as part of a wider musical and cultural ecosystem in the city, and to shift the model from a conventional music school to an interdisciplinary neighbourhood cultural centre.

Behind this change was also an urge to listen more to the evolving city and the soundscapes of its neighbourhoods: Colombian music, tango, salsa, rock, hip-hop, and so on. The leadership reimagined the Red's educational process as starting with an analysis of the local territory, via activities such as sonic cartography and barrio excursions. "We're pursuing a Red that reads the territories and their sound-worlds," said Giraldo (Vallejo Ramírez 2017). In one meeting, Giraldo described the city as "a living organism in constant movement and transformation, to which we have to adapt in order to generate relevant and consistent proposals [...]. We are no longer in 1996 or 2005 [...]. We must revitalize and enrich our model of music schools."

The aim was also to diversify and complexify the forms of connection with the territory: not just performing occasional concerts *for* the community but also learning *about* the community. The social team was concerned that students often just turned up and played at concerts without knowing much about the location or the reason for their presence. The team described the Red as failing to read its surroundings—as disconnected from the city (e.g. "Informe" 2017b). The goal was now to research, share, and collaborate in a two-way process of dialogue and exchange. Territorial activities were thus envisaged as pedagogical ones.

A further critique concerned the lack of spaces for reflection and genuine participation. Students performed in large ensembles, but historically they had a limited role in reflective or decision-making processes; the *degree* and *nature* of their participation were therefore limited. Managers argued repeatedly that rather than *playing* instruments, the students *were* instruments: they had been instrumentalized by the program and its adult figures of authority. Leaders claimed that the Red had historically been adult- rather than student-centred: it had revolved around providing work for adult musicians and focused more on their needs, desires, and knowledge than those of the students.

"This shouldn't just be a program designed to do what adults think— we want to listen to the voices of our students," said Giraldo (Vallejo Ramírez 2017). Therefore in 2018, the Red instituted a methodology of project-based learning (PBL). The intention was to move away from the conservatoire model of teachers depositing knowledge in students and towards co-construction. Each school and large ensemble developed a central project for the academic year, which was to be created in a participatory manner by students and staff together, rather than decided just by the director. This new approach rested on the belief that full participation required more than just playing music, and that students should play a larger role in proposing ideas, taking decisions, and choosing actions. The principal aim was to make the Red less top-down and put young people at the centre of the program, engaging in multiple activities rather than just playing their instruments and leaving the rest to the staff. The creation of the committee of student representatives was a step in this direction. As Giraldo put it, learning to construct collectively was a priority for Colombia, and therefore it should be a priority for a social program like the Red.

PBL was where the strands of diversity, identity, creation, reflection, territory, and participation could (potentially) unite and flow into practice. Its adoption was an attempt to connect the Red's artistic activities more deeply to the program's context and multiple constituencies. It was the primary means for realizing the leadership's vision of the Red as "spaces of collective, participatory, and inclusive construction, built on reflection, performance, research, and creation" ("Propuesta" 2018, 8).

These initiatives represented the latest stage in the shift that had begun in 2005 and gathered pace in 2013: loosening the Red's ties with El Sistema's orchestral training model and bringing it in line with the priorities of Medellín's Ministry of Civic Culture and then the Cultural Development Plan 2011–20. (The latter focused on democratic cultural citizenship and emphasized the now-familiar themes of participation, inclusion, diversity, creativity, and critical reflection.) They also emerged from analysis of key questions by the Red's new management. Considerable resources were devoted to this process: it was the main focus of the social team in 2017, and an array of consultants was hired in 2018 to bring in fresh perspectives. There was no complacency or resting on laurels. Rather, the emphasis was on identifying problems, generating new proposals, and enacting change. During the first year, the leadership undertook its diagnosis, and in the second and third years they took actions to address the issues described above (with varying degrees of success, as we shall see).

There were other problems that were identified, but acted on only partially, if at all, during the period of my research, due to overload (the program's hectic work rhythm and the sheer quantity of new strategies that the leadership wished to pursue) or the depth and complexity of the changes that they implied. For example, Franco articulated the management's desire to increase the program's inclusivity. It advanced on one front, creating a Laboratory of Neurodiversity and thus catering to more students of differing abilities; but in other ways inclusivity remained something of a good intention and a work in progress. Open pedagogies did not progress beyond an aspiration, sidelined by more pressing operational issues. At the first music-school performance that I attended during my first week in Medellín, Giraldo whispered to me ruefully: "look, there are hardly any black people here." There was sensitivity to this issue at management level—the leaders were enthusiastic advocates of Afro-Colombian music—but the racial diversity of the program changed little. Only 2% of students identified themselves as other than mestizo, while around 12% of the city's population was Afro-Colombian ("Propuesta" 2018; Álvarez 2016). Some of the problems were so deep-rooted that they resisted quick solutions.

Another critique that remained largely at the conceptual level concerned the character of the Red (like many large SATM programs) as a pyramid.[9] It had a broad base of beginners (in 2018, 57% of students were in the first two years of study) and a narrow apex of advanced students. This raised some major questions, particularly for Franco, the pedagogical coordinator. Firstly, the apex was where musical quality was taken most seriously and was the part of the program that was visible to the outside world; as such, it consumed a disproportionate amount of the program's resources. The leadership repeatedly expressed concern that the largest expenditure other than salaries went on transport for the integrated ensembles on Saturdays—activities in which only a minority of students were involved. They asked whether this was a fair or desirable use of limited funds. In contrast, only eight of the Red's 150-odd teachers worked in the musical initiation program, where 35% of the students were found. This disproportionate allocation of resources, effort, and attention to the musical activities of the most advanced students was an incongruent feature of what was supposed to be an inclusive social program. The management wanted to redress this imbalance, but they ran out of time.

Secondly, the pyramid spoke to a high dropout rate. In 2018, there were 1860 students in the first year, 1147 in the second, and 707 in the third. As one manager put it, simply looking at the population pyramid tells you more about the program's flaws than any amount of fieldwork. Two key issues were identified, both of them relating to the transition from Year 1 to Year 2: a significant increase in intensity (from one day a week to as many as three or four); and a major change of approach, as musical initiation was replaced by instrumental initiation. The unique selling point of SATM has long been to place orchestral instruments in students' hands from early on in the learning process and to push children fast and hard. But for the Red's pedagogical team, the high dropout rate indicated that the switch to this approach after Year 1 alienated

---

9   For a critique of the pyramid model of music education in the UK context, see Lonie and Sandbrook (2011).

many children, and the increased intensity was another off-putting factor (because of the potential for clashes with other extra-curricular activities and homework). They regarded the shift from Year 1 to Year 2 as too abrupt: the ludic aspect of the first-year classes went out of the window, and the children were now taught predominantly by *maestros de instrumento*—teachers who were trained as classical performers—in an atmosphere that the team characterized as "serious" and "keep quiet!" The management began to question whether a program like the Red really needed expert performers to teach children their first notes on an instrument, and to imagine hiring more pedagogues specialized in the early years of learning and fewer instrumentalists. This would have the added benefit of allowing more room for creative activities in the first phase of the program and not just via workshops with advanced students. However, such a shift would have constituted a challenge to the foundational practice and ideology of the Red, and it thus remained largely on paper during my fieldwork.

The leadership dreamt of a program that was shaped less by its end point (large-ensemble performance) and more by its starting point (playful, creative activities). They would have liked musical initiation to be a genuine foundation for a more ludic program rather than a brief prelude to the non-sequitur of orchestral or band training. Some staff concurred, arguing that an earlier shift to introducing starter ensembles called *pre-semilleros* halfway through the first year of instrumental learning had been a negative development, putting pressure on teachers to impart the technical basics too quickly and curtailing the more relaxed, ludic aspects of the preparatory year.

The leadership also critiqued the characterization of the schools by the needs of the program rather than the territories in which they were situated. There were thirteen string schools and thirteen wind schools, situated not because of local musical strengths or interests but because of a decision by the Red, which wanted to train string and wind players in equal numbers for its showcase ensembles. The leaders imagined schools that were more autonomous and distinctive, reflecting the socio-cultural characteristics of each barrio. But here, too, the rethinking pointed at changes that were impossibly radical for the Red at that time.

A further critical conversation involved communications. The leadership was keen to move from a top-down approach to communications to a participatory one. It reimagined the program's public face as an educational space where students would learn or improve communications skills, rather than a product delivered by adult professionals. The new idea was that schools and ensembles would be the principal actors, proposing and implementing their own publicity strategies with advice and support from the communications team. Rather than having a single, program-wide operation, the singularity of each school or ensemble project might be reflected in its communications. Accordingly, the new head of communications in 2018 told one ensemble: this is *your* project, and I'm here to help you develop *your* ideas about communications. However, like some other new initiatives, this plan was restricted in practice by limited resources and excessive workload.

PBL in Action: San Javier School

The music school of San Javier developed a project called GC13, or Gira Comuna 13, which ran over two years. "Gira" means tour, and Comuna 13 is the school's neighbourhood—an area particularly associated with Medellín's dark history of violence. The project focused on taking the music students out into the surrounding territory and bringing the neighbourhood, and particularly some of its iconic musicians, into the music school. Students were to learn about and interact with other cultural actors and explore their relationship with community spaces. An underlying question was how the San Javier school might permeate and have a positive impact on the barrio. The school's director, Andrés Felipe Laverde, emphasized to students that they were fortunate to study in the Red and had an obligation to their neighbourhood.

Fig. 10. GC13 Project, Armonía territorial, San Javier (2018). CC BY.

The 2018 version was named "Armonía territorial" (territorial harmony). The music students went out to visit and perform in places such as the local library and fire station, and they made a point of going on foot so that their instruments and therefore the school were visible on the streets of the barrio. The project thus included both excursions and concerts, both local institutions and community spaces. The school also enacted *"improvisajes"* in public spaces. *Improvisaje* is a neologism that combines *improvisar* (to improvise) with *paisaje* (landscape), and thus connects sound and territory. The first one took place in the local cemetery and was dedicated to the victims of the urban war in Comuna 13. As Laverde explained, these improvised musical actions were intended to reclaim, resignify, and heal particular spaces in the barrio: "This isn't just the corner where X was killed—this is also the corner where the kids from the music school played that wonderful piece."

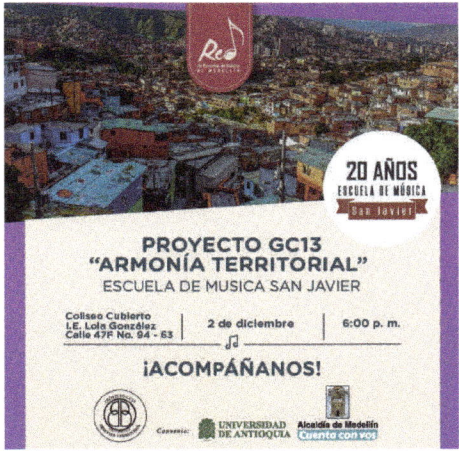

Fig. 11. GC13 Project, Armonía territorial, San Javier (2018). Archive of Red de Escuelas de Música. CC BY.

The school collaborated with well-known rappers (C15, el AKA), vallenato and mariachi ensembles (Colombian and Mexican genres respectively), rock and pop musicians, and traditional Colombian music and dance groups. All performed together at a concert that finished with a song written by Laverde about Latin American unity and ancestral knowledge.[10] The musicians performed it as a kind of bonding ritual

---

10   Andrés Felipe Laverde, "Abya Yala—Únete Latinoamérica", YouTube, 10 November 2017, https://www.youtube.com/watch?v=WoYIFs9pYNs&feature=youtu.be.

for the audience, who were encouraged to hug their neighbours. Some musical elements were improvised on the night. The guest musicians were not simply drafted in for the performance, but also invited to the music school for a social and cultural exchange beforehand: as well as rehearsing for the concert, they talked about their music and their personal histories, explained their instruments and learnt about the students', and shared food and drink.

For 2019, the project was subtitled "Talentodos: Aprendiendo unidos." *Talentodos* is another neologism, combining *talento* (talent) with *todos* (everyone), and encapsulating the idea that everyone is talented, rather than just a chosen few. The school focused on student creativity this year: students wrote songs themselves or chose music that they liked, and Laverde arranged the pieces for orchestra. As a result, the concert repertoire was entirely popular music. Laverde was classically trained and led a chamber orchestra in the school that only played classical repertoire, but the central project was led by the students' interests and compositions. Creating space for song writing and not only instrumental performance turned the school's activities into more than just a musical exercise: writing lyrics provided students with a valuable outlet for self-expression, and the results revealed much about them and their realities.

Fig. 12. Talentodos project, San Javier (2018). CC BY.

For the director of a music school, Laverde showed an interesting mixture of passion and ambivalence about music. Whenever I visited him, he would always show me the music that he was arranging for the students, play me recordings of their compositions, and pull up videos of their recent performances. Yet even though he led the school's orchestras, he did not want to play a conventional role—"I'm not a conductor," he said, "I'm a motivator"—and he dismissed standard orchestral rehearsals as "the most boring thing in the world." He mixed up his own rehearsals, handing over the baton to students, telling stories, making jokes, and sometimes even abandoning music for another activity. He believed that learning technique and repertoire was the least important thing that went on in the school; for him, it was a place for young people to go and share experiences and talk about their lives—a place where they might express more than at home. He was interested in the social bonding, not the musical product. For him, the purpose of the Red was to heal social wounds, which meant that students needed to express what was going on in their lives.

Laverde made a short documentary to present the project, and the opening music was a rap song by El AKA, "¿Que es arte?" (What is art?).[11] At one string orchestra rehearsal that I observed, he discussed the song with the students. El AKA was a friend and Laverde had invited him to come to the school and work with the students. Laverde held up the rapper and the questions raised by his chorus—"What is art if it doesn't name the struggle? What is art if it doesn't serve the community?"—as something for the school to reflect on and aspire to. He presented it as an example of socially committed art. This was not inclusion but rather interculturality in action. In the same rehearsal, they worked on a huayno (a traditional Andean genre) from Bolivia. Laverde began with a five-minute contextualization about colonialism, the silver mines of Potosí, and the extraction of resources from Bolivia to Europe in centuries past. He wanted the students to put themselves in the shoes of the silver miners and imagine their exploitation and deaths. This is their lament, he said, before they began to play. The choice of this huayno was not just about diversifying the repertoire; it was about naming the struggle, as El AKA put it, and the students making the struggle theirs.

Laverde encouraged students to gain as much experience as possible beyond learning to play an instrument in the school: to explore other arts, other activities, other spaces in the barrio. How can you express yourself in music, he asked, if you don't have anything to express? How can you play pieces about love or sadness or anger if you don't have these experiences in your life? He wanted students to go out and learn about the world, not just play music the whole time.

---

11   El AKA, "¿Qué es arte?", YouTube, 30 May 2012, https://www.youtube.com/watch?v=bYJSUVzlzR8.

He also focused on strengthening bonds between students, families, and the community, and again, music was secondary—an excuse that brought people together rather than an activity to consume all the students' time and attention. On Saturday mornings and during holidays, he would organize activity days in the school—making handicrafts, or learning about cinema, literature, or photography—or go out on an excursion in the barrio, for example visiting urban vegetable gardens. In 2019, they made a documentary about the history of the neighbourhood, filming important sites and interviewing older community members.

Underpinning the projects was a critique of the Red, in which Laverde had previously been a student and a teacher and was now a director. "We're in a comfortable place," he said; "we need to discomfort ourselves." He felt that the school had been somewhat closed off to the community in the past and was therefore little known; he wanted to open its doors, break down the idea of the Red as an exclusive island for a privileged few, and make the school take its place in the larger cultural movement of the barrio. Everyone wants to travel overseas, he said, yet they don't even know their own neighbourhood well. His dissatisfaction with the Red's old ways can be felt in notes he made for the project: "to unsettle ourselves in order to generate movement or chaos, leave our comfort zone, discover relationships, new forms and blueprints of thought, new processes, new ideas." He proposed a "critical, open, flexible curriculum" and argued that "we cannot develop our work with our backs to reality."

PBL: Other Projects

GC13 is just one example of the dozens of projects that flourished across the Red in 2018–19, and it illustrates how management proposals about diversity, identity, creativity, territory, and participation crystallized into practice. PBL had the potential to bring all these strands together. San Javier was one of the schools where this potential was most fully realized, but many other schools and ensembles made interesting advances. There were projects focused on ecological issues, on local history, and on significant musicians and musical genres in the barrio. When I revisited the Red in 2019, the second year of the PBL strategy, I saw evidence of new connections to local culture, spaces, and organizations. This frequently involved an element of research, as students and staff mapped communities and their music, sought out knowledgeable figures and written information, and delved into the past as well as the present. A number of schools carried out a participatory social cartography exercise: students and their families drew maps of the barrio, marking on it places of positive and negative significance to them. In the words of one school director, the project thus sprang from the vision and desires of the community, as articulated by the community, rather than from what she *imagined* that the community needed. If the focus on territory was bearing fruit, then, so was that on participation: student committees and surveys of the desires and interests of participants and their families sprang up across the Red. A number of projects involved elements of artistic creation such as composition and improvisation as well as performance.

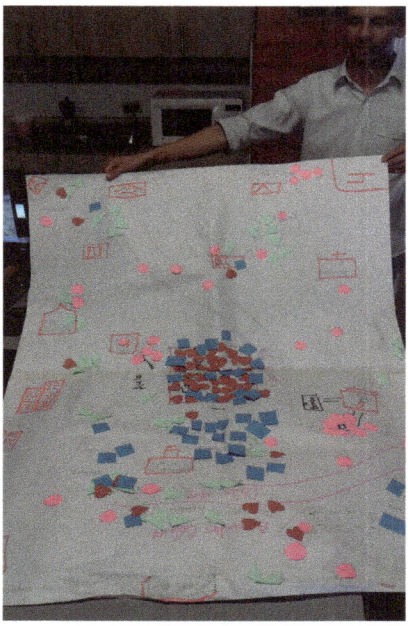

Fig. 13. Social cartography exercise. Photo by the author (2018). CC BY.

As a consequence of these initiatives, traditional and popular music were more in evidence. Pockets of the Red moved beyond diversifying repertoire to engage with issues of popular style, technique, and pedagogy, and to connect with significant popular musicians in the local neighbourhood—for example, those who had helped to give the barrio a particular musical identity. Such was the case of the Benjamin

Herrera school, which collaborated with important families of "tropical" musicians in the surrounding Barrio Antioquia. The 12 de Octubre school surveyed students and their families about their musical tastes. The former were most interested in rock and urban music, while the latter preferred Colombian and romantic music. They placed classical music in third and fifth place respectively. The school's director then looked for allies in the local community (such as a rock group) that could help the students learn to play their favourite music.

The shift to PBL led to some productive processes of self-examination and reflection, as schools took stock of what they were and where they wanted to go. The Independencias school, too, carried out a survey, not just of students' musical tastes but also their perceptions of significant musical places in the barrio. Most named neither classical music nor their own music school; hip-hop was the genre that was cited most often. The director was struck that the students did not seem to recognize either their own music-making or their institution as important elements in the musical life of the neighbourhood. This exercise shed light on the much discussed disconnect between the Red and its territories, revealing a self-perception of the program and its music as somewhat peripheral to the barrio. The school resolved to forge new alliances and explore a greater variety of genres.

The Pedregal school was created with a focus on Colombian music, but it also developed a student-led project about gender equity. Concerns from both girls and boys about gender relations in the school and surrounding neighbourhood led both students and staff into extended critical discussions of feminism and gender equality, and to settle eventually on gender equity as their preferred ideological formation. This was a novel way to approach the peace-building that is so central to the aims of social programs in Medellín such as the Red. Alongside more theoretical debates, the school took practical actions such as encouraging girls to take leadership roles and to play instruments such as percussion that are widely considered to be masculine, and putting a transgender student together with a boy from a conservative Christian family as stand partners. The latter exercise was a real challenge, the director confessed, but he was determined that the school should genuinely work on coexistence in concrete cases rather than simply repeat fine words.

The school in the neighbourhood of Popular devised a project in conjunction with SATMED, the System of Early Warnings of Medellín, a government program devoted to protecting the rights of children and adolescents. The project sought to identify and counteract violations of rights (such as sexual abuse and gang activity) by naming and analysing them via collective conversations and workshops with specialists. They took their project to the highest level, performing in the chamber of the city council. On a simpler level, the school director organized a meeting with students and their families and asked them why they were in the Red and what they would like from it. It turned out that they wanted to play and listen to more varied repertoire, particularly more "everyday" styles like the music that they listened to at home and on the radio, and the families wanted to watch their children playing solos or duets and not just in a large ensemble. The director changed the format of the school's concerts accordingly.

The school project at La Milagrosa emerged from a collective cartography exercise, which involved identifying the community's problems and concerns with relation to the surrounding territory and then discussing possible actions. The selling of drugs was the principal issue, so the school decided to focus on prevention of consumption among young people. The project entailed composing a musical about a mammoth who was faced with various temptations and risks but ended up making his way to the music school, where he found a more positive atmosphere and values. The following year, the school focused its project on a local fruit tree that had once been found widely in the neighbourhood but had now almost disappeared. One thread was ecological (working with a local seed bank and focusing on planting), while another was historical (students interviewing older inhabitants and comparing the past and present of the barrio).

A number of projects were underpinned by critical reflection on social realities and the Red's relationship to them. For example, the Alfonso López school decided to focus on the family, and particularly on students' connections to their families and the wider community. There was acknowledgment that despite two decades of work, the Red had had rather limited effect in this barrio: it had not transformed families or the neighbourhood or the place of culture in the life of the community in any significant way. The school project did not focus on doing something radically new, but rather on aligning the practice of the Red more closely with its theory. This entailed both naming social goals and forging concrete strategies and actions in order to realize them, rather than assuming that the social effects would happen automatically as a consequence of learning music. This project illustrated the move towards more targeted social action that was part of the Red's new philosophy.

Fig. 14. Alfonso López school project, outdoor rehearsal. Photo by the author (2018). CC BY.

Fig. 15. Alfonso López school project, outdoor rehearsal. Photo by the author (2018). CC BY.

1. *Creating, Redirecting, and Reforming the Red* 85

Fig. 16. Alfonso López school project, "Family is…" Photo by the author (2018). CC BY.

Fig. 17. Alfonso López school project, "Family, pillar of my dreams." Photo by the author (2018). CC BY.

The Santa Fé school alighted on the theme of freedom—again, underpinned by a critique of the Red's past. Freedom was explored through creation (improvisation, composition), expanding the repertoire (rock was an important focus), and highlighting important figures who symbolized music and freedom, such as Nina Simone. There were also discussions of the different forms that freedom takes. A huge poster with the word "freedom" at the top was stuck up in the foyer of the school, and students and staff contributed ideas over the course of the year on post-it notes.

Fig. 18. Santa Fé school project, "Rock, a song of freedom." Photo by the author (2018). CC BY.

In general, the shift to new ways of learning and working was more of a struggle for the integrated ensembles, which were the spaces most dedicated to high-level concert performance. One exception was the popular music ensemble, which already had a more progressive approach before the shifts of 2018. In rehearsals that I attended, the director created moments for collective reflection, and he urged the students to listen widely and research. He criticized a tendency among some musicians to skip over the listening and research parts and go straight to the score. He urged them to be thinkers as well as musicians, declaring that he was not interested in people who could only play the notes in front of them.

The REMM (Red de Escuelas de Música de Medellín) Ensemble emerged from the ashes of the hybrid ensemble that went on tour to the US in 2018. In its new incarnation in 2019, its emphasis was on putting students in charge of learning. They were encouraged to take decisions and occupy leadership roles. The ensemble was also framed as a space for acquiring twenty-first-century skills.

Some of the most progressive initiatives took place in new ensembles that were given the title of "laboratories." If introducing PBL was an attempt to reform the operation of existing structures (schools and integrated ensembles), the laboratories created new spaces for more radical ideas to flourish, circumventing rather than confronting the inertia that any large, longstanding institution generates. The Laboratory of Intercultural Creation was based on a critique of the idea of social inclusion, which its director described as trying to squeeze one social group into the worldview of another. This laboratory was underpinned by the more sophisticated philosophy of critical interculturality. It was designed as a space for getting to know oneself and interacting with others, and for creation, fantasy, and making mistakes, using not just music but also visual and plastic arts, literature, painting, and theatre. It also aimed to make both cultural and practical connections with local contexts; for example, the advanced students had a project called "Expanded School" that opened the doors of the laboratory to different forms of music-making in the surrounding territory. The Early Years Laboratory, meanwhile, took an interdisciplinary form: classes were led by a pair of teachers from two different art forms, so that a musician would be joined by a dancer, actor, or visual artist.

A New Vision of SATM

There were a few discrete moments in 2017–18 when a different approach to SATM flourished for a day or two. These were activities in which the management was closely involved and the program was briefly liberated from its longstanding traditions by the involvement of visiting staff or unusual students. They gave fascinating glimpses of a reinvented SATM.

One such event was the two-day "Afro laboratory" in October 2017. It brought together musicians from the Red and the Moravia cultural centre with Afro-Colombian dancers from the Red's sister program, the Dance Network, to learn music and dance from Colombia's Pacific coast. Two prominent Afro-Colombian musicians from the coastal Chocó region joined Giraldo as leaders of the workshop. Most of the dance students' families were originally from Chocó as well, and with few Afro-Colombians in the Red, the event was an opportunity for the young musicians to learn more about their own city and its diverse inhabitants and cultures, as well as about music and dance from the coast. (One participant admitted that she had had little interaction with Afro-diasporic cultural expressions before, despite her school being located in a cultural centre that also housed capoeira and traditional percussion groups.)

Alongside the artistic activities (which included the musicians learning to dance and vice versa), the event was marked by several eloquent and extended speeches by Giraldo and the invitees from Chocó, which were notable for their critiques of the Eurocentrism of music education in Colombia and their insistence on the importance of learning about the country's diverse cultures. One of the Afro-Colombian guests made repeated references to colonialism, slavery, and domination, and he highlighted the country's history of valorizing European knowledge and relegating indigenous and African culture to the margins. Giraldo proclaimed that the Red should invite more local master musicians like these, and not just foreign orchestra or band conductors.

A couple of weeks later, Giraldo also led an away day for the Red's administrative staff. The focus of the event was not administrative matters, though, but rather music. The staff spent the day playing musical games, trying out percussion instruments, writing songs in groups, jamming, and dancing, but also having lengthy and open discussions about music. Giraldo put his key topics (diversity, identity, interculturality) squarely on the table and encouraged the administrators to reflect on music and its relationship to their personal and emotional lives. Many talked about the role of music in their childhood, the genres they grew up around, the tastes and abilities of family members, and their favourite dance styles. The exercises allowed the administrators to emerge as individuals with rich musical lives. Almost all highlighted popular music, whether Colombian, Latin American, or North American. Why, then, asked Giraldo, is the Red so focused on classical music? He spoke to the administrators about cultural colonialism, the importance of horizontal dialogue between musics, and banishing an inherited sense of shame about local and national musics that has been so prominent in Colombian musical history. He also talked about music as a form of resistance and liberation.

These days were opportunities for Giraldo to put into practice his new ideas and explore what really mattered to him, without the constraints of the Red's traditions and expectations. The contrast with the program's usual activities was striking. There was less emphasis on instrumental teaching and more on a broad range of activities (listening, talking, creating) and ways of learning (playful, corporeal). These events created more spaces for fun (there were games, dancing, and laughter throughout the away day) but also for serious discussion of cultural history and politics. Both events involved participants in two artforms (music and dance). In short, these days saw the Red serve up a more varied, balanced, and enjoyable cultural diet. They gave a glimpse of what SATM might look like if it tore up the old model of symphonic training and started again.

The Red in Comparative Perspective

There were many parallels between the Red and El Sistema in the years around 2000. Both were founded by famously charismatic male leaders with an extraordinary capacity to inspire young people, their families, and funders. They shared a quasi-religious aspect, with a leader like a high priest and a cohort of devotees who were so committed and absorbed that the program almost became their life. Both Abreu and Ocampo were adored by their many fans. After a day of fieldwork, D. wrote to me: "The whole thing with Juan Guillermo [Ocampo] is a very emotional topic, it's like the feeling that many people had who knew Abreu. A kind of hyper-intense idolatry. Everyone who knew [Ocampo] and talks about him cries when they tell me the story." But critics characterized their programs as cults of personality. The newspaper headline that announced Ocampo's fall—"apostle of Medellín's child musicians imprisoned in the US"—captures the striking, paradoxical atmosphere of sanctity and scandal that surrounded these leaders.[12] Both programs, behind rosy public narratives, displayed deep contradictions that stemmed directly from their founders, complex characters who were idolized by some and abhorred by others—a tension captured in the labelling of Abreu as "the Philanthropic Ogre" (Rivero 1994). The intensive seminars in Medellín led by Venezuelan teachers were characteristic El Sistema-style events: the young musicians were shut away morning, noon, and night for two weeks of boot-camp-style training, and emerged playing the same orchestral repertoire as in Venezuela. The Red was like an adopted son of El Sistema.

The first phase saw the foundation of the program and a rapid-fire series of crowning achievements and successes. It also saw the construction of an almost mythical narrative about its founder and the power of music. Ocampo's arrest and imprisonment were like The Fall, and the dramatic nature of this rupture led to a process of critical scrutiny and organizational change that has lasted to this day.

The year 2005 saw an institutional break with El Sistema, as the Venezuelan program's closeness to Ocampo and Amadeus seems to have precluded collaboration with the Red's new management. But it also saw the beginnings of a more gradual separation at the levels of ideology and practice, rooted in successive internal investigations that shed critical light on the model and dynamics that had been developed in Medellín under El Sistema's supervision. Arango's 2006 report set out clearly, if briefly, a fundamental problem with the orthodox model of SATM: the Red aimed and claimed to generate peaceful coexistence yet in reality was found to encourage arrogance, exclusion, and disrespect in many of its most successful participants. This was a bombshell finding, and it was expressed not in an external report that could be ignored and quietly shelved, as had happened in El Sistema (Baker and Frega 2018), but rather in a foundational document written by the program's leader. It struck at the heart of the orthodox SATM philosophy that positive social action results automatically from collective music education.

The social team's reports, meanwhile, underlined the gap between the orchestra as metaphor and reality. As Pérez, the municipal cultural

---

12　See Baker 2014; Araujo 2017; and my blog post "Abreu's phantom PhD", https://geoffbakermusic.wordpress.com/el-sistema-the-system/el-sistema-blog/abreus-phantom-phd/.

official, noted, the metaphor is very powerful: "the kids sound together, in a society that struggles to sound together"; SATM is "the search for harmony in a society that still can't find it." Yet the social team found that sounding together was perfectly compatible with social discord. The tales of rivalries and hierarchies between players of different instruments will ring a bell with anyone familiar with orchestral culture, and they raise questions about the suitability of the symphony orchestra as a tool for peaceful coexistence.[13] At the very least, they showed that the search for coexistence in the Red had a long way to go.

Students and staff were ambivalent about the program's social goals and indicated the prioritizing of musical results over social processes. Echoing earlier interviews with members of El Sistema (Baker and Frega 2018), testimonies from across the Red's constituencies undermined claims—commonplace in SATM circles—that the pursuit of musical excellence is in itself an effective form of social action. In reality, the Red appeared to have as many social problems as any other large organization. The social team proposed an array of extra-musical strategies and interventions such as "coexistence away days" to deal with the problems, illustrating their conviction that music-making alone did not resolve such issues—indeed, it sometimes generated them. They argued that excessive belief in the power of music was not only misplaced but had also led to complacency, allowing social problems to flourish. These realist portraits of the ups and downs of SATM, the heterogeneity of opinions within a single program, and the tensions between theory and practice, provide a fascinating contrast with the dominant public narrative of SATM.

These internal analyses, starting in 2006, formed the bedrock of a process of continual self-critique and reform that continues to this day. Over time, the Red drew steadily away from El Sistema. The repeated changes of director, and their selection from outside the organization, led to much more debate and adaptation in the Red than in the monolithic Venezuelan program, which remained under Abreu's conservative thumb for forty-three years and was handed on to his protégé and

---

13   The furore that erupted when the bassoonist Francesca Carpos conveyed the culture of the professional symphony orchestra to students at the Royal Academy of Music illustrated just how complex and potentially controversial the dynamics of this ensemble actually are (see Rahim 2019).

chosen successor. These management changes in the Red allowed for self-evaluation and evolution. El Sistema, in contrast, developed unimpeded as a cult of personality, so reforms have tended to be small and slow. Growth, rather than change, was Abreu's priority. Even after his death, the program has insisted on continuity with his vision; room to critique his philosophy has been non-existent.

The timeline exercise with which this chapter began is a good example of the distance that opened up between the programs. Staff were encouraged to reflect publicly and critically on the Red's past and to join in collective construction of the future. The social team deliberately opened up a space for multiple histories, contrasting visions, and thus a polyphonic and at times dissonant narrative. In contrast, El Sistema's approach to history is obfuscatory: after forty-five years, no official record has been written, and key phases are shrouded in mystery. There has been much to shroud: for example, Abreu's past as a close ally of Hugo Chávez's political foes, or El Sistema's discursive makeover as a social program in the mid-1990s, not to mention the question marks over Abreu's personal history. There are no past regimes; the program's history is presented as a seamless whole, a simple story of the single-minded pursuit of one man's dream. An event like the timeline meeting would have been inconceivable in Abreu's hermetic, hierarchical institution, whose ethos was summed up as "everyone needs to be fully in tune in order to achieve unison" (Borzacchini 2010, 7). The Red's management argued that the Medellín of 2018 was not the Medellín of 1996, and that the program needed to change along with the city. El Sistema, however, remains bound to the original vision of its founder.

If Abreu and his lieutenants struck a consistently idealistic, propagandistic tone, both internally and externally, Giraldo was refreshingly realistic and open about the Red's defects and challenges, and he generally avoided utopian statements about the program or music as a model for society. He described music as "a complicated profession." The program had highlights and lowlights, he said; it was neither a panacea nor a disaster. As he told a group of senior students, "the Red displays the full human comedy."

The Venezuelan program has played up the issue of poverty as a marketing strategy and selling point, and its success in attracting funding illustrates that this approach has been highly successful. In

Medellín, however, there has been considerable and overt distaste for musical "poverty porn" since 2005. The Red has not gone down the path of carefully selecting individuals and dramatic anecdotes from the most deprived corners of the city in order to appeal to foreigners and funders, recognizing this approach as stigmatizing rather than empowering.

The Red has also moved towards a critical approach to the notion of social inclusion, which has been the bedrock of El Sistema since the 2000s. In Venezuela, this notion has been conceived narrowly in economic terms—as opening the doors to those with few economic resources. Other kinds of exclusion, such as race- or gender-based, have been largely overlooked. The framework of social inclusion has served to perpetuate educational conservatism: the underlying presumption is that existing practice works but is simply insufficiently disseminated. The way to social inclusion, for El Sistema, is widening access, not transforming practice. Behind this discourse lies a high-performance program that relies on high-functioning young musicians, and while it has separate branches for children with major, diagnosed disabilities, the main program—with its demanding, intensive, conventional musical training—is exclusive to children with less pronounced or undiagnosed learning difficulties, and indeed to children who simply do not fit easily into that training mould. In the Red, however, there was a growing awareness that access is not the same as inclusivity: for example, the number of black students and participants with disabilities was low in the Red, even though there were no formal barriers to their involvement. Many staff felt uncomfortable that they did not have the training or tools to deal with children with common disabilities and disorders. By embracing the more critical concept of interculturality and invoking open pedagogies, the management both critiqued inclusion and aspired to a deeper form of inclusivity than just access to standard music education.

The flaws in orthodox SATM's claims of social inclusion are evident in the high dropout rates from El Sistema, the Red, and other SATM programs, revealing that this kind of music education does not appeal to many children. In the Red in 2018, nearly 40% of students dropped out within a year; in El Sistema, 44% of students who were offered a place failed to complete two semesters (Alemán et al. 2017). The Portuguese El Sistema-inspired Orquestra Geração experienced a dropout rate over the first two years ranging from 38–49% (Mota and Teixeira Lopes 2017), and Sistema Aotearoa's rate was 38% (see Baker, Bull, and Taylor 2018). There are important questions to be asked about programs that include young people through music only to see many of them leave again soon afterwards. But dominant narratives of SATM usually focus on the musical achievements of a small number of older students and ignore the reality that many participants drop out within a year or two of starting. The many for whom SATM does not "work" simply disappear from view in publicity and media accounts. El Sistema historically deflected questions on this topic; for years, even the program's biggest supporters were unable to elicit figures. Booth (2008, 4) noted that "a number of students leave around age 12 (percentages were not available….)." Borzacchini (2010, 101) asked the then executive director Igor Lanz a straight question: "What is the percentage of children who leave the orchestras?" "One cannot talk about dropping out," replied Lanz evasively. The truth came out in a 2017 evaluation (Alemán et al. 2017): the IDB could and did talk about students dropping out, in considerable numbers. This issue may have been avoided by El Sistema, but it was a prime concern for the Red's pedagogical team in 2018.

A similar deepening of reflection can be seen in the area of participation. El Sistema succeeded in getting many more young people to participate in classical music, but it failed to make classical music more participatory. The *quality* of the participation did not change, even if the *quantity* did; the basic values of conventional concert music remained in practice, even if the discourse turned more participatory halfway through its history. In the Red, though, from Arango onwards, participation became a topic for analysis and reform. Successive directors reflected on what participation really meant and how it might be boosted. Their conceptions of participation varied, but all understood that simply playing in an orchestra was not enough.

It is also instructive to consider the parallels between the Red's long internal process of self-critique and external research on the Venezuelan program and its offshoots. For example, Arango (2006, 10) wrote that the Red lacked a coherent and consistent pedagogical model, "despite presenting itself as an alternative proposal for education." Ana Lucía Frega drew a similar conclusion after studying El Sistema as a consultant for the IDB in 1997 (Frega and Limongi 2019). There are also striking similarities between the Red's internal reports and Eva Estrada's (1997) evaluation of El Sistema for the IDB in the same year (see Baker and Frega 2018). Estrada found widespread disillusionment and "contradictions between the stated values and the actual practices of El Sistema" (1997, 6). Musicians accused the program of "fomenting behaviour and attitudes in the students that are contrary to those values" (13). Gaps between theory and practice were glaring. In the words of one musician: "the musical world could be as bad or worse than what you saw on the streets, I thought that a world of sensitive people would be something very attractive, very interesting, I had high expectations, and I saw a lot of cruelty, a lot of meanness, apathy, ignorance" (5). Its orchestras were presented as generating negative social dynamics such as competitiveness, favouritism, dishonesty, hypocrisy, and betrayal. One musician stated: "What I thought a musician must be isn't the reality [...] there is jealousy and a bloody battle to stand out." The report also highlights the narrowness and poor quality of the training, described by one musician as "producing musicians like sausages" (21). A fundamental problem was that developing positive values was of lesser importance to the program than "merely ensuring that the repertoire is ready. The organization, the pedagogical style, and the administration of employees are based on making the orchestra sound" (23). El Sistema may have been reframed as a social program by this time, but in reality it was still all about the music.

The similarities between Estrada's evaluation of El Sistema and the Red's internal reports would be uncanny had the Medellín program not operated as a satellite of the Venezuelan one. As it is, they reach similar conclusions because they describe the same model, illustrating that what emerged in both locations were not aberrations but rather inherent features. Where they differ significantly is in their reception: Estrada and Frega's reports were ignored by Abreu, whereas the Red's counterparts formed a cornerstone of efforts at reform.

The evidence that the Red generated mixed responses and effects is matched by research on other SATM programs (e.g. Sarazin 2017; Rimmer 2018). The overlaps between the Red's internal reports and my book on El Sistema are too many to list, but the presence of social problems such as competition, bullying, and hierarchization, and the frequent voicing of critical opinions by students and staff, stand out. Indeed, there was a certain element of déjà vu in my Medellín fieldwork. In 2014, I critiqued El Sistema's construction of practical and philosophical separations between students and their surrounding social reality. In 2018, the Red created a territorial team to address precisely this issue. In 2014, after visiting a problem-based urban cartography project on the periphery of Medellín, I wondered "how could a music education project strive to offer a comparable experience?" (Baker 2014, 313). Four years later, the Red embarked on PBL. In 2014, I reflected on the narrowness of the conception of social inclusion in El Sistema and the importance of extending inclusivity to curriculum and pedagogy. The Red's management was thinking along similar lines in 2018. I also critiqued the narrowness of the music education in orthodox SATM. In 2018, the Red made a concerted effort to broaden its offering in the Red beyond instrumental skills and ensemble performance. I raised questions about the dominance of classical music. The Red had been asking similar questions for years. My analysis of the absence of student voice, empowerment, genuine participation, reflection, and creativity found a clear echo in the efforts of successive Red managements and social teams.

Management critiques in the Red thus reinforce and are reinforced by the academic literature on SATM. The Red's process of self-critique and change underlines the point that has been gaining traction in the international research field in recent years: behind the grandiose, utopian rhetoric of SATM, the reality is usually more complicated. The findings from Medellín (and other programs) confirm that key issues identified in critical studies of El Sistema are not specific to that institution but are rather problems with the model itself. Comparison with international research, meanwhile, shows that the Red's reform process should not be viewed as simply the whims of a series of senior managers in Medellín.

The Red's trajectory constitutes a significant challenge to SATM's orthodoxy from the inside. There have been numerous critiques of SATM published since 2014, but mainly from the academic world.[14] It is therefore highly significant to find similar perspectives emerging from *within* a major program. It is also noteworthy that these internal and external analyses developed in isolation from one another. The

---

14   Though see Dobson (2016), Fairbanks (2019), and Godwin (2020) for insiders' analyses.

reports discussed in this chapter were written before any critical research on SATM was published, and since they were internal, they were unknown to SATM scholars. That both research strands arrived independently at similar conclusions is very suggestive. Similarly, the Red's transformations in 2018 echoed my 2014 book in numerous ways, yet the program's managers had not read my research. There are profound implications for the future course of debate about SATM: it will be much harder for critiques to be ignored or brushed off in future, as has often been the case to date.

The Red's pursuit of diversity, identity, creativity, territory, and participation shows parallels not just with the critical literature on El Sistema but also with international scholarship more broadly. The Red distanced itself from El Sistema, but it drew closer to critical and reformist currents in research on music education and youth development. The Red's recent priorities and initiatives look eminently familiar from the point of view of volumes such as *The Oxford Handbook of Social Justice in Music Education* (2015) and *The Oxford Handbook of Community Music* (2018), with their emphasis on issues such as creativity, critical reflection, student voice, and place-based learning. Researchers of youth in Medellín, too, have argued passionately for centring such approaches in activities for young people (*Jóvenes* 2015). Leaders' urge for the Red to transcend technical training and engage more directly with the social and cultural realities surrounding its schools is mirrored throughout Elliott el al.'s (2016) volume *Artistic Citizenship* and in Hess's (2019) vision of music education for social change. Distaste for salvationism has been articulated by researchers of music education (Vaugeois 2007; McCarthy 2018) and CM (Howell 2017; Mantie 2018), who have understood it as reinforcing oppression and inequality. Concerns over Eurocentrism and the coloniality of the Red find a clear echo in the growing academic interest in decolonization and music education, particularly in Latin America.[15] As far as I am aware, none of this international research was known within Red circles, yet the Medellín program seemed to be moving in a comparable direction.

Observing critiques and reforms in Medellín through the lens of senior management tells us much about both the Red and its abandoned

---

15 See, for example, special issues of *Revista Internacional de Educación Musical* (5:1, 2017) and *Action, Theory, and Criticism for Music Education* (18:3, 2019).

progenitor, El Sistema. Nevertheless, this narrative of crisis, self-examination, breaking away from the old model, and imagining more progressive alternatives tells only part of the story. The clue is in the repetition that I have deliberately conserved in this chapter in order to convey both my own experience of researching the program and an essential characteristic of its history. It was easy to grasp the new management's critique when I arrived in 2017, but over the course of a year of fieldwork, as I interviewed former employees and read old documents, I came to realize that attempts to address these issues were not new but rather had been recurrent in the history of the Red. Since 2006, senior managers had been urging that the social side needed to be taken more seriously; that the Red was a public program and therefore ought to be more participatory; that it should distance itself from dynamics of pity and charity; that it should strive for greater musical diversity; that students should have more voice; and so on. That they were still doing so more than a decade later is a strong indication that self-critique was one thing, change another.

This reiteration suggests that these were deep-rooted issues and real sticking points. There was some consensus at management level over problems in the orthodox model, but it was easier to identify them than to solve them. The repetitiveness of the critiques implies that such issues spring from this model of musical-social work and are therefore difficult to eliminate while maintaining it. It also points to the fact that critical analysis and reform efforts generated operational friction, tensions, counter-critiques, and resistance.

2. The Red Pushes Back: Tensions, Debates, and Resistance

> The Red saves children. But it eats adults.
>
> Former general director

In August 2018, the Red gave a workshop at an event for municipal employees, "Intermediaries of Civic Culture." Javier, a member of the social team, led a brainstorming exercise in which participants listed "virtues of a public servant" and "virtues of a citizen" on posters and discussed their ideas. Afterwards, Fabién, a music teacher, led them in a rendition of Pharrell Williams' "Happy." At the end of the day, they stayed behind to discuss the following day of the workshop; they had too much material and needed to cut some. However, the conversation soon became heated. Javier accused his musician colleague of not listening to the organizers' instructions about the importance of the social aspect and instead proposing ordinary musical activities. Fabién snapped back that Javier had said nothing in advance about leading a conceptual exercise, otherwise Fabién would have planned his own contributions differently; he also complained that he had already been obliged to cut his musical activities because the social exercise went on too long. "I'm a musician, I was invited here to do music," shouted Fabién; "I'm confused."

Fig. 19. Virtues of a citizen, Intermediaries of Civic Culture. Photo by the author (2018). CC BY.

"When Did We Lose the Enchantment?"

The previous chapter examined reform efforts by successive Red managements. Here, the focus is on how staff and students responded. The program of reform from 2017–19, as described so far, might sound like something out of a progressive music education textbook. The reality was rather more complex. The management's critiques and new initiatives generated tensions and were met by counter-critiques and resistance. Indeed, relations between management and staff were variable and at times quite discordant. This tension was manifested as a passive atmosphere of disengagement in large meetings; when certain topics were presented, mobile phones, tablets, and earphones came out in greater numbers. A week-long event to showcase new initiatives coincided with the 2018 football World Cup, and some staff, while obliged to be present, conspicuously watched the games on various devices at the back of the hall. There were also occasionally more actively critical responses on such occasions, and complaints were frequent in private conversations. Despite the euphonious sounds emerging from its classrooms, the Red was not a harmonious institution during this period. As Aníbal Parra, the head of the social team, said to the musical staff in one meeting: "we need to ask ourselves, when did we lose the enchantment?"

Resistance grew over time. 2017 was a year of watching and waiting; 2018 saw more restlessness; and in 2019 discontent escalated to the point of open rebellion, which coalesced as a formal letter of complaint from the school directors to the Red's operator, the University of Antioquia. Yet tensions were not a recent development. Former general directors acknowledged that the changes they had introduced had produced some discomfort or discord at times, including power struggles within the management team and increased turnover of staff and students.

It was not just management and staff who criticized each other; tensions between most constituencies were visible at some point. Certain relationships were more fraught than others, though. The social team and the musical staff were most clearly at odds with one another. At times the tension was evident in body language or disengagement in meetings when the social team spoke or organized activities, but there were also more open disputes.

A year of fieldwork allowed me to observe the grinding of the institutional gears as changes were implemented. In official narratives, SATM appears as a seamless whole, from the vision at the top to the practice at the bottom. The Red showed the reality to be quite different: in a multi-layered program, there is the potential for gaps and tensions at every step. New strategies forged by management are mediated and filtered by directors, teachers, and administrators, and may be embraced or rejected by students. It is a mistake to assume that a SATM program is simply what its leader states publicly; the mediators and participants may have other ideas and do otherwise in practice.

The point here is not that the Red is a dysfunctional institution; in some ways, its open disagreements point to the opposite conclusion. A certain amount of internal friction is par for the course in large institutions, particularly during moments of change, and dissonance may actually be the sound of a healthy organization. Nevertheless, the Red's internal dynamics of tension and resistance are worth exploring because public and academic discussion of SATM has barely touched on them, creating an illusory picture of harmony and unity, yet they help us to understand the field better. These sticking points in the Red illuminate points of tension in SATM more broadly and throw up some important questions for the field: how should SATM compare to conventional music education? How to balance the musical and social sides? How to mediate between the conflicting desires of different constituencies in shaping the program? Are teachers properly trained for this job? Does SATM "work" for them?

If the previous chapter focused on growing, this one centres on the accompanying pains. What is of interest here is not friction or disharmony per se, but rather what lay beneath it. Hence this chapter focuses on tensions that were underpinned by conflicting visions or ideologies, rather than personal differences. These debates allow us to grasp the Red as fragmented rather than unified, contested rather than consensual, and thus SATM as a complex set of choices and challenges rather than a singular, guaranteed recipe for success.

The main organizing principle is that of "first-order" debates. These debates were foregrounded in the program, regularly articulated by a wide array of actors, and therefore particularly audible and visible. They revolved around what were widely recognized as the Red's major issues.

Music and the Social

"There's a weak point in the program, it's always been a strong tension: where does the social end, where does the musical begin? How does one accompany the other?" said Diego, a school director. One of the general directors placed their fists together, knuckles to knuckles, to depict the struggle between the musical and the social. This striking gesture encapsulated the fiercest and most prominent debate in the Red, based on fundamental disagreement over what SATM should look like.

In its first phase, the program adopted the El Sistema view that collective music education *is* social action. After it changed operators in 2005, there was a recognition that some students suffered from psychological problems, so the program hired Jiménez to provide individual psychological consultations. Soon, there was a shift to focusing on collective problems and solutions, so Jiménez led a team that offered psychosocial workshops and training to the whole program. Under Restrepo's leadership, more emphasis was placed on a socio-affective approach, which led to greater efforts to integrate social development into the music curriculum, rather than equating the social with the extra-musical. Under Giraldo, the social team refocused its efforts on research, but a year later the social team morphed into a territorial team (as detailed in Chapter 1). This thumbnail sketch is enough to illustrate that the Red's approach to social action has shifted continually over the course of its history. Far from being the rock on which the program has been built, the social goal has been more like shifting sands, generating much of the unsteadiness and debate that has characterized the Red since 2005.

To return to the Red's first phase, the social aspect of the program—in Ocampo's account of his philosophy of SATM—revolved around key words such as "heart," "love," and "hug." Sara, a student from that period, remembered the music schools as "a space for a different kind of affectivity." The Red's social philosophy was never clarified at that time, she said, but in practice it was about being together and looking after each other. Ocampo was like a father to her, and everyone adored him. He had an extraordinary capacity to remember everyone's name and details about their life. She stressed the emotionality of students' interactions with Ocampo; he made them feel special and loved. Norberto, a fellow first-generation student, concurred that the social aspect of the Red was implicit at that time. The mere fact that a child went to music school *was* social action, because many left the house as little as possible due to the city's dangers. Creating spaces for fraternizing within violent barrios was a social act.

The transition from Ocampo to Arango in 2005 was an abrupt change in many ways, including from an emotional to a more rational approach to SATM. Ocampo's leadership style was charismatic and passionate, and he was somewhat dismissive of intellectual analysis. In contrast, Arango was a sociologist by training and a university employee, and her first major action was to undertake a critical examination of the program. The creation of the psychosocial team, too, evidenced a turn towards a more reflective approach. There was also a shift in the understanding of the word "social." For Ocampo, it was about the heart and the emotions. For Arango, however, its primary meaning was "public." She saw social action as empowering citizens to take responsibility for the Red as a public program.

2005 was a definitive turning point. It saw a splintering of understandings of SATM that continued under each successive leadership. Also, there emerged a distinction between implicit and explicit framings of social action. At first, social action was considered to flow spontaneously from music education, aided by Ocampo's warmth, charisma, and inspirational speeches. But in Arango's phase, senior figures increasingly conceived of the social objective as something to be named, analysed, and pursued more overtly. Social action was not an automatic consequence, then, but rather a possible outcome, which required reinforcing some existing elements and adopting new ones.

The "social as implicit" argument came under pressure as soon as the program passed from a nominally public but in effect private operation run by a classical music figurehead (echoing El Sistema) to a genuinely public program open to external scrutiny and with a non-musician in charge. As discussed in Chapter 1, internal investigations revealed that while collective music education was capable of generating positive socialization, it could also produce more questionable social effects and fail to teach some important social skills. The transition in 2005 thus saw not just a shift in the meaning of "social," the word at the heart of the Red's mission, but also questions raised about the effectiveness of the program's original approach. The result was the creation of the psychosocial team and the consolidation of the "social as explicit" perspective. There were now two different ways of understanding SATM, giving rise to the program's major tension.

Former Student Perspectives

One might imagine that successful students from the first phase would have embraced the implicit argument, but in reality their views were quite varied. The social team's 2008 report revealed that many staff doubted that music education alone could achieve the Red's social objective. I encountered similar critiques and mixed opinions in interviews with graduates from the first phase who had gone on to become directors or teachers in the Red. Their career path indicated their talent, love of music, and commitment to the program; their ambivalence cannot therefore be put down to failure or incompatibility.

Daniel remembered the Red's beginnings as "magical," but the work rhythm of the first years, when the program was "a mirror of El Sistema," overseen by Venezuelan musicians, was intensive. The long rehearsals were an opportunity to escape from the problems of the city, but the atmosphere was "very military." Rehearsals had no finish time. In this sense, "it wasn't all so pretty"—it was "an education based on fear as well." Many dropped out. "We lost out on a lot of family life," he noted; "the school practically became our home." He was sceptical of his peers who described that time as the Red's "golden age." There was "a level of competition that's incredible, that's not very pleasant, that comes from that training." They were "good performers, but perhaps people who are very rigid and who see the person next to them as a competitor and not a person who is doing a collective task." He believed that the Red's approach built character but also made students more tyrannical. Some went on to become music teachers without reflecting on their own experiences, he said, meaning that the Red continued to be a bit like *Whiplash* (2014).[1] "The first phase had its dark side," he concluded, "which was to create these people. I don't know to what extent that is the society that we want."

Estefanía cried with nostalgia as she recalled the Red's first phase. Today the program's musical level had dropped, she said, partly because El Sistema no longer sent teachers. Yet she also talked about "the Nazi-Venezuelan System" and described the present-day Red as more balanced: now "the Red is part of life, rather than life being the orchestra."

Norberto recalled how the Venezuelans brought their repertoire and set very high goals. When they came, the students would drop everything for one or two weeks of solid rehearsals, eight to ten hours a day, including weekends. At the time he regarded this as normal, as it was all he knew, and while he still had fond memories, now that he was a music school director his feelings were more mixed. He had spent years turning down social invitations in order to rehearse or perform at weekends and had sacrificed friendships outside the Red to create a new "family" within it. He too was critical of a tendency to romanticize the Red's past. Some of his peers talked about the program as though it were perfect in the Ocampo years, he said, but it wasn't. The staff's treatment of students was sometimes harsh because of the pressure to produce results: shouting, swearing, calling the children "idiots," humiliating them in front of their peers. If the children answered

---

[1] *Whiplash* (2014) is a film about abuse in music education: "A promising young drummer enrolls at a cut-throat music conservatory where his dreams of greatness are mentored by an instructor who will stop at nothing to realize a student's potential", https://www.imdb.com/title/tt2582802/.

back, some teachers "practically got the belt out." He characterized the Venezuelan-style approach as rushed and demanding, which worked well for the best students but was a "torment" for others; even he, one of the more talented, sometimes got to the point of thinking "we're no longer enjoying but rather suffering music." One consequence of the high musical goals was that there was no time to reflect on social questions; what mattered was preparing the repertoire for the upcoming concert.

Raquel pointed to this same contradiction: the Red talked a lot about the social objective, but its key activities were concerts and all that mattered was to sound good. Music doesn't make you good or bad, she said; you can be a good person without music, and a bad person with music. Some people who studied in the Red ended up in trouble after they left. The Red was a good option for young people in Medellín, but "having been in the program doesn't guarantee anything." Estefanía concurred: "That whole thing about [exchanging] a violin for a weapon has never been relevant. I had lots of friends who played [music] and were still bad [people]. That was a discourse that worked very well at the time but that's not the real backstory."

Diego reflected on Ocampo's unique charisma. He likened rehearsals to being in church with a priest, only with the focus on music and dreams of the future rather than religious doctrine. Ocampo was a true leader who did everything: he secured resources, sponsors, and tours, but also talked to families and knew every student by name. He convinced people with his rhetorical skill; they felt listened to and supported. "Juan Guillermo became almost like a god": whatever he said, people supported him 100%, because he set out dreams like playing for the Pope and made them come true. And yet, he had human flaws. He was not a great administrator, and he promised many things that did not happen. Diego was not entirely surprised at how Ocampo's history with the Red had finished. But people stopped seeing his faults, because their devotion to him bordered on fanaticism. There were tears when Arango ordered the removal of photos of Ocampo from the schools, even though he had been jailed for a serious crime. Diego concluded that Ocampo deserved gratitude for establishing the program and making a positive contribution to Medellín, but the fanaticism concerned him.

Ocampo had tremendous charisma, concurred Sara, the only one of these graduates to go on to a non-musical career. He had such ability with words that it was hard not to be moved by him. She had seen him as a father figure, and today, part of her retained this image of him. But subsequent experience and maturity—not to mention Ocampo's incarceration—had also given her a contradictory perspective: looking as an adult, putting aside her emotional attachments, she described him as "a snake charmer." Thinking about all the effort the children had put in, all that they had sacrificed, she concluded: "it was abusive. I felt used—I felt used for his benefit."

In these interviews, as in the internal reports, the Red appears as much more ambiguous than one would imagine from media stories, which painted the program as a kind of miracle. A question mark hangs over the social side, in particular. With their accounts of an atmosphere that was militaristic, sometimes oppressive, with little time for social reflection, some former students queried whether peaceful coexistence or an education in values—the program's raison d'être—were achieved or even seriously pursued. Their testimonies placed the "social as implicit" argument in doubt.

In the 2008 report, most constituencies expressed concern about the prioritizing of the musical in practice. Some staff recognized the Red's social deficiencies and requested that action be taken. Consequently, Jiménez urged the program to give the social dimension more emphasis and visibility and to unite behind "the goal of going beyond artistic and musical training to provide a rounded human education with social impact on the communities in which the schools are inserted" ("Informe" 2008, 3). Henceforth, the newly formed psychosocial team had its hands full organizing extra-musical workshops and activities to tone down the disciplinarian, time-consuming, all-absorbing culture that the Red had inherited from El Sistema and to pursue the social objective more purposefully. The "social as explicit" perspective moved into the ascendency. Staff responses to the team were noted as largely positive: they appreciated that "the Red was showing concern for them as people and not just as musicians" (7) and expressed the desire for the process to continue.

The picture in 2008 thus shows some consensus about the contradictions of SATM and the need for new strategies. Certainly, opinions varied, but many staff revealed mixed feelings about the social side and encouraged more involvement by social professionals. Yet by the time of my fieldwork, around a decade later, the relationship between the musical and the social, and between the musicians and social team, had become the program's major sticking point.

Music *versus* the Social

One day in 2018, Parra, the head of the social team, walked into a management meeting. He sat down and with no preamble declared: "this is not a social program." Around the same time, a musician from the first generation lamented that the program had lost its musical focus and become all about the social side, which was *una pendejada, una cagada*—a load of nonsense, a pile of crap. How had the Red come to generate such exasperated and diametrically opposed interpretations? Why had the ideal of SATM come to look so fraught in practice, acted out in mutual suspicion and tense encounters between musical and social staff? Why had combining music and social action become so complicated?

If there had been some agreement on the nature of the problem, there was less consensus on what to do about it and who should do it. The different approaches (psychosocial, socio-affective, territorial) that were tried in an effort to rebalance the musical and the social led to criticism and dissatisfaction from many musicians, who came to see the social team as a destabilizing force. The social team, meanwhile, viewed such responses as resistance to change.

Social team reports and musicians' testimonies point towards a fundamental, structural tension between the goals of social action and musical excellence in the Red's orchestras and bands. From its creation, the social team questioned the priority given to musical excellence over social action and proposed a shift in balance. Thus the relationship between the social and musical employees emerged as one that was in some sense antagonistic: the social team took on the role of providing a critical perspective on the musical side. The musicians had been working for a decade without anyone criticizing them (on the contrary, they were used to fulsome praise), so the sharp vision of Jiménez and her assistants was something of a rude awakening. The creation of a social team with a critical role was thus the initial source of division. As the social team wrote a decade later: "The social [side] is the one that sees the complexities, the musical [side] sees everything as fine" ("Informe" 2017c, 72). Now the Red tried to pursue two distinct goals—musical excellence and social action—at the same time via two distinct teams, and the priorities and practices of the musical and social staff were not just different but also often in contradiction.

The division into musical and social sides led gradually to polarization. In 2008, the social team was a novelty. However, a decade of workshops, training sessions, discussions, and urgings led not to a closer embrace of the social goal but rather to a generalized sense of fatigue. By the time of my fieldwork, a significant proportion of musical staff regarded any social activity with suspicion and were resistant to non-musical initiatives. Many musicians came to see explicitly social activities as extra work, a distraction, or a waste of precious rehearsal time, and the social team as a thorn in their side. Meanwhile, the social team (and leadership) considered the program to be too focused still on musical technique and performance and too obsessed with issues such as the details of the music curriculum, reducing its social efficacy.

Some musicians reacted against the increasing profile and activity of the social team by retrenching in the "social as inherent" view. Some members of the first generation, in particular, began to hanker after the simpler days of their youth, when all efforts were devoted to music and explicit social activities were considered unnecessary. The Red had worked for them, and what they saw over subsequent phases was increasing meddling and a decline in musical quality. We never needed psychologists or territorial managers, said one, because Ocampo made us believe in him: that was the social part. According to a school director, the social discourse about children taking up instruments rather than weapons was for the politicians who provided the funds; internally, the focus was on preparing repertoire, raising the artistic level, and working with invited musicians. There was no need for a psychologist: Ocampo was a great motivator and his powerful rhetoric kept the momentum up. The whole social side is a load of nonsense, said another director; the best form of psychological attention is putting an instrument in a kid's hands and teaching them to play music. One teacher kept repeating in our interview that he was a musician—this was his identity. "This is the Music Network," he said, "not the Network of Social Inclusion with Music as a Medium." What emerges from these accounts is a sense of nostalgia for simplicity—for a program driven by one man's vision, with one focus: the music.

The implicit/explicit debate played out in a long, drawn-out dispute over constructing a new form for the directors' monthly reports. The leadership believed that the Red's social objective ought to be identifiable in specific activities, and those activities should be describable on the report form. The directors argued back that the social was inherent in everything that the Red did, and it could not therefore be tied to particular activities or spelt out in a report. For the former, if the social was the central objective of the Red, then it had to be named and narrated; for the latter, if the social was the essence of the Red, it could not be named and narrated. This long-running debate over a superficially boring, administrative matter encapsulated key dynamics in the Red, which is why the management organized repeated, painful meetings to thrash it out: not just the division over implicit versus explicit conceptions of SATM, but also the question of top-down versus collective construction. Ironically, the management insisted that the directors should be involved in creating the form, while the staff wanted the management to present them with something ready to use.

Attitudes were certainly not uniform, however, and some musical staff continued to be sceptical about the idea that social action was implicit in music and displayed more openness to the idea of reinventing themselves and the Red. One director criticized her colleagues' recalcitrance: "introducing the socio-affective part in the lesson activities was very difficult, people put up a lot of resistance because they said that music already in itself exercises a social function. [They said:] 'The fact that I play an instrument very well makes me a better person, I don't need to be taught values.'" Another director regarded music education as a positive force at first, one that removed children from problematic environments and gave them another way of seeing the world. But after a certain point, he said, the ones who take it more seriously start to become increasingly egocentric: "it's all about me and my instrument." He claimed that musicians who spent hours practising and staring in the mirror ended up thinking that the world revolved around them. He found that advanced students were sometimes unwilling to give back to the Red. "We are very egotistical," he said, "and I don't know what we need to change this, because as a program we shouldn't be like this." A third director remarked: "if music is the most sublime art, that which is closest to God, if it is something so great, then musicians should be humbler, but on the contrary they have a huge ego. How does one reach the divine full of pride?"

The issue of the musical and the social became a battleground because the splintering of conceptions of SATM had practical as well as ideological consequences. There are clues in the 2008 report. The musical staff generally thought that the social objective was important, but some felt that their responsibility was musical and that the social aspects were a matter for others, particularly the social team and the corporal expression teachers. This was the Red's initial approach post-2005: employing a professional psychologist, which kept the social work separate from the musical training. But as time passed, the management and social team began increasingly to question this division of labour, and as the social staff drew closer to the musical coalface, the tensions grew. Once the psychosocial team started organizing activities in rehearsal time, relations began to deteriorate—and they worsened when the management inserted a socio-affective component into the music curriculum. The more the social team did to address social issues, they more they intruded into established musical practices; and while musical staff may have recognized underlying issues, there was less enthusiasm for rethinking their role, sharing their spaces, or giving up rehearsal time.

Many musicians supported a division of labour, seeing other professionals as more suited to the social aspects of SATM, and became unhappier as the social team encroached on their terrain. The social team was created as an attempt to take the social side of SATM more seriously, but for many musicians it had the opposite effect, reifying a distinction between musical and social work. The incarnation of the social in a critical team gave rise to two interlinked imaginaries: the social as a problem, and the social as someone else's problem ("Informe" 2017c).

The reconfiguration of the social team as a territorial team in 2018 was a case in point. After some initial confusion about what this new role entailed, it gradually became clear that there were conflicting visions of whose responsibility it was to do the territorial legwork. For the leadership, music education should be more connected to its surrounding community, and the territorial team would act as a catalyst, advising the musicians on making stronger connections with their communities. The leaders sought to reimagine the role of the musical staff, adding a spatial dimension. Many directors and teachers, however, argued that their hands were already full in the schools; for them, community relations required walking the streets—just the job for the *gestores territoriales*, or territorial managers, as the social team were now known.

The issue was not so much resistance to the social team, then, as differing views over its desired role. Ever since its creation, the social professionals had sought a more expansive role than simply providing psychological consultations: one that engaged with the full array and complexity of social dynamics in the Red, developed participation and citizenship formation, and generated dialogue with the city and its realities. They sought to promote reflection among the musicians and to foster greater emphasis on social skills within the music training. But many musicians preferred to see the team's purpose as social work writ small: fixing problems and thereby making the teachers' lives easier, allowing them to focus on the music. They measured the social professionals using that yardstick, and the more ambitious and expansive the social team's aims, the shorter it fell in many musicians' eyes.

An important obstacle to reform was the fact that the Red had not been designed to include explicit social strategies; it followed El Sistema's "social as implicit" line. It was constructed as a presentational program (one focused on performances to an audience), if one with a participatory discourse (Turino 2008). In practice, then, it was geared around learning technical skills and repertoire. As the social team wrote: "According to the objective of the Red, music is a tool, and the ultimate goal is a contribution to building citizenship and the rounded education of human beings; but in practice it is clear that the ultimate goal is music, performing, touring. The inconsistency is apparent" ("Informe" 2017c, 7). Thus, efforts to strengthen the social side often appeared as trying to insert something into a program where it did not fit. The Red's schedule was already full. Where and when were these social activities supposed to take place? With what budget? Many of the social team meetings that I attended were devoted to thinking of strategies with which to insert a social component into what was supposedly already a social program. The social employees perceived themselves as trying to squeeze into small or non-existent cracks in a musical edifice; the musicians felt squeezed by these efforts and saw the edifice weakening.

The invisibility of what was supposed to be the Red's primary goal was a frequent topic in reports and meetings. The social team pointed to the detailed musical curriculum but no social equivalent, and the Red's displays of its musical side but never its social processes. Similarly, the social was not measured or evaluated. The team felt sidelined in the planning of activities. They criticized the Red for neglecting the human aspect—particularly in the integrated ensembles—and for avoiding the major issues in students' lives, providing few opportunities for them to express their emotions or chew over their dilemmas. Parra likened the Red's musical instruments to a shield or barrier between students and such questions, rather than a tool for working through them.

Time was another source of tension between the musical and the social. From 2008, the social team was concerned that the Red left students little free time for leisure, family or non-musical relationships. The philosophy of SATM was that free time was a problem and a gap to be filled, whereas for the psychosocial professionals it was a necessity and needed to be defended. They waged and won a battle over reclaiming Sunday as a free day.

Parra lamented regularly that there was no time for social reflection in the Red; the curriculum was full (of music), the work rhythm of rehearsals and performances was excessive, and meetings were usually taken up with logistical, technical, and musical matters. We need to create time in the everyday routine, he said, otherwise we will be condemned to a peripheral existence. But the Red's traditionally presentational character constrained such efforts. The program had always given regular showcase performances across the city, so directors felt pressure to produce musical results and many resisted the "distraction" of non-musical activities. One former social team member recounted that she would try to organize in-depth sessions on social topics only to be met with responses like, "we've got a big concert coming up, we need to rehearse, can you do half an hour in the break?" A school director argued that society judged musicians solely on their ability to play, so he focused on the skills needed to produce decent concerts at short notice. Even an ensemble director who was sympathetic to the need for change said that he was trying hard to make the learning process more participatory, but there was only so much he could do with the deadline of a major concert looming; he had to put on a decent show when the ensemble appeared at the University of Medellín's concert hall.

Attempts to soften the Red's somewhat militaristic approach, too, were widely perceived as weakening its presentational side. As one school director put it, the musical staff "believe that the social [side] stops them from doing their job, this is evident in their thinking that the social team does not allow them to be demanding." A teacher confirmed this view: we're creating a society of useless people, he said, because now there are so many rules around teaching and everything risks being called out as bullying or mistreatment. Today you can't say anything to the kids; you can't simply tell them that they're no good at music. You need to be able to make demands on students, he said, otherwise we're just "educating bums."

Resistance to the social team had another practical dimension. Many musicians connected the hiring of more social professionals to the elimination or reduction of flagship musical activities such as festivals and foreign tours. A number complained that the Red spent money on social staff, who did not add any musical value to the program, instead of resolving longstanding equipment and facilities issues or raising salaries. As one social team member quipped, when they were active, the musicians complained ("why are they interfering?"); and when they were passive, the musicians also complained ("what do they do all day? Why are we wasting money on them?").

Yet even removing the social team from the picture, there were some tensions within the musical side over musical excellence versus social action. The Red's attempt to be both a musical and a social program meant that it treated music as both a professional goal and a pastime, and striking a balance was not straightforward. As one school director explained: "there are rivalries [within the orchestra] between those who go to the rehearsals and those who don't; at the moment there are many problems in my orchestra about this, because it's not fair that those who always go have to put up with someone who doesn't know their part and never goes." At times, the Red felt like two different programs forced together in an uncomfortable marriage. In the morning, the musical staff would urge the management to focus on raising musical standards and projecting musical results on prominent stages; in the afternoon, the social team would argue for more emphasis on the social objective. Not only was the Red unable to meet fully these conflicting demands, but also, by trying to pursue musical excellence and social action at the same time, it left both sides somewhat dissatisfied.

Intermediaries of Civic Culture

In 2013, Medellín's city government created the Network of Artistic and Cultural Practices, which grouped together the Red and three smaller arts education programs in dance, theatre, and visual arts. During 2017–18, the four networks were invited to take part in a city government program called *Mediadores de cultura ciudadana* [Intermediaries of Civic Culture]. It brought municipal employees ranging from traffic policemen to helpdesk staff together for two-day workshops run by the arts networks. The workshops were repeated several times over the year with different participants. Their aim was to use arts education to develop social skills in public servants who worked as intermediaries between the government and the citizenry, and thereby to boost public trust in city functionaries and improve civic culture.

The purpose of the music workshop was thus essentially the same as that of the Red—social action through music—if with a very different constituency. Yet the Red's initial offering was quite distinct from its everyday activities. Its workshop focused on playing, but percussion instruments and Colombian music rather than symphonic ones. Subsequently there was considerable debate at management level and the offering changed, moving even further away from the norm of SATM. New facilitators were brought in to shift the emphasis away from teaching music towards imagining, creating, listening, and connecting. The final workshop I attended included creating soundscapes, relaxation/meditation exercises, working with sonic memory, connecting rhythm and life, and multi-sensorial activities. Interestingly, although the facilitators were Red employees (two school directors, a corporal expression teacher, and a social team member), much of what they brought to Mediadores came from their work outside of (or before joining) the Red, in traditional and popular music. While the workshop had elements of musical initiation and corporal expression, one of the directors likened their new approach to music therapy.

There are distinct echoes of the Afro laboratory and administrators' away day described in Chapter 1. To an even greater extent, Mediadores served as a laboratory of SATM, freed from the constraints of the Red's historical model. Indeed, some senior figures described it in precisely these terms. Here, the management had the freedom to bypass the Red's traditions, select facilitators with specific skills, and pursue social action by any musical means they deemed fit. By its very contrast with the Red's everyday activities, Mediadores underlined the extent to which the Red was still shaped by its history rather than more progressive management visions; the program's form was the outcome of struggle, in which tradition still had the upper hand over reform, rather than consensus.

Mediadores was itself a site of struggle, but not between old and new ways. Neither the starting point nor the end point resembled the Red's normal operations. Rather, the struggle was once again over balancing the musical and the social. It was at Mediadores that the near-fight with which this chapter began occurred. The misunderstanding between the musician and the social team member dramatized the struggle at the heart of the Red. As Fabién noted wryly afterwards, once tempers had calmed, it was ironic that two Red employees had nearly come to blows during an event to which they had been invited to teach others about listening, tolerance, and peaceful coexistence! Their dispute, at the end of an afternoon of upbeat musical activities, illustrated both a hole in SATM theory (no necessary transfer from the musical to the social realm) and the depth of the problem of the musical versus the social. Harmonizing these two sides was a lot more complicated than simply having representatives of both involved.

Much of the debate within the management board and with the organizers concerned aligning music's offering with the aims of Mediadores. At two of the events, a Red ensemble performed at the opening general assembly before the workshops. These were attractive concerts, but as a city arts official noted, they had no connection to Mediadores. It was unclear what these performances were supposed to teach the audience or how they related to the theme of mediation; rather, the Red appeared in its familiar guise as an urban ornament. In contrast, an actor delivered a presentation called "Improv for life," which not only entertained the audience but also provided them with

2. The Red Pushes Back: Tensions, Debates, and Resistance 117

specific and easily memorable life lessons from improvised theatre. After the first workshop, another city official raised a similar point. She had received positive feedback from participants about how much they had enjoyed the music workshop, but the objective of the scheme was not for public servants to enjoy themselves; it was for them to learn something useful for their work. I had observed that workshop and indeed, it was clearly a fun break and a good bonding experience, but it did not provide participants with any obvious tools for their work as civic intermediaries. In this sense, as the officials noted, the Red had somewhat missed the point.

This distinction between enjoyment and fulfilling social aims is very relevant to analyses of SATM. Also relevant is the debate over implicit versus explicit social action. The workshops began in orthodox SATM fashion: involving participants in relatively conventional music-making, and then engaging in a social reading of the activities afterwards. But the Red's social team and city officials criticized this approach and over the year the management moved towards the more challenging method of designing the activities with specific social outcomes in mind. Here the Red's central debate played out in miniature. Participating in these events obliged the Red to invert its usual formula of music taking the lead and think more like a social program. In fact, the many meetings and conversations about the Red's role in Mediadores often resulted in discussions about changing the program itself. As one manager said, Mediadores was an opportunity to strengthen the Red, and he proposed taking the workshop around all the schools.

The Red's sister programs (dance, theatre, and visual arts) also participated in Mediadores, and they offered more innovative workshops. This put further pressure on the Red to up its game. The comparison with the other networks was doubly revealing: while they shared regular activities with the participants, the Red had to invent something new in order to resemble a socially oriented arts program.

The musical versus social debate did not go away, but the obligation to put on a series of events under the watchful eye of culture ministry officials forced it towards a resolution within the microcosm of Mediadores. Change went faster and further compared to the Red as a whole. Here was the Red with much of the resistance removed, working with carefully selected staff and different students, positing music as a means rather than an end, and developing rapidly and innovatively when the weight of history and tradition was put aside. The speed and extent of transformation over one year in Mediadores contrasted with the Red's slow pace and limited reforms over the previous dozen.

These brief moments of florescence suggested how different SATM might look if torn up and started again from a twenty-first-century perspective. They also evoked a question posed in Chapter 1: if such activities were the clearest route to social action, why were they abandoned in the Red after one year of musical initiation so that students could move on to conventional orchestral or band training? Why did the Red not look more like Mediadores?

Staff Training

The answer to this question lies not just in the Red's history but also in the training of its musical staff. They had a variety of profiles and trajectories, so they were not a homogeneous group. Nevertheless, the primary route into the Red was via the music departments of the city's universities, particularly the University of Antioquia, where students received a conventional conservatoire-style education. There were two music degree programs that students followed: the *licenciatura* [bachelor's degree], a broader program with a pedagogical component, aimed mainly at aspiring teachers (but not specifically SATM); and the *maestro de instrumento* [instrumental diploma], which focused more narrowly on performance (primarily of classical music). Many of the Red's teachers came in via the latter path. Additionally, wind and brass players often had a background in directing or playing in municipal bands. There was no professional training available that prepared musicians specifically for socially oriented music education. If the Red did not look more like Mediadores, it was partly because many of the Red's staff did not look much like the Mediadores facilitators.

Judging from its fame, one might imagine that SATM had a curriculum and pedagogy designed by educational experts and delivered by specially trained teachers. The reality is often quite different in Latin America. Rather than creating a distinctive, socially oriented pedagogy, El Sistema borrowed a mixture of existing methods, and it passed on this approach to the Red and other programs. Abreu was a conductor and performer rather than a pedagogue, and his "method" consisted of long, demanding, repetitive orchestral rehearsals. El Sistema's approach to collective music-making was summed up in two words of advice for a conductor who visited Caracas to work with a local youth orchestra: *apriétalos* (squeeze them, i.e. be tough on the musicians) and *repítelo* (repeat it, i.e. keep going over the repertoire until they get it right). Its theory, in contrast, is quite vague, resting disproportionately on Abreu's aphorisms. Somewhat ironically, then, considering how its name has been understood around the world, El Sistema is not a pedagogical system (Frega and Limongi 2019).

Accordingly, Abreu showed little interest in teacher training, which was unnecessary for this kind of approach, and El Sistema's teachers are not required to be certified or qualified. The program's philosophy is "teach how you were taught." For El Sistema, just as collective music education *is* social action, an excellent orchestral musician *is* an excellent SATM instructor. Similarly, the Red did not provide initial training—unlike the visual arts network, which prepared its teachers full-time for two weeks before they began working.

The Red's efforts to impact on pedagogy were therefore focused on the annual pedagogy seminar, a two-to-three-day event. My impression from attending the 2017 seminar and speaking to participants was that these seminars were widely valued by staff, but they were too short to make a significant impact on practices that had been established over many years or decades. There was also a Catch-22 element: the further a workshop departed from established norms, the less likely it was to be adopted into everyday practice. A decade of seminars had generated some interesting experiences and reflections, but it had not been enough to forge a distinctive, program-wide, socially oriented pedagogy. This is not to suggest that the program lacked skilled and engaging teachers, but rather that it had fallen short of the goal articulated in Arango's 2006 report—to create a pedagogical model, document it, and spread it to all the schools—and that skills were therefore unevenly distributed.

Hence there is little mystery over the central tension of the Red. The program's objective was social, but professional musicians in Medellín were not trained to fulfil it, and many received little pedagogical formation. As long as the social element was treated as implicit, this contradiction could remain buried. But from 2005 onwards, neither the leadership nor the city government was willing to let the Red continue running simply as a music program with a social discourse. With their attempts to redress this situation, the tension began to be felt.

The disjuncture between the program's social objective and musicians' training could be observed in the gap between the elaborate descriptions of social and critical pedagogy in official documents (e.g. *Documento* 2016) and the minimal appearance of such pedagogy in everyday practice. Arango noted that, in theory, the program used "the model of dialogical community practice of Paulo Freire, which is reinforced by the liberatory pedagogical theory of Rebellato and Girardi" (2006, 9). In practice, each director applied their own method, and "neither directors nor teachers have a clear understanding of applying one method or another" (11). Furthermore, the elements that could be identified came from standard music education methods such as Suzuki, Orff, and Dalcroze. In reality, then, teachers applied the tools that they had learnt through their own training, and the Red resembled less the radical theories of Freire, Rebellato, and Girardi than the conventional learning experiences of its staff. Eleven years later, the social team devoted pages to making the same point ("Informe" 2017a, 173–79). This gap was hardly surprising; where teachers were supposed to have learnt social and critical pedagogy was a mystery.

In higher-level meetings, the conversation returned repeatedly to the issue that educating the students in social skills required retraining or shifting the thinking of their teachers, otherwise the Red's chances of fulfilling its social objective were limited. The social team was particularly struck by the gulf between conservatoire training and the skills needed in a large social program, but there were also recurrent discussions at management level about the desirability of staff unlearning their university training and relearning new skills for SATM. In meetings, the official objective of transforming students' lives often took a back seat to discussions of how to transform their teachers.

At one management meeting, a senior figure argued that the Red's staff had not internalized the social aspect of the program: it is a job for them; they do their contracted hours, but they have little sense of a social mission. The Red had important work to do in raising consciousness among its own employees. Another manager responded that some school directors from the municipal band tradition treated their role in the Red as similar to that of a town band director. A third argued that the Red would only progress if it began hiring more pedagogues and fewer performers.

All four of the city's arts education networks faced the same problem to some degree. At the first meeting of representatives and researchers from the four programs that I attended, teacher training was the most prominent topic of discussion. Those present concurred that socially oriented arts education programs needed teachers with particular skills and not just conventional artistic training. They lamented that local universities generally followed a Eurocentric paradigm that left many arts graduates unprepared for and ignorant about the contexts where they subsequently went to work.

Part of the problem was that in Medellín, as in the classical music world more generally, teaching was sometimes seen as a consolation prize for aspiring performers. It was not just that many Red staff were not trained as teachers; some did not particularly *want* to be teachers. As one teacher put it, some musicians saw the Red just as a place to make some extra money or subsist while waiting for a better opportunity to come along. Quite a few teachers are in the Red because they have nowhere else to go, said one school director; they would leave if they got a better offer, but what else are they going to do in Medellín? As the principal employer of musicians in the city, with 150-odd teachers, the Red was an obvious pragmatic destination, and there was not a wealth of alternatives for the classically trained. Some saw the frequent hiring of instrumentalists rather than pedagogues as evidence that the Red had become more about providing jobs for musicians than educating students.

A school director told the social team: "The majority of the Red's teachers see the program as a source of income, not as a vocation, and this hinders the development of creativity and a rapprochement with pedagogy" ("Informe" 2017a, 75). Indeed, some of my interviewees did not see a particularly good fit between themselves and their work and did not imagine themselves staying in the Red over the long term.

The issues of training and vocation thus lay behind the sluggishness of pedagogical reform.

Some musicians, though, were attuned to the need for a shift among teachers. The 2008 social team report saw a number of musical staff doubt whether their education had prepared them properly for musical-social work. In interviews with the social team, some school directors were notably critical of their musical colleagues. "We're stuck in an old-fashioned music education, repeating things from centuries ago; we carry on with the technical aspect and that's it," said one ("Informe" 2017a, 71). Another argued: "We musicians don't have a social function within the community, we're just 'harlequins,' via our education at university we become just 'note-bashers,' we don't think, we're musicians and that's the only thing we know how to do" (73). A third argued that the program lacked joy: "this is linked to the teachers' conservatory training; they lack pedagogical skills and so they transmit a rigid training that does not change with the present context of the city and the new context of education. This kind of training bores the students and distances the educational process from the objective of the program, reducing the enjoyment" (75).

Similar points emerged in my own interviews. For example, Daniel was critical of the attitude of many performance majors (*instrumentistas*) in the Red. According to him, some saw learning new teaching methods as a waste of time and were particularly dismissive of more experimental approaches. He was irritated that musicians who lacked important skills resisted straightforward opportunities to acquire them. Norberto, too, underlined the difference between *licenciados* and *instrumentistas*: the latter generally were more technically focused and had fewer students and more dropouts. He saw some of them as "out of context" in the Red. Carolina, also a school director, claimed that many teachers did not actually see the Red as a social program. They might be good musicians but this did not mean that they had relevant skills for a social project. She wondered why no Medellín university offered suitable training, given the size and prominence of the Red.

Some advanced students, too, expressed criticism of the teaching staff. One told me that he had seen high turnover among staff with performance degrees: they did not seem to want to be teachers and tended to leave as soon as they got a better offer. Two others students claimed that there were numerous teachers with limited pedagogical skills and enthusiasm for the work. A meeting between student representatives and program leaders saw members of the principal youth orchestra question the attitude and teaching level of some staff. One student asked the managers outright: when is the Red going to update its pedagogy? Music is changing, she said, but the Red is stuck in the past. Another student claimed that some teachers used the notion of the Red as a social program as an excuse to provide a second-rate music education. But an important gap also opened up. If the management wanted to move the Red away from a conservatoire model, many advanced students desired the opposite.

Current Student Perspectives

Resistance to the new management proposals also came from some of the program's most experienced students. Those who remained in the Red in their late teens and early twenties often had expectations and desires shaped by many years in the program and by the wider classical music sector, and a shift in the Red's priorities was not to all of their liking. One of the new management goals, alongside diversity, creativity, and inclusion, was greater student voice—and some senior students used their new voice to express their suspicion of diversity, creativity, and inclusion.

Members of the student committee of the youth orchestra, having spent years climbing the institutional hierarchy, were keener on performing European masterworks than playing Colombian repertoire or composing their own music, and they *wanted* the orchestra to be exclusive. One described how she had cried in her audition—and then argued that aspiring members should have to go through the same experience. These students were concerned that opening the doors wider would lead to a drop in musical level. They were more interested in musical challenges (playing great works) and opportunities (high-profile concerts, festivals, competitions, tours) than in social inclusion. The Red's management was pushing for a more participatory ethos, but the most advanced students wanted a more presentational emphasis. There are echoes of Bull's (2019) finding that members of the UK's National Youth Orchestra disagreed with efforts to foster greater equality. They had been socialized in the competitive ethos of the classical music world and wanted to retain a system of unequal rewards. As Bull reveals, young classical musicians can be conservative, defending the existing system of hierarchies and inequalities. Those who rise to the top of a competitive system tend to be socialized in its beliefs and unlikely to agitate for major reform—an important point when considering the slow evolution of SATM.

I also observed a survey at the start of a rehearsal by the symphonic band. The conductor asked the students: why are you here? Three main reasons emerged: high-profile concerts, challenging repertoire, and more specialized technical training. On another occasion, this conductor stated that every year he asked the students what they wanted to play, and they always named canonic works of the international symphonic band repertoire. Again, there was an obvious gulf between the desires of the leadership (for more creation, experimentation, and exploration of Colombian music) and the students (focused on conventional skills, repertoire, and opportunities). The students never mentioned the social objective, complicating any intention to move the program towards taking it more seriously.

Advanced students were nearing the end of an educational process that could last up to eighteen years. For most, the priority was to reap the rewards and project the results as far as possible; changing the process was of less interest. The older the students, the more likely they were to be studying music at university and aspiring to be a professional musician. The most advanced often dreamt of progressing onto a more specialized orchestral program like Medellín's Iberacademy (discussed below) or the Colombian Youth Orchestra. Improvisation classes or territorial workshops were simply a distraction for most of them. Adding reflection or creation felt more like an impediment than an opportunity for those who had already decided upon a classical career path. Tellingly, an attempt to radically reconfigure the integrated ensembles in early 2019 was the only new initiative under Giraldo's leadership that was roundly reversed, due to the scale of student resistance.

Conversations with advanced students were revealing from the perspective of SATM and educational change more broadly. These students were generally very focused on music and often disliked activities organized by the social team. Most saw the social aspect of the

Red in terms of enjoyment and socializing with their peers rather than grander goals such as peaceful coexistence or social change, confirming Wald's (2009; 2011; 2017) findings concerning SATM in Buenos Aires. Many were less keen on discussing or acting on social issues, viewing explicit pursuit of the Red's social objective as affecting musical quality and a hindrance to their musical studies. They tended to complain that the program already tilted too much towards the social aspect and ought to provide a more serious musical training, in some cases to help them get into a university music department. One senior student told the social team that the Red was "a social program... unfortunately." When I asked another about the social side, he responded immediately: I wish it granted more importance to the musical part. He wanted more pressure so that students played better. Two of his friends defined the "social" in SATM as "undemanding."

Since students generally showed limited interest in social action, they were sometimes at odds with the social team. Javier, an advanced student, explained his perspective at length:

> we had two years when the social side attacked us and we seemed like an orchestra of psychologists. We'd go to a rehearsal and they'd say: today we're going to do a psychosocial activity. And we'd be like, OK... but when are we going to play? [...] During the administration of [Mayor] Gaviria, it was always all about life... Workshop for life, this for life, that for life... Lots about values, and I feel that the [musical] level dropped a lot during that time... a lot of psychology and psychosocial and we neglected the music.

He talked about how the students found the reflective activities boring, stopped paying attention, and rarely felt moved to speak up:

> Now when someone talks about social, I think the word has become kind of derogatory. It's like the social side has impacted so much on the musical that we've come to see it as something repulsive. When someone says social to me, I see it as something that's going to get in the way of the musical process. [...] I think that the rhetoric about keeping the kids here so that they're not taking up a weapon is no longer relevant, and keeping the kids here passing the time in a mediocre fashion without pushing them isn't enough.

The integrated ensembles like the youth orchestra were where the contradiction between the musical and the social was most apparent. For the management and social team, they offered the greatest possibilities for fostering coexistence and dynamic social experiences, since they brought together young people from different neighbourhoods and social strata. But they were also the showcase groups with the highest musical demands, and the musical staff and students saw them as the artistic pinnacle of the Red and thus the place to take the musical side most seriously. The social team noted that, in practice, these ensembles did not focus on their social aspect but rather on preparing and performing demanding repertoire and representing the program ("Informe" 2017a). It also pointed to these ensembles as focal points of negative dynamics such as excessive demands, bullying, competition, and exclusion, as a consequence of the emphasis on musical results. For the social team, the integrated ensembles showcased the worst of the Red.

The story of the REMM Ensemble—the new ensemble created for the US tour—is illustrative. It adopted an innovative approach, creating all its own music via two distinctive laboratories. In 2018, with a tour guaranteed, demand for participation was very high, and large numbers of the Red's best performers auditioned for much fewer places. In 2019, the ensemble announced its continuation, but this time without a tour. The take-up was now so low that the original plan had to be shelved: the large, high-performance, freestanding ensemble had to be reconstituted as an elementary project in one of the music schools. It appeared that travel rather than pedagogical or musical innovation had been the real draw. The leadership had imagined the tour as a catalyst for wider changes, but the students had other ideas.

Foreign tours were a major source of motivation during the Red's first phase, according to some students-turned-teachers. Going on tour was the big attraction: not because of the music, said one, but because it meant travelling with friends, away from school and family, and seeing new places. They didn't give up all their weekends just to give concerts for their parents. "Typical adolescent thinking," as he put it. But in recent years, such thinking has fallen somewhat out of sync with that of the Red's leadership, focused as it has been on social, territorial, and pedagogical reform at home.

Social Action versus Pre-Professional Training

These findings lead us to a central paradox in SATM in South America. Programs like the Red and El Sistema are closely articulated to and feeders for the classical music profession and its institutions, and as such, they share its value system. Many teachers are or have been professional classical musicians, or have at least trained for this profession, and many older students aspire to this goal. Classical music is a highly competitive world and students who hope to make a career in it are therefore obliged to focus on their musical studies; it is their musical level that will determine whether they get into university, pass their degree, and succeed in an audition. In other words, as SATM students rise through the levels and become more advanced, they generally move closer to the professional world and the values that underpin it, and further from the supposed raison d'être of the program—social action. As a consequence, the "star students" of SATM programs often resemble conventional conservatoire students (indeed, they often *are* conventional conservatoire students), and they can be among the least engaged with the official objective and most critical of attempts to realize it more fully.

The Red's relationship with Iberacademy illustrates this issue. Iberacademy is an elite orchestral training program based in Medellín but with tentacles reaching out across the Americas and a strong focus on touring and placing students in overseas conservatoires. It is funded by the Hilti Foundation, which also supports El Sistema, and the two programs are closely aligned. Iberacademy was an object of desire for advanced students in the Red. A number joined or aspired to join Iberacademy; sometimes they remained in the Red as well and sometimes they left, but their comparisons between the two programs rarely favoured the Red. None of this is at all surprising: one might expect advanced students, after many years learning music seriously, to admire a high-level program like Iberacademy; one might also expect them to be the most critical of the Red, since they were the ones most invested in the elite classical training that the Red's leadership now questioned. Parra was blunt: the Red is not really a social program but rather a school of technical and artistic training that revolves around playing and touring, so it is little wonder that the best students want to leave when something like Iberacademy appears, offering better playing and touring opportunities. Nevertheless, the fact that advanced students looked longingly at an elite classical scheme like Iberacademy illustrated the challenge that the Red's management faced in pushing the program towards greater musical diversity and social engagement.

Both programs took the professional symphony orchestra as their model and operated within the wider value system of the classical music profession. El Sistema began life as a pipeline into the orchestral profession and the two Medellín programs also served that role. Both were embedded in a local, national, and international context in which performing excellence is valued above social or pedagogical excellence and the measure of an orchestra is closely bound up with the repertoire that it plays and its touring schedule. As a result, the most talented students generally prioritized tackling harder repertoire and performing it on distant stages. In twenty years of operation as a large, flagship "social program," the Red had not shifted those values or expectations; on the contrary, it had positively fostered them. This approach eventually created a dual tension: on the one hand, with the more appealing Iberacademy; and on the other, with the less appealing official objective of social action for the benefit of the local community.

Unsurprisingly, then, there was no traffic in the other direction. The Red was not an object of desire for music students in anything like the same way as Iberacademy. Older students rarely developed a significant thirst for social action; they were mainly concerned about musical quality. Most saw the Red as a mediocre version of Iberacademy, its wings clipped by its social objective, rather than a program that offered something distinct but of equal value.

This imbalance reflects the fact that neither El Sistema nor its two Medellín disciples had forged a genuinely distinct philosophy and practice that went beyond a justificatory or publicity discourse and elevated social action to a central concern and a position of high status. Despite its stated social objective, the Red lacked indicators or criteria for evaluating social action. An advanced student was one with advanced technical ability on an instrument, not advanced ideas about social issues. Student promotion was dependent "on the achievements reached in instrumental playing [...] according to the criteria of musical quality and fulfilling a certain number of performances" (Arango 2006,

14). There was no social route to promotion, such as civic performance or community service.

These programs do not create role models for social action, only for musical success. Graduates who rise to the top ranks of the classical music profession are loudly celebrated, but in two years of fieldwork in Venezuela and Colombia, I never saw these programs hold up a music student who went on to become an exemplary citizen, a social leader, a community figurehead, or a catalyst of social change.[2] What is more, the figures at the top of the SATM pantheon—particularly conductors like Gustavo Dudamel—are those who have established themselves in orchestras overseas; they symbolize an ideology of music as a means of individual social mobility and transcending the local, rather than as a catalyst for collective social change within and for the community. Here we see a paradox in orthodox SATM: an idealization of the collective (the orchestra), yet an individualized conception of success (the young musician who "makes it" in the profession).

In sum, these "social" programs have historically reproduced the value system of classical music rather than social or community activism. It is hardly surprising, then, that social action figured minimally in many advanced students' understanding of what mattered, or that there was some resistance to the leadership's progressive reforms in 2017–19.

Family and Student Expectations

At the other end of the student age scale, there was a more subtle kind of resistance, and it too revolved around expectations concerning the musical and social sides of SATM. Several members of staff made the point that children (or their parents) do not generally sign up for the Red because of its social objective; they sign up to learn to play a musical instrument for free. The social objective justified the Red's funding and was central to its official discourse, and there was a continual pull towards strengthening the social side from the city government, program leaders, and the social team; but families usually just wanted free music lessons and a place to keep children occupied. In other words,

---

[2] Hess's (2019) vision of music education for social change provides an illuminating contrast. She built her model around individuals with or without music industry success but with a clear focus on changing society through music.

in a context where SATM is the main option for free music lessons, a gap opens up between the official vision (a social program) and the public vision (a free music school). What this meant in practical terms, according to my interlocutors, was that participants were generally more interested in what was supposed to be the means (music) than the ends (social action), and their musical expectations limited the scope for more ambitious social work. As one school director told the social team: "This is a musical program with a social angle. Whatever we do, we have to start with music. *If this were a social program, we would really go and impact the communities that are in difficult contexts*, but people come here because it is a music program, [...] they come to learn music, the social is a consequence" ("Informe" 2017a, 69; emphasis added).

Another school director put it bluntly: the kids aren't really interested in doing anything other than playing their instrument. When she tried to broaden the offering and put on non-musical activities like watching a film or tidying the park or painting a mural, few turned up. A third director lamented that few older students ended up taking part in his school project; most wanted to play difficult, well-known repertoire and be the best school orchestra in the Red, rather than engage in more innovative, creative, participatory activities with the younger students.

Howell (2017, 115–16) reveals that this multiplicity of motivations in musical-social work is not limited to the Red:

> Organisers may emphasise instrumentalised value in their stated aims in order to build a compelling argument for donors, but simultaneously remain committed to the delivery of music opportunities as their raison d'être. Conversely, participants are often motivated to participate because of the immediate (intrinsic) appeal of the artistic undertaking; for them, the arguments around social development or healing (for example) provide little initial persuasion.

A clear official vision does not therefore make for a unified program in practice. But as we have seen, in the Red this was not just a case of students shrugging their shoulders at the formal aims; some experienced those aims as a negative factor and actively resisted efforts to realize them more fully.

A major question thus emerges: how to balance the goals of the funder and leadership with those of the participants? Should the Red be led by progressive ideas about expanding the horizons of students and deepening impact on the community? Or should it be shaped by the more conventional expectations and desires of those same constituencies? One school director explained this tension in 2018:

> Now [the students] are obliged to be creative. But no one asked them if they wanted to create. [...] If you ask the kids about being creative, a lot will tell you that [the leadership] has lost its way. [The students] just want to play like the Colombian Youth Orchestra. [...] The kids say: this [i.e. creativity] is no use at all. I want to play better so that I can join Iberacademy or the Colombian Youth Orchestra.

She concluded: "Here in the Red we're trying to change things, to revive our culture. But that doesn't mean much to the kids."

Classical versus Popular Music

Parra regularly referred to "the theme of the year." These were the issues that generated most debate and discontent during Giraldo's tenure, beyond the perennial ones such as the musical and the social. In 2017, according to Parra, the theme of the year was classical versus popular music. This was the moment that a popular musician took over as general director and began to promote an agenda of diversity and identity. In reality, the issue of classical versus popular music had been circulating since Arango's 2006 report, but now the reappraisal was led by an active performer of popular music, for whom this question was therefore a personal one as well.

This topic became the theme of the year because not all the Red's musical staff were enthused by the popular turn. Various counterarguments were made. Some staff articulated a historical argument (classical music had always been the hallmark of the Red); others a technical one (classical music was better for developing instrumental technique); others a practical one (there were few teaching materials for Colombian popular music). But there were also those who questioned the initial premise that the Red was weighted towards the classical, arguing that Colombian repertoire had always been prominent. This question was further blurred by the issue of repertoire, formats, and instruments. When a symphony orchestra played an arrangement of a popular Colombian piece, some observers focused on the repertoire (Colombian) and others on the format (European). The lack of consensus on the basic question of whether or not the Red *was* a classical music program only intensified the debate about what it might *become*.

In our interview, Ocampo explained: "What really carries weight in the world of music is not the wind band, it's the symphony orchestra." He argued that the orchestral repertoire was rich and demanding, while bands were much more limited. Although his argument was framed in pragmatic terms, it should be recalled that the Red emerged from Ocampo's classical music company and music appreciation activities. A classical focus would therefore appear to be not only a strategic decision but also a personal and professional inclination.

However, to complicate this picture, the Red was originally created in 1997 as the Network of Bands and Music Schools of Medellín—no mention of orchestras. The newspaper article in March that year ("Escuelas de música" 1997) projected a future in which classical music appeared almost as a footnote:

> around two thousand children and young people from popular barrios will be part of a huge band. But a symphonic band. The whole city will be able to listen to its youth performing [popular tunes such as] "Antioqueñita," "La Ruana," *pasillos, cumbias, guabinas,* and other Colombian styles, as well as classical, popular, and tropical music, and pasodobles and other tunes from around the world.

Ocampo's remarks about bands and orchestras were made as a parenthesis during his account of his relationship with Abreu. He claimed that he only discovered El Sistema after the Red began. When he made his first visit to Venezuela shortly afterwards, he thought, "why reinvent the wheel?" Abreu agreed to provide teachers and the years of close alliance began. Students from that period recalled that the Venezuelans brought El Sistema's repertoire. It thus appears that the surprisingly eclectic, distinctively Colombian vision at the start quickly gave way to something closer to the Venezuelan model, which had been created by a classical conductor with minimal interest in or sympathy for popular music.[3] The program may have begun life in 1997 as the Network of Bands, but in 1998, a new municipal agreement was

---

3   On Abreu's distaste for popular music, see my blog post "Scam, Voodoo, or The Future of Music? The El Sistema Debate", https://geoffbakermusic.wordpress.com/el-sistema-older-posts/scam-voodoo-or-the-future-of-music-the-el-sistema-debate-2/.

signed, bringing the Red's youth orchestras and choirs into existence, and looking back two decades later, Ocampo's preference was clear. This ambiguity at the very outset might be seen as sowing the seeds of 2017's theme of the year.

Behind the debates and pragmatic arguments lay differing ideological positions with regard to classical music and its role in a society like Medellín's. Both defenders and critics of classical music focused on questions of difference and, less explicitly, superiority. For the defenders, classical music's difference was a strength and source of success. As it was somewhat alien to the popular barrios where the program began, classical music symbolized distance and exception from the violent social context and the destructive social norms that underpinned it. Classical music, in its very difference, was heard as the sound of Medellín's youth turning over a new page in the city's history. Classical music's association with elevation and distinction made it ideal for projecting a "new image of Medellín to the world," as the program's publicity slogan went (see Chapter 4).

As one school director told me, he was happy for the Red to diversify somewhat but it should not lose its essential character as classically-focused, serious, academic, and formal. Classical training allowed students to learn music properly from a technical perspective and to join together in large ensembles; but also, popular music was ubiquitous and so it did not generate the same response in students or their families. For novelty and personal growth, people needed a different genre to the norm. Also, he associated popular music with drinking and excess. Adults might enjoy it, but did they really want their children to learn it? When you have a symphony orchestra playing European music in a barrio, he said, that attracts people's attention; popular music, improvisation, creation, and so on simply would not have the same impact.

For critics, however, this distance was perceived more negatively. They saw the Red as reproducing old dichotomies and hierarchies of classical versus popular, cultured versus uncultured, "good kids" versus "bad kids." They argued that distancing a few children from Medellín's violent realities did little to tackle those problems, to help those left behind, or to generate attitudes of empathy. Some at leadership level and in the culture ministry saw the perpetuation of a colonialist ideology dating back to the Spanish Conquest, which treated European music as superior to indigenous or African and as a tool of salvation and civilization. As the social team wrote: "We need to grant value to our own music, we only play international repertoire, it is as though we did not have our own history. This happens even in school, first we teach universal history and only if there is time left over, Colombian history—we disrespect ourselves" ("Informe" 2017a, 73).

This issue became the subject of lively debate in 2017. For the new leadership, opening up not just to popular repertoire but also to popular instruments, techniques, and styles was an inherent part of giving the program more of a local and national identity, embracing the musical diversity of the city, and starting to decolonize music education. For some popular music specialists in the program, talking about repertoire was something of a red herring (if the pun may be excused); the problem was not that the program did not perform popular music, but rather that it did not perform popular music *well*. The director of the popular music integrated ensemble issued a challenge to the players in one rehearsal: when we play classical music, the Red sounds good; when we play [Argentinean] tango, we sound good; but when we play [Colombian] cumbia, *porro*, or *gaita*, we sound weak. This is true even for us, the most specialized group in the program, let alone in schools where directors know less about Colombian music. We can play the rhythm, he said, but the feel isn't there. We've been so colonized musically that we sound worst when we play our own music. What are we going to do about this?

Fig. 20. Archive of Red de Escuelas de Música. CC BY.

The social team argued that the atmosphere of concerts was transformed as soon as the ensemble struck up a popular tune, with both performers and audience immediately livelier and more engaged than with classical repertoire ("Informe" 2017a). A school director voiced a compatible view: "the worst thing is that we play music for an audience that doesn't exist. We play classical music, and we've been playing that for twenty years, but we haven't developed an audience that really likes classical music. Our audience is the Red parents. We haven't created a real consumer of art or [classical] music in the city." But other musical staff defended a focus on classical music and were concerned about a shift that they saw as potentially eroding the historical identity, musical quality, and pedagogical foundations of the program.

Matters had changed by the time of my return in 2019, when I saw a notable shift of emphasis towards popular music in the music schools and ensembles. The key driver, it seemed, was not ideological debate or management exhortation, but rather the move to project-based learning (PBL)—the "theme of the year" in 2018.

Pedagogy

From January 2018, when the new approach was rolled out, until I left Medellín in September, there was tension and open debate over PBL. The management understood PBL as a flexible, non-prescriptive, participatory approach to education, and as such, it wanted each school or ensemble director to seize the idea and flesh it out with their own individual proposals, together with their staff and students. Many directors, however, simply did not understand what the management was looking for, and they requested clear and detailed instructions—something that, for the management, went against the spirit of PBL. The leadership felt that the directors were resistant to new thinking, while the directors complained that the management was incapable of explaining the new approach.

Nevertheless, when I returned a year later, and the Red was halfway through the second year of the PBL strategy, I was struck by the variety and imagination on display during a two-day "projects fair" in which all the schools and ensembles participated. Ironically, the staff were in open mutiny against the leadership over the direction of the program, yet large advances had been made. It appeared that much of the incomprehension and resistance of the previous year concerning PBL had been overcome as the idea had become more familiar, and now this approach was producing some impressive results (as outlined in Chapter 1). Particularly notable was the new dominance of popular and traditional music. PBL was allied with the shift to a more territorial focus, meaning that many projects focused on local history, culture, spaces or ecology. It seemed to be easier to explore and illustrate these themes with music that had a direct connection to the barrio around the school, rather than classical music from distant times and places.

The backdrop to the introduction of PBL was a wider debate—another one that dated back to 2005—over formal versus non-formal education. The Red was officially described as a non-formal program, but under Arango it began to take on many formal characteristics, such as fixed levels and educational cycles and a curriculum. For some, this change brought welcome order to a program that had been somewhat chaotic and improvised in its first phase. For others, the Red came to resemble a conservatoire in all but name, to the detriment of its official social objective. The adoption of PBL was linked to the new leadership's perception that the pendulum had swung too far in the direction of formalization. The social team, too, argued that non-formal education was a source of freedom and offered spaces for developing positive social dynamics such as self-expression and listening; they were more suspicious of the elaborate curriculum ("Informe" 2017a). However, this shift caused discomfort among many staff, particularly among those who had invested considerable time and energy over a period of years in constructing the curriculum. Non-formal approaches were quite alien to many who had received a formal training themselves.

This debate played out in discussions over ludic versus serious approaches. Franco, in particular, advocated for a more playful, spontaneous attitude towards music learning, building up from the base of musical initiation, and he perceived many of the Red's activities as overly rigid and serious, dictated from the top down by the norms of professional classical music. The Red is too much like school, he said at one meeting; it should be a different kind of experience. He described the Red as twenty-seven little conservatoires offering conventional classes, and he dreamt of more innovative, varied, dynamic experiences.

With PBL, then, resurfaced longstanding debates over whether the Red should resemble an ordinary music school, but with a broader social constituency and a different atmosphere, or a social program, embodying a profoundly different approach to music education.

"Happy Students, Teachers in Adversity": SATM as Work

If there was one topic that rivalled the social in terms of the passions that it aroused, it was the staff's contract with the city government via the university. The directors and teachers were on rolling contracts with no fixed duration, but typically nine to ten months in recent years. Each Christmas, they had no guarantee that they would be rehired in the New Year, and even if they were, the start date was usually unknown. From the end of one year to the beginning of the next, they remained unpaid and suspended in a sense of uncertainty over whether or when their services would be required. This situation did not just affect the staff—until their contracts began, there were no activities in the music schools for students either.

The nature of the contract and the precarity that it produced were a constant source of tension, and in a number of important meetings, at least one school director stood up and gave an impassioned speech on this topic. It regularly overshadowed discussion of new priorities such as diversity, identity, and creativity. Some of the musical staff were outraged and incredulous that after more than two decades as a flagship program of the city government, the Red still did not offer permanent contracts. They spoke of the effect not only on themselves and their families, but also on the Red's capacity to retain existing students and attract new ones. Delays to the start of the academic year saw participants and potential recruits drift away to other programs that had already begun.

This issue could not have been more different from the musical and the social: one complex and conceptual, the other straightforward and practical. At first, I mentally switched off a little when this topic was raised in meetings; I instinctively saw it as less interesting than the philosophical intricacies of SATM. But over time I came to understand it as a specific example of an issue that is both important and commonplace in SATM: a gap between the (supposed) benefits for students and the more ambiguous realities for their teachers.

The theme of musicians as workers is largely absent even from academic discussions of SATM, let alone media narratives. Stories and images focus on engaged and enthusiastic students; we do not see disgruntled, underpaid, or precariously employed staff who keep the wheels in motion. Belfiore (2021, 15) points to this darker side of socially engaged arts practice more broadly, as well as to the reason why it is rarely discussed: "the importance of maintaining good relationships with funders [...] perpetuates silence around the realities of working conditions within social engaged practice and works against positive change." In writing on SATM, the focus on beneficiaries has generally elided the experience of the crucial intermediaries between SATM's theory and its practice, thereby overlooking what was, for many musical staff in the Red, the most important topic in their professional lives: pay and working conditions.

We can see here another of the central paradoxes of SATM in older South American programs. For some musically talented students, being "rescued" or "transformed" by music education morphs into becoming low-paid, precariously employed instructors to the next generation. Music may provide a new life path for some students, but those who are good enough to become professional musicians but not good enough (or connected or lucky enough) to secure an orchestral or other performing position often end up as teachers—a destination that is more ambiguous than the celebratory narrative about transforming lives would allow. There is a certain irony in a social program that trains low- to middle-income students over many years for a competitive, uncertain, precarious, and modestly remunerated profession.

This issue of SATM as work came into greater focus with the decision to open the Red's schools on Saturday mornings as well as Monday to Friday. Saturday opening became 2019's "theme of the year." The management and culture ministry wanted to open up the music schools more to the surrounding community. But for the school directors, it was the straw that broke the camel's back, pushing hardworking staff beyond their limit and creating clashes with family and outside musical commitments. The resulting conflict was a reminder that behind the elevated rhetoric, SATM depends on workers and labour rather than angel-musicians and miracles.

In a moment of sympathy, a member of the social team reflected that the musical staff were resistant to the social side because they saw it as extra work, and they already had too much on their plate (full-time teachers were supposed to give thirty-two hours of lessons a week); this is why they wanted the social team to take care of it. Similarly, this high workload was also an impediment to teachers' engagement with PBL, since the new approach implied adapting their teaching to each school and therefore potentially more preparation time. SATM work may be coveted by some, particularly those fresh out of higher education and with high ideals or desperate for income, but as with many jobs, its demands can lead enthusiasm to give way to ambivalence. The Red was a major provider of work for classical music graduates but not necessarily a dream job. The social team noted a feeling of monotony and a loss of motivation and interest among some staff ("Informe" 2017a). Considering SATM as work not only brings its elevated rhetoric down to earth but also, as Belfiore suggests, opens up the possibility of positive change.

The timeline meeting discussed in Chapter 1 ended with proposals from staff. Many revolved around their contract, working conditions, (in)stability, and motivation—in other words, around the Red as work rather than as social action. One teacher stood up and described the Red as "happy students, happy families, teachers in adversity."

Stress and burnout were found among all the adult constituencies in the Red. Despite its ambitious social claims, or perhaps because of them, SATM can be a challenging place to work, and employees do not always seem to feel the power of music. One of the Red's general directors quipped, tongue only half in cheek: "the Red saves children. But it eats adults."

Improvisation

One of the major and rising sources of tension in 2017–19 was organizational dynamics. The musical staff argued that the leadership lacked organizational skills and were incapable of communicating their proposals clearly and effectively. The leadership, in turn, criticized the musical staff for an unwillingness to listen and a resistance to change. This is not the place to adjudicate the rights and wrongs of this particular argument, but it is worth considering the notion that this broken communication represented not (or at least, not only) deficient capacities and attitudes but rather the fact that the leadership and staff were not speaking the same language.

The most obvious example was the struggle of some musical staff to understand Parra, an anthropologist by profession. Yet communication between the other two leaders and the staff was sometimes little more fluid, despite the fact that all were musicians. Most of the staff had trained as classical or municipal band musicians, whereas Giraldo and Franco were rooted in Colombian traditional music, jazz, and composition. The relevance of this distinction becomes apparent when one considers the word that lay at the heart of staff criticisms of the leaders' organizational style: improvisation.

For Giraldo and Franco, improvisation was a word with positive connotations, and it underpinned the musical changes that they tried to instil in the Red. They instituted improvisation classes for the teachers, at which Giraldo would sometimes show up and participate, and they created more space for improvisatory musical traditions. More broadly, they wanted the music schools to loosen up and the directors and teachers to stop worrying so much about the curriculum and the timetable and to become more flexible and creative. They aspired to a looser, more informal approach to music making, with more joy and less routine. Franco loved nothing more than walking into a school to find little groups of students doing their own thing, without adult supervision; he was less impressed by large, adult-directed ensembles.

Fig. 21. Archive of Red de Escuelas de Música. CC BY.

2. The Red Pushes Back: Tensions, Debates, and Resistance

The leaders were also keen to foster a more consensual organizational culture, which implied keeping plans partly formed in order to leave space for staff and student input, and more of a trial-and-error approach. They were happy to depart from business-as-usual, to take risks, and to leave outcomes uncertain. They saw leaping into the unknown as part of the creative process—organizationally as well as musically. Giraldo's conception of the management's role with regard to PBL was that of a jazz improviser: don't wait for us to tell you what to do, just get on with it and try things out, and see what works and what doesn't. Don't worry about making mistakes; learn as you go along. This is a non-formal program; if anywhere is the place for flexibility, experimentation, and error, it is here.

However, the word "improvisation" was used against them by staff as a criticism of their approach to leadership. For the school directors, in particular, there were few things worse than improvisation (in an organizational sense). What the leaders perceived as consensual and emergent struck many staff as confusing and confused. The management dreamt of a different kind of Red; the staff criticized them as distant from the schools and unmoored to reality. The directors did not want looseness, risks, uncertainty, trial and error, leaps into the unknown, or endless discussions; they wanted order and clear instructions. This was how most had been educated themselves. Furthermore, many of them had joined the Red in the Ocampo or Arango years, when there was a strong leader who told them exactly what to do. The role of staff was to implement plans, not to agree or disagree. Arango's leadership style provoked diverse responses, but even her detractors acknowledged that she was clear and organized and everyone knew exactly what was expected of them. Many staff harked back to her as an example of effective leadership; few held up improvisation as an ideal.

Improvisation was thus at the heart of both the new proposal for the Red and the staff's scepticism towards it. There were important ideological differences over the musical versus the social, classical versus popular, and formal versus the informal; but there were also copious debates over *how* the changes were implemented. The centrality of the word "improvisation" suggests that beneath the discontent over problems of organization and communication lay further ideological differences, this time over order versus chaos, fixity versus fluidity.

These ideological differences were themselves rooted in the different kinds of musical training that the various parties had received. In fact, the issue of training might be seen to underlie all of the tensions and debates in this chapter. The new approaches implemented from 2017 onwards were a challenge for many music graduates. The way that the Red had developed over the years (particularly the adoption of a relatively formal, conventional curriculum and pedagogy) reflected closely how its staff were trained, and the efforts to transform the program bumped up not just against its history and the kind of inertia that is commonplace in large institutions, but also against the limitations of this training. The new leadership's focus on popular and traditional music, creativity, improvisation, non-formal learning, PBL, participation, and territorial connections demanded skills that went far beyond those that most staff had acquired at university, though there were some notable exceptions. Musical improvisation is not a practice that is associated with classical music or conservatoire training, at least in Colombia, and therefore it was not something with which the majority of the Red's workforce was particularly comfortable. In 2018, school directors were asked to assume a role akin to a *gestor territorial* (territorial manager), one that was unfamiliar to many and demanded a kind of mobility that contradicted the longstanding static model for this role. It is unsurprising that resistance was quite widespread among those who were now asked to turn their training and previous experience on its head, transform their own role in unfamiliar directions, and develop skills in students that they themselves lacked. Much of the friction and debate stemmed from this gap between expectations and training.

Norberto, the school director, held up the example of creativity. It was hard for most staff, he said, because they came from a system—the Red and the university—where they had learnt "like parrots... just play, that's it!" More broadly, he reflected that classical musicians were used to being told what to do and not having to think; so when the new leadership arrived and asked the staff what they proposed, many "went into shock [...] What we wanted for so long, we now have—and we don't know what to do with it."

Franco dreamt of music schools that were freer, more flexible, and more playful: less carving up of time and space into formal lessons and rehearsals, and more creative spaces where students came together to try different instruments and jam and compose with others of varying ages and abilities. This picture of loose, creative, collaborative activities was one that Norberto and many other directors struggled to imagine, let alone enact. Many lacked a background in composition, improvisation, and other creative activities. For them, music education meant giving children a serious, solid technical grounding in one instrument and then in a conductor-led ensemble. The rapid shift was a significant practical and ideological challenge, and some advanced students and teachers argued that the leap was simply too big.

Franco had done much of his previous music education work in villages. He recalled the eagerness and openness to new ideas in such contexts, where participants were like sponges. He was somewhat shocked to find that his proposals generated so much resistance in the Red. Giraldo, meanwhile, had a background in jazz and popular music ensembles, with small formats and informal approaches. Their experience in the Red might be seen as a culture shock as they came up against the traditions of the orchestral and municipal band worlds. As one school director said, "the teachers and directors don't have experience of research, they have no idea how a project works, so how can you ask this of them? First you need to train them, then maybe. You need to convince them why it should be done this way." The leaders, in contrast, came from backgrounds where such activities were normal.

This was not just a matter of the Red. Most of the new leadership's primary objectives were somewhat alien to large ensemble culture more generally. This was obviously the case with improvisation or traditional music techniques, but it was also a challenge to embed a more participatory approach in the Red and shift to a more horizontal, student-centred dynamic, because many staff had been formed in and reproduced the vertical, teacher-led ethos of orchestras and bands. This gap between training and objectives became very visible with the raft of new initiatives from 2017, yet it was not new. As seen in Chapter 1, it became clear during the diagnostic phase at the start of Arango's tenure that many of the musical staff found the Red's social objective laudable but also overly ambitious, and they doubted their capacity to fulfil it. From the first internal reports, then, tensions and debates were founded on a gap between the staff's musical training and the goals that the program set for them.

Conclusion

Shortly after I began my fieldwork in 2017, the social team produced a 210-page internal report summarizing its research during the first year of Giraldo's administration. Over time, I discovered that many of the issues it highlighted had been raised in reports dating back years. In fact, the Red had been grappling with largely the same questions since 2006. The Red's repeated efforts at reform and limited progress epitomized the cultural field as a place of "vigorous and dynamic struggle" (Martin 1995, 180–81). The Red emerged as a complicated and contested organization, for all the simplicity and rosiness of its public representations. This is an important conclusion, given that the primordial objective of such programs is often expressed as fostering social harmony, and struggle is elided from most publicly available accounts of SATM.

Official accounts of SATM usually portray the pursuit of musical excellence and social action as going hand in hand, but the relationship between the two halves of the SATM equation turned out to be the Red's biggest headache. Behind the upbeat rhetoric about transformation, the social appeared as a prime locus of tension. The testimonies of students and staff revealed that, as Estrada had found in Venezuela in 1997, the pursuit of musical excellence led to a neglect of the social objective and/or the generation of negative social dynamics (see Baker and Frega 2018). Yet a shift to more active pursuit of social goals led to widespread complaints that music education was being disrupted and artistic standards compromised. For many, the Red was like a zero-sum game, in which the musical and the social were locked in struggle. The conflicts between the social team and musicians serve as a dramatization of this tension.

There are many different and at times contradictory ways of understanding and pursuing SATM. The history of the Red shows multiple changes in social strategy and a lack of consensus over how SATM should work. Having initially borrowed a model from Venezuela, the Red's history since 2005 appears as a long-term and probably unending search: a succession of approaches in constant transformation. From a synchronic perspective, the Red shows similar variation. The diachronic and the synchronic are connected: the Red included staff hired during all its different phases, and thus those phases and their ideologies were all present in some form in 2017–18. They both coexisted and competed in the program, since they represented distinct philosophies of SATM. The Red cannot therefore be reduced to a single philosophy or approach at any single moment, much less over time.

The bagginess of the term "social" lies behind this central issue. There were major variations in what this word signified in relation to the Red: a quality of personal interaction, a space for socialization, a focus on disadvantaged populations, a collective pedagogy, a public ethos, mixing of social classes, instilling discipline and responsibility, and so on. While debate might seem inevitable in a program of this age and size, the atmosphere pointed more to competition and tension than to happy diversity when it came to the coexistence of differing visions. In Medellín, SATM appeared less like a harmonious blend between the musical and the social than a serious game that both teams were trying to win.

While debates often fell into a binary dynamic, the period that I observed also presented a three-way internal debate in which different ways of understanding SATM came into tension. The two musicians at the head of the program saw diversity, identity, creativity, and interculturality as the way forward; the social team repeated the decade-old call to take the social side more seriously; and many musical staff saw both these paths as distracting from the large ensemble performance that was the program's calling-card and their own speciality. This three-way tug-of-war could be observed clearly in relation to the integrated ensembles: the musical coordinators wanted to shake up the pedagogical approach; the social coordinator urged more space for thinking about social questions; while the conductors and students wanted to raise the musical level and perform and tour more.

Similarly, the dynamic between the management and staff cannot be reduced only to a dichotomy of critique versus resistance. The social team interviewed all the school directors in 2017, and as with the first social team report nine years earlier, the staff conveyed a complex picture ("Informe" 2017a). Some pointed to issues such as the absence of suitable professional training and a lack of critical reflection and citizenship education by their musical colleagues. The directors were not therefore a monolithic group, nor were they unaware of problems or resistant to change per se; the tensions revolved as much around the direction and pace of change and the way that it should be managed. Complicating matters further, individual musicians sometimes had contradictory views or saw both sides of the coin. One school director described the social team in two terms: "1. A balm that soothes the injustices and tough demands on the teachers, administrators, directors, and students, and softens the rigidity of the musical processes. 2. Interventions that make no sense" (148).

A "glass half full" perspective might be to argue that dissonance is desirable in both musical works and democratic societies (Fink 2016), and that its absence would be a worrying sign. The debates, then, would suggest that the Red is fundamentally healthy. A "glass half empty" version might regard the Red as having lost its unity of vision and purpose after Ocampo's departure, never to fully recover. It might see considerable irony in a program for peaceful coexistence that has produced such tensions. However, it is possible that both visions are valid at the same time. What was experienced negatively by many, as tensions and disagreements, may also be analysed as a sign of healthy debate and necessary adjustment. We are back to growing pains.

The process of change itself was thus ambiguous. Successive leaderships believed that change was necessary, but it also generated discontent; it was felt as unnecessary and counter-productive by many of those affected. The 2019 projects fair was a good illustration of this ambiguity. Outside the hall, in the corridors and coffee stands, staff dissatisfaction was reaching fever pitch. With the directors having sent a formal letter of complaint to the university, the Red was experiencing its biggest crisis in years. Yet inside the hall, positive achievements were amply on display. It seemed as though the directors had taken the new PBL approach on board and were producing results. I saw a program more aligned with progressive currents in music education.

Tension arose from the conundrum of how to foster participation and change at the same time. Directors were given ample opportunity to voice their views in meetings and interviews. Yet since their requests usually revolved around strengthening conventional musical features, they were routinely ignored by management, who had a different agenda, one that was influenced by the culture ministry and the city's cultural policy. Changing the Red meant attempting to break with the past and therefore not acting on the wishes of the program's old hands—undermining the goal of participation and stoking frustration.

Ironically for a music program, listening turned out to be delicate topic. Directors felt that they had spaces to speak but that they were not listened to by the leadership. But the reverse was also true, and the large staff meetings sometimes offered concrete examples (teachers with earphones in, watching the football, playing chess, and so on). On one such occasion, a musical consultant, having observed the low level of attention, told the audience: "we musicians are not good at listening. In fact, there are few who are worse at listening than musicians. This meeting is an example."

A further ambiguity concerns the notion of change itself. In practice, what took place from 2017 was not so much changing old ways of working as layering new ones over the old. The Red had relatively fixed commitments, expectations, and resources. Since the city continued to demand regular concerts in multiple venues, and the musical staff had (and wanted) to maintain the existing practices, the Red continued with its former approach—conventional music education to prepare students for public performances—while a number of new initiatives were rolled out alongside. Hence the new initiatives often became (and were experienced as) extra responsibilities, and for musical staff who already worked long hours and had multiple obligations, the strain on their time and mental capacity was evident.

Change thus meant more work, and also less money for what had historically been the Red's core operations. There was considerable discontent from the musical staff that there was money for new laboratories, ensembles, directors, consultants, and managers, yet not for the program's creaking infrastructure, deteriorating instruments, or stagnating salaries. What appeared as interesting innovations to some struck others as unnecessary extra costs added to an overstretched budget.

The reality of the Red was clearly more complex and conflicted than the public narrative about such programs. What deserves further elucidation is what lay behind this panorama. Within the program, criticism tended to focus on the perceived personal and professional failings of particular constituencies and individuals. Yet as an external researcher, I saw ideological tensions or incompatibilities that could not be so easily reduced to questions of right and wrong or pinned on a particular group or person.

From this perspective, the kinds of social problems identified within the program were not the fault of students or teachers, but rather a structural consequence of a program set up in such a way that it generated such problems and did not have strategies to deal with them. They were a result of the model. Similarly, the rising tensions during Giraldo's tenure were not only a matter of communication and leadership style, but also a result of attempting to align the Red's actions with its goals and to graft progressive educational ideologies and practices onto a program that had long been imagined and organized in quite conventional ways. As one school director put it simply: "[some teachers] don't like change or adopting new pedagogies. But that comes from the way that they all learnt. Many in the Red are inherently conservative."

From this perspective, the conflicts tell us about tensions between progressive and conservative tendencies in music education and between core elements of SATM, such as musical versus social goals, classical versus popular music, music as art versus music as work, and training versus education. The grating noises within the Red were the sound of a new vision grinding against an old system. This was the fault of neither the management nor the staff; both their perspectives made sense on their own terms, but they were not easily compatible. Beyond a story of one side pushing too hard and the other pushing back, it was the sheer distance between positions and practices that lay at the heart of the matter. Had the management's progressive ideas not been so far from SATM's origins and the norms of classical music culture, the leadership might have been able to convey them more clearly and the staff might have been able to grasp them more easily. When Giraldo told a staff meeting that creativity was the Red's problem and its solution, one teacher replied: fine, maybe you're right, but we are mainly symphonically trained, the curriculum is symphonically focused, and our teaching is focused on technique, so you are talking about changing the program completely. This exchange highlighted the scale of the challenge to bring the Red into line with Medellín's cultural policy and orthodox SATM into line with contemporary educational thinking.

The first-order debates within the Red point to key challenges and dilemmas in the wider SATM field. Take teacher training, for example.

The exponential growth of SATM programs has not been remotely matched by a transformation in the education of professional musicians, meaning that there is a shortage of appropriately trained teaching staff with experience of social work and a strong understanding of social issues. Only a few years ago, Kratus (2015) argued that many teachers came out of conservatoires having received a training that differed little from that of nineteenth-century performers. As a result, it is not uncommon in SATM to find a gap between social goals and the skills and experience of some staff. As Godwin (2020, 13) notes, the international SATM field faces "insufficient numbers of teaching artists with both musical expertise and skills in teaching large groups of children with diverse learning or behavioural needs, and an absence of the necessary materials and pedagogy." This problem is exacerbated by a tendency in some quarters to hire fresh conservatoire graduates who may not even know the local context, much less have a deep understanding of its social issues and appropriate ways of tackling them, reproducing El Sistema's philosophy that classical performance training is the perfect preparation for such work. The Portuguese El Sistema-inspired Orquestra Geração actually boasted of hiring inexperienced recent graduates (Mota and Teixeira Lopes 2017). Yet as Schippers (2018, 29) notes drily, "the skill set that would have prepared graduates brilliantly for their role in a nineteenth century German town may not be appropriate for twenty-first century realities." To return to Ndaliko's point from the Introduction, this is an example of an approach that would be ludicrous if proposed in most other fields, and it makes it harder to take such programs seriously as social work.

Some issues appear particular to SATM. For example, there are echoes of the Red in Veloso's (2016) portrait of an Orquestra Geração student who aspired to be a professional clarinettist but struggled and failed to make the transition from the program to conservatoire. The risk that SATM runs in attempting to cover both pre-professional training and social action is doing both mediocrely. Other problems are found much more widely in music education. For example, numerous scholars have identified a gap between progressive educational theory and conservative practice and have pointed the finger at the training of future teachers in higher education (e.g. Carabetta 2017; Waldron et al. 2017; Wright 2019). Some issues, such as music education as work, sit somewhere between the two. In El Sistema, I found that many teachers were poorly paid, with few benefits, working in poor conditions, and with little control over their employment. I have heard similar complaints from some SATM teachers in other countries. Certainly, this issue is not unique to SATM; but the field's idealistic rhetoric brings this problem into sharp relief.

More detailed, critical, ethnographic studies of SATM programs are required in order to have a clearer picture about the extent of such issues across the field. It may be that, for example, programs in the global North that have taken El Sistema's name but have remained much smaller than their South American counterparts have avoided some of the problems. An issue like rivalry, for example, may be proportional to the number of students and ensembles. Programs that are newer and less intensive than the original SATM model, and/or aimed at a younger constituency, may be considerably more distanced from the classical music profession than El Sistema or the Red.

Nevertheless, there is ample evidence to suggest that the issues discussed in this chapter are neither unique to nor particularly severe in the Red. Rather, I see them as somewhat typical and predictable, a consequence of the orthodox model of SATM rather than local problems in Medellín. The Red followed the El Sistema approach under direct Venezuelan supervision, and the problems discovered from 2005 match closely those found by researchers in Venezuela.

Yet there are also major differences between the Red and El Sistema. The tension between the musical and the social never came to the surface in El Sistema because the Venezuelan program did not actively pursue its social objectives, but rather treated them as an inherent feature and automatic consequence of musical training. It added the social ingredient in the mid-1990s, halfway through its history, but as a discursive construct that barely affected the educational practices. El Sistema (and its more orthodox derivations) is essentially a social reading of and expanded access to conventional music education. But in the Red, since 2005, there have been consistent attempts to go beyond naming the social to actively pursuing it. This rethinking and redirecting of SATM introduced a tension between the musical and the social that never went away. Living up to an official mission of social action while maintaining musical excellence is not easy; indeed, it is a problem that no SATM program has entirely resolved. It is much easier to pay lip service to social action and focus on the music. The Red took a harder path.

Furthermore, El Sistema followed a much stricter line than the Red with regard to tensions and debates: it provided no room for them to be expressed or to flourish, preferring to present a single, unified, utopian vision at all times. Tensions between the musical and the social run right through Estrada's evaluation—most of her interviewees described a striking dissonance between theory and practice, between social ideals and musical priorities—but El Sistema did not allow them to surface publicly and become a topic of debate, and it had the means to construct a powerful official narrative that painted the opposite picture. It is an institution with a strong party line. In contrast, the Red has allowed much more space for debates to play out. I appreciated the critical reflections of the general directors and the ambivalence and realism that many employees showed, publicly as well as privately. The Red presented a refreshingly honest, self-critical contrast to its progenitor.

One consequence of El Sistema's single-minded focus on orchestral training and performance and its relentless dissemination of its official narrative is that, particularly at the apex of its pyramid, it can appear highly efficient. The multiplicity of visions and voices in the Red, and the greater openness with which they are expressed, makes its problems more apparent, and more time is spent on discussion and trying out alternatives. Hence the Red can seem rather chaotic in comparison, but the idea that its problems are deeper or more numerous is an illusion. Indeed, the ways that problems are hidden, suppressed, and denied in El Sistema speak volumes. Behind its public image of continuity and constancy lie educational stagnation, organizational dysfunction, and an allergy to critical thinking. If there is more evidence of tensions in Medellín, it is because the program has attempted to document, analyze, and resolve them since 2005 and has had a social team dedicated to this process. The Red's struggles might be seen not so much as a sign of failure but rather as a consequence of greater honesty and social ambition. The atmosphere in the Red was more openly charged and conflictive than in El Sistema, yet it signalled that groupthink did not dominate, employees were willing to be critical and self-critical, and differences of opinion could be expressed publicly. Clearly the Red was not perfect, but, in its very fractiousness, it seemed a healthier environment than El Sistema.

In sum, now that we have seen the Red through the eyes of management, staff, and advanced students, SATM appears more like an educational puzzle than a magic bullet, one that raises many questions. What approach would allow musicians and social professionals to pursue musical excellence and social change at the same time and in harmony? Can and should a program move towards greater inclusivity and more targeted social action if many students and staff would prefer to focus on the music and keep it demanding and competitive? Can progressive change be achieved through a participatory, collaborative approach if key stakeholders are sceptical of such change? How well can teachers prepare children for the music and society of the future if their education was rooted in a nineteenth-century conservatoire model? Does diversifying SATM require diversifying its staff? If so, where could more appropriately trained teachers be found? SATM appears as a multi-faceted conundrum, which would explain why it generated so much debate in the Red.

3. The Red through a Social Lens

> Teaching people that their love of Schubert makes them better people teaches them nothing more than self-regard, and inspires attitudes that are the very opposite of humane.
>
> Richard Taruskin, "Is There a Baby in the Bathwater? (Part II)"

With the characteristic friendliness and generosity of the *paisas*, as the inhabitants of Antioquia and surrounding provinces are known, the Red opened its doors to me, and I got to know representatives of all of its constituencies. I followed the reform efforts of the management (described in Chapter 1), and I investigated how those efforts were received by directors, teachers, administrators, and students (Chapter 2). Yet it was in the social team that my research questions about citizenship and social development found their natural home. The social team was at the heart of the matters that most interested me: both the principal source of critical thinking *about* the Red and also a focal point of criticisms *by* the Red's musical staff and students.

When I arrived in Medellín, I was met with two pleasant surprises. The first was that with the appointment of the new leadership at the start of the year, the Red's social team had switched its focus to internal research. The second was that the four members of the social team shared many of my questions and concerns. This convergence of activities and perspectives served us all, if for different reasons. I hoped to develop a collaborative angle to my research, and an internal social team exploring similar questions offered the perfect opportunity. Furthermore, they did not know my publications on El Sistema, so their views on SATM served as a triangulation point on my own. It quickly became apparent that while we had independently studied different programs in different countries at different times prior to meeting in September 2017, we had come to similar conclusions. All four were Colombian and employees of the Red, so their subject positions were very different to mine, but there was no obvious distinction between local and foreign perspectives on SATM or internal and external critiques. I thus saw their work as cross-checking, illuminating, and reinforcing my earlier work on El Sistema, critical scholarship on SATM more broadly, and my new research on the Red.

The social team was also interested in collaboration and corroboration, but for different reasons. They saw me as a useful ally: firstly, because I was a senior foreign researcher; and secondly, because I was a musician with a masters in performance from a European conservatoire and a PhD in musicology. As they explained, the former (rightly or wrongly) provided me with extra kudos in Colombia, and the latter meant that I could talk to the Red's musicians as an equal, which the social scientists felt they could not, and thus help with connecting social science concerns to the musical world.[1]

Why did this matter to them? The social team occupied a peculiar position in the Red: at the heart of its mission and its discourse, and yet strangely marginalized in everyday practice, constantly trying to carve out spaces and justify their existence within a sceptical musical community that often saw them as a burden or an obstacle. The social team struggled to find a role for itself in a program that was supposedly social in orientation but in which few staff wanted more than psychological support for specific students with problems. The team's experience was frequently one of frustration, its members worn down by battles to persuade staff to engage more fully with social questions. The social team thought that the Red and even the city government would be more likely to listen to them if I were on board. Indeed, as we will see below, the issue of artistic citizenship moved up the agenda as a result of our shared interest and collaboration.

---

1   The social team documented this point, noting that my arrival "can strengthen the possibility of translating the social to the musical. [...] It is important that he be part of our research as a team member" ("Informe" 2017a, 64),

Like the social team, the questions addressed in this chapter are simultaneously fundamental and somewhat peripheral to the Red: they lie at the heart of what SATM does and claims to do, yet they were not day-to-day topics of discussion in the way that the issues in Chapters 1 and 2 were. The main organizing principle here is that of "second-order" debates. These were issues that reared their head on occasion but without ever being fully and publicly debated. When discussions did occur, they were generally limited—behind closed doors in a small meeting, in a private conversation, or in the pages of an internal report that few people read. While such debates were less urgent and thus had a lower profile than those in the previous chapter, they are just as important for a thorough understanding of SATM. They hovered in the background for the Red, but in the foreground for its social specialists. This chapter amplifies such issues and gives them the prominence that the social team and I believe they deserve.

Here, then, the emphasis shifts towards the voices of the Red's social team, though not exclusively so. The involvement of social scientists (particularly psychologists and anthropologists) in key roles has been a significant and consistent feature of the Red since 2005. The social coordinators have been high-ranking and influential figures, working alongside the general directors. The first (Rocío Jiménez) lasted a decade, the second (Aníbal Parra) four years at the time of writing; other team members, too, spent years in the program. This long-term, full-time involvement contrasts with the more fleeting contact by most external evaluators of SATM programs, and it gave the social team a much more detailed and accurate picture of the central issues than appears in any published evaluation of SATM. They also took a more critical approach than most evaluators, since their role was to analyze and improve, not to justify funding; it was an inward-facing role more than an outward-facing one. As one member put it, the team's job was to move the staff out of their comfort zone and stretch them in new directions. Although theirs was an internal perspective, they observed from a position of critical distance, without the rose-tinted glasses of classical music ideology. Placing enquiry at the heart of the program, the social team understood the importance of "going beyond an idealized view of the Red" ("Informe" 2017c, 27).

I worked with or interviewed over a dozen current or former members of the social team, and they all held positive views about arts education and the Red's social objectives; however, most gave fairly short shrift to ideas that were prevalent among the musicians, such as music education as inherently socially beneficial. Most were concerned by some of the social dynamics that the Red generated and felt that musical training alone did not make a genuine and effective social program. Lacking musicians' socialization into the norms of symphony orchestras or bands, and with training and experience directly related to the Red's social objective, they felt the gaps between theory and practice more acutely than many of their musical colleagues.

The voices of the social team blend considerably with mine, since what began as an observer/observed relationship developed immediately into something much more collaborative. After a year of meetings, conversations, and reading internal documents, it was sometimes hard for me to know where one perspective ended and the other began. As far as possible, I will try to differentiate them, but a certain blending simply reflects one of the most salient conclusions from my fieldwork in Medellín: there was little that separated the social team's internal critiques of the Red from my decade of research on SATM.

Citizenship

At the first meeting of the student representatives in 2019, described in Chapter 1, Giraldo asked what the fundamental purpose of the Red was. "To form good citizens," came back the answer. He nodded approvingly. Indeed, citizenship discourse was regularly invoked in and around the program. The Red was supported by the Ministry of Civic Culture and stated that its pedagogy was based on "citizenly values." In 2006, the program's primary objective was stated as "education in civic and citizenly capacities" (Arango 2006, 5). Yet discussion of what a "good citizen" or "citizenly values" might actually be was rare during my fieldwork. This might have been due to a widespread assumption that everyone meant broadly the same thing when they invoked such terms, but in fact they did not. Citizenship is a notoriously complex and multifaceted concept, so it is perhaps unsurprising that beneath the linguistic surface lay conceptual disjunctures.

A prominent citizenship campaign undertaken by the administration of Mayor Federico Gutiérrez (2016–19) was based on the slogan "Pórtate bien" [behave yourself]. It involved attempts "to eradicate the main forms of behaviour that upset civic coexistence, such as quarrels, loud music, and poor disposal of rubbish."[2] This campaign was viewed askance by some of the city's more liberal inhabitants, including several of my interlocutors. In the cultural sphere, the touchstone text was the city's Cultural Development Plan 2011–20, produced under the earlier administration of Alonso Salazar. Here one finds a very different vision of citizenship, emphasizing democracy, participation, inclusion, diversity, creativity, and critical reflection. Culture is portrayed as "rooted in political ethics" ("Plan" 2011, 31), and: "The citizenry should be understood as active, critical, and proactive in relation to the major problems that confront the city as a whole and as a protagonist in cultural policies; but this requires civic participation and public deliberation" (48).

This urban-level dichotomy—behaviourist versus political conceptions of citizenship—was replicated quite closely within the Red. Interviews with school directors pointed to understandings of citizenship formation in terms of the inculcation of values such as discipline, order, responsibility, punctuality, and respect, and behaviours such as asking permission, not interrupting, and saying hello, please, and thank you. In the Red's official history, one director stated that the program taught students to be better citizens by instilling four values: discipline, respect, responsibility, and order (*El libro* 2015, 20). The centrality of such values has been in evidence since the first evaluation of the Red ("Medición" 2005), in which teachers highlighted discipline, work rhythm, organization of time, perseverance, and concentration as the main social impacts of the program. This was consistent with a pedagogy based on inculcating citizenly values, as declared in the program's mission. If this conception of citizenship echoed what Bull (2019) calls classical music's "ethic of correction," there are also parallels with the city campaign of *pórtate bien*. Parra's social team, however, held a vision of citizenship that was much closer to the Cultural Development Plan. This proximity was partly because of a shared intellectual grounding and partly because the

---

2   "Campaña pórtate bien", https://www.medellin.gov.co/irj/portal/medellin?NavigationTarget=navurl://3c3092487d6a9ab5522a091106130533.

social scientists explicitly rooted their analysis in the city's official plan so that it might be perceived as having as having a solid foundation, rather than being a matter of intellectual caprice or personal preference. The social team upheld a political rather than behaviourist conception of citizenship: it was concerned with the "political subjectification of students via music"—or rather, its absence.

The cultural plan imagined artistic education as forming "active, critical, proactive citizens" ("Plan" 2011, 100). It spoke of "developing potentialities and capacities more than giving instruction or information to the citizens, and it is aimed at developing a civic consciousness capable of living freely and being autonomous, and thus it does not seek the standardization of behaviours; as a result, it privileges active and reflexive pedagogies over instructive and directive pedagogies" (95). The 2017 social team saw a clear gulf between this cultural policy and the everyday practices of SATM (which exemplified precisely what the plan rejected), and so it developed a critique of citizenship formation in the Red. Its report was blunt:

> although the Red has citizenship formation as its mission, it does not fulfill this because it is not found in the curriculum and because the kind of training that it offers via the symphonic format—whose characteristics do not allow for reflection—does not foster critical subjects, as Martha Nussbaum puts it, nor people who construct collectively with others. The information collected to date speaks of *values education and not citizenship education, which is more political*. ("Informe" 2017a, 28, emphasis added)

Its diagnosis was that in focusing on technical and aesthetic matters and inculcating good behaviour, the program failed to develop the political subjectivity of students or their capacity to reflect critically on the world through music. The team doubted whether values education through music was sufficient "to educate citizens with the capacity to participate actively in the life of their community and the city" (187), and it therefore questioned whether the Red constituted citizenship education at all.

The social team's critique revolved around the program's focus on musical matters and its relative neglect of key constituent elements of citizenship such as reflection, voice, and agency: "[Belief in] the Red as salvation and social impact via concerts detracts from the (social) need to connect art with the fostering of subjects' agency" (115). Both the social team and the management board more generally often characterized Red events as students turning up, playing, maybe listening to some adults talking, and then leaving again. An earlier report insisted on the importance of including the voices of the students in decision-making, otherwise the program would lose legitimacy as an exercise in civic participation and students would stop believing in the possibility of dialogue and conflict resolution for social transformation (*Jornada* 2014). In other words, citizenship needed to be modelled and practised through real participation in taking decisions; just playing in an ensemble was not enough. But solutions were elusive. Three years later, another report noted: "Sometimes the students are treated like an object or an instrument; the only real interest would seem to be the music itself, rather than the musicians; the aim is for [the music] to sound. We don't ask what the students want" ("Informe" 2017c, 72). In a large staff meeting around the same time, a manager asked: are the students *participants in* the Red or *instruments of* the Red?

For the social team, the main problem was the symphonic format. They simply could not find evidence of a connection between large ensemble training and the stimulation of critical thinking, creativity, dialogue, respect for diversity, capacity to read the city, civic participation or the formation of "autonomous and free citizens" (188). Rather, they connected this training to "the conservative character of the Red" (98). "What kind of citizen does the symphonic format produce?," asked the report. "What kind of citizen does the Red form?" (31). Its answer was: a subject who followed norms and did not question. The team argued that the Red's values education might distance some young people from drugs and violence, but that it also pointed to "the formation of a 'good citizen' who is characterized by thinking that is conservative and uncritical with respect to their surroundings" (98). Their report suggested that the Red's students "will probably be citizens who comply with the norms and regulations of authority, but they will struggle to question them when they disagree or their interests are affected" (195). "To what extent can a musician in a symphonic format become an agent of their own transformation?" (31), asked the team. Not a great extent, they concluded, since this format demanded obedience, following a script, and keeping quiet (as the conductor had the last word). A school director revealed the social values inherent in conventional orchestral culture: "I have always said that music is social by its very nature […]. In the orchestra they learn to be disciplined, responsible, to know that they have to obey the rules, to look after their instrument." Where, then, would autonomous, critically reflective citizenship come from? How would a student learn to become "an agent of their own transformation"?[3]

However, such critiques were not unique to the social team and management; they were also expressed by some musical staff. One school director stated:

> I think that I've done nothing as regards aspects like politics and citizen education, perhaps just be an example. [...] The very fact that in music the recognition goes to one person already closes off the possibility of equity and critical reflection. [...] The Red is lacking in the formation of political subjects, it's something that has not been developed; what is taught is to be always a group, to move in the same direction; when have you seen a kid criticizing something?" ("Informe" 2017a, 71–72)

Another director mused: "I wish the Red taught us to be more critical [...] we're like sheep, we just follow, we don't teach the kids to have their own opinions." A third director decided to focus on developing critical thinking after finding that "in a rehearsal, when faced with various questions, the students 'go blank' because they lack their own voice to express what they think about the place they occupy in the ensemble, the school, and their context; it is common to find that the students constantly want to be told what to do" ("Informe" 2017d, 47–48).

The social team acknowledged positive dynamics in the program, such as a closer connection and greater degree of human warmth between staff and students than is the norm in ordinary schooling. Some directors and teachers took on a kind of a parental role. The team recognized the usefulness of values such as discipline, commitment, and pursuing goals. The schools offered potential for positive socialization, then. But the social team believed that the Red needed to go further, rather than just reinforcing the same norms and values upheld by other societal institutions (such as school and family), and to educate "human beings with a civic consciousness" (186). They envisaged a more socially comprehensive education, in which students could take lessons from

---

3   There are distinct parallels between the social team's critique of the Red and Spruce's (2017, 728) argument that "[c]onformity lies at the heart of Sistema discourses. [...] Conformity becomes a condition of participation where voices are heard only when they articulate accepted discourses."

the music school and apply them to their community and the city at large. In this way, young musicians might

> advance in their understanding of their role as citizens and not just as students who carry out duties to achieve goals. The question is how to create consciousness and stimulate the exercise of citizenship, the valuing of the public sector, and the sense of belonging to a city, along with an understanding of the role that they play, as musicians and artists, in the society of which they form part. (195)

There were close parallels here with my earlier work on El Sistema. Confronted with Abreu's pithy statement that "when you educate musicians, you educate better citizens," I had asked whether this was really the case. This question gave rise to a chapter in the volume *Artistic Citizenship* (Elliott, Silverman, and Bowman 2016), in which I reflected on the lack of voice or political participation of El Sistema's students (Baker 2016a). I compared the realities of playing in a conventional large ensemble with the characteristics of citizenship education, which the Ancient Greeks called *paideia* and had "the overall aim of developing the capacity of all its members to participate in its reflective and deliberative activities, in other words, to educate citizens as citizens" (Fotopoulos 2005). In citizenship education, emphasis is generally placed on modeling democracy, involving students in decision-making, and promoting critical and creative thinking. In comparison, El Sistema appeared to be designed to produce loyal subjects, trained to obey authority, rather than good citizens, educated to participate in democratic processes.

I drew on Roger Hart's (1992) famous study of children's participation. Hart argued that participation is the fundamental right of citizenship, but he was careful to break it down into eight categories, which he conceptualized as a ladder. It is only when we get toward the top of his ladder of participation, where we find child-initiated and shared decisions, that participation shifts away from tokenism towards citizenship. The bottom three steps on the ladder—manipulation, decoration, and tokenism—may *resemble* participation but, according to Hart, they are not the real thing, and so they do not foster citizenship. I argued that most of El Sistema's activities fell within Hart's category of tokenism, which describes "those instances in which children are apparently given a voice, but in fact have little or no choice about the subject or the style of communicating it, and little or no opportunity to formulate their own opinions" (9). As the program became more overtly aligned with the Venezuelan government in the twenty-first century, it showed increasing signs of decoration and manipulation. Hart's study provides good reasons to be sceptical of Abreu's optimistic claim that playing in an orchestra necessarily constitutes an education in citizenship.

Citizenship is thus intimately connected to participation, and as Brough (2014, 50) explores, numerous scholars have nuanced the latter term, distinguishing between "functional" and "transformative" participation, "deep" and "narrow," "nominal" and "transformative," "pseudo" and "authentic," and minimalist and maximalist "participatory intensities." Many writers agree that participation often positions those who participate as beneficiaries rather than citizens. Brough states that "a participatory culture should be characterized as such based upon whether participants have meaningful influence over decisions that affect themselves, their communities of practice, and ultimately the culture itself" (202). She argues that expanding access to technologies and skills does not necessarily promote a more participatory public culture or bolster the power of citizen voices; such efforts must be linked to communicative practices and spaces characterized by *horizontality*, *dialogue*, *openness*, and *autonomy*. Brough uses these four categories to analyze the extent to which digital programs in Medellín promoted a participatory culture and thus youth citizenship, and a similar process could usefully be applied to SATM programs that aim to educate citizens, and indeed to the label "participatory music making." Her argument that digital citizenship requires a lot more than simply giving people access to a computer and some Microsoft software and teaching them how to use it is equally relevant to music education.

We must therefore dig beneath citizenship discourse and observe closely the processes that lie beneath. "Discourses of participation can easily be appropriated to serve a variety of ideological (and economic) agendas while the corresponding practices of participation may, in fact, be minimal" (319–20). With its focus on putting students on display rather than entrusting them with taking decisions, orthodox SATM is a presentational rather than participatory culture (Turino 2008) and thus resembles Hart's tokenism more than citizenship education.

Returning to the Red, a useful analytical perspective is provided by Westheimer and Kahne's (2004) article, "What kind of citizen? The politics of educating for democracy," which poses precisely the same question as the social team in its 2017 report. The authors identify three answers or categories in citizenship education in the US: the Personally Responsible Citizen, the Participatory Citizen, and the Justice Oriented Citizen. They argue that each vision has positive aspects but is also incomplete. Of particular relevance to SATM is the Personally Responsible Citizen—one who is respectful, obedient, attentive, hardworking, and well mannered. Westheimer and Kahne argue that these are important values, but they

> are not *inherently* about democracy. Indeed, government leaders in a totalitarian regime would be as delighted as leaders in a democracy if their young citizens learned the lessons put forward by many of the proponents of personally responsible citizenship: don't do drugs; show up to school; show up to work; give blood; help others during a flood; recycle; pick up litter; clean up a park; treat old people with respect. These are desirable traits for people living in a community. But they are not about democratic citizenship. (5–6)

The authors suggest that democratic citizenship education must go beyond values education to encompass participation (in Hart's and Brough's senses) and social justice.

In Medellín, the vision of the musical staff aligned closely with the first category, while the social team's perspective had much in common with the second and the third. There were clear parallels between the social team's critique of the Red's approach to citizenship and Westheimer and Kahne's critique of the Personally Responsible Citizen. However, the social team's conception of citizenship did not fit precisely with either the second or the third category. What became more marked in the Red in 2018 was a focus on territory and the relationship between citizenship and the city.

The Red was founded in a decade of extreme violence in Medellín, and its aim was to provide *entornos protectores* [safe spaces] for young people. The Red began as an attempt to contain the issue of violence by isolating young people from negative influences. One of its key slogans became "transforming lives." Twenty years on, there was mounting concern at the management level that this approach was outdated;

the city continued to be a challenging place, but the levels of physical violence had declined substantially since the 1990s. The leaders now viewed the schools as somewhat divorced from the city and its cultural currents, and they questioned the extent to which the Red fostered reflection and action on issues outside its walls. The social team sought to broaden the conception of citizenship in the program from correcting individuals (transforming lives) to addressing issues facing urban society (transforming the city).

The team concluded its argument for a shift from values education to citizenship education:

> there is a consciousness and care in transmitting some values through musical practice. Despite this, it is necessary to generate strategies that allow the development of capacities like creative imagination, critical thinking, and active, deliberative participation by the students, not just in relation to the learning process, but also in relation to the role and contributions that they as musicians can make to the positive transformation of their immediate surroundings: the barrio, the community, and the city. ("Informe" 2017a, 202)

This vision is underpinned by the city's cultural plan, which states: "The challenge for the educational system is to promote a citizenship education that acts on the city, which implies viewing the latter as an object of analysis and a source of learning" ("Plan" 2011, 96). In an article connecting Westheimer and Kahne's work with arts education, Kuttner (2015) proposes that future research might seek to test and go beyond the former's three categories and explore what other kinds of cultural citizenship arts education programs may be encouraging. What the social team (and the management and culture ministry more broadly) sought to form, I would argue, was something akin to a Locally-Oriented Citizen—a young person in dialogue with their neighborhood and committed to its transformation.

Our shared interest in the issue of citizenship led the social team and I to have regular discussions on this topic, and as a result the program incorporated artistic citizenship as a strategic priority in 2018. The Red also offered me a formal role as its consultant on artistic citizenship. Unfortunately, I was unable to take up the offer for contractual reasons, so the Red hired a local researcher. But before I left Medellín, I gave two presentations to the program and proposed a model for thinking about this issue. I presented a vision of artistic citizenship based on the notion of the citizen as an individual who plays a role in the creation and changing of the social order, and artistic education as an important domain in which to develop the necessary capacities. I offered a very simple model, focusing on four notions: *reflection, creation, participation,* and *action*. Reflection and creation allow students to build agency and an autonomous voice, while participation (in Hart's sense) and action encourage them to project that voice, dialogue with others, and put their music to work in their communities and city.

This proposal attempted to draw together relevant external research with the Red's internal deliberations and priorities since 2017. On the one hand, I sought to translate (literally and figuratively) and condense ideas that were in circulation elsewhere so that they might be easily accessible to the Red. I drew on my earlier work and the sources already mentioned, but I also took considerable inspiration from Brad Barrett's (2018) DMA thesis, which had built on the volume *Artistic Citizenship* (and my chapter within it) to construct a model for an El Sistema-inspired program at the Conservatory Lab Charter School in Boston. I was also influenced by the work of the Red's sister program, the Network of Visual Arts, which had articulated a vision of citizenship that focused on transforming the social context (*Organismo vivo* 2016; *La ciudad* 2017), in contrast to the Red's "transforming lives"; and by Hensbroek's (2010) argument that cultural citizenship requires co-authorship (creative input) and not just visibility (performing someone else's script). On the other hand, there was nothing in my proposal that had not already been discussed or tried out somewhere within the Red. One school director, for example, emphasized to students that they had a responsibility to society and should give something back to the community in return for the free education that they received; she took actions such as taking the school orchestra to play in an old people's home. My aim was not novelty but rather to draw together promising threads from the Red with wider international currents, present key ideas in as simple and memorable a form as possible, and use my privileged position to help the social team give citizenship education more prominence within the program.

Like the social team, I founded this proposal on a critique of the equation of citizenship formation with inculcating good behaviour. The work of scholars such as Michel Foucault (1991) and James C. Scott (2012) suggests that inculcating discipline may actually be antithetical to fostering citizenship. SATM programs generally strive to produce "good citizens," but if they are to pursue social change, they need to ask: "does the role of educators imply an obligation to help students learn to be 'bad citizens'—to make their own artistic political or social statements?" (Bradley 2018, 79). Vujanović (2016) argues for the social importance of "bad artistic citizens"—those who are critical and disobedient. For dominant groups, a good citizen is usually orderly and obedient, but from the perspective of social change, a good citizen might be the opposite (think, for example, of civil disobedience in pursuit of social justice).

In the realm of SATM, El Sistema seeks to forge "good" citizens (loyal, obedient), but some participants in recent years could also be seen as "bad" citizens (disengaged from democratic processes, propping up a dubious political regime). Gustavo Dudamel was criticized in Venezuela for avoiding discussion of politics and thereby failing to model a good citizen (see Baker 2016a). Who were the good citizens, the musicians who obediently performed as propaganda for Venezuela's government or those who disobeyed and rose up against South Africa's apartheid regime (Hess 2019)?

"[B]ecoming and being an artistic citizen does not come about automatically; artistry must be integrated with other forms of knowing and doing," suggests Bowman (2016, 81). More specifically, "[s]tudents cannot and will not become fully engaged citizens unless they are prepared to penetrate, unmask, and transform their worlds positively. This is what full-blooded citizenship, and artistic citizenship, involves and demands," argue Silverman and Elliott (2016, 100). Action is thus crucial to artistic citizenship, but it is a very different conception of action than in orthodox SATM. In the latter, music education and performance are considered to *be* social action. But as a Red school director admitted, "concerts are like band-aids because people go back home and find the same problems waiting for them" ("Informe" 2017a, 78). Artistic citizenship, however, implies engaging in some way with those problems waiting back at home and not just providing a space for avoiding them. It entails action in and on society, which springs from critical reflection and has ethical, political, and civic dimensions, rather than disciplining oneself. Artistic citizenship entails putting the arts to work. As Bowman (2016, 65–66) writes, "the notion of artistic citizenship suggests a necessary relationship between artistry and civic responsibility. [...] Artistic citizens are (or at least aspire to be) socially engaged, socially aware, and socially responsible." This was something the social team grasped fully. They quoted the city's cultural plan: "citizenship should be understood as active, critical, and proactive with regard to the major problems that challenge society at large" (cited in "Informe" 2017a, 201).

In short, my proposal represented an effort to take seriously the issue of citizenship formation in the context of SATM programs, where citizenship discourse has been quite prominent but deeper reflection rather less so. It appeared from interviews that many Red staff and students had not thought much about this topic before; that in-depth, collective discussion had been somewhat absent outside of the management team; and that the program consequently lacked a clear, shared conception of citizenship education. My hope was to contribute to the social team's efforts to stimulate further reflection and action around the goal of citizenship formation, and to distinguish this objective from other SATM aims such as social action or inclusion. Here, my intention is to highlight an important question for a field with aspirations to citizenship education: what *kind* of citizen?

Question Marks over Citizenship

Reflecting the complexity of this topic, a number of doubts began to exercise me after presenting on artistic citizenship to the Red. In a spirit of promoting self-critical reflection, I will outline three of them here.

The Ambiguity of Citizenship

The Red's official objective, *convivencia* [coexistence], is the central term of *cultura ciudadana* [civic culture], a widely-used concept in Colombia that is associated with regulating citizenly behaviour and promoting positive social norms. The Red falls under the Sub-Ministry of Art and Culture, which forms part of the Ministry of Civic Culture. Institutionally, then, culture (narrowly defined, as in the arts) forms part of a wider strategy focused on culture (broadly defined, as in norms and behaviours). In other words, for all that the values that the Red upholds may be positive ones for living in a community, as Westheimer and Kahne acknowledge, the confluence of culture and citizenship appears here as a form of government. The Red, with its historical emphasis on producing well-behaved, "responsible citizens" (Barnes and Prior 2009), looks like a conduit for a behaviourist or disciplinary conception of citizenship within a behaviourist urban ideology of civic culture. The program aims to produce subjects that accord with the dominant political ideology, and effects that are sought and claimed are ones that are politically sanctioned. Even the social team's attempt to inject more politics into the program involved alignment with official policy, if a more progressive one (the Cultural Development Plan).

The Red exemplifies a governmentalization of culture that dates back to the nineteenth century. Culture was instrumentalized to serve as a tool of social control, aimed at changing the behaviour of the urban poor (Belfiore and Bennett 2008; Mantie 2018). This period saw a blossoming of claims that the arts promoted moral progress and public order and attempts to push the working classes towards "rational recreation" (the cultural pursuits of the middle and upper classes).

There are close links between the Red and Medellín's "Metro Culture" program, which seeks to promote good behaviour on the city's metro system. As Brand (2013, 10) writes: "'Correct' behaviour is permanently reinforced by the 'Metro Culture' programme [...], with its messages concerning the 'good citizen' and the values, attitudes, and everyday habits which it expects of users. The Metro system offers classical music and book-lending facilities of local authors. The culture it promotes is bourgeois and traditional; a strategy of 'social improvement.'"[4] The Red's alliance with Metro Culture, in the form of offering concerts in metro stations, illustrates its role in propagating an official, behaviourist notion of good citizenship.

Accordingly, there was some scepticism over citizenship discourse from less institutionalized branches of Medellín's cultural scene. Acosta Valencia and Garcés Montoya (2013) note that youth collectives generally saw citizenship as a somewhat empty, official discourse of the

---

4   See https://www.metrodemedellin.gov.co/cultura-metro.

state and preferred to speak of empowerment. In a public debate on culture and citizenship, Lukas Perro from the audio-visual collective Pasolini characterized citizenship as a civilizing, disciplining, normative discourse directed from the centre to the periphery and underpinned by a will to control. He was more interested in disruptive voices from the margins.

It is worth comparing the Red, an official musical response to violence in Medellín, with local scenes such as hip-hop and punk, which have offered a more critical, resistant vision, not just of violence but also of the dominant order that contributes to its production. Wiles (2016, 27) evokes this kind of dichotomy when he asks: "What is the purpose of art—to bind people together into some kind of community, or to provide a radical dissenting voice that subverts an unthinking status quo?" So too does Vujanović (2016, 114–15): "One of the most powerful potentials of art [...] is to produce an affective knowledge wherein the images and narratives of actual society can be discussed, distorted, perverted, and confronted by images of what the arts and society might be and could be." Hence, "as a public activity, art is more 'bad' (rebellious, noisy, disturbing, thought provoking, on the edge of being punished) than 'good' (silent, obedient, keeping the public order)." Such perspectives question the use of the arts (and arts education) as a support act for dominant ideologies.

Citizenship is thus an ambiguous, contested term, and it is often employed by dominant groups to further their aims. As Levinson (2011, 281) notes, "elite-legitimating, authoritarian citizenship is alive and well." This was clearly the case in El Sistema, which used the term liberally while systematically denying participants any political voice. But in a more subtle way in Medellín, citizenship was a discourse that tied together a disciplinary, corrective conception of music education with the priorities of city politicians and policy. Music education that is focused on values education appears as a vehicle for a top-down, official, behaviourist conception of citizenship: *cultura ciudadana* and *pórtate bien*. In return for free music education, the target population was expected to assume the subject position of self-disciplining citizens who behave in appropriate ways (Nuijten 2013). As such, music education conformed to the norm in citizenship education in Colombia: legitimating political elites and the dominant social order, and eliding fundamental problems of inequity, injustice, and exclusion (Galeano and Zapata 2006).

However, the ambiguity of citizenship can also be exploited. As a hallowed official discourse, it can be used to smuggle in a more progressive or even radical agenda without scaring institutions and funders. For the Red's social team, invoking citizenship was a way to open up space for thinking about forming young people as autonomous political subjects and not just obedient robots. In the visual arts program, citizenship was bound up with imagining youth as agents and creators of their own social reality. The latter program (discussed further below) serves as an example of using the officially sanctioned language of citizenship to push arts education in more innovative and progressive directions. Some conceptions of citizenship, such as "insurgent citizenship" (Holston 1999) or "subversive citizenship" (Barnes and Prior 2009), appear promising from the perspective of social change.

The discourse of citizenship thus has conservative and progressive valances, and it covers (or covers up) both social reproduction and social change. Dagnino (2007) writes of a "perverse confluence," since the language of citizenship and participation can hide very different political positions, ranging from radical democracy to neoliberalism. Even within Medellín's city government and its policies, the word "citizenship" did not have consistent or stable connotations. In part, this was simply about changes of mayor and government every four years, but it also reflects citizenship as a contested and ambiguous field.

Consequently, citizenship is both a risk and an opportunity for SATM; it can support either stasis or change. It may act as a kind of Trojan horse. It can open up space for more progressive agendas; but it can also be used to smuggle conservative ideologies and practices into progressive spheres. There is nothing inherently progressive about citizenship discourse, so it needs to be scrutinized and handled with care. A risk is that artistic citizenship could be divorced from critical debates and employed as a new label for conventional practices. It is a notion that holds great potential, but the trajectory of terms like citizenship, participation, and creativity suggests the importance of guarding against neutralization or cooptation to other (including neoliberal) agendas.

Citizenship in Latin America

I also had ideological doubts that made me question my own perspective on citizenship. I began to ask whether a normative approach, deeply rooted in European thought, was really justifiable in a Latin American context. Did it rest on or perpetuate a colonialist notion of Latin American peoples as deficient and in need of correction (Rosabal-Coto 2019)? Was my proposal not just as much a manifestation of coloniality as the El Sistema model that it critiqued and sought to supplant? Would a version more closely based on Colombian realities rather than European norms not be more appropriate (Galeano and Zapata 2006)? Why did I give such prominence to autonomy and critical reflection, which are much less salient in indigenous systems of knowledge? And yet, I had spent a year talking to the Red's leadership and social scientists and reading their reports; my proposal chimed with their thinking and was well received by them. They had, after all, offered me a job as a consultant on artistic citizenship. Was I now being more papist than the pope?

I do not have easy answers to these critical questions. I continue to find considerable value in the notion of artistic citizenship, and I still believe that a program that embraced reflection, creation, participation, and action would be stronger than one that did not; however, the questions are also valid. I suspect strongly that this model requires further elaboration in a Latin American context (and I offer some pointers in Part II). It may simply be that this topic does not lend itself to conclusive solutions, and that, rather like SATM more broadly, honest investigation of citizenship education will be an unending search with more questions than answers. Perhaps we need to be skeptical of all models, including mine.

Action or Activism?

Growing out of the critique of a normative approach is a question mark over action—the last of the four words in my model. This choice of word itself reveals my doubt, because in *Artistic Citizenship* and other recent work on this topic (e.g. Hess 2019), the emphasis is on *activism*, with its more political connotation. While I support this approach in theory, I am also aware that activism implies something different in Colombia than in much of the global North. Activism is potentially dangerous in

Colombia—the regular murder of social activists is a national scandal—and so many shy away from it. Hence there are reasons to be cautious about framing artistic citizenship as *necessarily* centered on activism.

One might also question whether a constant pressure to engage in action or activism might be a burden and/or limitation on music education programs, whatever their context. Consequently, I prefer to think of action as a possible or desirable outcome, rather than a necessary one. It is also one that might take place beyond the music program (whether outside or later). By promoting reflection, creation, and participation, music education might give young people tools to engage in action or activism in other areas of their lives or when they are older, if they so choose. In a context like Colombia, this would mean SATM laying the groundwork and fostering activist capacities rather than putting students on the line. This view finds an echo in Hess's vision of music education as "set[ting] the conditions for activism" (156) rather than guaranteeing action.

There are undoubtedly other critiques that could be made, and I hope that they will be. I do not believe that there is a blueprint for artistic citizenship within SATM. But I do believe that approaching citizenship as a question to grapple with and not just a publicity discourse would be a productive path for the field to follow.

"Music Education Is Political"

The issue of citizenship is closely tied to that of politics; indeed, it might be argued that politics is what differentiates citizenship education from social action. Mullin (2016) suggests that "deep" artistic citizenship is politically reflective and engaged, and, for the social team, citizenship education was inseparable from political subjectification. Politics was a "second-order debate" par excellence in the Red: it ran through much of what I observed yet was rarely a subject of direct discussion outside the social team. This is also the case in SATM more broadly, so it is well worth bringing this topic out into the open for further discussion. In the case of the Red, there was little open debate because politics is something of a dirty word for many people in Colombia. It is frequently associated with *politiquería* [politicking, or the "dark arts"] and corruption. Some confuse being a political subject with politicking ("Informe" 2017a).

Within the context of arts education, politics can therefore be a sensitive issue. Nevertheless, the efforts of the new leadership from 2017 might be understood as profoundly political.

The social team tackled the issue of politics head on in urging the Red to focus more on "the political subjectification of students via music." In a presentation to all the directors in 2018, Parra included a slide entitled: "Music education is political." In fact, constituting and empowering students and their families as political subjects had been a concern for leaders since the time of Arango, and it had been the principal goal of Jiménez, Parra's predecessor as head of the social team, who had regarded the value of SATM as lying primarily in the sociopolitical processes that it could catalyze. Such views were underpinned by the city's cultural plan, which portrayed culture as "rooted in political ethics" ("Plan" 2011, 31). For successive leaders and social teams, then, the Red was at heart a political project, and its success or failure ought to be evaluated in terms of political notions such as agency and voice.

Giraldo, too, engaged with politics in an explicit way, for example during his opening words to the new student representatives in 2019. But his and Franco's re-envisioning of the Red through lenses of diversity and identity also constituted a form of cultural politics. Their frequent evocation of terms such as horizontality, agency, and *diálogo de saberes* [exchange of knowledge] underlined that their new initiatives were driven by political and not simply aesthetic considerations. Their promotion of creation in addition to performance was about representation as well as innovation. The adoption of PBL was explained as a route away from autocratic dynamics towards participatory construction, illustrating a concern with the Red as an embodiment of a political ideal. But Giraldo also invoked art as counterculture and a tool for questioning society. These musicians pursued somewhat different routes to the social scientists and used different language, but their diagnoses and their political goals were quite similar. In their own way, they were equally concerned with constituting students as political subjects.

An important strand of their cultural politics was their embrace of interculturality and their critical response to colonialist dynamics in Colombian music education. The Red is not an academic space, so words like "colonial" and "decolonial" were not a regular part of everyday discourse, but these terms came up frequently enough in smaller meetings and private conversations that it became clear that they informed the leaders' thinking. The leadership did not dismiss classical music or suggest that it should not form part of the Red, but rather they criticized the colonized mindset that foreign is better than local and focused their efforts on bolstering the (historically weaker) popular and traditional side of the program. From 2018, they increasingly used the traditional music school, Pedregal, to showcase the program at external events. By championing Colombian music and embracing terms like interculturality and horizontality, they made it clear that they intended to move the Red away from a colonialist hierarchization of culture that placed European classical music on a pedestal. Giraldo stated explicitly that the new emphasis on diversity, identity, and horizontality had a "powerful political backdrop." Mignolo and Walsh (2018, 57) provide more detail on that backdrop, describing interculturality as "both a complimentary political, epistemic, and existence-based project and an instrument and tool of decoloniality's praxis," which they distinguish from "a politics of inclusion that, more often than not, is tied to the interests of the dominant order."

In contrast, El Sistema—which has operated under the banner of inclusion since the early 2000s—has always disavowed politics and presented itself as apolitical. Following the lead of his mentor Abreu, Dudamel steadfastly refused to discuss politics for his first decade in the global limelight; his public relations handlers made it clear to journalists that he did not wish to talk about this topic, and when pressed, he responded: "El Sistema is far too important to subject to everyday political discourse and battles. It must remain above the fray" (cited in Baker 2016a). Politics is another area in which the Red broke away from El Sistema in 2005, to the point of offering a profoundly distinct vision of SATM.

In reality, all music education is political, as Parra's slide declared; what vary are the kinds of politics and the degree of openness. Both El Sistema and the Red are state-funded and directly overseen by politicians. El Sistema operates out of the Office of the President and has leading politicians on its board of directors. The Red's director answers directly to the Minister of Civic Culture. Their imbrication with formal politics has been a source of their success but also of criticism, whether from inside or outside the organization, since their position has made them subject to political dictates.

El Sistema's claims to be apolitical are simply a strategic discourse. Abreu was a politician before he created the program, he became a government minister while directing El Sistema, and he was widely known as a master of *politiquería*. The program has always worked closely with Venezuela's governments, and this relationship became even closer under Presidents Chávez and Maduro. In recent years, El Sistema has openly danced to the government's tune, clearly contradicting its continued claims of political neutrality. This overt political alignment has made the program an object of increasingly strident criticism from Venezuelans in recent years (e.g. Esté 2018; Kozak Rovero 2018), though the apolitical fiction still has a considerable hold over the public imagination in the global North.

In the case of the Red, the criticism has been more internal and more muted, and has come particularly from the first generation. Some musical staff saw a long process of formal politicization of the Red, starting with the shift from a private company (Amadeus) to the city government, and accentuated with the mayor's appointment of the general directors from Zuluaga onwards. Zuluaga and her successors were tasked with aligning the Red more closely with the priorities of the culture ministry and the city administration. These changes were viewed askance by some staff, who remembered a "golden age" when the Red was more independent and who resented the idea of being at the whim of politicians.

Both programs are also political at a more micro level. As Ansdell et al. (2020, 138) note about CM, "the intimate and personal work of musicking with people in a variety of ways and settings is also necessarily micro-political." El Sistema's strict limitation of the agency of students, to the point of even telling them whom to vote for in elections, and its openly autocratic approach, built around discipline and male figures of authority, are just as political as the Red's concern with empowerment and political subjectification.[5] A denial of politics and ideology is often

---

5   A 2015 Venezuelan newspaper report alleged that music school directors were ordered by top figures in El Sistema to take their employees to vote for the government in the national elections ("Denuncian hostigamiento" 2015). Luigi

a sign of an implicit conservative agenda, and this is the case with El Sistema, as numerous scholars have attested.[6]

While the Red's progressive politics contrasted with El Sistema's conservatism, in practice the distinction between the two programs was somewhat less clear. The fact that the social team was still struggling with the same issues a decade after its creation was indicative: the Red evolved as a satellite of El Sistema, and it did not change overnight with the arrival of new management. Parra's overriding concern in 2017 with the political subjectification of students reveals the extent to which Jiménez's earlier intentions, dating back a decade, had been frustrated or subsequently reversed. Hence the Red's more political approach, focused on empowerment and voice, might best be understood as a management vision, one that was constantly curbed to a greater or lesser degree by the deep-rooted philosophy of discipline and correction that ran through the heart of the program (and indeed of classical music education more broadly). The Red thus appears in reality as a space where different approaches to SATM coexisted in tension, rather than a pure example of a different model of SATM. Nevertheless, however partial the advances in practice, the leadership's critiques of Eurocentric, colonialist ideology and their embrace of goals such as horizontality and interculturality began to destabilize some of SATM's more conservative political foundations.

Holding up El Sistema and the Red together allows us to question the dominant notion that SATM is or ought to be independent from politics, and to understand how a more openly political approach is tied to a more progressive agenda and is therefore more promising if social change is the goal. El Sistema's "apolitical" SATM, beneath the rhetorical carapace, is more focused on strengthening existing values than generating new ones, as will be discussed in the next chapter. El Sistema is something of an outlier among socially oriented music programs in its negation of politics; in fields such as CM or social justice in music education, individuals are commonly driven by political beliefs and organizations

---

Mazzocchi, too, recalled that El Sistema's leadership had issued directives as to how orchestra members should vote (Scripp 2016b).

6   See the special issue of *Action, Criticism, and Theory for Music Education* 15:1 (2016). One of the many paradoxes of El Sistema is its top-level and discursive alignment with the socialist government and its perpetuation of Abreu's conservative leanings further down the organization and in its actual workings.

frequently frame their activity in political terms. Politics are also more prominent in some other parts of the Latin American SATM field.[7]

It is also interesting to compare the Red to SATM programs in the global North. Of course, there is considerable variation across the latter. Nevertheless, the "power of music" ideology is widespread in advocacy and public discourse there, whereas it was entirely absent among the Red's management during my fieldwork. I never heard the leadership explain music's impact in terms of cognitive or psychological effects, or IQ or test scores. Instead, they were interested in encouraging young people to find a voice, to connect to their cultural heritage, and to act on issues in their barrios. For Parra, music's value was as a means for students to reflect on and express who they were and what they experienced. Social change would emerge from cultural creation and political participation, not invisible changes in students' heads. There was no talk of miracles or salvation; benefits were seen as depending on the program's pedagogical and political stance and the ways that it did or did not allow students to develop as social and political subjects.

These kinds of issues are sidelined not just by the dominant model of El Sistema but also by the evaluative culture prevalent in the global North. The Red was funded by the city government as a program for peaceful coexistence. In this sense, its overarching objective was both political and virtually unmeasurable, and indeed, one of the few challenges that the program did *not* face was an obligation to prove its value via regular impact assessments. It might seem that a lack of evaluation would be a recipe for poor quality, but another perspective is that it allowed the program's management to focus on the issues that really mattered to them rather than those that could be measured by others. In the case of the Red, this meant that the cultural and political aspects of SATM moved to the centre of the debate, and measurable indicators such as cognitive effects and academic achievement were relegated to the margins.

In this vein, I was struck by how indifferent Giraldo's team seemed to studies that did not address cultural or political questions. They showed little interest in quantitative or psychological evaluations, but not for the

---

7   For example, politics were central to the presentations and debates at a one-day conference on youth orchestras in Latin America that I co-organized with Ana Lucía Frega in Buenos Aires, Argentina, in November 2018.

reasons sometimes found elsewhere (an unshakeable belief in the value of the program). On the contrary, they clearly believed that a SATM program that failed to foster a *musical* and *political* voice in students was deficient, and no amount of studies on other topics was going to change this assessment.

In sum, politics is a topic to be embraced if we are to understand SATM more deeply, yet it has often been avoided, even in much research. If we start from Parra's idea that "music education is political," and assume there is no such thing as apolitical music education, we are more likely to understand the macro- and micro-political forces that structure programs and run through them. Every program is enmeshed to some degree in national, regional, or local politics, and aligning seamlessly with dominant individuals and ideologies is not the same as neutrality. Every program embodies a form of cultural politics through its choice of curriculum and pedagogy, and such politics is no less real for being implicit. Every program is involved to some degree in constituting political subjects; the question is, what *kind* of subject?

The Bubble

One director described his school as a kind of oasis: a place where everyone left their troubles at the door and breathed a different atmosphere. Nora, a member of the social team, had a different take. She viewed the program as creating a separation between the school and the barrio, and constructing dichotomies of "good kids" versus "bad kids," *culto* versus *inculto*: those who are educated and cultured versus those who are not. She characterized the attitude of some Red students to their peers as "you, so simpleminded, just listening to reggaetón and me, so sophisticated, listening to Beethoven." This was not the fault of the students or teachers, she said, but rather inherent in the Red. She argued that such binaries could have been productive if they had been taken as topics for discussion; instead, they just generated prejudice. "This is the most dangerous dynamic that the Red produces—because it shouldn't be about pointing a finger at some people and putting others on a pedestal." She saw this as the opposite of what the program should really be doing, which was promoting empathy and acting for the benefit of others. Rather than tarring youths caught up in the urban conflict as "bad kids," rather than fostering a binary of "I'm a musician and you're a criminal," the Red should be trying to humanize others and understand them.

Nora went on: "what we're doing, or what is generated here, is that those kids don't have a critical vision of those realities and those barrios but rather simply want to distance themselves." If I'm a music student within a violent context, she said, but I stay in my music bubble, I'm not doing anything to improve that context; I'm not doing anything to transform the reality of other people who live alongside me. She described the dynamic as *huir pero no devolver*: to escape but not give anything back. Students treated the music school as a refuge, but a counter-movement or return to the community had been much more partial. "So at the end of the day, the impact that the Red has is limited to the music school and doesn't go beyond it." Her conclusion? "If we're creating that bubble, we should burst that bubble."

Nora's explanation was particularly detailed, but the underlying view was not unique to her. Parra alluded regularly to the Red's historical imaginary of good kids and bad kids, those who were saved and those who were left behind. The social team's 2017 report critiques the construction of a self-enclosed world:

> Another aspect found in interviews and the collection of information in the field (school visits and meetings) is the limited attention of the communities to the program's performances, in other words, how little impact there is for people who are not connected to the Red; and the resistance of teachers and directors to open up to other possibilities that would broaden the perspective of the work and allow students to explore other spaces. ("Informe" 2017a, 99)

It continued that the pedagogical model and performance focus limited students' comprehension of the social realities of other young people in the city. In a meeting with directors, Parra pointed to the contradiction between the Red's supposed employment of critical pedagogy, according to official documents, and what he described as "a total negation" of the question of violence in many schools. He asked: is the Red forming political subjects or people who take refuge in music and isolate themselves from society?

Lucía, one of Nora's predecessors, stated that the "bubble issue" had been a major topic of discussion during her time. She described the Red as an "elite" program that took children out of their everyday surroundings, gave them new knowledge, and opened their eyes to other realities; but it also opened up gaps between them and their contexts, their families, and their communities. This meant a constant risk of tension or conflict with their everyday lives, one that the Red had never really dealt with. Echoing Nora, she claimed that the students became distanced from reality and no longer lived fully in their territories. They "levitate" as they walk through the barrio, she said (an image that evokes the opposite of "down to earth"); they believe they are on a higher plane than their peers.

María, one of Nora's colleagues, criticized the Red's original intensity (long hours, seven days a week) for disrupting students' relationships and activities with their families and friends. She also looked askance at the widespread discourse of the Red as a family: no, she said, it's *not* a family, it's a public program and it shouldn't supplant the family. Most of the participants already have a family and should spend some time at home.

Evidence of such visions dated back more than a decade. The first social team report noted that among student motivations for joining the Red was "to be different from others (better)" ("Informe" 2008, 5), and that "the students in the schools feel proud and different, even within the context of the barrio itself" (23). The 2005 evaluation was clearer still:

> the beneficiaries have a sense of belonging to the group of musicians, which they see as something positive, attractive, but which makes them different. Different because they have a talent that they should put at the service of others, because they are more sensitive to the world and to those around them, because they learn tolerance and recognition, and because they are an example to the rest of the children of their age or family. ("Medición" 2005, 13)

It also notes: "the teachers try to foster a lot of confidence so that [students] can assume the role of being different" (4). The repetition of the word "different" is striking. Furthermore, under the category of social inclusion, the report highlights the affection of the participants for each other, with whom they spend much of their time.

What emerges from these reports and testimonies is a clear sense of the Red as cultivating bonds among an in-group (music students) and distinction or separation from an out-group (other peers). There are parallels with studies of SATM programs in other countries. Wald (2009; 2011; 2017) found that young SATM musicians in Buenos Aires had a strong "us versus them" worldview—a clear sense of difference and distance from their non-musical peers, whom they regarded as problematic and less worthy. She argues that the programs were not so much transforming the most vulnerable youths as providing an outlet for young people from popular neighbourhoods whose families were economically stable, already shared the middle-class value system of SATM, and were committed to their children's participation. Hence the programs exacerbated the imagined distance between the two groups. In their study of Portugal's Orquestra Geração, Teixeira Lopes et al. (2017, 207) note that "this strong environment of unity also ends up having a negative side given that sometimes the orchestra functions somewhat like a little world isolated from everything else, 'a very closed sphere.'"[8]

Sarrouy (2018) paints a detailed portrait of a group of mothers who spend every afternoon waiting for their children outside a Venezuelan El Sistema school. He notes a contrast between children inside the school, who are smartly dressed, and those outside in the streets of the barrio, shoeless and dirty. He asks the mothers about this. They reply that those outside come from families who show less concern for their children. One says: "they are above all single mothers who suffer from alcoholism and gambling; they prefer to spend the afternoons watching soap operas and they're not concerned about their children, who spend their days in the street and become delinquents" (50). In this account, El Sistema appears not as a program of social inclusion aimed at the most excluded but rather as a motor of social separation, drawing a line between children from more and less supportive families.

Boundary drawing is a major theme of Bull's (2019) study of youth classical music in the UK. Its appearance in SATM programs in South America thus seems not coincidental but rather a consequence of the shared building-block of classical music education. Bull opens her book with a self-critical account of her own experience as a young classical

---

8   Teixeira Lopes and Mota's (2017) recommendation that the program adopt a territorial approach, moving beyond students and their families to engage with local groups, associations, institutions, and movements, has many resonances with the Red's policy in 2018.

musician, which has unmistakable echoes of the social team reports on the Red: she describes "a sense of being somehow apart from the rest of the world—everyday concerns didn't touch my fellow musicians and I because we were doing something much more important than everyone else" (xi). Together with her argument that being a classical musician was a powerful social identity for the young people in her study, this brings us to a little-understood point about SATM: the characteristic dynamic of the collective in SATM is not the much-touted teamwork—of which the conductor-led orchestra is in fact a strikingly poor example (see Baker 2014)—but rather tribalism.

In its first phase, the Red had a motto, *Siempre juntos* [always together], and a hymn of the same name. The sense of in-group bonding is obvious in the words themselves and was underlined by the fact that members of the first generation still used this motto twenty years later. Some employees echoed Bull's characterization of young classical musicians as "being somehow apart from the rest of the world," describing Red students as "going along with their heads in the clouds" because they played classical instruments, or as disconnected from other youth cultures. Coexistence, the central objective of the Red, was generally imagined as among music students, rather than between music students and the rest of society. Such tribalism is particularly marked in El Sistema. In its publicity discourse, the notion of "one big family" is constantly reinforced, but the other side of this coin is a striking insularity and exclusivity. Mora-Brito (2011, 60) describes "a closed and inhospitable system for outsiders," while an experienced orchestral administrator quipped: "it's one big family... like the Sicilian mafia" (see Baker 2014, 223).

Developing friendship, bonding, and belonging among likeminded people is a recognized characteristic of music education and it may be seen as a positive process (Hallam 2010). Shieh (2016) notes some positive aspects of El Sistema's "bubble" philosophy, though he also raises numerous critical questions. Collective activities potentially offer considerable benefits to societies fragmented by neoliberalism, political polarization, and new technologies. One Red director stated: "The kind of friendship that is generated in music schools is not the same as in [ordinary] schools." He argued that students became more like siblings or soul mates, as they were there out of choice and shared interest rather than obligation.

But what has emerged from analyses of the Red and other programs is the other side of the coin: in-group bonding at the cost of solidarity or empathy with others, and thus the construction and maintenance of social divisions. As Bowman (2009b, 122) writes: "The other sides of music's inspiring capacity to forge unity amidst diversity are its erasure of at least certain dimensions of individual difference and its creation and reinforcement of boundaries that separate and distinguish insiders from outsiders." Similarly, Daykin et al. (2020), in their study of the role of social capital in participatory arts for wellbeing, argue: "The data suggest some negative aspects of social capital. For example, bonding can create in-group identities and, by definition, can reinforce exclusion of out-groups." SATM appears to fortify rather than contest an evolutionary dynamic of in-group solidarity and out-group hostility, raising doubts about its contribution to peaceful coexistence and social harmony. Moreover, the discourse of "one big family" has served to normalize and cover up troubling dynamics in music education institutions, including sexual abuse, in the UK (Newey 2020) as well as Venezuela (Baker 2014).

Central to El Sistema's philosophy is the notion of the symphony orchestra as a training ground for life. Yet a conventional orchestra is a bounded unit that fosters insularity and limits exchange with wider society in various ways (such as entry requirements and the design and use of space). In an educational context, it trains students to bond with those who have similar skills and interests and separates them from others. In the case of orthodox SATM, with its intensive time commitment, students often describe the curtailment of their wider social connections as their life revolves increasingly around the music school and other music students. A miniature world that limits inhabitants' dealings with strangers with different tastes and ideas is hardly "a model for an ideal global society," as Dudamel claims (Lee 2012).

One kind of tribalism, then, is SATM versus the rest. Nora's pithy summary—"you, so simpleminded, just listening to reggaetón and me, so sophisticated, listening to Beethoven"—indicates how this tribalism is mediated by musical genre as well as activity. While SATM may be analyzed positively as participants' acquisition of cultural capital, Daykin et al. (2020) note: "Cultural capital is sometimes observed to reinforce hierarchies through aesthetic judgements and distinctions based on taste, repertoire, creative skills, accomplishments and experiences." Wald (2017, 72) makes a similar point with particular reference to SATM: "The aesthetic experience of classical music contributes to constructing the identity of the collective, that 'us,' the different ones." The dismissive attitude of SATM musicians towards reggaetón is something that I too have observed repeatedly. Reggaetón is a style of popular music that is very widely consumed across Latin America, and while it has cross-class appeal, it is particularly associated with the popular classes. It is distinctly ironic that programs that are supposedly focused on social harmony and aimed at popular barrios in fact breed disdain for the music most widely consumed there. SATM programs could approach the issue differently: for example, challenging students who complained about the genre's musical and lyrical impoverishment to write a good reggaetón song; or teaching them about all the popular musical genres going back to the sixteenth century that have been initially despised by social elites and have then gone on to become hallowed national symbols in Latin America (like tango, samba, and rumba) or staples of classical music (like the chaconne and the sarabande). Instead, SATM often fosters a division between supposedly high-minded classical musicians and low-minded reggaetón fans.

Cheng (2019, 59–60) writes: "What's actually in short supply—what lies at the root of so much injury and injustice—is people's limited capacity or willingness to understand, tolerate, and dignify the different things that *other people* find beautiful. Think of all the strife that erupts when society's inhabitants fail to empathize or put up with one another's tastes and interests." Should programs that claim to focus on inclusion or peaceful coexistence through music not aspire to build bridges between consumers of different genres rather than using music to divide them?

Another kind of tribalism is a feature of the orchestral world, found most obviously in the attribution of distinct characteristics to string, woodwind, and brass players, or the jibes at the viola section. Its presence in the Red can be seen in the internal reports discussed in Chapter 1, with their references such as "a lot of rivalry and jealousy between the woodwind/brass and strings and between instruments," and "real or imaginary hierarchies that may be at work and being reproduced in the ensembles, generating discontent, discrimination, and exclusion." One of the viola teachers reacted angrily after a colleague made a viola joke in a staff training activity that I attended. We're supposed to be trying to move away from the dynamic of the symphony orchestra here, she snapped; we're supposed to be equal. I have to put up with viola jokes all the time in orchestras; I shouldn't have to put up with them here. This brief incident illustrated how the tribalism of orchestral music infiltrated even a supposedly social program, and how its jibes and stereotypes can foster separation and tension rather than the official goal of coexistence. The evidence from the Red raises questions about the suitability of a musical collective traditionally marked by internal and external divides, hierarchies, and competition as a model of and motor for social harmony.

I understood the Red's new territorial approach in 2018 as, in part, an attempt to counteract the construction of social dichotomies and distinctions, which contradicted the program's central objective of promoting peaceful coexistence. In the 1990s, the music schools were founded as refuges from the city's problems and as bastions of musical difference. However, the 2005 evaluation of the Red revealed that 88.2% of students surveyed felt safe in the barrio where they lived. In other words, within a few years the idea of the music school as a refuge from violence had become of lesser relevance to the vast majority of students, yet it continued to define the Red. Twelve years later, the social team noted that "the Red is often seen as a refuge that protects students or keeps them away from coming into contact with or thinking about the problems that affect the community or immediate surroundings of the school" ("Informe" 2017a, 199). One team member held up an example: the narrative in one school is that there is a drugs dispensary nearby but the students walk past it without even looking because they are "good kids." There is a clear dichotomy in the school's imaginary: good kids in here, bad society out there. What had been lacking in the history of the Red, she said, were strategies to bridge the two. The notion of safe spaces was fundamental to the Red's thinking. As such, it had separation, both social and cultural, in its genes.

Over time, the Red began to ask how its students might act as agents of positive change in the city and not just within the music schools. From 2017, the new vision was for the program to open its eyes, ears, and doors; "to get to know the territories and communities, and devise strategies so that the students dialogue much more with their surroundings, in pursuit of a social transformation that impacts at the level of the city and nation" ("Informe" 2017a, 106). Connection and exchange, rather than escape, were now the order of the day.

This entailed a different vision of SATM, not one based on a narrative of individual salvation but rather asking, what is the responsibility of music students towards the rest of society? Parra criticized an imaginary of the Red as a group of escapees from the problems of the barrio. What was it doing for those who remained, he asked? Here we find a political conception of SATM allied to a spatial one: a concern with "those out there" as well as "us in here," with wider social relations as well as individual transformation and in-group bonding, with the community at large and not just students and their families.

In one management meeting, there was a discussion about how the Red might contribute to constructing the social fabric, rather than simply going out to perform concerts. How might the music schools serve to foster the community and solidarity that were lacking in the neoliberal city? The program began to ask: if the spaces around the school are dangerous, what could the school do to make them safer? If they are ugly, how could the school make them more beautiful? The social team's cartography exercises were a concrete example of this shift away from conceiving of the wider social context as a problem to be avoided and towards recognizing, engaging with, and even repairing the outside world. Laverde, the director of San Javier school, spoke often of the importance of breaking down the idea of the Red as an exclusive island for a privileged few and reconnecting it to the barrio; the school's project was dedicated to this end. Its *improvisajes* were imagined as a form of territorial healing.

Such a conception of SATM treats young people less as potential delinquents to be rescued and transformed by the power of music, and more as political subjects in formation and prospective agents of social change. Rejecting older ideas about distancing and "saving" children from their social realities, it places more emphasis on their capacity and responsibility for acting on the city's problems. It recognizes that music students are often in a position to serve others who are more disadvantaged or isolated. The social team conceived of music as a tool for naming and working on social realities, not avoiding them, urging the program to go beyond constructing safe spaces *from* violence to fostering critical reflection *on* violence "and in this way transform society through the formation of reflective subjects with their own judgment" ("Informe" 2017a, 116). It asked how safe spaces might be created not just within music schools but also across the barrio. The team highlighted Nussbaum's contention that citizenship education entails fostering the capacity to think about the common good and not just a local group (198).

The dominant conception of orthodox SATM has been that students *receiving* music education equates to social action. There is a vague notion that values spread outwards from the children to their families and wider society—though there is little explanation or evidence of this process, and Sarrouy's (2018) data suggests the opposite (see Chapter 4). What is largely lacking from this osmotic model is the idea that social action entails students *giving*—in other words, a conception of social action built on service to others. "Social impact" was normally shorthand for benefits for students. Now the Red was paying more attention to the potential benefits for wider society, not just for the 5000 participants in the program but also for the city's three million inhabitants.

Hess (2019) explores music's potential in this regard. She elaborates a "pedagogy of community," which emphasizes connection on three levels:

> First, youth engage with each other in the local classroom community, fostering a mutually-supportive environment in which they learn to value their own contributions and those of other community members. Second, youth connect music to its sociopolitical and sociohistorical context in a way that allows them to understand their own lives and the lives of Others in a wider matrix of social relations. Finally, youth encounter unfamiliar Others through examining different musical traditions that provide a window into both the local community and the wider global community. (152)

Hess thus expands the one-dimensional bubble philosophy of orthodox SATM into a three-dimensional model that looks outwards as well as inwards, across time and space as well as at those present in the here and now. As Sachs Olsen (2019) argues, the challenge for socially engaged art is not to promote solidarity between likeminded people but rather between groups that are quite different. Similarly, Silverman and Elliott's (2018) vision of artistic citizenship is concerned with many "others" and not just participants and their immediate circle:

> an 'ethic of care' should not be limited to one-on-one pairings, small groups, or local circumstances alone. Part of moving beyond 'the self,' beyond the one-to-one relationship that is common with local community music programmes, is a purposeful 'seeking out' of much larger community needs. Therefore, what is 'good-for' multiple 'others'? What does it take to understand and serve the larger needs of those we don't necessarily engage with on a local or daily basis? Part of the answer rests in the nature of self-other responsibility that is, or should be, at the heart of artistic citizenship. (369)

The fourth element of the model of artistic citizenship presented above—action—attempts to capture this alternative approach to SATM: treating students as agents of social action, as citizens and not just beneficiaries. In the context of a social program, music should be considered as political and ethical action and an exercise in civic responsibility (Elliott, Silverman, and Bowman 2016), which implies an outward movement towards society, rather than an inward one towards disciplining a few young people. Artistic citizenship revolves around putting music to work for the betterment of others; it entails an ethic of care directed towards society and not only the individual. This model rejects the deficit thinking that lies at the heart of El Sistema, articulated in its official mission as "rescuing children and young people from an empty, disorientated, and deviant youth," and the pathologizing of individuals that takes place when large ensemble music education is imagined as correction or cure (Mantie 2012).[9] Spruce (2017, 725) summarizes the deficit model in music education: "Young people are characterised here in terms of [...] what they do not have—rather than in terms of what they might bring to the sites of music education as sentient musical beings often embodying rich musical and cultural heritages." Artistic citizenship follows the latter route; its focus is not on what young people lack but rather what they could contribute to culture and society. In Mantie's terms, it "lean[s] more in the direction of *education* as ethical enterprise rather than *training* based on presumed lack and necessary acquiescence" (120).

---

9   El Sistema, "¿Qué es El Sistema?" [what is El Sistema?], https://elsistema.org.ve/que-es-el-sistema/.

Eun Lee, clarinettist and founder of the activist orchestra The Dream Unfinished, uses the analogy of a car to represent different levels of musical engagement with social justice (Robin 2020). Level 1 is the hood ornament: superficial, focused mainly on stances and displays. Level 2 is the engine: everything is in place, it is all set up properly, but the car is still parked. Level 3 is when the car actually moves. In the case of The Dream Unfinished, their 2020 theme was civic engagement and voting rights. Level 3 meant, for example, performing concerts in communities that historically had low voter turnout and having voter registration available: "So that it's not just a concert *about* something, but you can actually *do* the something at the concert." The Dream Unfinished offers a suggestive example for SATM: treating music education as opening up opportunities for social action rather than as a form of social action in its own right.

In regarding young people less as a problem to be solved than as a potential solution, the Red also moved away from the deficit ideology of Medellín in the late twentieth century and towards contemporary progressive thinking about youth, culture, and politics. In Medellín in the 1980s and 1990s, youth were widely perceived as either dangerous or vulnerable, and therefore to be contained or protected. The Red was formed under the dual influence of this ideology and El Sistema, hence its practice of shutting young people away for long hours playing music and its discourse of "a child who takes up an instrument will not take up a weapon." But in the early 2000s, youth increasingly became political protagonists in the city, assuming positions of responsibility (for example, within the city government). By 2007, there were nearly 300 youth groups in Medellín, many of which had a cultural or artistic focus (Brough 2014).

There was a shift towards perceiving youth as political agents and resourceful producers of culture. This shift is amply documented in a recent volume in which researchers of youth in Medellín roundly rejected a deficit model in favour of positive youth development. Its title speaks volumes—"Young people: a vital flame" (*Jóvenes* 2015). Yet the Red lagged behind, despite efforts at management level. It remained rooted in a twentieth-century vision of youth focused on lack and risk rather than a twenty-first-century vision centred on potential. Its bubble approach protected young people from social problems and provided them with a safe alternative, but it also fostered disconnection with positive new youth dynamics and movements in the city. The Red's changes from 2017 might be seen as a renewed attempt to catch up with recent developments in urban youth culture and politics and with social and cultural organizations now found all across the city.

Fig. 22. Archive of Red de Escuelas de Música. CC BY.

Comparing the Red to such organizations would be a revealing exercise, if one that goes beyond the scope of this book. A member of the social team expressed her ambivalence about the Red to me: on the one hand, the program had clear limitations and there was much room for improvement on the social front; on the other hand, some schools operated in challenging circumstances, and just doing their basic job of teaching music was already an achievement. Perhaps it was wrong to expect the Red to do more than keep children off the streets and out of trouble, she mused. Then, answering her own argument, she continued: but there were many other organizations that were working in more challenging circumstances, higher up the hillsides, with fewer resources, yet they managed to keep social and political questions at the heart of what they did. This is something that the city's famed hip-hop schools were able to do. They managed to look outwards as well as inwards. So why not the Red?

The Pipeline

During the first years of the Red, there was a musical "pipeline" that worked well. The program began in an era when Medellín's professional training and orchestral scenes were significantly depleted. As such, there was a relatively clear route for the most serious students, which ran from the Red to university music departments (particularly at the University of Antioquia) to the city's two professional orchestras, the Medellín Philharmonic Orchestra and the EAFIT Symphony Orchestra (EAFIT is a prestigious private university). I was told repeatedly that a significant proportion of these orchestras in 2018 were Red graduates.

Over time, however, this pipeline became more constricted. As the Red expanded, the competition for university places grew as well, and as the city's orchestras filled up with young Red graduates, the number of professional opportunities declined. Two bottlenecks thus emerged. This issue was raised as early as 2005, when the evaluation of the Red noted that whatever its stated social goals, the program was producing a considerable number of musicians with professional aspirations and supply had quickly outstripped the city's demand.[10]

Initially, then, the orthodox SATM approach served to foster a more vibrant orchestral scene in Medellín (as it was designed to do in Venezuela). But as the Red grew, the capacity of the city to absorb so many musicians did not. Medellín moved steadily towards saturation point. Yet the production line of musicians continued, posing the question ever more insistently: where would they all go? What were they all going to do for a living? The emergence of Iberacademy and the Antioquia Symphony (another youth orchestra) only contributed to the problem. In 2018, Medellín had three orchestral training schemes yet only two professional orchestras, an imbalance of supply and demand that exacerbated concerns about the future prospects for students. The Red's second decade also saw greater priority accorded to the program's social objective. This led to increasing questions over the extent to which the Red *ought* to serve as an orchestral pipeline or whether it ought to focus more on other kinds of processes and outcomes.

---

10   Howell (2017) reveals a similar disjuncture at the Afghanistan National Institute of Music (ANIM) between the musical training and the limited subsequent options available to those who had been trained.

Franco argued that there were a wide range of musical paths and careers in Medellín, yet the Red prepared students for just one of them, the orchestral profession—and it was one that only a tiny proportion would end up in, given the competition. Another manager agreed. The musical world is changing, he said, so the Red needs to change with it; our students need to be versatile and have broad skills if they want to make a living out of music in the future. Such views were not limited to management. One school director was blunt: it makes little sense for the Red to be a production line of symphonic musicians when there is so little work for them. Another discussed inviting speakers to give talks to students about different careers, arguing that it was important to show them that there were other possible professional routes. A third director told the social team: "In focusing on the formation of musicians and not citizens, the program has produced many musicians for the city over twenty years, but there isn't the capacity to provide all these professionals with musical work" ("Informe" 2017a, 75).

Even one of the program's best-known teachers, one of the first generation, told me that classical music had become a saturated professional field in Medellín and he generally steered his students away from it. His career advice was to carry on playing but to study something else at university. He was critical of higher music education that taught students a large amount of classical repertoire that they would never play in public outside the institution's walls. If they were to make any money from music, he said, it would be from playing salsa not a classical concerto.

Nora from the social team stated: "We should ask whether we're actually harming them by putting music as a life goal, if this is a market that is already over-supplied with musicians." Popular music was a bigger field with more opportunities, but the Red only provided limited preparation in this area. She argued that matters would be different if the Red were using classical music as a means to provide a rounded humanistic education to young people in the barrios, because then professional saturation would be less of a concern. But "we're not giving them tools so that they can reflect on their context;" instead, the program provided a narrow, technical training, preparing students for a small and shrinking profession, and devoted only minimal resources to the kind of social education that justified its funding and would be much more widely applicable.

The result was a growing clash of expectations. As competition increased and opportunities narrowed, musically ambitious Red students became more concerned about the quality of the preparation that the program provided. As we saw in Chapter 2, they often saw the Red's social character as lowering the level of the program and thus counter-productive to their professional aspirations. Meanwhile, the pressure from management and the social team was in the other direction—towards musical diversification, broadening the educational offering in order to prepare students better for other musical opportunities; and/or providing a rounded social education.

In theory, the latter positions gained the upper hand, since they were supported by the culture ministry as well as the most senior figures in the program. In practice, though, they were not favoured by advanced students or staff, and the Red did not have sufficient employees with suitable training to enact them fully. The Red was somewhat locked into a pattern that was hard to break, precisely because it was one part of a pipeline and a wider educational and professional ecosystem that was still quite wedded to the norms of conservatoires, and it had little control over the other parts. The Red was the first link in a chain that included higher education and the profession, both of which fed back into the program by supplying its teachers and shaping the aspirations of its students. The Red was thus caught between three stools: no longer willing or able to serve predominantly as an orchestral pipeline, yet struggling to shift decisively towards either musical diversification or social action.

In 2018, Medellín offered an ambiguous example. On the one hand, its Network of Cultural and Artistic Practices was the envy of other cities; on the other hand, opportunities for their graduates were not plentiful and, in the case of music, were shrinking.[11] A city cultural official reflected on this ambiguity. She admitted that it hurt her to see artists of different kinds (musicians, mimes, circus performers) busking at traffic lights across the city for a few coins. Public social-artistic programs are very complicated in a country like Colombia, she said; if those coming

---

11 In 2020, the Network was awarded the 4th International Prize, CGLU (Ciudades y Gobiernos Locales Unidos)—Ciudad de México—Cultura 21.

out of them end up scraping a living at traffic lights, then something is not working.

El Sistema's current travails illustrate that such dilemmas and struggles are a part of SATM more broadly. El Sistema was designed to train professional orchestral musicians quickly, and particularly after its rapid expansion in the 2000s under Chávez, it produced a large and ever-growing number of young musicians who set their hearts on an orchestral career. Yet outside Venezuela, the orchestral profession is extremely competitive, and in most countries, opportunities were stagnant or shrinking even before the global upheaval of 2020. Until around 2014, this tension remained hidden, as high oil prices and Abreu's political power created a classical music bubble economy in Venezuela. Abreu had sufficient influence and resources to take dramatic measures, such as professionalizing all the regional youth orchestras and creating semi-professional orchestras in Caracas at will. But that bubble burst with the national crisis, and the collision between El Sistema and reality could be observed over the following years as an exodus of the program's musicians took place and they could be found busking on trains and street corners across Latin America and Spain. All- or majority-Venezuelan orchestras were created in several big cities outside Venezuela, not as a source of paid work but rather as a social focus for the immigrant musicians and, in some cases, an attempt to gain a first, if largely symbolic, foothold within the local cultural industry (see e.g. Fowks 2019). Such sights generated pride among many Venezuelans, yet they also pointed poignantly to the superfluity of musicians that El Sistema had produced, an overproduction that had been sustained for many years and presented as a glowing success story only because it had been underpinned by the world's largest oil reserves and a political and economic genius adept at channelling them into music. But now reality had bitten.

Today, the question—not only in Medellín but also across orthodox SATM—is: can it really be considered "social action" to train up large numbers of young people from popular barrios for such a challenging and shrinking career path? If orchestral training provided the best *social* education available, that question would be largely answered. But the Red's social team was unconvinced, and it was not alone.

The Orchestra

Franco once joked to me that the program should really be called the Network of Symphonic Music Performance (rather than the Network of Music Schools). This was one of the myriad ways that he expressed to me his critique of the orchestral focus of the Red. He regarded the centrality of large ensembles as constraining possibilities for acquiring skills other than performing notated music. Imagining a more independent musician with a fuller toolkit, he urged less emphasis on melodic instrumental performance in large ensembles and more on learning rhythm, harmony, composition, and improvisation. He urged the Red to create more space for smaller ensembles of eight to ten students, arguing for less focus on quantity and more on the quality of the social dynamics and relationships. In his eyes, the Red cultivated dependence on the ensemble and its conductor. What happens when students step out into the world and neither the conductor nor the ensemble is there, he asked? While he appreciated the symphony orchestra from an aesthetic point of view, he was more critical of its organizational dynamics. He spoke of "principal chair syndrome": how the hierarchization within orchestras can generate arrogance. More broadly, he was concerned that the Red inducted students into what he saw as a rather unhealthy culture and infected them with the bad habits of some professional orchestral musicians while they were still young. In fetishizing the orchestra, the Red imitated the orchestral profession, warts and all.

It was striking to hear such a view from the pedagogical coordinator of a prominent SATM program, and his perspective was not unique. Other managers made remarks about the Red turning students into "automatons" or "robots," and they also critiqued the figure of the conductor and the atmosphere of orchestral rehearsals. The leadership sought to migrate away from the conventional SATM model of the director/conductor as an authoritarian stick-waver towards a more horizontal, participatory dynamic, with more power granted to students and the director/conductor replaced by a mixture of educator, manager, and communicator. During my year in Medellín, several of the program's conductors with the most conventional professional profiles were dismissed and replaced by individuals with a wider range of musical skills and a less vertical way of working. The contrast with El Sistema, a program created by an authoritarian stick-waver and operating as a production line of conventional orchestral conductors (Govias 2020), was striking.

The social team held a similarly critical view of orchestral culture. As seen above, its 2017 report is permeated by a critique of the symphonic format, which is seen as impeding the development of citizenly capacities ("Informe" 2017a). The previous team elaborated conceptual foundations for the program from the perspective of rights, based on the notions of dignity, autonomy, and freedom (*Fundamentos* 2016). Autonomy was defined as the capacity to define one's own course and find one's own solutions, with help and support from others; freedom as the possibility to take decisions to realize one's own ambitions. It is not hard to see a tension here with the functioning of a conventional large ensemble.

It was even more striking to hear critical perspectives from teachers who had been students in the first phase of the Red. In the middle of telling me his life story, Pepe confessed:

> orchestras bored me, orchestras stressed me out, because it was always the same story, and because I started in a system at eleven years old playing in orchestras, at twenty-four I was fed up with being in an orchestra, of the rigidity of an orchestra, the monotony of an orchestra, that nothing happens in an orchestra... as a human being, I got bored.

Daniel described his mixed feelings about his education in the Red:

> I felt that negative part—the experiences I had in an orchestra were that people gave you dirty looks, or that you were nervous about what the others would say about how you were playing, or what you were playing, or how you measured up to others... the atmosphere was very heavy... even the conductors, they were tyrants, they would arrive and shout at you, and I would think, "oh, if this is music, I don't like this part."

Both teachers now led large ensembles themselves, illustrating how individual reservations about SATM may be swept away by necessity in institutions such as the Red. Pepe, in particular, was an embodiment of SATM's ambiguities: he expressed a profoundly negative view of the orchestra as a mode of musical organization, yet he was also a passionate enthusiast about SATM and perpetuated with gusto that same mode that had left him "bored" and "stressed out" as a student. They were not the only ambivalent conductors in the Red. One school director questioned "the one-way relationship and authoritarianism of the conductor with respect to the orchestra: do this, play, stop!" ("Informe" 2017a, 142). Another director reflected on the hierarchy and competition that the orchestra inculcated in students, with its system of principal chairs and rules about who has the right to speak up. Having recently changed schools, she saw a mixed bag of social behaviours in her new orchestra, with some students reluctant to help each other and resistant to new ideas. She described leading the orchestral rehearsals as "a punishment" and "the most annoying thing in the school."

These were not isolated findings. Social team reports from 2008 onwards homed in on negative dynamics generated within and between the Red's large ensembles. Similarly, many of the criticisms articulated by El Sistema's musicians in Estrada's 1997 evaluation related to the program's symphonic focus, which was seen as producing social problems and limiting educational possibilities (see Baker and Frega 2018). These findings should cause little surprise. There is now half a century of academic studies exploring the complexities and tensions of symphony orchestras (see Baker 2014). In the last few years, critical scrutiny of orchestral culture has intensified with the rise of #MeToo, the breaking of numerous scandals concerning famous conductors and orchestral musicians, and more openness in mainstream and social media about the darker sides of the profession (see e.g. Johnston 2017; Miller 2017; Ferriday 2018). Attitudes are thus changing, and in this sense the Red's management, with its critical perspective on the orchestra, was moving with the times. But large ensembles were so central to the Red's history and imaginary, to the expectations of staff and students, and to the demands that the city placed on the program, that spaces for debate were limited and progress slow. It is indicative that the biggest reversal of Giraldo's leadership was the forced abandonment of its attempt to reform the integrated ensembles.

In short, much research and journalism present a deep challenge to SATM's foundational notion that the orchestra serves as "a model for an ideal global society." On the contrary, they reveal the orchestra as at the heart of negative dynamics that are found in some of the best-known SATM programs: authoritarianism, hierarchies, cliques, imaginary divides, pedagogical narrowness and rigidity, and lack of student agency. The evidence from Medellín supports that from Venezuela in pointing to the orchestra as a problem rather than a solution. In Medellín, this model necessitated the creation of a social team in order to counteract the problematic dynamics that it generated. One of the issues that preoccupied the social team has also been at the heart of recent critiques of orchestral culture more broadly: gender relations.

Gender

Members of the social team sometimes made comments about the Red as a system of "mums and dads." A proper exploration of the theme of gender would require a separate study, so my intention here is simply to flag it up as one deserving further attention. Even though four of the Red's six general directors (as of late 2020) have been women, the program has largely reproduced the patriarchal dynamics of both *paisa* culture and classical music. During my fieldwork, the three top figures and most of the management group were men; the exceptions were the communications director and the three rank-and-file members of the social team. All the instrumental integrated ensembles (orchestras and bands) were conducted by men; only the choir had a female leader. Three-quarters of the school directors were men. The twenty-seven school administrators, however, were all women.

These figures point not only to a predominance of men in the upper echelons of the program, but also to a distinct gendering of different kinds of labour. When the social team muttered about "mums and dads," they were in part making an empirical point. The figure of the school administrator had in fact emerged from an informal system of parental helpers in the early days of the program, and a number of mothers of Red students were given jobs as administrators when the role was formalized. There were still some of these mothers occupying this role in 2018. But the social team was also pointing to a division of labour according to conventional gender norms. The majority of schools were run by a duo of male director and female administrator. Musical leadership was generally the province of men; the more "social" roles—the social team, administration, and communications—usually fell to women. (The gendering of the musical and the social sides sheds further light on the priority given to the former in practice.)

Once again, the Red is not an isolated example. Both the Red and El Sistema may be seen as patriarchal systems created by charismatic male leaders. Abreu liked to surround himself with men, leading the Venezuelan author Gisela Kozak Rovero (2018) to describe El Sistema as "a sort of masculine brotherhood of Knights Templar of classical music, with Abreu as the focus of the cult." When Abreu eventually embraced the idea of social inclusion, he interpreted it solely in class terms, meaning that other systemic exclusions have been perpetuated rather than challenged. The result is a glass ceiling for women that is much more glaring than the Red's (see Baker 2014; 2015) and makes a mockery of rhetoric of social inclusion or justice.

As such, programs like El Sistema and the Red embrace progressive discourses such as social inclusion and social change, but in practice they often show more signs of reproducing the conventional, conservative gender dynamics of their surrounding societies and perpetuating the historical gender inequalities of orchestral culture. The Red is the more ambiguous of the two, with its four female leaders, and the female-dominated social team made continual efforts to tackle gender issues through workshops and discussions. Parra had a longstanding academic interest in gender and masculinities. Nevertheless, the effects on the higher echelons were limited, and several women told me privately of their dissatisfaction with the gender dynamics of the Red, pointing to a historical resistance to female leaders and a tendency of male staff to give female colleagues instructions rather than treating them as equals. Looking at outcomes rather than intentions, the organization as a whole still leaned more towards reproducing the status quo. Perhaps this should come as no surprise, given that this is a pattern found in the classical music sector elsewhere (see e.g. Scharff 2017; Bull 2019).

Music and Other Arts Education

Music was by far the largest and best funded of the city's four arts education programs, but Parra remarked to me several times that the others were interesting and that it would be well worth observing the Visual Arts Network in particular. As a result, I spent some time in that program, participating in their teacher training, attending a two-day workshop, visiting a school, speaking at length to some of its senior figures, and reading many materials that it had published. I also made several visits to the dance program. These experiences gave me a clearer picture about the extent to which the Red's issues had to do with context (Medellín, its government, arts education, and so on) or with music.

When I sat down in the director's office on my first visit to Visual Arts, I saw that the walls were lined with critical and theoretical books on the arts and architecture. In the teacher-training sessions, the discussions were much more socially, politically, and conceptually oriented than I was used to in staff professional development activities in the Red (which did not even have a teacher-training program). Whereas the Red was shaped by the staff's own musical training and the goal of putting on concerts for the city, I observed the theory and pedagogy of Visual Arts being built up from scratch by the new teachers, starting from the foundation of social goals (such as peace and citizenship). I understood why the other programs did not have a social team: the social side was woven into the teachers' work. A valorization of critical thinking and a willingness to ask hard questions were constantly apparent. Such questioning was not absent in the Red, as I have detailed; nevertheless, there had always been a struggle to integrate this process of reflection into the practice. In Visual Arts, though, critical theory and practice went hand in hand. Conversely, I heard minimal reference to key concerns of formal education such as technique or curriculum, which were prominent in the Red. In Visual Arts, they were considered to have little to do with social impact. In fact, very little that I saw related to visual arts in the everyday sense of the term (drawing, painting, and so on); the focus was squarely on conceptual art. Classes were therefore freer and more creative than in the Red, with its focus on acquiring technique in order to perform existing repertoire.

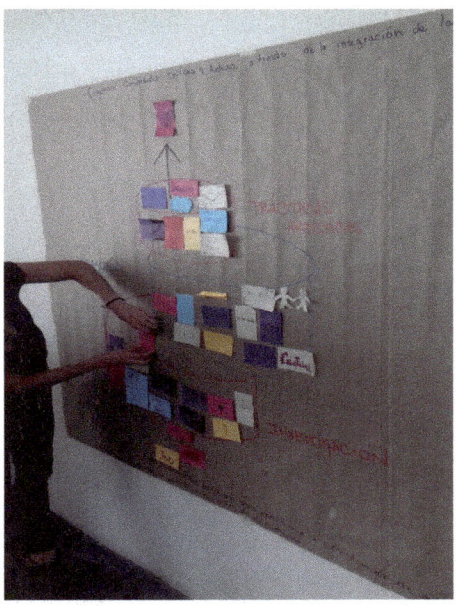

Fig. 23. Constructing theory and pedagogy, Network of Visual Arts. Photo by the author (2018). CC BY.

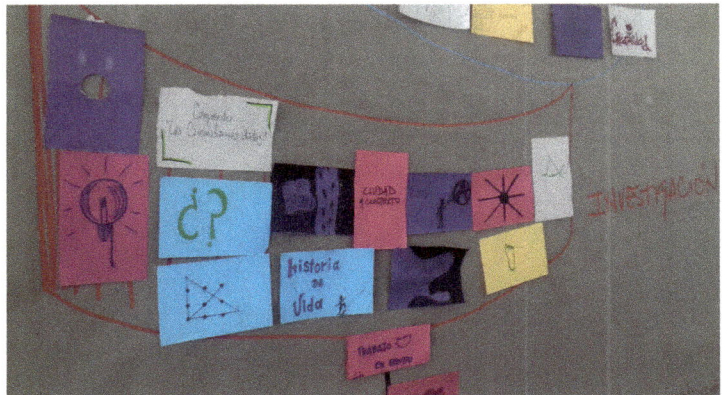

Fig. 24. Constructing theory and pedagogy, Network of Visual Arts. Photo by the author (2018). CC BY.

Fig. 25. Constructing theory and pedagogy, Network of Visual Arts. Photo by the author (2018). CC BY.

The Visual Arts Network described the work that it had undertaken during 2016 in a book whose title, "A living, mutating organism," underlined that organizational change was central to its identity (*Organismo vivo* 2016). Its director, Tony Evanko, wrote about an earlier shift of focus from technical training to "forming citizens with the consciousness, capacities, and confidence to generate changes in their lives and their surroundings" (9). The network saw itself as a pedagogical laboratory and "an adventure in transformation" (23), focused on creation, critical thinking, and key issues in the construction of society, such as human rights, identity, citizenship, and peace. Participants formulated projects or activities that stemmed from their own interests, realities, and needs. The program sought to strengthen a range of citizenly skills: respect for and trust in oneself; learning through creating; gaining a voice; recognizing and respecting difference; developing a critical position and the capacity to take decisions based on reflection and arguments; undertaking concrete actions directed at transformation; and constructing collectively and collaboratively.

Pedagogical principles included care, questioning, allowing mistakes, prioritizing process over results, and seeing problems as opportunities. The importance of connecting research and pedagogical practice was underlined. And lest this all sound entirely theoretical, much of the book was devoted to analysing the artistic work carried out in the Communal Creation Laboratories and explaining how it exemplified the program's aims.

The following year's work focused on fostering critical thinking, creation, autonomy, agency, empathy, and cooperation (*La ciudad* 2017). The network positioned itself clearly as non-formal arts education, centred not on learning techniques or training artists but on generating reflection. By organizing "unlearning laboratories" to move staff out of their comfort zone and encourage them to deconstruct and reconstruct their professional selves, and by valorizing participants' existing knowledge, they questioned a vertical teacher-student relationship in which the former is the one who knows, and the latter, one who does not. In a self-critique of their previous work, they moved away from a focus on artistic projects to one on urban and social interventions—on transforming the city. These interventions included actions on themes such as public spaces, animals, and waste, and activities such as writing a song, making a video clip, painting murals, and gardening. In these interventions, they also experimented with different methods of social organization and encouraged participants to exercise responsibility and share leadership. The self-critical spirit is evident near the end: "As we close this volume, we return to the questions: how much have *we* changed? How far are we willing to change, personally and institutionally, to achieve that society that we imagine?" (105).

I now understood why Parra had been so keen for me to see Visual Arts. In the Red, such ideas arose sometimes in meetings or internal documents as theories or aspirations for the future, but in its sister network, they were well established in practice: these books were reflections on work already done, and in my visits I saw such work in progress. The gap between the programs was glaringly apparent. It turned out that there had been a revolution in the city government's arts education networks several years earlier—with the exception of Music. Consequently, the Red was widely recognized to be the most conservative of the programs. Indeed, it was revealing that between

2017 and 2019, Giraldo's administration was attempting to align the Red with the city's cultural plan for 2011–20, even as that plan was about to expire.

Pérez, the former culture ministry official, explained the evolution of the networks to me. The administration of Mayor Aníbal Gaviria (2012–15) catalyzed the process of transformation, seeking to shift the focus from fine arts and the acquisition of technique to more contemporary artistic developments and a more experiential approach to education. The programs broke with traditional methods and shifted to a more horizontal, experimental "laboratory pedagogy." Visual Arts was the first to make the about-turn, and Dance and Theatre followed soon afterwards—but Music did not, "because it was captured by traditional symphonic musical training." In the other artistic fields, there were small civil society organizations that were agile and flexible and thus ready to take up the challenge of transformation, but Music was run by a huge, slow-moving entity (the University of Antioquia) and had a large budget. There was no other cultural organization in Medellín that was willing and able to take on such a sizeable contract, plus taking the Red away from the university would have come at considerable political cost to the mayor. As a result, Music stayed put and continued as before. It was not until 2018 that the Red began to experiment with laboratories, several years after the other networks, and then only as small pilot projects alongside the traditional offering of orchestras and bands. Ironically, then, the Red's power was the source of its weakness. Its size gave it much more prominence in the city than the other networks, and its staff (despite their complaints) had better contracts than their counterparts; however, its size was also an impediment to evolution, leading it to become the least innovative of the programs over time.

This gap was evident in the Intermediaries of Civic Culture events (Mediadores), in which some programs took an experimental approach. Visual Arts had participants plan, prepare, and cook a communal meal. Theatre took attendees out into the streets. In contrast, it took considerable debate and rethinking for Music to go beyond simply teaching participants to play instruments. If Music struggled to come up with something suitable for Mediadores, the other programs adapted more easily, since their regular activities had already been through a process of redesign to bring the social goals to the fore. As a city official who oversaw the process observed, the other programs had already digested the issue of culture and citizenship, whereas Music had remained focused on playing—and it showed in the preparations for Mediadores.

While practical considerations clearly played a large part in the different trajectories of the sister networks, there are also wider artistic trends to consider. One of the social team members spoke of how theatre and visual arts had gone through major ruptures in Latin America, breaking away from classical traditions. He argued that such a shift had been more limited in the art music sphere, and so he was unsurprised that among the varieties of arts education offered in Medellín, music was the one that most resembled a form of social control. The social team's report underlined the conservatism of music education in comparison to other arts education, which had been revolutionized by avant-garde movements ("Informe" 2017a).

Music thus appeared as the odd one out in terms of public arts education in Medellín: simultaneously the most favoured in terms of budget, facilities, and exposure, and the most conservative in its approach. This does not appear to be simply a Medellín issue, however. A comparison between orthodox SATM and the volume *Art as Social Action* (Sholette et al. 2018) points to a similar divide and to fundamentally distinct understandings of the words "social action" in SATM and other arts education.

The approach to social action in SATM was encapsulated by Rodrigo Guerrero, the director of El Sistema's Office of International Relations: "the students are so excited by and dedicated to the musical fun and creation, they don't realize until they leave El Sistema that it is really a social development program more than a musical one" (cited in Booth 2008, 11). In El Sistema, social action supposedly happened automatically or by osmosis, so there was no need to actually *do* anything. Paradoxically, social action was supposedly so subtle that students were unaware of it yet so dramatic that the program deserved hundreds of millions of dollars in social funds. The available evidence suggests that SATM was invented as a discursive ploy in the mid-1990s, and involved simply describing what El Sistema had always done (orchestral training) as social action; as such, there was no need to change anything. In short, there is a striking lack of social *action* in orthodox SATM. Indeed, given that a "social action approach" to social change through the arts is associated with *political* action and radical Latin American figures such as Paulo Freire and Augusto Boal (Dunphy 2018), SATM could be seen simply as a misnomer for Abreu's influential approach.

Art as Social Action (ASA) presents a very different conception of action to orthodox SATM. It showcases a variety of arts projects with what might be loosely called social justice aims. If SATM is largely inward-looking, acting primarily on participants, ASA is outward-looking, acting on society. In SATM, learning to play music is considered itself to be a form of social action; in this sense, there is no difference between means and ends. ASA positions art as a means to the end of acting in and on society. SATM tends to reinforce the existing social order, while ASA or socially engaged art tends to question it. We may find a concrete example in the attitudes to citizenship in the Music and Visual Arts Networks, as discussed above. The dominant conception of citizenship in the Red revolved around social order and resembled Westheimer and Kahne's Personally Responsible Citizen. In Visual Arts, the focus was on social change and the aspiration more akin to the Justice Oriented Citizen.

The discrepancies between SATM and other types of socially oriented arts education are illuminating. The global success of El Sistema illustrates that many classically-trained musicians and elite institutions do not see anything particularly strange in pursuing social change through conventional artistic practices, but key figures in Medellín's culture ministry and cultural sector were more sceptical, and the other arts abandoned this approach. The Red may have been the biggest, most visible, and most famous of the city's arts education networks, but having been "captured by traditional symphonic musical training," it was the least innovative, and it was shown up by the more diverse, flexible, experimental, emancipatory approaches of its sister programs. As Parra suggested, there is much that SATM could learn from other approaches to arts education.

Conclusion

The issues explored in this chapter may have been "second-order debates" in the Red but they related to fundamental objectives and characteristics of the program. Unsurprisingly, then, we find many parallels with El Sistema, and the debates therefore resonate for the wider SATM field. The bubble issue is quite characteristic of SATM, since it relates to the field's distinctive ideology of rescuing, saving, and distancing. Questions over citizenship, politics, and gender are found more widely across music and arts education, but they may be more insistent in SATM, where the stated prioritization of social goals means that they are thrown into sharp relief. Large ensembles and music education as a pipeline to the profession are far from unique to SATM, but idealization of the orchestra is a fundamental characteristic of this field, and there can be few places in the world where such a high proportion of professional orchestral musicians come from a single training program as Venezuela and Medellín.

While the Red had taken important steps with regard to the bubble issue, on other fronts it had not gone much beyond identifying the problem and so it lagged behind other forms of arts education in Medellín. The comparison between SATM and *Art as Social Action* suggests that this lag was not just a local feature. However, by bringing in comparison with other arts education programs and linking the Red's debates with research on topics such as artistic citizenship, bursting the bubble, and music education for change, I have also highlighted advances in adjacent fields and thus pointed to ways forward for SATM. There is a lot that can be learnt from broadening the lens beyond SATM in this way to include a wider range of practices and studies. It may be sobering for some readers to learn that music has moved slowly and ended up behind the curve of other arts education in such contexts, but this information should provide an added impetus to reform.

It would clearly be a mistake, then, for SATM to isolate itself from research on music and other arts education, but this is historically what it has done, particularly in Venezuela. In its heyday, El Sistema showed little interest in contemporary currents in research or pedagogy; despite having ample resources to do so, it did not hold conferences or send staff to overseas events such as the ISME World Conferences, even though the latter had an El Sistema Special Interest Group. It paid little attention to alternative approaches, let alone critical perspectives. Its special invitees were usually conductors or performers, rather than pedagogues or researchers. This belief that El Sistema already had the answers to music education's questions stunted the program's evolution and rubbed off on some parts of the SATM field, which have organized Sistema-only events and sought inspiration from Venezuela or sister programs more than from the much larger and more developed fields of arts education and music education research. Many, in Medellín and internationally, have grappled with the kinds of issues raised in this chapter. If the problems are not unique, nor are the solutions; there is no need for SATM to reinvent the wheel.

4. The New Image of Medellín to the World

In August 2018, the Red received a delegation from Harvard University's John F. Kennedy School of Government. The visit was organized by Medellín's Agency for Cooperation and Investment (ACI). The delegation was in Medellín to find out more about the city's social and cultural transformation—to see the Medellín Miracle first hand. Representatives of the Red gave a presentation about the program, and the Colombian music ensemble from Pedregal school followed up with a performance. Judging from their delighted faces and admiring comments, the visitors were impressed.

Ironically, this event to demonstrate the city's success in overcoming its history of violence took place on a day of major student demonstrations, which had their focal point at the university, just across the road. In fact, the Harvard delegation had to be smuggled in and out through the back entrance, because at that precise moment there were blockades, protests, and missiles being thrown in the surrounding streets. Inside the building, the Red and the ACI presented a harmonious vision of Medellín to the foreign visitors; outside, just out of earshot, the discordant realities of urban life continued.

Since its early days, the Red has served as an image of the city transformed. It was awarded the title of "The New Image of Medellín to the World" by UNESCO, and this slogan became part of its publicity. More recently, the Red has partnered with the ACI to sell an appealing image of urban renewal for international consumption. But the Harvard event brought into focus several major questions. What are the implications of music education serving as a form of urban marketing? And looking past the image to the messy reality outside, how effective is SATM as a social program? Did the Red really (help to) transform the city? SATM and social urbanism have been described in identical terms ("the Venezuelan musical miracle," "the Medellín Miracle"). Should we believe in miracles?

In this chapter I move away from the debates that I observed in the Red and focus on my own questions, ones that have interested me since I started studying SATM in 2007 and particularly since I first visited Medellín in 2012. The relationship between SATM and social urbanism is specific to Medellín, but examining the connection between music education and urban society resonates much more widely. The questions about the effectiveness and philosophy of SATM—does it work? Is it a program of social *change*?—relate in one way or another to the entire international field.

Does SATM Work?

One might expect this to be a burning question for the field, but it is not. Rather, it is widely assumed that SATM does work, and effort has been focused largely on generating evidence and arguments to support that belief. There was very little critical scrutiny of the claims of the largest SATM programs before the mid-2010s, decades after the field's emergence. As Belfiore and Bennett (2008) argue, the ideology that the arts are inherently beneficial for society has become dominant since the 1980s, and nowhere is this truer than SATM. To question this ideology publicly is to arouse great suspicion, and to hold a contrary view, despite its two and a half millennia of precedents, is to be treated as a heretic and burnt at the metaphorical stake by prominent supporters. Yet an important role for academic research is to test out supposedly common-sense ideas and see whether they stand up, and the more dominant and influential the ideas, the more important it is to inspect them. Answering such a simple question as "does SATM work?" may in fact be impossible (see Ramalingam 2013), but we may learn much by trying.

Evaluations

On the surface, existing studies of the Red present a positive picture. A 2005 external evaluation concluded that the program had a significant impact on reshaping the values of participants ("Medición" 2005). A more recent economic study also drew positive conclusions, arguing that the program reduced the probability of participants becoming involved in conflict and brought academic and cultural benefits (Gómez-Zapata et al. 2020). However, closer examination muddies the picture.

The lack of baseline data or randomized assignment to treatment and control groups means that the 2005 study shows only correlation, not causation, and since aspiring participants were both auditioned and interviewed, and only around 30% were accepted, pre-existing differences between the music students and the others are a likely cause of the findings. Furthermore, the numerous internal studies discussed in previous chapters provide extensive counter-evidence that contradicts the external evaluation: the Red's own social scientists repeatedly found pervasive problems that the evaluators had either missed or ignored. The categories analysed by the evaluators were confidence, inclusion/exclusion, skills for conflict resolution, attitudes to the body, perseverance, and discipline. The Red's social team found problems within some of these categories (particularly inclusion/exclusion), but it was also primarily interested in issues such as participation and empowerment, which were not measured. This difference in focus further explains the discrepancy between the positive account of the external evaluators and the critical accounts of the internal team.

I asked Arango whether the evaluation had impacted on her own diagnostic study the following year. A little, she replied, but it was only one of a range of sources that she used. Her report was based mainly on her own "ethnographic" reading of the Red, which resulted from spending a lot of time visiting the schools and talking to everyone that she could. The text of her report is even clearer. Arango cited the positive conclusion of the external evaluation, and then continued immediately: "However, in the everyday workings of the program one can observe a certain deviation from this social achievement and/or goal" (2006, 17), and she went on to drop the bombshell about the contradiction between the objective of peaceful coexistence and the problematic behaviours of advanced students, as detailed in Chapter 1. At the time, then, the Red's general director directly contrasted the evaluation with her own findings. It is striking to see a SATM program secure a positive external evaluation only to then question its value and repeat the process internally. Arango's greater trust in ethnography than evaluation, and the gulf between the 2005 study and the raft of subsequent internal reports, raises important questions not just about this specific case but also about the reliability of evaluations of SATM programs more generally (see Baker, Bull, and Taylor 2018; Logan 2015b).

The 2020 study, meanwhile, made no mention of the now-extensive critical literature and debates on SATM and cited only two questionable evaluations of El Sistema, revealing limited knowledge of this topic and a one-sided approach. Still, one might have expected the Red to be thrilled with the outcome, but during my last visit to Medellín, senior figures privately expressed doubts over the value of an economic lens and the robustness of the methodology, and they did not take the findings very seriously. The study did not address the kinds of social, political, and cultural questions that, for them, determined the quality of a program: for example, the degree of diversity, creativity, and participation. In general, I found senior figures somewhat sceptical of researchers who had little knowledge of the day-to-day workings of the program, engaged only minimally with the Red's social scientists, and seemed determined to draw only positive conclusions. Managers spent their days dealing with an array of complex issues, and they had limited patience for researchers who were unable or unwilling to grasp the Red's challenges.

El Sistema presents an even more ambiguous picture. Assessing El Sistema's effectiveness is complicated by the lack of clarity and consistency over its goals. The program is widely presented as a seamless whole, yet comparing sources from the 1970s with those from the 2000s reveals a major shift in stated objectives.[1] It started out simply as a program for training orchestral musicians, yet since 2000 it has been widely described as a social inclusion program. The program's current official mission and vision emphasize personal transformation on moral, spiritual, and behavioural planes (see Baker 2016c). Abreu also presented El Sistema as a remedy to poverty: "when [a child] has three years of musical education behind him, he is playing Mozart, Haydn, he watches an opera: this child no longer accepts his poverty, he aspires to

---

1   See my blog post "Professionalization or rescuing the poor? The origins of El Sistema (in Abreu's own words)", https://geoffbakermusic.wordpress.com/el-sistema-older-posts/professionalization-or-rescuing-the-poor-the-origins-of-el-sistema-in-abreus-own-words/.

leave it behind and ends up defeating it" (cited in Argimiro Gutiérrez 2010). The UN's multimillion-dollar contributions to El Sistema have been made in the name of "social inclusion and the eradication of poverty through music education" ("FundaMusical" 2017). The IDB's loan in 2007, however, was justified by a prediction that it would be effective in reducing crime, and Abreu has stated: "Orchestras and choirs are incredibly effective instruments against violence" (Wakin 2012). El Sistema's goals are thus shifting, highly ambitious, and extraordinarily diffuse.

Here, the conclusions of evaluations are even more questionable (Baker and Frega 2018; Baker, Bull, and Taylor 2018). The first two evaluations, in 1996, were roundly contradicted by two more the following year. An IDB report produced a decade later was used to justify a loan of $150 million, but the bank subsequently distanced itself from this study. The report's central plank was a speculative calculation that every dollar invested would reap the equivalent of $1.68 in returns. However, El Sistema never carried out the major element of the proposal—to construct seven regional music centres. In reality, then, the loan only produced a fraction of its expected return, and the report's speculation about the likely effects turned out to be misguided.

For many years after the IDB started supporting El Sistema, it hypothesized SATM's benefits rather than demonstrating its efficacy in practice. It eventually decided to evaluate the program's theory of change via a one-million-dollar experimental study (Alemán et al. 2017). Reflecting El Sistema's expansive claims, the study measured twenty-six primary outcome variables. Only two significant outcomes were found, and they depended on using an unusually low threshold for statistical significance (90%). Mark Taylor, an expert in quantitative analysis, scrutinized the IDB's data and methods and raised four separate question marks over the two supposedly positive results, concluding that they were almost impossible to take seriously (Baker, Bull, and Taylor 2018). There were no significant outcomes in twenty-four areas, even at the low threshold of 90%, and the researchers "did not find any full-sample effects on cognitive skills [. . .] or on prosocial skills and connections." In an added twist, the original evaluation proposal had stated: "The data will be used to evaluate rigorously the impacts of El Sistema on school dropout, risky behaviours, incidence of crime, and prevalence of unplanned pregnancies" ("Evaluación" 2011, 3). However, the published study made no mention of these issues, nor did it give a reason for dropping them. It is therefore unclear whether the researchers intuited that they would not find evidence of such social effects or sought them without success.[2]

Had this report uncovered robust evidence that El Sistema reduced poverty, crime, and violence by effecting personal transformation on moral, spiritual, and behavioural planes, the program would truly have merited the label of "the Venezuelan musical miracle." As it was, this study by El Sistema's own funder found no social impact of genuine significance, revealing its theory of change to be more of a fantasy story. Coming in the wake of a wave of independent critical academic studies, it would have taken the shine off the miracle narrative had it not been almost entirely ignored by the SATM field, the media, and even most researchers.

Orthodox SATM's hypotheses have been undermined by events as well as research. The evidence for social change in Venezuela, home of by far the largest and longest SATM experiment, is thin bordering on non-existent. The Venezuelan pianist Gabriela Montero writes of "the bitter irony that South America's musically and minerally richest nation is also the continent's most corrupt, most violent, most economically imperilled, and most morally disembodied."[3] Venezuela was the wealthiest country in Latin America when El Sistema was founded; it is now the poorest, and one of the most dangerous places in the world. This shift has complex causes, and it does not prove El Sistema's inefficacy; it does, however, raise further questions about the claims of transformative social effects. El Sistema has raised and spent impressive amounts of money, but much of it has gone not so much on social action as on monumental buildings in central Caracas and top-of-the-range instruments, salaries, and international tours for its showcase orchestras. Many ordinary music schools operate in poor conditions, and solid evidence of reducing poverty and crime is lacking. The exodus

---

[2] It may be relevant here that a meta-analysis of twelve studies of after-school programs in the United States suggested that such programs had a small and nonsignificant effect on delinquency (Taheri and Welsh 2015).

[3] "PUTIN POWER: musicians sound their outrage (a statement of support)", Facebook, 11 February 2021.

of El Sistema musicians since Venezuela's crisis began to bite in the mid-2010s sheds further doubt on the idea of SATM as a remedy to major social problems.

The Theory of SATM

El Sistema and programs inspired by it in Latin America tend to have similar broad features: a focus on large ensembles; an emphasis on the middle to lower end of the socio-economic spectrum (in the Red, Medellín's popular barrios; in El Sistema's mission statement, "the most vulnerable groups in the country"); and an argument that putting these two together provides benefits for individuals and society. These benefits supposedly result from changing the attitudes and behaviour of participants (in the Red, instilling civic values; in El Sistema's mission, "rescuing children and young people from an empty, disorientated, and deviant youth"), and thereby reducing the incidence of negative phenomena such as poverty, violence, and crime. There are myriad problems with this picture as a theory of social development.

Firstly, it rests on a conservative and largely discredited ideology that links social problems with individual deficits. In Abreu's vision, poverty rests on a lack of individual aspiration and can thus be surmounted by raising ambitions. He also claimed that "a child's physical poverty is overcome by the spiritual richness that music provides" ("El Sistema" 2008). Yet expert opinion is much more likely to attribute serious social problems like poverty and violence to structural causes and to treat material deprivation in a less glib fashion.[4] For example, in outlining the core of social justice social work, Baines (2017) writes: "Key to this practice is the understanding that the problems faced by an individual are rooted in the inequalities and oppression of the socio-political structure of society rather than in personal characteristics or individual choices."[5] Maclean (2015) identifies Medellín's urban violence as rooted in the city's extreme inequality, and thus as a perpetuation of social and political norms rather than a breakdown in the social fabric. Such problems are therefore unlikely to diminish noticeably by disciplining

---

4 See Bates 2016 and Baker 2016b for discussion.
5 Quotation taken from the book's blurb at https://fernwoodpublishing.ca/book/doing-anti-oppressive-practice1.

individual behaviour or raising individual aspirations. It is likely that a few individuals will alter their social position (social mobility) but improbable that such an approach will shift the problems or structures beneath them or the numbers affected (social change).[6] Abreu's deficit vision—the foundation stone of orthodox SATM—is thus contradicted by a wealth of social science. Cheng (2019, 43) is rightly scornful of claims that poverty is a "state of mind" or a lack of "richness in spirit," and his tracing of such a view to (among others) Donald Trump's minister and acolyte Ben Carson speaks volumes about the politics behind Abreu's philosophy.[7]

Secondly, it is questionable whether music education can have a significant influence on knottier social problems. The evidence that arts and culture have a significant impact on material poverty, as opposed to the effects of poverty, is slim (Mamattah et al. 2020). It is worth recalling that even many of the Red's staff had doubts about their capacity to address serious social issues and regarded the program's objective as overly utopian. In Chapter 1, we saw that social team investigations found teachers frustrated and overwhelmed because they were expected to respond to complex social or family problems, yet lacked suitable training or skills.

Thirdly, it is highly debatable whether the most vulnerable or marginalized groups in society are a major source of social problems such as violence and crime—a position that is implicit in Abreu's framing of orchestras and choirs for poor and vulnerable children as "incredibly effective instruments against violence." Such groups are by definition relatively powerless. If social change were genuinely the aim, a more rational approach to SATM would be to target social elites—the small segment of the population that has disproportionate control over the structural forces that produce violence and crime (see Chapter 5). Even Medellín's ex-mayor Alonso Salazar (2018) has argued that the city's elites have the greatest responsibility for its "moral ruin."

---

6   As Folkes (2021) notes, there is a vast amount of evidence contradicting the position that equal opportunities and social mobility have the capacity to alleviate structural inequalities.

7   Similarly, the attribution of poverty to personal deficiencies (or character or personality traits) in the UK in recent times has been a feature of the conservative Coalition government (Folkes 2021).

Similarly, since promoting coexistence and civic values is the principal goal of the Red, it bears asking whether young people from popular neighbourhoods are really the right target. As Bates (2016, 3) states, "evidence shows that the poor already possess strong personal and social skills." He draws on several studies to argue that compared to the wealthy, the poor tend to be more ethical, compassionate, and altruistic, are no more likely to abuse alcohol or drugs, and are just as hard-working and communicative. Solidarity is a characteristic feature of the working class and its organizations such as trade unions, whereas individualism is more marked among higher social classes. Why, then, is the supposed remedy for a lack of coexistence in Medellín aimed at the popular classes in the city's barrios rather than the rich who live in gated compounds in their own urban enclaves? Why is it assumed that the poor need lessons in collectivity, solidarity, and listening, rather than the rich? As Holston (1999) and Caldeira (1999) note, the segregation of the wealthy has a deleterious effect on sociability and public life, and by underlining inequalities and a lack of commonalities, it may promote rather than prevent conflict. "Cities of walls do not strengthen citizenship but rather contribute to its corrosion" (136). Who, then, really needs lessons in civic values and citizenship?

Demographics: Whom Does SATM Serve?

A final but major weakness in SATM's theory is that programs often fail to reach the most vulnerable or marginalized groups when offered as a voluntary, extra-curricular activity. The 2005 evaluation of the Red found that students came from better-off, more stable, and more educated households than a control group; for example, they spent more time out of school accompanied by their parents. Wald's (2017) research on similar programs in Buenos Aires revealed that students who thrived came from more economically stable families. The programs generally included the most includible young people (Escribal 2017): those who lived in popular neighbourhoods but were closest to the middle class in terms of both family employment and values. Picaud (2018) found that students in the French SATM project Démos generally came from families with higher-than-average levels of education and employment; their parents lived in poorer zones but were relatively well-off in terms of cultural capital. Godwin (2020) presented analogous findings in her study of an Australian SATM program: children with traditional forms of disadvantage constituted only around 15% of the program, and half of them dropped out within a year. Many participants had aspirational parents with a middle-class outlook who saw the program as a source of free music lessons. The emergence of similar results from such widely dispersed programs points to a struggle to reach the most vulnerable or marginalized groups as a feature of the orthodox SATM model.

Most strikingly of all, El Sistema's 2017 evaluation estimated the poverty rate among entrants at 16.7%, whereas the rate for the states in which they lived was 46.5%. In other words, the children entering El Sistema in the study were three times less likely to be poor than all six- to fourteen-year-olds residing in the same states. Consequently, the researchers concluded that their study "highlights the challenges of targeting interventions towards vulnerable groups of children in the context of a voluntary social program." El Sistema's own funder recognized this flaw in the model. While striking in its demolition of the El Sistema myth at a stroke, this finding is hardly a surprise from the perspective of research on education and youth, in which it is widely recognized that less privileged families are less likely to support extracurricular activities for their children, whether for reasons of money, time, logistics, or values (e.g. Lareau 2011).

Over time, the social makeup of the Red has been further affected by two contrary movements. On the one hand, Medellín's expansion has meant that the areas of greatest poverty—the urban margins—have moved steadily up the hillsides of the valley and away from the centre of the city. On the other hand, several of the Red's outlying schools (such as Independencias, Villatina, and 12 de Octubre) have been obliged to move in the opposite direction—down the hillsides—for security reasons. One, La Loma, simply had to close. There are major practical impediments to the Red working in the poorest barrios. Safe access for staff and students is one; another is a lack of suitable buildings. Some of the Red's schools operate out of rented premises, and the poorest areas simply do not have buildings for hire that could accommodate all the instruments, an orchestra or band rehearsal, and several lessons taking place simultaneously. Whatever the desires of its leaders and staff, such a project is not designed in such a way as to be easily accessible to the most disadvantaged in society in the 2020s.

Nevertheless, one consequence of a salvationist streak in SATM (and the "poverty porn" approach of some reporting on it) is a tendency to exaggerate the level of disadvantage and thus stigmatize participants. This is clearly the case with El Sistema, where there is a gulf between the IDB's demographic findings in 2017 (which echoed those in my 2014 book) and media accounts and public perceptions of slum-dwellers rescued from a life of crime. The challenges of Medellín's barrios are undeniable, but as a recent volume by an array of local youth experts argues, most young people are not significantly at risk, nor are they a risk to society (*Jóvenes* 2015). Of those that are, few find their way to the Red.

At the first board meeting I attended, a member of the social team stated that the Red's students did not generally see themselves as poor, vulnerable, or in need, and they rejected this kind of categorization. Similarly, Wald (2011) argues that the public narrative around SATM in Buenos Aires both stereotyped and stigmatized its social contexts (as places of crime, drugs, violence, and unemployment) in order to play up the transformative effects of music. Not only did most participants not fit this bill, but they also dissented from such portrayals and were explicitly critical of the melodramatic media narrative woven around them: "they talk about us as though we were savages who have a violin instead of a bow and arrow," said one. Wald emphasizes the heterogeneity of popular neighbourhoods in Buenos Aires—an important point for understanding SATM, since it underlines that not all inhabitants of such zones in Latin America (and much less, all participants in SATM programs) are "at-risk kids," as is commonly stated in the global North.

Managers and directors gave plenty of clues about their perceptions of the social composition of the program. One of the general directors told me that the Red had become "gentrified" and asked why the program was not working in the city's most disadvantaged contexts. Is the Red transforming Medellín, they asked? Or is it subsidizing the music education of a certain sector of the city's population?

Reflecting the findings of studies elsewhere, it appeared that this "certain sector" generally represented not so much the most vulnerable or marginalized groups but rather an aspirational, educationally committed fraction of the popular class. While there were exceptions, most students in the Red did not fit with the commonplace SATM narrative of social rescue. Many were from socio-economic strata 1–3 (Medellín has six official strata, with 1 the lowest), but as one school director put it, the majority of his students came from a good family environment. They might not live with both parents, but there was a family head who took care of them, and the vast majority of parents were concerned about their children.

Some staff shed light on the character and behaviour of students. One director changed schools during my fieldwork, and he compared the two contexts. There were more difficulties in his new school, he said, citing issues such as drug use and disrespectful behaviour; he estimated that there were around ten critical cases, out of a population of nearly 200 students. At his previous school, he did not have a single difficult case to hand over to his successor. Another director described the children in his school as nice and polite, with few personal or social problems. A third painted his students as "humble, they don't have much money," but also "very wholesome people." Their parents had financial difficulties but made a big effort to push their children, making for exemplary students. He saw the social work of the school not as transforming children but rather encouraging and supporting their positive traits and showing them off to the community as an example. A member of the social team expressed her exasperation with the commonplace idea that the Red was saving 5000 children from Medellín's urban war. I asked her how many she thought would have become delinquents without the program: "two or three," she replied.

Other staff pointed to the socio-economic profile of students. One day, a manager described a visit to a neighbourhood cultural program for children who, as he put it, had *nothing* (such as street children). In contrast to the Red, the program was run on a shoestring. His immediate response was: "this is what we should be doing. We have so much! Why aren't we working with these people? This is what the Red is supposed to be about." A school director argued that the Red was fighting for the same students as other public leisure programs rather than striving to reach underserved parts of the city.

Another director stated that the Red had begun with the aim of removing youth from the reach of the urban conflict, but that the situation had changed over time; the risks, while still real, were much reduced, and the school had become simply a destination for children who wanted to learn music. He continued: it's generally the children from strata 3–4 who do best in the Red.[8] They tend to have parents who are committed to their children's education. Children from strata 1–2 are more likely to drop out, he said; they may be sent off to work by their family, have problems at home, or move barrios.

Sarrouy's (2018) portrait of the El Sistema núcleo of Santa Rosa de Agua is again illuminating. The group of mothers who spend their afternoons waiting for their children outside are generally educated (the majority have a university degree), devout, and concerned with values and morals. Their mere presence outside the núcleo speaks volumes about their concern for their children's education and wellbeing. Sarrouy portrays them as playing a vital role: keeping the children off the street, making them presentable, and encouraging home study. The families may be poor, but they are also organized and supportive. This picture chimes with the Red, but it bears little resemblance to El Sistema's official mission to "rescue the most vulnerable groups in the country." Rather, what we see are children from conscientious families that would like their children to change from one set of leisure activities that they consider unwholesome (hanging out on the street, playing with the computer, watching TV) to another activity that they consider more wholesome (playing music).

An obvious question immediately arises: what happens to children without supportive families—ones who might genuinely be described as vulnerable or even in need of rescuing? In Sarrouy's account, they appear to be outside, "playing in the streets of the barrio, shoeless and dirty." They rarely make it to the music school—or perhaps they are among the large numbers of students who drop out early on—because their families cannot or do not want to take them every day, sit outside all afternoon supervising their study, and encourage them to practise at home. The visual contrast between the smartly dressed El Sistema students and their shoeless and dirty non-musician peers is neither coincidental nor a consequence of the former having been "saved" by music; it is indicative of the pre-existing social differences between

---

8   Strata 3–4 correspond to a local lower-middle to middle class—the same constituency that historically predominated in El Sistema.

El Sistema and non-El Sistema children discovered by the IDB's 2017 evaluation.

The implications for understanding SATM are profound. El Sistema appears here not as a means of social inclusion, but rather of social differentiation and stratification. Recall the "bubble" from Chapter 3, and Wald's finding that SATM students who thrived in Buenos Aires not only came from more economically stable families but also developed a distinct "us versus them" worldview. Similarly, research on Sistema Scotland found that its immersive learning approach might make program engagement difficult for students with additional needs or difficult home circumstances, and that children from an ethnic minority, with English as a second language, or with additional support needs dropped out more frequently—pointing to systemic exclusion of the most disadvantaged (see Baker 2017a). Godwin (2020) paints a picture of a SATM program in which the most disadvantaged or challenging students often dropped out or were excluded, since the program was ill-equipped to support them. Such findings suggest that systemically speaking, SATM tends to separate out relatively advantaged children— those from more stable, aspirational families with a higher level of educational commitment—from relatively disadvantaged ones, and to support predominantly the former. In other words, SATM appears as a process of social hierarchization that exacerbates a micro-class division within popular neighbourhoods.

To use the terms that my collaborators in Medellín used, which were already in big quotation marks, the students of such programs *are* generally speaking "good kids"; and they are also *constructed* as "good kids" through participation in SATM programs. They are imagined as different from and superior to the "bad kids" hanging out on the streets and provided with an educational boost. In the eyes of the social team, the Red was not so much transforming "bad kids" as giving a leg-up to "good" ones, exacerbating the distance between the two.

These programs thus benefit primarily an aspirational, educationally committed fraction of the popular class, and while they broaden the constituency for classical music, their effect on unequal and divided societies is more questionable. It is not just that, in contrast to claims about "rescuing the most vulnerable groups in the country," few of the most vulnerable are included; it is also that a boundary is drawn, widening this social divide rather than narrowing it and thus excluding the marginalized even further in relative terms. This finding ought to be of considerable concern to programs that pursue goals such as social inclusion or peaceful coexistence between disparate groups, since it suggests that SATM may actually deepen the inequality that is at the root of many of Latin America's gravest social problems. But it should not be a surprise to scholars of music education: it coincides with Bourdieu's well-known argument that education reproduces inequality by allowing benefits to accrue primarily to those who already have them, which has been influential in the sociology of music education (see e.g. Wright 2010).

Family Values

Sarrouy's data raises another important question over the functioning of El Sistema and, by extension, SATM more broadly. The official narrative is that the program "rescues" vulnerable children by instilling in them values such as discipline and responsibility. Furthermore, the theory is that these values then spread outwards to their families and wider society. As Abreu put it in his TED prize speech, "the child becomes a role model for both his parents." Yet Sarrouy's data tells a different story. He writes: "it is the mothers and grandparents who insist on their children and grandchildren being dedicated, hardworking, and responsible" (50). Furthermore, he relates that the group of mothers constituted an unofficial "union," one of the roles of which was

> to put pressure on the teachers who tend to miss lessons. The women meet and talk with the teacher, insisting on valid reasons. There are teachers who miss classes with unsatisfactory excuses, but the pressure that is put on them obliges them to turn up regularly, otherwise they will have to face the group of mothers, the director, and even the students, because they too become demanding. (51)

In other words, rather than values radiating outwards from El Sistema to children and then their families, the dynamic that Sarrouy describes is the precise opposite: the mothers are the point of origin of key SATM values such as discipline and responsibility, and their influence converges via their children on El Sistema, culminating in the striking image of parents and students policing the music teachers. Here, it is

El Sistema's adult musicians—not their pupils—who are undisciplined and the families who discipline them.

Support for this picture comes from many other sources. In my own research in Venezuela and in Medellín, it became clear that successful music students were often socialized in the value system of the program by their families before joining it. A Red teacher from the first generation told me a typical story: "a lot comes from the home... in my house, at least, hanging out on the corner was never an option, never... they always drilled into me that I had to be someone, that I was going to study." His father had not finished school but always said: "you can't be like me, you've got to get a university degree." Several directors suggested that the Red was more likely to work for a child if their family was interested, committed, reliable, and responsible—in other words, if there was a fair degree of prior alignment with the values of the program.

Wald (2009, 61) drew similar conclusions in Buenos Aires: students reject the official discourse of SATM programs and "affirm that the frame of reference that shapes their values and the majority of their practices comes from elsewhere: from family guidance and, to a lesser extent, their religious beliefs." The students examined in depth in Mota and Teixeira Lopes's (2017) portrait of Portugal's Orquestra Geração (OG) were poor but supported by an extended family. Only two out of thirty-five identified dissonance between family and program values. The researchers found "a tendency for the strengthening of dispositions that had previously been created within the young participant's families," "flows of consonance and interdependence between family, home and the OG," and "inter-generational transmission of the family's educational resources" (Teixeira Lopes et al. 2017, 224–25). Rimmer (2018; 2020) found that students' enjoyment of In Harmony Sistema England depended to a large degree on an aspirational outlook, parental support, and commitment to schooling. El Sistema has been sold as an approach for disadvantaged children, but Rimmer found that those from less supportive, interested families were more likely to find it boring or oppressive and/or be put off by the challenge of music education guided by ideals of discipline and hard work. Consistent dynamics can thus be identified in SATM across several countries, with music education appearing regularly as a conduit and beneficiary of family values rather than a source.

Successful students frequently received and depended on considerable family support during their studies. SATM is very time-intensive: in the Red, students might be expected to attend three to four times a week by their second year; in El Sistema, this could quickly rise to five or more. Such a schedule would pose a great challenge to a child without a supportive family, unless they lived very close to the school. "Without the support of the families, we would be absolutely nothing," said one school director in Medellín. "There are people who manage to do it without a father or mother, but really the parents are the cornerstone." Another director stated: "the collaboration of the parents is fundamental in the school [...] if the parents don't commit themselves, we cannot function." Here, we see clearly the program's dependence on existing family values.

The Red appeared to be set up in practice to favour those who were already socialized into its norms, suited to its requirements, and backed up by more stable and supportive families. The Red operated an explicit selection process in the form of interviews and meetings to filter out children and parents who seemed a poor fit with the program. As Mosse (2004, 652) notes in his research on overseas aid: "There is always an incentive for staff to select those people who already possess the characteristics that a project aims to create." The result, as Wald found in Buenos Aires, is that the primary dynamic of SATM is a reinforcement of values shared by families and programs rather than a transformation.

Exclusion

For all the talk of inclusion, SATM can have exclusive aspects. One is the time pressure placed on families. In Medellín, one mother said: "There's a problem that I see, and it's that if he's going to practise, I have to bring him [to the school] to practise, and I can't because I have to look after his little brother and do my chores." Wald (2017) notes the intense demands placed on students and their families: frequent rehearsals and activities, often conflicting with domestic routines and requiring family support. There may also be associated economic pressures. A 2013 sociology thesis about Montalbán, El Sistema's showcase núcleo in Caracas, included a report on a focus group of students' families:

All the mothers agreed that a poor family cannot remain in El Sistema. [...]
They all agreed that in El Sistema there are no poor people because
they would not be able to keep up with the routine expenditure that it
requires, and that on the contrary, those who spend their time there have
a basic level of economic resources that allows them to pay for travel,
food, instrument maintenance and repairs, uniforms, etc. [...] [T]he
mothers agree that many children drop out along the way because their
families don't have the resources to keep them there. "Many children
don't continue here for that reason, because seriously, it's a sacrifice, you
need to have parents who can help you." (Pérez and Rojas 2013, 126–27;
emphasis in original)

Here we see clearly the problem of constructing SATM as a (supposedly) meritocratic system, in which those who work hardest and have most ability in theory rise to the top.[9] It is widely recognized by scholars that meritocratic systems tend to privilege those with more resources. Society is not a level playing field: some children enjoy better supporting conditions for hard work than others. Conversely, if their families lack key resources like time or money, children may face insurmountable barriers irrespective of their application or ability. However, the survivorship bias of most SATM writing and research has seen little attention paid to exclusion.

Similarly, the issue of student retention is rarely raised in public discourse, but as we saw in Chapter 1, it was high enough in the Red to cause concern among the leadership, and evidence from several SATM projects suggests that up to half of new students may drop out in the first year or two. One Red director's suggestion that children from the lowest social strata were the most likely to drop out is particularly noteworthy, since it points to a fundamental problem at the level of social inclusion. The program appears to filter out the most disadvantaged, who may not even be able to access it and may be disproportionately likely to leave if they can.

"The Red is a closed system," said a city official in one meeting. Its policy was that students had to be in school and achieving reasonable grades. If students dropped out of school, they could be expelled from the Red. But this is supposed to be a social inclusion program, exclaimed

---

9   In actual practice, El Sistema is far from meritocratic, since influence and string-pulling play a significant role (Baker 2014).

the official; why does it exclude precisely the kind of young people that it should be helping? The focus of the Red should be the children with problems, not *los niños más juiciosos* [the best-behaved children].

Ironically, then, SATM may be least accessible to those at whom it is supposedly most targeted. It is hard for children to join the program and remain in it for any length of time without a modicum of family stability, support, and solvency. There are also geographical constraints: students in the higher parts of the barrio live further from the music school and are more likely to be cut off by a deterioration in the security situation. Such programs appear relatively exclusive from the perspective of the most vulnerable children in the most marginalized zones.

SATM may also be a struggle for all parties without a fair degree of prior alignment in values. One director described the difficulties of SATM work when families are not on the same page as the school:

> In his work with the children he struggles with the accompaniment of the families. There is a lack of understanding of the need for a minimum of daily practice. He shares a study guide with them but they do not accompany their children. They have a conception of the school as a day-care centre. They do not bring what they need for the lessons […]. This can be seen in the rehearsals, where the individual affects the collective. So, in the face of this lack of joint responsibility by the families, he has ended up getting cross with them, though not with their children, since the students cry and get frustrated by their failure to fulfil their commitment when they find themselves in the ensemble. ("Informe" 2017d, 43)

This director elaborated further that students from less committed families tended to hold the others back, because they ended up practising in rehearsals rather than beforehand. He described having to make the more committed students sit and wait for up to fifteen minutes while he went through the basics with the others. He did not attempt to hide his frustration. As his account reveals, symphonic training can be a challenge without the prior socialization of children into educational norms such as discipline, obedience, and commitment.

The social team also noted that its interviews with directors raised questions about the program's ability to deal with students from more conflictive backgrounds, those with drug problems, or "those who don't manage to settle into the dynamic of music education because they are not disciplined or do not have the musical level that characterizes the program" ("Informe" 2017a, 117). A member of the team told me bluntly: the Red is not music therapy; it is very hard for the schools to deal with young people with serious problems. SATM is poorly equipped to serve those who do not already fit the SATM template of a "good kid" and might benefit most from a social program.

These findings suggest that SATM depends on the prior existence of the key values that it supposedly produces in order to function properly. The real dynamic appears to be in direct contrast to the official one: family values are the prime force shaping the child, and music schools rely on children arriving with such values already instilled in them and families who are willing to support students through the intensive program. As such, these programs depend on and reinforce the values, dispositions, and resources of an aspirational, committed fraction within popular neighbourhoods. Rescuing the most vulnerable and transforming lives may be the headline story but it is only a small part of the real work. There may be a widespread belief that music education serves to put children on a straight path, but the evidence suggests that the aspiration and commitment are often already there in the home, rather than being handed down from the musical gods. Contradicting the deficit ideology that underpins El Sistema, it is community social *assets* that keep SATM's wheels in motion.

My argument here relates to large, iconic, high-profile programs in Latin America. There may well be parallels elsewhere: for example, Howell (2017) explores the disjuncture between narratives of hope within and around the internationally celebrated Afghanistan National Institute of Music and the despair and downward trajectory of the country outside its walls. As with El Sistema, discourses of social transformation jar with inescapable realities and limited likelihood of change, and many musicians have left. The leaders of such programs have become international celebrities on the back of their inspirational storytelling, but it is highly questionable whether their aspirations have been converted into outcomes. However, I am not claiming that SATM cannot or does not work anywhere. Rather, the evidence from El Sistema and some of its largest and oldest offshoots in Latin America suggests that we would do best to start from a position of ambivalence or skepticism rather than overly optimistic assumptions. There is no question that such programs provide many participants with opportunities for socializing and enjoyment, and particularly when goals are framed in vague, multiple or changing ways and numbers of students are high, some aims will inevitably be achieved some of the time in some cases. But a realist account of SATM also needs to consider the many holes in the official narratives and the many students for whom such programs do not work, and to distinguish between official objectives, real dynamics, and demonstrable results.

My argument also relates specifically to El Sistema and similar versions of SATM: voluntary, non-targeted, and extra-curricular. The evidence suggests that SATM designed in this way, while bringing with it the positives of conventional music education, is unlikely to lead to the kinds of impressive social outcomes that are widely claimed. It might be that a SATM program designed and run in a different way could have a larger impact.

Ultimately, any attempt to answer the question of SATM's efficacy will need to grapple with the looseness of the term "social" and the scale and duration of possible effects. If social action is considered quite narrowly in terms of short-term, small-scale effects on successful individuals (i.e. survivors) and their families, then a more positive evaluation might be justified. If, however, the excluded and the dropouts are considered too and longer-term effects on communities and society are sought—and it is precisely such effects that official narratives tend to claim or imply—then the picture becomes muddier. Accounts of SATM and similar programs tend to focus on individualized effects, particularly individual stories of redemption, because they are easy to capture and convey. Documentaries, in particular, usually home in on extreme cases because they make for better television, and such an approach serves programs as well, making it easier to convince politicians, funders, the media, and the general public of their value. Societal impacts, though, are much harder to measure and so are often the subject of vague, hypothetical claims. Olcese and Savage (2015, 724) strike a balance on the social potential of art: they regard "aesthetics as empowering subjectivities and identities," allowing "innovations and the prospect of change, where change is not seen in epochal terms as an external condition of social life, but as imbricated in the everyday and routine." This perspective suggests a more modest vision of SATM than the norm:

it keeps open the possibility of small-scale change in individual lives, but points away from grandiose discourses of social transformation.

As more research appears, the weakness of some of the more extravagant hypotheses becomes clearer, but gaps in logic may be apparent even without such research. Is it really likely that a few thousand "good kids" retreating into a bubble of classical music is going to reduce poverty, crime or violence in a city of millions? Is it really likely that an institution that does not require staff to have even pedagogical training, let alone social training, will be an educational standard-bearer and motor of social change? A glass-half-empty perspective would be that at the level of policy, such programs are really a sticking-plaster over major problems rather than a solution. A glass-half-full vision might focus more on success stories, good intentions, and efforts to do something positive for a city or community, but it would still struggle to produce convincing evidence that SATM works either for the most marginalized or for society as a whole.

Does Music Work?

A subsidiary question is what the role of music might be in SATM. Is it a special ingredient that brings benefits or effects that other activities do not? Or could it actually be social action through anything? The "power of music" literature provides many reasons to believe the former; but a contradictory picture may emerge from ethnographic and sociological research. It is not just a matter of doubts over the scale of the effects of SATM, but also over their source.

A striking aspect of the Red was that there were more signs of social action *around* music than *through* music. It was non-musical figures that were widely signalled as the key sources of social action: most obviously the social team, but also the teachers of corporal expression and the school administrators. The corporal expression teachers came from theatre or dance backgrounds, and they were identified by the musical staff in the 2008 internal study as responsible for delivering the program's social component. Several interviewees, including musicians, described corporal expression as where the Red's most interesting work took place—quite a telling remark about a music program. One corporal expression teacher reported:

You see a lot of things. The child hasn't got their instrument but rather their body. Sometimes you see some marks that aren't normal, that aren't just "I fell over and scraped myself," and they tell you: "oh Miss, my father hit me." "Does he do it often?" "Yes!" And when we're in these classes with the body like an open canvas, these things come out.

She was also gently critical of the Red's music education per se: "I feel like learning music is like putting them in a little box... very rigid, very stiff." As the students get older, "they slowly lose that capacity to play and create. They lose the ability to surprise. [...] Maybe the very process in the [music] school squeezes them or boxes them in a bit." She portrayed corporal expression as in a losing battle with the musical training: "I see them playing [music] and I don't see any corporal expression." She put this down to fear of being judged and of making mistakes. "Everything has to come out perfectly. Making a mistake isn't acceptable." She asked: "if this is a social program, why is it so important that the musical part be perfect?"

Fig. 26. Archive of Red de Escuelas de Música. CC BY.

The administrators, meanwhile, played a pivotal role in the schools. They were the main intermediary between the program and the students and their families, particularly at the elementary levels. They were usually located near the entrance of the school and their roles included that of receptionist, so they greeted or said goodbye to everyone who came and went. They often engaged in long conversations with parents who were waiting or had a problem, so they tended to know everything that was going on. Many of the schools' social interactions pivoted around these figures. Although there were variations across schools and over time, the female administrators were often figuratively as well as literally more accessible to families (usually represented by women) than the directors, who were figures of authority, usually men, and more likely to be shut away in an office or a rehearsal. A social team report summarized the main interests of the Red's different constituencies, and it portrayed only the administrators as focused on the social element; management, directors, teachers, and the integrated ensembles were depicted as concerned above all with musical and operational issues (*Síntesis* 2014).

A school director described the administrator as akin to the students' therapist. She was a person to whom they could talk about their personal problems. A manager described the directors as the Red's musical leaders and the administrators as "the social intermediaries of the program." An administrator confirmed this view: the director takes care of the musical side, she said, and I take care of the social side. Such findings raise questions about the notion of social action as flowing through music and musicians.

When teachers reflected on their time as students in the first phase of the Red, they often identified positive experiences with socializing in the times and spaces *around* music-making, while the most negative comments generally focused on music-making itself (endless rehearsals, overbearing teachers, boredom or stress in the orchestra, and so on). For example, Juan, one of the program's iconic figures, described the social aspect entirely in terms of non-musical activities: sharing food with friends, hanging out in the park after rehearsing, going on tour, even mundane activities like cleaning the school. In his account, the social equated to socializing, sharing experiences and stories, hanging out and laughing with his friends. Not once did he mention the experience of playing music together as socially formative. Music appeared as the excuse for socializing, rather than the channel through which social action flowed.

In general, musical staff had clear ideas about the values and behaviours that the Red ought to instil, but fewer about how they might be inculcated through music itself. Values such as discipline, order, responsibility, punctuality, and respect could just as well emanate from martial arts training, for example (which would also be cheaper and simpler to teach than classical music). As the social team noted, "any discipline, practice, or study that involves a teacher-student relationship could claim the same achievements" ("Informe" 2017a, 187). There is nothing specifically musical about learning to ask permission, not interrupt, and say hello, please, and thank you. Some staff portrayed the Red as an alternative space to home and school and as fostering social relationships with a special quality, but their accounts suggested that this special atmosphere derived from having a shared and freely chosen interest more than from music itself.

This evidence from the Red complicates the popular idea of SATM's social action as revolving around the power of music. It leaves two questions hanging: is music actually a trivial part of SATM and one that could easily be replaced by another activity? Alternatively, could music-making be reconfigured so that it boosted the social aspect of SATM—so that social action flowed *through* music as well as *around* it? Music itself seems to do relatively little work in orthodox SATM. How could it do more? This question will be picked up in Part II.

Social Change or Social Reproduction?

So far, this chapter has raised questions not about whether SATM has social effects, but rather about what those effects might be and who might be affected. While such programs have positive impacts on individual lives, there is much less evidence to support the more grandiose rhetoric that often accompanies them—in particular, discourses of social change or transformation. It is questionable how much music education can really do in the face of major social problems. But beyond this, it is worth asking whether, beneath the discursive surface, social change is even the goal of SATM, and whether music education may actually, in some instances, reinforce those problems rather than resolve them.

We return here to the ambiguity of music. Denning (2015) argues that music may serve as a force for social ordering or reordering. For Hess (2019, 50), "while musicking can potentially generate change that challenges the status quo, it can also reinscribe it." Music education, too, may support social reproduction or transformation (Bates 2018), and in CM, "depending on the amount and type of 'intervention', a music teacher/practitioner could be viewed as an agent of social change or an agent of social control" (Ansdell et al. 2020, 144). Boeskov (2019) argues that social reproduction may be as much in evidence as social transformation even in musical-social work directed explicitly at change. Which side of these binaries does SATM fall on?

Some interviewees in the Red articulated the idea that the program reproduced salient features and dynamics of the city. Medellín is known for its Cs: commerce, Catholicism, and conservatism. It became the industrial and commercial heart of Colombia in the early twentieth century. Franz (2017) traces the emergence at this time of an industrialist elite from the traditional oligarchy, which had historically embraced a paternalistic religious vision, authoritarian, hierarchical rule, and a rigorous work ethic. Hylton's (2007) account of Medellín's industrial culture emphasizes personalized authority, modes of domination characteristic of domestic servitude, demands for loyalty and obedience, vertical ties to *patrones* (bosses), expectations of prompt and efficient execution of orders, and an ideology of good works (the obligations of social elites to perceived inferiors). Maclean (2015) identifies traditions of clientelism and caudillo-style leadership, with authority often focused on a single (often militaristic) leader; "the patronage for which the region is famed affirms vertical power relations" (36).

The parallels with orthodox SATM are not hard to spot. Both El Sistema and the Red had religious overtones in their heyday, revolved around a charismatic, patriarchal founder, and implemented a hierarchical system centered on male figures of authority and a culture of unrelentingly hard work. Culturally, classical music might be marked as different in Medellín's barrios, but this model of music education reproduced the city's traditional social dynamics—something that did not go unnoticed. One of the Red's senior managers described the program as *Medellín en chiquito* (Medellín writ small), holding up as examples its conservatism, resistance to change, and tendency to formalize. Another senior figure claimed that the Red's historical elision of the indigenous and African populations and cultures of the department of Antioquia was typical of *paisa* culture, which he described as white, Catholic, and conservative. María, a member of the social team, described Medellín as a city with a progressive surface (evident in the iconic policy of social urbanism) but ruled by conservative cultural structures at a deeper level. For her, the Red was the same. She viewed the program as part of Medellín's progressive façade, but, at heart, an archaic model for the modern city, particularly in relation to its gender dynamics. Daniel, one of the most critical school directors, analysed the Red's tensions, manoeuvres, power games, and political pressures and influences, and he concluded: "it's like Colombia in miniature."

Such perspectives from within the Red clearly trouble a discourse of social transformation. In Medellín (as in El Sistema), we may see music education not so much transforming as mediating and reinforcing certain existing values of local society. In building El Sistema as a cult of personality around a charismatic but authoritarian leader, Abreu mirrored the dynamics of the Venezuelan political culture in which he was steeped and which has caused the country such problems in the twenty-first century. He and his approach were archetypical representatives of Venezuela's "magical state" (Coronil 1997). That is not to say that SATM does not bring benefits and pleasures, but rather that they are accompanied by significant strains of social reproduction, and the social features that are reinforced, such as male-dominated hierarchy, often jar with the progressive image of such programs.

To break the cycle of reproduction and pursue social change would require a clear and concerted effort to critique and unlearn problematic social and cultural values and relearn new ones in their place. As Matthews (2015) argues, good intentions are not enough to prevent complicity with systemic problems; self-critical examination of beliefs and prejudices is required. Unlearning and relearning has to begin at the top, but this is not something that SATM has managed in any consistent way. The godfather of SATM, Abreu, was famously unbending, and he allowed no one to question his vision or actions. As Bull (2019, xxiii) argues, orthodox SATM draws on "the most conservative and authoritarian aspects of classical music culture" rather than "music's potential as a form of radical critique." One of El Sistema's core mottos speaks volumes: "teach as you were taught." The Red, in contrast, has made efforts to grapple with such issues. Nonetheless, critique has tended to focus on behaviours (trying to reduce negative ones like shouting and promote positive ones like listening and respect) rather than power dynamics and social structures. Without a deeper process of self-critique and change, without more profound unlearning and relearning, such programs may be destined, despite good intentions and efforts by staff, to be limited in their transformative effects and even to perpetuate injustices.

Gender is a good example. If it is not raised as a critical issue in music education, then the gender oppression of wider society tends to be repeated (Matthews 2015), and this is what has happened in programs such as the Red and El Sistema. No amount of proclamations of social inclusion will disrupt gender inequity if patriarchy goes unmentioned and gender is not considered a relevant topic for discussion. Changing society requires challenging its rules, whether explicitly or implicitly or both. Instead, SATM has largely avoided discussing many big issues and focused on technique and performance—an approach that works well for producing skilled musicians, but that does little to alter societal dynamics. However, the Pedregal school project, mentioned in Chapter 1, provides a valuable counter-example. Students and staff at this school reflected on how perpetuating gender inequities countered the Red's social aims, and thus took steps towards rebalancing. The seeds of unlearning and relearning had been sown.

It is instructive to return to Sarrouy's (2018) account of an El Sistema school here:

> A certain responsibility to act as a masculine figure falls on the male teachers. "With my students I try to be authoritarian and demanding, but only after establishing a relationship of trust," explains the double bass teacher. The teachers say they feel a certain weight of parental responsibility, as an exemplary figure. They try to transmit notions of "commitment," of "responsibility," setting out "objectives to fulfil" for their students. (48)

This vignette sheds further doubt on attempts to link El Sistema with progressive notions such as social change and social justice. Progressivism rests—to put it in very simple terms—on the idea that society is flawed, hence the need for change. For example, progressives often regard social structures of gender and race as unfair and thus in need of transformation. This is not what we see in Sarrouy's description. There is no questioning of parental or gender roles or hierarchical relationships. The underpinning ideology is not that social norms are problematic, but rather that they are weakened and need to be reinforced. This is classic conservatism. The mothers in Sarrouy's study believe in values such as discipline and responsibility, and they take their children to the music school to have such values reinforced.

Above, we saw evidence that a number of SATM programs that have been subjected to critical scrutiny cater primarily to children whose families already share its values. Social reproduction is thus the primary dynamic. SATM's role here seems to be to channel and put on display the existing values of a particular social sector. A similar point emerges from the social team's report on its interviews with school directors. Noting that symphonic training upholds values like discipline, commitment, and obedience, it continues: "These values appeal to some families, like the possibility of ensuring that their children fit in more easily with social norms" ("Informe" 2017a, 112). Music education appears here as a normalizing force, adapting young people to society rather than vice versa. Ironically for a program that has become a symbol of the socialist Bolivarian Revolution, conservatism runs through El Sistema, from the politics and ideology of its founder to its derivative pedagogy and limited, repetitive curriculum. As such, it makes little sense to regard orthodox SATM as a form of music education for social change.

The role of classical music once again comes into question. Conventional classical music education is designed to educate classical musicians, not to transform society, and if unchecked, it often reproduces problematic social dynamics rather than challenging them (Bull 2019). It is naïve to think that the attractive strains of classical music necessarily counter discordant social dynamics in the outside world, and there is abundant evidence to the contrary.

Another way in which classical music culture mirrors Medellín's structural problems concerns division and violence. We have already seen ample evidence from the Red and other SATM programs of the creation of social divisions between individuals and groups as well as in-group bonding. Behind comforting discourses such as coexistence and "a big family," we have witnessed the reproduction of standard divisions and rivalries between instrumental groups within orchestras and the mockery of standard targets. Here too, then, we can see the mixture of change and reproduction that Boeskov highlights. On the one hand, in its first phase the Red moved young people out of harm's way and into a protective bubble, and the recollections of those involved at that time point to a focus on forging strong affective connections.

On the other hand, there is also evidence that the program fostered an "us and them" mentality and shielded children from the most extreme manifestations of violence, rather than questioning or transforming the dynamics that lay behind it.

Music is in no sense inherently counterposed to violence. Indeed, Alex Ross (2016) has examined a variety of ways in which "music is violence." Quadros (2015, 502) notes: "Power in a choir, as in an orchestra, band, and other conducted ensembles, is constituted by a quality of authority that is almost unrivaled in any other aspect of civic life, resembling the absolute authority in the armed forces and other areas of uniformed life." This issue is certainly not alien to music education, as Quadros makes clear. If the film *Whiplash* brought it to public attention in a dramatized (and rather over-dramatic) form, there is plenty of evidence and research to suggest that it is a genuine problem. Indeed, it has long been something of an open secret in classical music education, and in recent years it has become the focus of more concerted attention. Fernández-Morante (2018) has studied psychological violence in music conservatoires, while Pace (2015) has written about the increasingly visible phenomenon of sexual harassment and abuse in music education. Estrada's (1997) external evaluation identified domination, humiliation, and bullying as features of El Sistema's pedagogical practice. In Scripp's (2016b) report on El Sistema, the word "fear" appears twenty-two times—surely a record for a music education article on any topic other than performance anxiety. He notes that one of Abreu's several unflattering nicknames was the Führer—hardly a sign of a pacific approach to leadership.

Recall also members of the Red's first generation from Chapter 2. Estefanía half-joked about "the Nazi-Venezuelan System" imported to Medellín, while Norberto claimed that staff sometimes shouted, swore, and humiliated children in front of their peers, and even "practically got the belt out." Daniel argued that by training students in competition, the Red indirectly trained them for conflict, even though its official objective was coexistence. Competition and violence are a big problem in Colombian society, he said; we don't need more of them, we need to foster cooperation and a peaceful society. He rejected the notion of healthy competition in music, arguing that this was a matter for sport. In short, there may have been some reflection on violence at a macro level (in the sense of a desire to offer an alternative to the dangerous streets of the city), but at a micro level there were signs of continuity between a violent society and the Red.

The variety and geographical and temporal spread of these examples implies that violence is not an aberration in music and music education but in fact, in some cases, a constitutive element. Recall Gaztambide-Fernández's (2013, 214) argument from the Introduction: "the orchestra sounds magnificent not despite but because of the militaristic regimes that rule how many musicians are trained." Fernández-Morante (2018) identifies violence as almost in the genes of conservatoires, with their hierarchies and imbalances of power and the veneration accorded to top teachers. He finds a fine line between the pursuit of excellence and violence, and a similarly fine line exists between violence and the discipline that is so central to such pursuit. Again, it requires more than good intentions and individual efforts to produce transformation; a thorough critique of the imbrication of violence with music, and a reflection on its permeation of the values and practices of conventional music education, would be necessary.

José spoke about suffering a crisis after eight years as a school director, when he realized that he was an archetypical "tyrannical conductor." This crisis was triggered by a student complaint, sessions with a psychologist, and the Red's new emphasis on the socio-affective aspect of music education. In other words, it took the confluence of three developments, all of them provoking critical reflection, to shake him out of reproducing violence rather than transforming it. José could hardly be blamed for his earlier behaviour; the tyrannical conductor is a historical norm in orchestral culture, and one that some continue to defend (Hewett 2020).

The solution to violence is not simply to flee to the opposite extreme. Harmony has often had a coercive streak throughout history (Baker 2008; 2010; 2014). Violence and conflict require resolution, not suppression or denial. Cobo's (2015) study of group music pedagogy underlines the importance of carefully managed conflict and constructive controversy for cognitive development. Indeed, she argues that teachers should *promote* particular kinds of conflict in order to problematize knowledge and foster collaboration between peers. Similarly, Henley's (2019) work with the prison program Good Vibrations is founded on the view that conflict plays an important part in pedagogy; the facilitators thus strive to create a safe environment, allow conflict to play out, and reflect on it afterwards. Vicenç Villatoro, speaking at a public event in Medellín, put it memorably: culture is not an instrument to win a battle or a hammer to hit a nail; it is a battleground where ideas come into contact and conflict and play out. Paradoxically, then, responding to societal violence by avoiding conflict and enforcing harmony may be counter-productive, as it does not allow participants to reimagine conflict as a productive force and to learn how to deal with it constructively. The unreflecting use of music under the banner of social harmony is thus unlikely to impact significantly on violence even when it avoids reproducing it.

Violence does not just take physical form. Fernández-Morante's study of conservatoires covers psychological and academic violence as well as physical and sexual. Matthews (2015, 240) argues: "Music educators are just as implicated in structural violence as anyone else, for it resides in their prejudices, in the way in which they see the world, and in the classifications that they impose on their students." Some decolonial music education researchers see Eurocentric music education in Latin America as a kind of epistemic violence—a continuation of historical forms of oppression dating back to the Spanish Conquest (e.g. Rosabal-Coto 2019). Conventional approaches to music education have been critiqued through the frame of symbolic violence (Powell, Smith, and D'Amore 2017). Joabe Cavalcanti writes of "the cultural violence committed against communities in the name of development" (cited in Ramalingam 2013, 91). Music educators do not need to be tyrannical conductors or "practically get the belt out" to participate in the reproduction of violence.

Even in this realm, then, where one might expect SATM's impact to be least ambiguous, there is evidence of complexity and contradictory effects. The 2005 evaluation found that Red students were more likely to be victims of violent crime than their peers (the authors' hypothesis revolved around the musicians' nocturnal movements). El Sistema's rapid expansion in the 2000s coincided with the worsening of Venezuela's security situation. The Venezuelan program exemplifies how violent dynamics may be perpetuated beneath discourses of peace and a utopian view of music education. There is much to reflect on here for those interested in the employment of SATM and of music education more generally in combatting violence.

A more subtle way in which SATM participates in social reproduction is in the definition of problems. In framing the issues that it is supposed to resolve in terms of individual deficits, SATM helps to distract from structural causes such as inequality and thus serves to perpetuate them (see Baker 2016b). El Sistema's formulation of its central problem as a lack of discipline or aspiration and "an empty, disorientated, and deviant youth" is particularly stark, but the Red's official description, while more subtle, still points to behaviour and correction rather than the structural causes of social problems: its fundamental aim is "to generate and strengthen processes of coexistence and civic culture through the education of children and young people via the enjoyment and learning of music."[10] As Boeskov (2019, 191) writes, such analyses "contribute to concealing and naturalizing the power relations upholding the status quo." He goes on: "musical practices promote or conceal specific conceptions of the social and political reality, with consequences for how musical agents can come to understand themselves and their possibilities for action" (221). When SATM states that values education is the solution, it implies that young people's values, rather than social structures, are the problem, and therefore limits the imagination of a different world. When SATM opts for discipline, it constrains the possibilities for action to challenge and change those structures.

In short, SATM has the potential to generate social reproduction or change or, as Boeskov argues, both at once. Greater awareness of this ambiguity can only serve those who look to SATM with hopes of social transformation.

Beliefs versus Evidence

In their study of Orquestra Geração (OG), Cruz, Mota, and Costa (2017, 78) noted: "the research team encountered fairly assertive affirmations on various occasions by OG members (nucleus coordinators and teachers) about the improvements made to the academic performances

---

10   This text appeared on the Red's homepage on 6 September 2017 (http://www.redmusicamedellin.org/).

of students when compared with other students." The researchers thus carried out a quasi-experimental study, the results of which led them to conclude: "we cannot consider that OG students turn in better academic results in comparison with other students in the same school that do not attend the orchestra" (84). The employees' beliefs about the effects of SATM turned out to be overly optimistic.

This study, placed alongside the questions raised about social impact and social change so far in this chapter, points to a further issue in critical research on this topic. On the one hand, the evidence of significant social impact is limited and questionable, and there is considerable evidence to the contrary. On the other hand, many who work in this field believe SATM to be effective. (This is not universally the case by any means; we have seen plenty of examples of ambivalence and scepticism in the preceding chapters.) Researchers have a duty to take such views seriously, whether or not we ultimately agree with them. Yet how can we take both the research and the beliefs seriously at the same time when they are in contradiction?

The way to square this circle is to understand such beliefs as logical and common-sense. The fact that research questions these beliefs does not make them illogical or foolish. There are good reasons why SATM employees might hold them. In cases such as the Red and El Sistema, many teachers were once themselves students in the same program, and so they may regard themselves as living proof that SATM works. Their beliefs are fuelled by personal experience; but personal experience is not always a reliable guide to general truths.

In Medellín and Venezuela, I repeatedly heard musicians claim that SATM was effective on the grounds that many of their neighbourhood friends who did not enter these programs ended up getting into trouble, going to prison, or even dying. This may be true, but it does not mean that these musicians were destined for such fates before they discovered music. Personality or family influence may have determined that these individuals chose music while their friends took other paths. Music may thus be an effect rather than a cause of a different life trajectory. The problem with any individual story of redemption is that there is no accounting for pre-existing differences and no control; such stories are based on what the individual imagines they might have become without music, and they are therefore susceptible to being skewed by ideologies of various kinds—including the commonplace notion of SATM as salvation. When a randomly-assigned control group is introduced, as in the IDB's 2017 study, matters look quite different—and even more so if the data is re-analyzed by an independent researcher (Baker, Bull, and Taylor 2018).

The effectiveness of SATM is also right before teachers' eyes, in the sense that they see successful students on a regular basis. The problem here (as above) is survivorship bias. In a voluntary program with a high dropout rate like the Red or El Sistema, failures tend to disappear rapidly from view while successes remain visible and become more prominent over time. It is perfectly understandable that a student who thrived in the program over a period of fifteen years would loom much larger in the mind of a teacher or a researcher than a student who struggled for a few months and left. When they consider SATM, it is perfectly logical that a teacher should think primarily of themselves and their peers who became professional musicians, rather than those (probably many more) who were less attached to the program and passed through it more fleetingly. Survivorship bias is not a personal failing, then, but it can easily lead participants to regard SATM as more successful than it is.

Survivorship bias is also a major issue in SATM research. Whatever a voluntary program of this size does, however good or bad its practices, some students will like it and others will not—and most of those who do not will leave, removing evidence of failure. Talking predominantly or entirely to survivors is likely to skew the researcher's impression of the program. It is very hard for researchers to avoid focusing on those who are present rather than those who are not, yet dropout statistics and accounts of failure are just as important as success stories in understanding SATM. The high rates of desertion in many such programs speak volumes; but such information is ignored even by many researchers, let alone in official narratives.[11]

---

11   Fairbanks (2019) is an exception: he notes that in the high school he studied, only a fraction of students even had the opportunity to enter the Sistema program, and an initial cohort of sixty diminished over the years to ten or fewer. In other words, "there are upwards of 50 'ghosts'—which incidentally amounts to five times the number of 'successful' high school orchestra musicians—who ultimately discontinued their participation in the orchestra programme" (177). Nevertheless, as the author acknowledges, his study focuses on the minority of survivors, not the majority of "ghosts."

Out on the streets of Medellín, extremes of violence and the murder rate declined notably over the two decades of the Red's existence. As a result, many people in Medellín claimed that the Red had transformed the city. However, the reality of urban renewal is more complex than this story (as we will see below). Also, the Red flourished at the same time as a wide range of other urban policies aimed at similar goals (van der Borgh and Abello Colak 2018). Without an experimental study, it would be impossible to isolate the effects of the Red from those of all the other policies, and to credit music education with any changes. Research on the arts and urban renewal in other countries gives plenty of reasons for caution over expansive claims (e.g. Belfiore 2002; Miller 2013; Lees and Melhuish 2015). Nevertheless, the Red was born with a discourse about coexistence, and the barrios have become considerably less violent since then; linking these two developments is thus a logical step.

El Sistema presents a much more contradictory picture. The program's explosive growth and international boom were followed shortly afterwards by a decline in social conditions in Venezuela and then a full-blown national crisis. Here, the persistence of positive beliefs about SATM in the face of mounting counter-evidence points to the central role of ideology.

Beliefs in the power of music go far beyond SATM. In Latin America, idealistic views about European music and salvation date back to evangelization campaigns during the earliest days of the Spanish Conquest. They have been taken up again in recent decades by cultural institutions, the music industry, governments, and the media around the world, becoming a dominant ideology of our age. Optimistic visions of the social impact of the arts are found everywhere today, forming a central plank of funding justifications and institutional marketing. Few are aware of the negative tradition, so comprehensively has it been displaced (Belfiore and Bennett 2008).

Nor is research immune. In both hard and social sciences, the publication process is biased towards positive findings and inflates effects (Lortie-Forgues and Inglis 2019; Clift 2020). Alemán et al.'s (2017) study of El Sistema is a case in point, as discussed above. Furthermore, some scientists working on music and cognition (e.g. Schellenberg 2019; Sala and Gobet 2020) suggest that their field is prey to confirmation bias.

Despite such inflation, research studies themselves do not generally articulate grandiose statements about miracles and social transformation; rather, some point to small cognitive or psychological differences and benefits, while others do not. The two largest randomized controlled trials (RCTs) in this field found no effect of music training on cognitive or academic skills (Haywood et al. 2015; Alemán et al. 2017). But in the translation into the public realm, many caveats and limitations are ironed out, and null or negative findings are generally overlooked, since there are no organizations in whose interest it is to promote them. As Sala and Gobet (2020) note, the two major RCTs above have been paid little attention by the media or even by other researchers, even though RCT is the gold-standard methodology. More positive studies are more likely to be picked up by advocacy organizations and to lead to a report in the media, in which small-scale and specific findings often become an expansive and generalized story about the power of music (Mehr 2015; Odendaal et al. 2019). Many musicians encounter headlines, summaries, and animations of such stories on social media. As a result, there is a significant gap between the mixed findings and caution of some researchers concerning the transfer effects of music education, and the more uniformly optimistic opinion that prevails among musicians and the general public (Mehr 2014; D'Souza and Wiseheart 2018).

There is virtually no appetite for questioning the dominant narrative in the public sphere, meaning that counter-arguments are rarely heard. The classical music industry and profession have lined up behind a story that benefits and flatters them, and many classical music journalists have followed suit. Few are willing to risk arousing the wrath of music lovers by presenting less positive research conclusions to a wider public.[12] The ambiguous picture presented in these pages will not be a surprise to many researchers in fields such as the sociology of music education or development studies, who are used to confronting counter-effects, unintended consequences, and gaps between aims and outcomes. In the public sphere, though, ambivalence about the power of music education is a rare bird.

In sum, positive—often glowing—accounts of music's effects are the norm and come from multiple angles. It is perfectly logical, then,

---

12   Sala and Gobet (2017) is an exception—but see also the comments below their article, which illustrate the resistance to null or negative findings on this topic.

for many within SATM to hold optimistic views. However, there is a growing amount of research to suggest that such views, for all that they reflect the dominant narrative, may not be accurate as an account of the field's social impact.

The social team makes for an interesting contrast. Its members worked full-time inside the Red, in some cases for years, so they knew the program very well. But they were not influenced by survivorship bias or dominant ideologies of music to nearly the same extent as the musicians, and as social scientists, they were trained to think critically about such questions. They reflected frequently on what many of them perceived as rose-tinted and poorly founded beliefs about music and social impact, and they often expressed scepticism over the Red's expansive claims. Where is the evidence, they asked?

Half a Miracle

The event for the Harvard delegation with which this chapter began illustrated the Red's partnership with Medellín's Agency for Cooperation and Investment (ACI) to convey an appealing image of urban renewal for international consumption. In some ways this might appear as a logical and unproblematic quid pro quo: in return for receiving considerable funds from the city, the Red supports the municipal government and its policies. However, senior Red staff who were present at the ACI event for Harvard confided to me afterwards that they were uneasy about the way the Red was being used to "sell" Medellín and the students were required to play the role of city ambassadors. Their critical comments encouraged me to look more deeply at this arrangement.

The obligation to play a marketing role clearly demanded that the Red transmit a positive image. Consequently, the Powerpoint presentation to the visiting delegation elided the nuanced, ambivalent views of the staff who were present and the complex issues that were discussed daily, and painted an entirely rosy picture. It exemplified the simplification that goes on in the self-presentation of SATM to the outside world.

Observers should not take this kind of institutional self-publicity too seriously, since it obscures as much as it reveals about the real dynamics of the project and the surrounding society. But all too often, this is precisely what has happened with SATM: marketing discourses have been taken up and repeated by the media, researchers, and other institutions as though they represented the whole truth. The story of El Sistema in the years around 2010 was one of a constant flow of delegations to Venezuela, where they were given a polished, carefully stage-managed, red-carpet tour (see Baker 2014) and went away convinced that the program was transforming the country and represented the future of classical music (neither of which, as subsequent events revealed, was true).

The Harvard event was thus a microcosm of the production and reception of the SATM story around the globe in recent years. It allowed me to observe the international reproduction of an idealized vision of SATM taking place in real time. A publicity narrative was conveyed to an enthusiastic audience with no easy way of assessing its accuracy and no reason or incentive to doubt it; this narrative became the truth, doubtless to be repeated back home (as happened after similar official visits to El Sistema). Meanwhile, outside in the streets, the student protests rumbled on, and in the schools, ensembles, and meeting-rooms of the Red, messy, complex reality continued unabated.

There was nothing untoward in any of this: it would make no sense to expect anything else from an event like this. No one was at fault; everyone was simply doing their job or gratefully receiving what they were offered. I would have done the same in their shoes. The story here is not about failure; it is about the idealization of SATM as part of its subservience to political and economic agendas. I knew all the adult representatives of the Red at the event quite well, and from long conversations with them I knew that they held complex and insightful views on their own work. Yet the institutional and political dynamics of the event obliged them to idealize SATM, and, through no fault of their own, to place music education in the role of promoting somewhat simplistic, utopian thinking rather than nuanced, critical reflection.

There are echoes here of Logan's (2016) characterization of El Sistema as a cultural veil draped over the inconvenient facts of everyday life. For music educators interested in critically reflective musicianship (Johnson 2009) or critical theory more broadly, it may be somewhat disconcerting to see music education drawn into this ambiguous role, obfuscating some inconvenient social realities as it highlights more palatable ones, and serving as an ornament on urban policy rather than a provocation to think and act. Given that this was not down to individual or collective failures, the question arises of whether music education can play both marketing and critical roles at the same time, or whether SATM in Latin America—because of its size and dependence on political patronage—is designed and destined to promote rather than question the status quo.

The issue of instrumentalization came up in my private conversations with staff after the event. This word usually appeared in the context of critiques of the utilization of students in pursuit of musical goals, but here the issue was rather the harnessing of young musicians for political and economic ends. At the Harvard event, they were used to market the Medellín Miracle to foreign visitors. Such a dynamic may seem relatively unproblematic to those who agree with the ends—in this case, presenting Medellín's government, policies, and record of urban transformation in a positive light. But as we shall see below, there have been many informed critiques of the miracle narrative, and more importantly, there is a principle at stake here about whether music students should be treated as means or ends.

The potential dangers of such instrumentalization have become painfully apparent in Venezuela in recent years. When the Simón Bolívar Youth Orchestra burst onto the international scene in 2007, its populist, nationalist display was seen as a relatively harmless bit of soft power on the part of a government that had considerable international support from the Left. For the next few years, El Sistema's showcase schools and ensembles were regularly wheeled out in polished displays for local and foreign delegations, in pursuit of funding, celebrity endorsements, political support, and positive media coverage. A decade later, such an approach looked much more problematic, as students were pressed into bolstering the Venezuelan government's dubious human rights record, celebrating its questionable political alliances, and decorating its propaganda campaigns. El Sistema had clearly descended to the bottom rung of Hart's ladder of participation (discussed in Chapter 3): manipulation. There are ethical questions around treating music students as pawns in an adult game, even if the pawns seem to be having fun. Venezuela illustrates that a laissez-faire attitude to such instrumentalization can lead to serious consequences.

The adult game in question in Medellín was urban renewal. Like many foreigners, I had been attracted to the city by the visible signs and effusive accounts of its urban renaissance, and particularly its iconic policy of social urbanism. But shortly after my arrival, I attended a public event entitled "Medellín pa' donde vamos" [Medellín, where are we heading?]. I was struck by the lack of complacency and indeed outright concern of the speakers and audience, who clearly believed that Medellín had a lot of work still to do. The opening keynote was given by Francisco de Roux, a Jesuit priest and leading figure in Colombia's peace process. The "Medellín model" had been acclaimed around the world, he said, yet inequity, sexism, and racism had continued, limiting life chances for a large segment of the population. He underlined inequality as a key problem in Medellín. The city was historically Colombia's centre of industry, trade, and capitalism, but also of paramilitaries, guerrillas, and drug bosses. Medellín had not overcome the historical trauma underpinning the city, he claimed, preferring to look away and forget rather than face up to the pain generated by violence. The result was an absence of reconciliation and solidarity and a divided society. A month later, the famous novelist and Medellín resident Pablo Montoya published a coruscating critique of the city's supposedly miraculous transformation, also under the title of "Medellín, where are we heading?" (2017). The author portrayed the miracle narrative as little more than an illusory spell cast by hubristic city leaders, covering up a reality in which corruption, criminality, poverty, inequality, racism, paramilitary activity, child prostitution, and environmental degradation were alarmingly prevalent.

These were not exceptional views. The shine has come off the Medellín Miracle somewhat in recent years. In a *Foreign Policy* article entitled "Half a Miracle," Francis Fukuyama and Seth Colby (2011) provided a more sober assessment, acknowledging the city's recent achievements but also attributing the decline in violence to the dominance of a single crime boss, known as Don Berna. When Medellín won the Innovative City of the Year award in 2013, the mayor was obliged to admit straight away that all was not rosy, and the archbishop issued a press release that further dampened the self-congratulation by denouncing a catalogue of serious urban problems (Brand 2013). As Hylton (2007, 89) notes, "Medellín's makeover rests on the graves of tens of thousands of its citizens."

Researchers, too, have poured cold water on miracle stories, arguing that while the murder rate has declined dramatically over the last twenty years, the cause was not so much social urbanism as increased paramilitary control and shifting priorities and alliances on the part of criminal organizations, which saw economic benefit in a more pacified city (Hylton 2007; Maclean 2015). Politicians and crime bosses agreed on the need to prioritize the requirements of foreign capital and thus security. There has been a mutation and diversification in violence and criminality more than a diminution: less homicide, but more extortion and other forms of criminal activity, meaning that the declining murder rate is somewhat deceptive (van der Borgh and Abello Colak 2018). According to Tubb (2013), the city government may have implemented an array of attractive social programs (like the Red), but most have had little effect on violence or criminality. He portrays the two as simply sitting side by side, like Medellín's stark poverty and immense wealth.

Meanwhile, social urbanism has been critiqued as a policy in the service of the local business elite, and an attractive way of avoiding the issue of inequality and income redistribution. According to Franz (2018), "the main beneficiary of [Mayor] Fajardo's governance formula was big capital." Maclean (2015, 3) notes that while there have been successes, "many of the policies associated with social urbanism reaffirm as much as challenge elite power and dominance."

Social urbanism has also been portrayed as a policy to change the city's image rather than attack underlying problems, in order to attract foreign investment and tourism. This policy was successful in some senses: it brought economic dividends (for some), and a recent survey found that one-third of visitors to Medellín came to see its urban transformation (Zambrano Benavides 2019). However, it did little to alter the sky-high levels of inequality in the city. In 2013, shortly after the eight years when social urbanism was dominant (2004–12), Colombia was reported to have the most unequal cities in Latin America, with Medellín the worst offender (Téllez Oliveros 2013). Inequality dipped a little and then rose again over the following years, and it was still rated as "very high" in 2017 ("La desigualdad" 2020). Since inequality is widely regarded as a significant cause of violence, researchers have blamed social urbanism and its successor policies for perpetuating many of the city's troubles.

A study of the famous outdoor escalator in Comuna 13 concluded that it boosted civic pride and Medellín's international image, but also that it addressed an ill-defined problem and had little impact on mobility or inequalities, and so it was ineffective as a motor of social development (Reimerink 2018). Similarly, Brand (2013) argues that social urbanism appealed to Medellín's residents, but in practice it did little to resolve the city's problems. Localized benefits did not translate across the city as a whole. Social urbanism produced a widespread *sensation* of social inclusion, but very meagre material improvements. For Brand, social urbanism was primarily about image, spectacle, and marketing, and the political benefits that they brought. Franz (2017, 143) concurs: "Socioeconomic conditions in the city are far from miraculous."

In a particularly illuminating study, Montoya Restrepo (2014) analyses the "social" in social urbanism, and she concludes that in concrete terms, behind all the hype, the policies simply enacted standard practices and basic obligations of the state. She argues that the word "social" was thus a justificatory, ideological prefix, and a strategy to bolster urban marketing (aimed internationally) and normalization and control (aimed at the local population). Behind this label, it was business as usual—in both senses of the word "business."

The Red was part of the Medellín Strategic Plan of 1997 that sowed the seeds of social urbanism, and it was taken over by the city government early in Fajardo's administration, when social urbanism flourished. Some of the Red's schools found a home in the iconic new library parks, one of the policy's signature features, and its ensembles performed in the stations of the metro, another emblem of Medellín renewed. Not only did musical and architectural change happen at the same time, but the Red also helped to populate and animate the new buildings and spaces, forming part of the symbolic transformation of the city.

The Red might be seen, then, as a microcosm of social urbanism: a half-miracle within a half-miracle. Like social urbanism, the Red is attractive, a new image of Medellín to the world, and a source of local pride and international acclaim; but as with social urbanism, there are also question marks. If Reimerink (2018, 201) argues that social urbanism created "islands of exception" within the city, there are clear echoes of the Red's "bubbles." Brand (2013, 14) could be describing the Red when he writes: "Vast areas remain untouched and a huge concerted and continuous effort would be required for social urbanism to extend effectively over the whole city. This only accentuates the symbolic importance of social urbanism, whose aesthetics are much stronger than its material impacts." Both programs are widely believed to have had a beneficial effect on the city, yet detailed research points more to positive images, beliefs, and feelings than to tangible social change for the city's poorer inhabitants. If Medellín's mayors have favoured "media-friendly visible interventions that convey an image of modernity" (Reimerink 2018, 192), the Red might be seen as the audible counterpart. The narratives of both the Medellín Miracle and SATM have been co-constructed and significantly boosted by ample media attention. City re-imaging, like SATM, depends on media willing to brand it a success and return to the story repeatedly, implanting a positive image in the minds of the public.

In both cases, miraculous appearances and attractive spectacles can be deceptive: behind progressive exteriors lie internal workings that are more ambiguous. Effects are mixed; positive results may not match those claimed in official discourse; causes are a matter of debate. The Red is one example of a broader phenomenon in Medellín: feel-good social policies that became world-famous despite showing modest results. They are symbolically important to the city, but it is harder to argue that they have had a significant material impact. As Maclean (2015, 123) writes in relation to Medellín's iconic urban policies, "it is unclear that they have represented a real challenge to the shape that the city would have taken were it simply to have obeyed the needs of capital." The effects of the Red on the city's destiny are similarly unclear.

Did social urbanism make Medellín a better place to live? Most would agree that it did. But I found far fewer residents inclined to self-congratulation. As Maclean notes, the image makeover was more believable to foreigners than locals. Love for their city did not preclude widespread criticism by its inhabitants; Medellín continued to be more complicated than the miracle story would suggest. Much the same could be said about the Red.

Performing the Medellín Miracle

The event for the Harvard delegation illustrated how the Red serves, among many other things, as a tool of urban marketing, aimed both inwards and outwards. With its frequent *conciertos de ciudad* [city concerts] and performances in urban spaces such as parks and the metro, the Red is part of Medellín's ceremonial apparatus: a presentation of a particular image of the city, to the city, funded by the city. Urban development inspired by the Barcelona model has an important component of spectacle (Brand 2013), and music may be seen as playing a part in Medellín's performance of urban renewal. How better to present the city reborn than displaying a large group of young people playing in harmony? What better spectacle of development?

As its slogan "The New Image of Medellín to the World" suggests, the Red has also taken pride of place in a wider program of city reimaging for external consumption. Juan Guillermo Bedoya, the mayor's director of communications from 2008–09, said: "any society that transforms itself needs symbols," and he spoke of visitors to Medellín "taking away the image of a city renewed" ("Medellín" n.d., 210). Since its early days, the Red has been pressed into service as a symbol to support this image. It is not just lives that the program is intended to transform.

The theme of narrating the city—of telling a new story or constructing a new imaginary—was ubiquitous during my time in Medellín, particularly in public debates and discussions at cultural events. It was a central pillar of the Red's tour to the US in 2018, with its city portrait composed by the students. At government level, the main aim of this reimaging has been to boost foreign investment and tourism; it is thus significant that the organizer of the Harvard event was the ACI—the Agency for Cooperation and Investment. The connection between the arts and tourism was made clear in 2018 with the creation of the municipal program *Ciudad de artistas* [City of Artists], which was aimed explicitly at using the arts to make the city more attractive to foreign visitors. Thompson (2009, 26) suggests that applied arts practitioners should always ask: "Which show are we part of?" The Red's musicians were part of the Medellín Miracle show.

However, as noted above, Medellín's urban policies have attracted sustained criticism from researchers for perpetuating urban problems. "Selling" Medellín's urban renewal internationally is not therefore a neutral or uncontroversial activity from a political or economic perspective. In playing a symbolic supporting role in relation to urban policies with mixed effects, the Red might be seen as occupying an ambiguous position. If the "new image" that Medellín has projected to the world in recent years is at least partly deceptive, where does that leave the Red?

Then there is the thorny question of the Red's imbrication with promoting investment. Franz (2017) provides an illuminating analysis of the ACI. This agency promotes Medellín not only as a destination for foreign direct investment but also as a flexibilized labour market, offering investors a city where workers have low wages, long hours, and few benefits. Yet flexibilization can have negative impacts on labour productivity (not to mention quality of life). The agenda that the ACI pushes is focused on "economic activities in the service sectors that either remain at the low-productivity end of the value chain or are skill-intensive tradable services that cannot generate much employment for the vast majority of Medellín's unskilled labor force" (139). This agenda serves mainly the interest of the city's capitalist class, and it has contradictory effects on economic development. The city's overall economy has grown, but because this growth is concentrated in service industries, it contrasts sharply with high unemployment and underemployment rates and increased precariousness of working conditions. For a music education program to partner with the ACI and support such an agenda raises obvious concerns—all the more so a program with a social objective and aimed primarily at the popular classes, who generally experience the most negative effects of such policies.

There are various ways to view the Red in the context of wider urban policy. One might regard it as one facet of an externally-directed policy of urban re-imaging. Or one might see the Red as just one of a vast array of public policies and programs in Medellín, and note that cultural policies often contrast with the wider economic and security program of the state in Colombia. Ochoa Gautier (2001, 379) describes "an exacerbation of extremes—implementation of democratization processes through cultural policy or other administrative and legal procedures, coupled with neoliberalization and escalation of armed conflict." During the year that I spent in Medellín, the government of Mayor Federico Gutiérrez placed a higher emphasis on security than his predecessors, and rising levels and perceptions of violence suggested that this policy was not working well. There was something of a contradiction between the Red, which sought peaceful coexistence through education and culture, and the more reactive, hard-line approach to security of the government that funded it. How to understand the role of the Red in this picture? Was it supposed to help mitigate the effects of tougher urban policies, giving back with the left hand what the right had taken? Or was it an attractive smokescreen for those policies—a cultural veil, in Logan's terms? If the city's security situation was worsening, then should the Red be seen as compensating for this decline, masking the problem, or simply ineffective?

The role of the arts in urban renewal is contested, and behind the positive official rhetoric, many scholars have critiqued their use as a handmaiden of neoliberal capitalist development (e.g. Berry, Slater and Iles 2009; Lees and Melhuish 2015; Mould 2015). Music education as marketing for urban renewal is thus an ethically and politically complex phenomenon, as ambiguous as the policies that it supports. Sachs Olsen (2019, 175) offers an alternative vision: one of socially engaged art that questions and fosters debate rather than "decorat[ing] urban space as part of a wider city-branding strategy." The comparison with the Red is illuminating.

Critical scholarship on social urbanism and the role of the arts in urban renewal illustrates the importance of a sceptical attitude towards supposed miracles, and, in encouraging caution about grandiose claims, it provides a valuable pointer to observers and researchers of SATM. It underlines that attractive-sounding policies and programs may not have the effects that are claimed for them, and that even when positive effects are observed, their causes may be quite different. This literature points up the weaknesses in the commonplace argument that the Red was created, the murder rate went down, ergo music education is an effective social solution. The causes of pacification identified by scholars have little to do with uplifting areas like culture and education, which feature prominently in official narratives of social urbanism, and more with obscure negotiations in the city's dark underbelly. The wealth of ambivalent scholarship on the Medellín Miracle supports a similar take on the Red.

Montoya Restrepo's analysis of social urbanism, in particular, is highly pertinent to SATM. Both phenomena have developed idealistic discourses and been heavily boosted by the national and international media, but up close, SATM, too, looks rather like the state fulfilling a basic obligation: in this case, to make artistic education available to young people. In Venezuela, the social discourse emerged long after the creation of El Sistema, also as a justificatory, ideological prefix; and Montoya Restrepo's argument that in Medellín's social urbanism it signalled marketing (aimed internationally) and normalization and control (aimed at the local population) is an uncannily accurate description of the Venezuelan music program. Behind the social label, El Sistema too was business as usual: the program continued to deliver the same conventional music education that it had always done, based on models dating back centuries; and Abreu secured a starring role for El Sistema in the international classical music industry, vigorously commercializing SATM with the help of agents, promoters, festivals, concert halls, and a leading record label. Montoya Restrepo (2014, 218) critiques the view that "the only way to include those who have been traditionally marginalized is one thought up from outside, a vision that reproduces the way of inhabiting the city imposed by foreign models." Much the same point could be made about a vision of social inclusion based on the European symphony orchestra.

The warm, fuzzy word "social" served, in El Sistema as in social urbanism, as an ornament on neoliberal thinking. In both cases, grandiose claims were made about the efficacy of the measures before any attempt to evaluate them. When such research eventually appeared, it poured cold water on many of the claims—yet it did little to loosen the hold of the well-established miracle story on the public imagination.

Medellín: Creative City

A final illustration of the ambiguity of the Red concerns the issue of creativity. This was a central focus of the new proposals under Giraldo's leadership and was championed by the pedagogical coordinator, Franco. While we have seen the practical obstacles in the Red, the logic behind making music education (and SATM in particular) more creative is strong, and there is a wealth of research to support such a move. Whether one looks from a musical, social or cognitive perspective, the benefits of creativity at an individual level are compelling.

The invitation to the Red to perform at the launch event for "Medellín: Creative City" in 2019 thus made perfect sense. Yet this event had only a tenuous relationship to creativity in the sense that Franco invoked it (musical composition and improvisation). It was a business meeting, organized by the chamber of commerce and launching a creative economy strategy for the city. The focus was squarely on culture as an economic resource. Music and other scenic arts found themselves grouped under the heading of a "business tourism cluster."

The use of the Red to adorn the launch of a creative city policy raises similar questions to the Harvard-ACI event. There is a wealth of scholarship critiquing the concepts of the creative city and the creative economy (e.g. Berry Slater and Iles 2009; Pratt 2011; Mould 2015; Stevenson 2017), on both ideological grounds (as an expression of neoliberal urban development) and practical ones (as producing mixed or downright pernicious effects on cities). So there are good reasons to think that this strategy might not be a magic bullet for Medellín. On one level, the Red's concert was simply another performance at another city event—a bread-and-butter activity; but on another level, the Red was drawn in as a support act for a much-questioned neoliberal ideology. In adopting creativity as a central discourse, then, the Red had sailed inadvertently into murky waters.

Ironically, the Red has little to do in its everyday practices with the creative economy. Indeed, one of the internal criticisms was precisely that it was too disconnected from the local music industry, and there was actually little effort in the program to promote entrepreneurialism or skills for the music business. Yet the Red was easily co-opted for marketing purposes and used to provide an attractive face for a complex, questionable policy, putting an auditory gloss on neoliberal urban development.

The convergence of music education and urban policy on the issue of creativity might be seen as another example, alongside citizenship, of what Dagnino (2007) calls a "perverse confluence." It further illustrates that SATM is not a neutral bystander, nor does it operate in a separate, autonomous realm; it is closely bound to the dominant social, economic, and political order, whatever the beliefs and localized actions of individuals within it. Thinking about SATM in this way helps to explain why it has received such support from governments in a number of Latin American countries. As ever, this is clearest in Venezuela, but in Medellín, too, the Red has propped up the dominant urban narrative: co-opted into international marketing, promoting government policy, and appearing in a local publicity campaign for the mayor's office in 2018. The Red's external effects are thus as ambiguous as its internal dynamics: it has been utilized to symbolize and perform a debatable conception of the city (the Medellín Miracle) and a debatable urban policy (the creative city).

Creativity encapsulates both the potential and the risks of SATM (and of culture more generally) in the neoliberal city. Creativity may be admirable in an individual musician or an ensemble, yet also more questionable when placed at the heart of urban policy. What works well at a micro level may be more dubious when it becomes a structuring principle at a macro level. Furthermore, as Kanellopoulos and Barahanou (2021, 150) argue, the radical potential of creative arts education is easily neutralized when it is instrumentalized within an ideological and political framework that views creativity as fostering an entrepreneurial attitude to work and life and "as a survival strategy in an uncertain neoliberal world."[13]

Creativity holds out the possibility of freedom and the new; yet it is also a core ideology of contemporary capitalism, and it has become a cover for poorly paid and increasingly precarious labour. Creative music education could form critical citizens who imagine alternatives to the status quo; but it could also prepare young people for an uncertain existence as workers of the creative economy. Creativity could become a tool of subtle subversion (Mould 2015); but it could also become a support act for the dominant urban agenda. What is clear is that creativity, like citizenship, is a double-edged sword.

Conclusion

The fundamental question of whether SATM works looks even harder to answer now that we have zoomed out from the micro-social and community levels to effects at a larger scale. Boeskov (2018) draws on Georgina Born's theory of four planes of sociality to explain how musical-social work may have multiple and contradictory effects simultaneously: "social music making that at one level allows for a transgression of some confining aspects of the social experience of its participants may at the

---

13 See also Kanellopoulos 2015.

same time also potentially reinforce other parts of the social formation in ways that may not serve the interest of the people involved" (94). Bull (2019) identifies a similar contradiction within youth classical music in the UK: those she studied often found enjoyment, a sense of identity, and a social scene, yet within a cultural and institutional context that reproduced gendered and classed structures of domination. Arts-led urban regeneration shows a comparable disjuncture: the arts may have positive local effects, yet "those effects may be peripheral to the underlying structural facts of economic restructuring and deployed simply to mask the realities of social displacement" (Lees and Melhuish 2015, 252). Critics of "artwashing" point out that artistic projects may generate pleasure while also contributing to gentrification. There is a clear pattern here: the arts may produce positive effects on one plane while concealing and reinforcing structures of inequality on another. Furthermore, the very pleasure that participation induces may enable that concealment.

There is no question that the Red has many positive aspects. Plenty of children derive enjoyment and benefit from studying within the program. However, serious analysis cannot stop here (and not only because of the problem of survivorship bias). The Red is also connected to urban reimaging in pursuit of foreign investment and tourism and to a creative city strategy, and such policies produce more questionable results on a different plane to students socializing and enjoying themselves. The program is implicated at the macro level in the reproduction of the problems that it is meant to resolve at the micro level.

Boeskov's adoption of Born's model helps us to understand that SATM may generate both positive and negative effects, both change and reproduction, at the same time. It is not just that there is little evidence of micro-level benefits rippling out to the macro level; it is also that the levels may actually be in contradiction. SATM may produce localized benefits for some participants while also supporting dynamics and policies that have more dubious impacts at urban and societal levels. The question then arises, to what degree should micro-level benefits for individuals be offset by macro-level drawbacks? How to weigh up a group of happy students in a classroom against urban policies that maintain inequality? How do socializing and pleasure stack up against coloniality, conservative gender norms, or hierarchical conceptions of culture and society? It may be tempting to focus on the more obvious and immediate benefits rather than the longer-term, more diffuse structural downsides. But El Sistema's most vociferous critics, like the pianist Gabriela Montero, have argued that it has helped to whitewash a government that has had a disastrous effect on Venezuela. In this view, the benefits that some individuals within the program may have accrued are outweighed by its collaboration in the downward trajectory of the country as a whole.[14] One of the many complicating issues in SATM is that what serves one small portion of society (participants and their families) may not serve society as a whole.

Considering SATM as operating on multiple levels simultaneously is something that many observers and researchers have failed to do sufficiently. Focusing on immediate impressions and ignoring or downplaying the structural and political planes has led to a proliferation of overly optimistic assessments, though there is now also a body of more critical studies that focus on those levels and offer a counterweight. Still, writing on SATM lags behind research on Medellín's urban renewal, in which the gap between a miraculous social narrative and more complex reality is now well recognized. With regard to SATM, many are still entranced by one part of the story. To be properly understood, SATM needs to be both observed closely and studied from a structural or political angle. That is not to say that every analysis needs both; however, the field needs both if interested readers are to gain a balanced picture of SATM, in all its complexity and ambiguity. Understanding the role of culture in urban renewal requires this kind of two-pronged or multi-planed approach.

Where Medellín differs from other places that have co-opted culture into urban reimaging is that its dominant, official narrative is not simply that culture makes the city a more vibrant or attractive place, but rather that it has overcome violence and renewed the city. The arts are presented as a transformative agent. Music has a particularly prominent role in stories of urban renewal in Medellín. Alongside the Red, there are innumerable media reports that have taken the hip-hop collectives Kolacho and 4ESkuela as drivers of the Medellín Miracle. Yet numerous scholars argue that social urbanism was espoused by the city's elites

---

14 Kozak Rovero (2018) and Esté's (2018) criticisms of Abreu as complicit in Venezuela's decline are somewhat analogous.

primarily for economic reasons and has served to perpetuate their dominance over and distance from the majority of their fellow citizens. Young musicians' participation in this narrative of culture overcoming violence is therefore not without its ambiguities. Those who benefit most from the *image* of a harmonious, culturally vibrant city are not necessarily those who participate in community arts programs, but rather those involved in the worlds of business and tourism. If this image has contributed to the maintenance of high levels of inequality, if it promotes Medellín as a flexibilized labour market and destination for foreign investment, it may actually constrain the very communities whose youth participate in its construction. Nevertheless, it is a narrative that appeals to all parties. Many people in Medellín believe that the Red has worked wonders, and it suits many people to believe so. Still, there are good reasons to believe only in half-miracles.

PART II

Fig. 27. Archive of Red de Escuelas de Música. CC BY.

5. Change

> In some sense our ability to open the future will depend not on how well we learn anymore but how well we are able to unlearn.
>
> Alan Kay

In her imagining of real utopias in music education, Ruth Wright (2019, 217) draws on Erik Olin Wright's vision of social justice-oriented research or emancipatory social science as focused on three tasks. Thus far I have focused on the first: "to elaborate a systematic diagnosis and critique of the world as it exists." I now pivot my attention towards the second—"to envision viable alternatives." Part II builds on the Red's search and fleshes out its rethinking of SATM, adding both complementary and contrasting analyses. To begin with, in this chapter I consider how changes in society and music education raise questions about orthodox SATM, how the search for alternatives to that orthodoxy has already begun, and where this path might lead.

Change in the Red

The original SATM programs were created at times and in places when most young people had few or no alternative activities, and keen students were willing and able to spend most of their non-school time studying music. Indeed, the idea became to occupy all their spare time to keep them off the streets. Abreu's main concern was training orchestral musicians quickly, but one of his many Victorian reformer-esque traits was a quasi-religious elevation of work and an explicit abhorrence of *ocio* (leisure, free time). Mantie (2018, 546) writes that "self-appointed moral guardians sought to impose their vision of proper behaviour through recommended free time activities. Concern over the conduct of others was often driven by a fear that people—that is, people of lower social classes—would not use their time appropriately." He is describing nineteenth-century advocates of "rational recreation," but he could just as well be referring to Abreu proposing to rescue disadvantaged youths from "an empty, disorientated, and deviant youth." The original SATM programs were essentially *intensified* versions of conventional music education, and their level was high because students dedicated so much time to them. There was no miracle, no revolutionary pedagogy: musical achievements rested on a huge investment of time and a leader who persuaded young people to make it through a mixture of charisma, incentives, and promises. El Sistema and the Red had two levels of intensity: high and higher. Weekends and holidays were seen as an opportunity to increase the workload, not rest. Even Abreu himself said that there was no secret: El Sistema was built simply on "work and study."[1]

But twenty years on, Medellín is full of free cultural and sports programs, and new technologies provide endless sources of distraction. The old model of intensity and exclusive focus is no longer so appealing to many students or their families. In the global North, programs inspired by El Sistema did not even attempt to adopt a similar level of intensity, acknowledging—sometimes grudgingly (see Mota and Teixeira Lopes 2017)—that it was impossible to recreate in their social contexts, but they did generally opt for a higher amount of instruction than was the norm. However, even this more modest attempt at intensity can be a source of friction. In their study of a North American SATM program, Hopkins, Provenzano, and Spencer (2017, 254) found that "increased intensity was the source of most of the benefits *and* challenges reported by the participants." The high level of time commitment required meant that attendance was a problem, and some students (and the researchers) raised concerns over the focus on excellence that accompanied the intensity. Most strikingly, "[i]n the student focus-group interview there

---

1 YOLA National at Home, "The Philosophy of El Sistema", https://www.youtube.com/watch?v=DMDTfTgFaOA.

was near unanimous opinion to reduce the number of meeting days per week or the length of the after-school rehearsals" (251). El Sistema's only unique selling point was thus difficult to implement in practice and unpopular with the students.

In the Red, too, intensity might be regarded as a major source of both benefits and challenges—another example of SATM's ambiguity. The program's "golden age" had been characterized by intensity not just of time but also of atmosphere. It shared with El Sistema teachers, repertoire, and methods, and also charismatic leadership, inspiring pep talks, total commitment and absorption, and a quasi-religious or cult-like aspect. For those who stuck with the Red, intensity had its upsides, and gradually rowing back from it since 2005 provoked a sense of loss and nostalgia for some members of the first generation. Yet it also incited more ambivalent and negative reactions, and most staff recognized that twenty years on, it was no longer possible or appropriate.

The Red started to acknowledge and tackle the downsides of intensity quite a few years ago, questioning the El Sistema-esque focus on endless playing in search of artistic perfection, and encouraging instead a diversification of activities and a less pressured approach. In 2014, the social team asked: "How can we minimize the [Red's] negative impact on formal education [and] guarantee space for family life [...]?" (*Síntesis* 2014, 5). Historically, the Red had absorbed time that would otherwise be used for recreation and domestic chores, but the social team recognized such activities as important and did not agree that music education should compete with them.

During my fieldwork, a number of teachers stressed that leisure time was important for students and that young people should not have an overly packed schedule. In one meeting, a director argued that it was scientifically proven that downtime, rest, and moments for doing nothing were important to human beings. This was a far cry from Abreu's demonization of *ocio* as a root of crime and social problems, but it was in accordance with local youth researchers: Rincón (2015, 132), for example, argues that youth "is a state where you have to lose yourself to find yourself, where it is worth wasting time, where free time (*ocio*) is gained to relax [...]. What have to be created are the conditions to waste time in useless projects and collective play, and thereby carve out time to be young."[2]

José, a school director, reflected at length on the issue of change and diversification since the 1990s:

> Before there was just music, [but] the offering has changed [in the city], now there is theatre, literature, photography, painting... For me it's great that a kid says: "Sir, I can't stay here till 9 pm playing like a crazy thing, because I've got to go to my art class." That was fine at the time, but... we've got to move on.

He was sceptical about the nostalgia of the Red's first generation, arguing that the first phase had been less rosy than they claimed:

> The Siempre Juntos generation never read a book, painted, played, no family time, cinema... it was all orchestra. How sad to have a life where you don't want to be in your own house. It didn't lead to social improvement in the sense of forming better citizens; rather, they created a parallel society where they enjoyed being together and that was it. Play, play, play [music], and nothing else.[3] [...] There were no alternatives, the only book that people had in the house was the Bible. Now that has changed, there are the library parks, Comfama, the public programs. There has been a big transformation in the city in recent years, now the kids don't want to devote themselves only to music and close the door to everything else. It's more important to be a rounded kid who reads and does other things and not just be glued to their instrument. [...] I prefer a kid who reads, who can talk about politics, than an idiot who just plays and plays.

Even nostalgic members of the first generation acknowledged that society and culture had changed, and with young people now presented with many more options and distractions, there was no going back to the intensity of the old days. One, now a school director, told me: Medellín is a different place today, and the Red should adapt to the world that the students live in, rather than trying to adapt students to the ways of the 1990s. Intensity—even the lowered level in comparison

---

[2] An increasing number of writers on work, productivity, and creativity, too, argue for the value of alternating periods of intensity and rest in order to improve the quality of work and allow for the incubation of new ideas. Unrelenting intensity can have both mental and physical costs.

[3] The Spanish word *tocar* does not have the dual meaning of the English "play." It simply means to play music.

with the past—was seen by many staff, students, and parents as an impediment and a source of attrition: they often remarked about older students dropping out because the Red took too much time away from schoolwork and hobbies. In 2018, both management and staff pointed to the rapid escalation of time commitment between the first and second years as an important factor in the high dropout rate among younger students. A first-generation student-turned-teacher noted that the age profile was much lower in 2018 than in the early years. Most of his students were now in the eight-to-ten age-range. His implication was that the Red was losing its hold on teenagers. Indeed, in 2018, 64% of students were twelve or under—a revealing figure considering that the Red's age range was seven to twenty-five and students could start as late as fourteen. Demand was still high at entry level, but interest dropped off dramatically. SATM had been very appealing when there were few alternatives but it struggled with retention now that young people had more options.

By 2018, intensity seemed to hang over the Red like a ghost: many of the Red's veterans lamented its departure, yet they generally acknowledged that it was gone and could never return. There was nostalgia for the first phase, but I never heard the argument that the Red should simply turn back the clock. The Red's past was a ghost that some could not quite let go of, rather than one they actively desired to bring back to life.

Practice and research in music education more broadly have changed considerably since El Sistema was created and spread across Latin America to places like Medellín. Greater emphasis on child-centred learning, creativity, and curricular diversity raises major questions about a narrow, top-down, repetitive model. El Sistema has been revealed as riven with operational and educational flaws, but allegations of serious irregularities have also emerged from El Sistema-inspired programs in Mexico and Guatemala, suggesting issues with the model itself.[4] Not only is it out of kilter with contemporary educational thinking, but it has also in some places reproduced rather than challenged societal problems such as authoritarianism and corruption.

---

4   See for example my blog post "'False philanthropy' in the Sistema-inspired sphere", https://geoffbakermusic.wordpress.com/el-sistema-the-system/el-sistema-blog/false-philanthropy-in-the-sistema-inspired-sphere/.

El Sistema was created to train orchestral musicians, and while this focus may have made sense in oil-rich, twentieth-century "Saudi Venezuela," as it was nicknamed, massifying this approach around the world is much harder to justify today. Since the late 1990s, El Sistema has claimed that its purpose is not in fact to train musicians, yet not only is this strategic discourse a denial of the program's origins, but also many students who are given this pre-professional training do indeed go on to develop professional ambitions (Agrech 2018). In Medellín, 20% of Red students were expected to go on to music performance degrees in 2006 (Arango 2006). Yet they are trained for a profession that, even before COVID-19, was not only hyper-competitive but also stagnant or shrinking in many parts of the world. The challenges of trying to make a career in classical music have become increasingly obvious in the twenty-first century. It is one thing to provide young people with music education, but another to provide them with training that encourages them to aspire to an orchestral career. Such training may be perfect for those who want to be orchestral musicians, but it is an illogical choice for mass music education in the 2020s. Whether one looks at the career prospects for musicians or the social goals of SATM, music education on this scale should be broader.

At the projects fair in 2019, the head of the Red's popular music ensemble gave a heartfelt and somewhat anguished speech questioning whether the Red was preparing students for the future. Today, he said, you don't need to play an instrument to make music or write notation to compose. Conventional figures like the composer and the instrumental performer are in decline. Young people have a different conception of music than adults. Major technological changes are happening and adults are being left behind by young people and their ways of working. How is the Red reflecting this new reality, he asked? How could it persuade young people to play instruments like the oboe or the tuba that do not feature in their lives? And why should it? Do we really know what music the kids listen to and want to make? Are we preparing them for the world of music that they live in and the one that is around the corner, or are we recreating the world of the past that we come from?

In short, the original model of SATM—long hours, exclusive dedication, little life outside music, preparing students for the orchestral profession—is poorly suited to the social and musical realities of the present in contexts of digital, cultural, and recreational abundance. In many places it is impossible to reproduce today. Its constituent elements have been much critiqued by music education researchers for many years. The challenge is therefore to create new forms of SATM that accord with current values, possibilities, and musical and technological realities, allow students to be involved in other extra-curricular activities as well, and can be pursued in more humane and time-efficient ways.

Giraldo spoke often about changes in the city and the wider world over the twenty years since the program's foundation, and he presented change in the Red as a logical and necessary response. *Reading the city* was central to the discourse of his team. When management and staff mentioned the old slogan "a child who takes up an instrument will never take up a weapon," it was often to point out its decreased relevance twenty years after the program's creation. There was widespread recognition that keeping children off the streets was no longer enough—that the Red had to imagine a new purpose and a new form.

SATM in Movement

The Red is not unique; change is in the air elsewhere too. In South America, Argentina's Programa Social Andrés Chazarreta is a national SATM program that focuses on Latin American traditional and popular music. It was founded on a critique of, and as an alternative to, Abreu's model.[5] Other programs have adapted over time. Eduardo Torres, musical director of the Brazilian SATM program NEOJIBA (Núcleos Estaduais de Orquestras Juvenis e Infantis da Bahia), wrote: "the management team of NEOJIBA read your book in November 2014, and in December, we presented, chapter by chapter, your findings and critical comments to our pedagogical team and to all members of the main orchestra, in order to foster discussion. Some strategic decisions we have been taking since then had influence from the book, and from these internal discussions."[6] These decisions included creating a psychosocial support team; producing annual reports on the social profile of beneficiaries; increasing the diversity of musical practice; enabling

---

5   Personal communication from the program's founder, Eduardo Tacconi.
6   Personal communication (cited with permission).

students to take decisions about repertoire and activities; and creating a more comprehensive but also flexible curriculum. Batuta, a nationwide program in Colombia, started with close ties to El Sistema, but it has forged a distinctive path in recent years. At the SIMM conference in Bogotá in July 2019, a senior Batuta representative presented a four-part model: collective musical practice, a constructivist pedagogical model, collective creation, and psychosocial accompaniment.[7] Of these elements, only the first derives from El Sistema (and it is hardly unique to that program).

In mid-2018, the Red participated in a three-day international conference in São Paulo organized by the Brazilian SATM program Guri and the international NGO Jeunesses Musicales. Entitled "For all: Youth and musical connections," the event explored issues such as autonomy, identity, youth development, collective composition, group improvisation, and the changing nature of the music profession. It thus addressed a number of SATM's historical weak spots, and with no mention of El Sistema in the conference program, it provided further evidence of moves to decentre the Venezuelan model and explore alternatives in some corners of South America. When Giraldo returned from Brazil, he talked about his desire to align the Red further with this progressive current. Inspired by this snapshot of life outside the box of orthodox SATM, he realized that the Red could work on bigger problems, in tougher contexts, with more innovative methods.

The label "El Sistema-inspired" (ESI), now widespread in the global North, therefore reflects a historical reality but also obscures a more nuanced contemporary scenario, in which some programs have distanced themselves from the Venezuelan program in practice and/or ideology. There was a clear rupture in the case of the Red, but my private conversations with staff in some other Latin American programs have revealed attitudes to El Sistema and its model that are more mixed than is commonly supposed. Argentina is an example of a country where there is a variety of orchestral programs with different origins, aims, approaches, and political leanings, including the Chazarreta, whose founder was scathing about Abreu's Eurocentrism. The reality is thus

---

7   Catherine Surace, "Batuta y su papel en la consolidación de un discurso sobre las artes y la transformación social", SIMM-posium 4, 26 July 2019.

more complex than the reverential "El Sistema-inspired" movement that some would like to imagine.

Shifting to North America, one of the first ESI programs to be created in the US, Orchkids in Baltimore, has emphasised the development of collaborative composition in recent years. In 2018–19, Sistema Toronto implemented a Social Development Curriculum, which looks like an attempt to prioritize social action in practice as well as discourse. Each month, students explored a theme such as teamwork, listening, or respect, and discussed its meaning and applications.[8] The El Sistema-inspired Sister Cities Girlchoir is a "girl empowerment choral academy"—a fascinating inversion of the Venezuelan "masculine brotherhood of Knights Templar of classical music" (Kozak Rovero 2018) with its glass ceiling for women and troubling gender relations. The YOLA National Symposium in Los Angeles in mid-2019 focused on topics such as power, voice, and creativity, thereby drawing much closer to critical scholarship on SATM. Such research may still have been viewed askance in some North American Sistema circles, but the gap in ideas had shrunk considerably; what had been controversial or even unmentionable just a few years earlier was now at the heart of the discussion. The 2020 edition of the YOLA event gave the impression of a program moving further away from El Sistema and closer to progressive music education each year.

Brad Barrett's work at the Conservatory Lab Charter School (CLCS) makes an important contribution to the topic of artistic citizenship, and if the school was initially inspired by El Sistema, its more recent work is worlds away from Venezuelan practice. According to Barrett (2018, 10):

> resident artists at CLCS have developed a learning community that balances technical development with creative practice, encourages reflective processes, and places importance on democratically run ensembles—with the overall intention of developing artistic citizenship. [...] At CLCS, there is a clear shift from simply supporting students to execute written music provided for them to guiding students who create music, text, and art for the purpose of examining and expressing their social realities.

---

8   Sistema Toronto, "Social development", https://www.sistema-toronto.ca/about-us/our-program/social-development.

In a study of SATM programs in Canada and Argentina, Brook and Frega (2020) argue that the field has moved so far from its progenitor that it should stop using El Sistema as a point of reference.

Beyond the labels, then, a decentring of the Venezuelan model is in progress, if to differing degrees in different places. One current in SATM has seen an initial burst of enthusiasm for El Sistema, followed by an awakening to certain weaknesses and a sotto-voce process of critical distancing. The Red started out as virtually an annex of El Sistema, yet today there are no connections and the Venezuelan program is not mentioned in any public-facing materials. The International Society for Music Education adopted an advocacy stance when it created an El Sistema Special Interest Group in 2012, but it changed the name and removed the reference to El Sistema in 2020, as the group had become both more wide-ranging and more critical. Such examples may point to a future in which there is more that separates SATM programs from El Sistema than links them, and the Venezuelan program is gradually sidelined within the field (except for publicity purposes).

The momentum behind change is thus building, in the practice sphere as well as within the research world. New paths are opening up, but much still remains to be done. The Red serves as a perfect example of both. It was a force for good in a complicated city, providing access to music education to many who might otherwise have missed out and also a space of socialization that had positive sides. Particularly in its first phase, it provided safe spaces for young people that were sorely lacking elsewhere. There *was* something miraculous about the emergence of this program in the dark decade of the 1990s. Yet as times changed, the need grew to conceive of music education as more than just an escape from the problems of the streets. A succession of Red leaders felt that the program ought to go further, that its social processes were incomplete, that students deserved more agency and voice. Other social programs—including arts-based ones—grew up around the Red and implemented more progressive agendas, treating students as protagonists, creators, and citizens. A comparative perspective did not flatter the Red. In 2017–18, the Red was engaged in an ambitious process of transformation, yet it remained the most conservative of Medellín's municipal arts education programs, the only one to have resisted revolution several years earlier.

The Red had achieved a lot in its first twenty years, yet like the city of Medellín, the miracle was only half-complete.

However, there is a curious paradox here. My research suggested that public perceptions of the Red were overly optimistic—that it was not quite the success story that was widely imagined. Yet when it came to internal perspectives, I had the opposite sensation: that they were sometimes overly pessimistic. The disruption that accompanied change meant that the glass looked half-empty to many staff and students, and even broken to some. But as a researcher who had spent the previous decade examining a flawed program defined by stasis, I saw the changes—however halting and contested—as a sign that the glass was half-full. To return to the notion of growing pains, many employees felt the pains more clearly, whereas what caught my attention was the growing. Recall Bartleet and Higgins (2018, 8) on CM: discomfort and tensions "are quite possibly a sign of health and growth."

The path has not been straightforward and progress has been bumpy at times, but the Red has taken important steps. It has recognized the need for change, identified important issues, and made a real effort to tackle them. Its leaders deserve credit for attempting to modify a large, longstanding, highly regarded program, especially given the larger hemispheric context where continuity has generally been the norm. External consultants hired by the IDB in 1997 urged major reforms on El Sistema, but Abreu ignored them, buried the reports, and continued to pursue his personal mission and his own formula of the same but bigger (Baker and Frega 2018). In contrast, I encountered the Red—also around the twenty-year mark—trying (once again) to change course, taking the need for reform seriously. It serves as an example that self-critique and change *are* possible in such programs, even if they are not easy.

If El Sistema is a supposed success story that turned out to be riddled with failures, the Red's changes of direction were often regarded internally as partial failures, yet some elements were successful and, from an educational perspective, they constituted a valuable experiment. As Bell and Raffe (1991) note, an operational failure can still be a scientific success if it contributes to knowledge and points towards more productive paths. The change in emphasis from transforming lives to transforming the city constituted a positive development from deficit thinking to artistic citizenship, and the fact that there was much more discussion in meetings of transforming the Red than transforming its students underlined the recognition that a paradigm shift was in order.

In this sense, there may in fact be more for the rest of the world to learn from Medellín than from Venezuela. With its vast size, its politician-leader, and its petro-state support, El Sistema at its peak was simultaneously the cornerstone of SATM and completely inimitable—a cultural manifestation of Venezuela's highly peculiar "magical state" (Coronil 1997). Medellín's combination of progressive surface and neoliberal underpinnings is closer to many of the contexts where SATM has taken root in the global North, and the possibilities and limitations of SATM emerge more clearly in this somewhat less baroque context. This is not to suggest that the Red's experiences will be equally relevant everywhere, but they provide a concrete example of El Sistema's adaptation, a word that has been central to the ESI field since 2007. The program's successes, struggles, and failures in adapting SATM may be instructive for many.

A Need for New Models

The discourse of SATM was created to advocate for Venezuela's orchestral culture and classical music education; it was in essence a funding and marketing strategy.[9] This approach has been widely reproduced with the international spread of El Sistema since 2007, which has seen SATM adopted by many symphony organizations. It is no coincidence that Los Angeles emerged as the centre of SATM in the US under the reign of the orchestral über-strategist Deborah Borda at the LA Philharmonic (see Fink 2016). If such institutions' priority is for SATM to contribute to their image and sustainability—justifying and promoting their work to funders, donors, the media, and the public, and pitching for new audiences—then perceptions may be paramount. As Rimmer (2020, 3) notes in his study of the English ESI program In Harmony, a policy may be ineffective as a program but perform well in terms of optics and political benefits; policies thus have symbolic dimensions and "questions of 'success'/'failure' are as much bound up with the ways

---

9   Hence it is unsurprising that the IDB's 2017 evaluation found so little evidence of social effects.

they are presented and perceived as their efficacy in achieving specified goals." His evidence suggests that In Harmony's social achievements have been modest, but the program has attracted outsized government, institutional, and media attention because it "appears to have provided a rhetorical platform from which to rejuvenate classical music's image at a time of diminishing cultural relevancy, audiences and funding" (5). In these terms, it has been a great success. As a support act for classical music, SATM is a winning formula and no change is needed.

From the perspective of social development, however, its effectiveness is much more questionable, and it raises myriad cultural, political, philosophical, and ethical questions. In the 1990s, Abreu mixed orchestral training with social development discourse and deliberately muddied the issue of what his real goal was. This blurring has continued as ESI programs have blossomed around the world. But those who are serious about SATM need to re-clarify this issue and ask: what is the ultimate goal? Is it social change or musical development? Are music students the ends, or are they the means to ends like diversifying, marketing, and funding music organizations? Is SATM at heart about rebranding and opening up new markets for orchestral music, or is the social objective paramount and therefore the format and genre up for negotiation? Is orchestral inclusion a response to demand from communities or is it driven by supply from the classical music sector?[10]

The answer to such questions cannot be "both," because marketing classical music and pursuing social development demand different approaches. If social change is the primary objective in reality and not just a strategic discourse, then new models are required. As Govias (2020) put it caustically, there is little sense in hoping that "outdated, deprecated or conservative pedagogies or models [...] will someday produce results different from the last 300 years of their implementation."

---

10 Godwin (2020, 16), who worked for an Australian ESI program, considers such questions, and her conclusion is clear: "the primary interest of the symphony orchestras running Sistema-inspired programs is to support the continuance of the institution of classical music and the orchestra." She pinpoints the moral ambiguity of this approach: "El Sistema, when appropriated by classical music organisations in Australia, is an effective tool to harness the hearts and wallets of donors, media and supporters. This appropriation, when done uncritically, enmeshes all involved in a deceit, unknowingly or knowingly, consciously or unconsciously" (19).

In other words, as successive Red managements have understood, the focus needs to shift from *changing the world* to *changing SATM itself*.

There is, put simply, little chance of the former without first embarking on the latter. Just as studies of development have put the spotlight on development organizations, SATM needs to re-envision itself before it re-envisions society. In their critique of the Canadian orchestral sector's engagement with Indigenous artists and artists of colour, Peerbaye and Attariwala (2019, 24) argue that inclusion is not enough; rather, a fundamental shift is required by symphony institutions, "to un-settle their own systems and structures: not only organizationally, but artistically and creatively." This is not a call that SATM—which recruits BIPOC students into orchestral culture around the world—can afford to ignore.

We have seen much evidence of past and present changes in the preceding pages. What might be key topics for attention in the future? Where might imagining new models begin?

Fig. 28. Archive of Red de Escuelas de Música. CC BY.

The Social in SATM

The most obvious place to start is by reconsidering the key elements of the SATM equation—the social and the musical—and the relationship between them. The word "social" is central to the SATM field, sprinkled over its activities like magic dust, but what does it mean? In Medellín it was a disputed term. The Red's founder, Ocampo, saw it as synonymous with "human" and criticized the tendency to use it as signifying "for the poor." There was a move in 2018 to understand it in more political, spatial, and relational terms: to conceptualize society as "those out there" and not just "us in here," and to focus on how students related to the former (community, territory, city, including those with no direct contact with the program) as well as the latter (other music students, families, audiences). In SATM more widely, the social is often interpreted by students as socializing, by leaders as moral and behavioural improvement, and by advocates as a cognitive and academic boost or a tool against poverty and violence. For Montoya Restrepo, behind the miracle narrative, the "social" in social urbanism was a mixture of basic state obligations, marketing, and control—a conclusion that is very important for an analysis of SATM, pushing us to think beyond emotive but problematic narratives about saving the poor and consider the social label in terms of power, politics, economics, and image.

The main practical effect of the word "social" has been to open the door to funding, prestige, and media coverage. The late twentieth century saw a move toward a utilitarian view of culture around the globe; increasingly, the prime way to convince government and business leaders to support cultural activity was to argue for its social and economic impact (Yúdice 2003). For example, the rhetoric of social inclusion entered the arts world in the United Kingdom during the 1990s, as a response to the previous decade's decline in public funding and questioning of high culture's automatic right to subsidy (Belfiore 2002). Social discourse has been central to the rhetorical transformation of classical music, particularly in the realms of education and outreach; it has increasingly displaced cultural arguments to justify training many young people in music that is a minority interest. "Social" is a word that, in practice, is closely tied to strategy and resources. If some of my interlocutors saw this word as charged with human meaning, others regarded it as an empty term that was increasingly attached to many cultural activities in a bid for public funds.

It is important also to consider the words to which "social" is attached—such as action, inclusion, mobility, change, justice, and impact—and how each one signifies a different and sometimes contradictory ideology.[11] There is often slippage and confusion, particularly as practices and terms cross international borders. In North America, El Sistema attracts labels like "social justice" and "social change" that are rarely if ever attached to the program in Venezuela, and in fact jar with Abreu's political conservatism.[12] In Chapter 4, I raised questions over the framing of orthodox SATM in terms of social change, given its propensity to social reproduction. Similarly, the term "social justice" should not be connected to a program founded on the ideology that social problems result from individual deficits, since social justice social work explicitly rejects this stance (e.g. Baines 2017; Nixon 2019). Nor should it be attached to a program whose social injustices have been repeatedly documented over a period of two decades and which has reduced music students to playing a propaganda role for an authoritarian government accused of grave violations of human rights. As Spruce (2017, 723) notes, partly in relation to SATM, "although there is a strong commitment to the ideals of social justice within the music education community, these ideals are often not underpinned by the conceptual and theoretical principles which might enable them to be argued for and acted upon." What is more, "an absence of conceptual and theoretical underpinning leaves social justice *as a term* vulnerable to being appropriated in order to promote and/or sustain approaches to, and discourses of, music education that work against these ideals."

"Social" thus covers a dizzying variety of meanings and aspirations. Bringing clarity and rigour to this conceptual proliferation and (at times) confusion is an important step towards sharpening understandings of the field, strengthening its theoretical base, and achieving greater alignment between ideals, discourses, and actions.

As leaders of the Red have argued consistently since 2005, if such an institution is to present itself as a social program, to claim social outcomes as its key purpose rather than an accidental byproduct, then it

---

11 For example, the UK's Labour Party abandoned social mobility as a goal in 2019 in favour of social justice (Stewart 2019). See also my blog post "Is Sistema a 'movement'?", https://geoffbakermusic.wordpress.com/el-sistema-older-posts/is-sistema-a-movement/.

12 El Sistema sponsor Hilti Foundation combines linguistic slippage with historical revision, confusing Abreu's "social inclusion" with "social change" and projecting it back to 1975, more than two decades before its emergence (https://www.hiltifoundation.org/music-for-social-change).

needs to take the social more seriously. This step has both conceptual and practical angles: analyzing the term "social" more deeply and specifying the objective, but also designing activities around that objective rather than musical goals. The word that the Red's social team used frequently was *intencionar*. This word encapsulated a sense of taking an active rather than passive approach to social action: shaping and directing activities towards specific goals rather than allowing processes to occur spontaneously (or not). The team was aware that positive social effects sometimes arose as a natural consequence of music-making, but it urged the Red to hone its activities so that they were focused on producing such outcomes more consistently.

The form that this directing or honing might take deserves further consideration. The Red saw a contest between two visions of SATM (as discussed in Chapter 2). The dominant (though not universal) view among the musical staff was that social action was an inherent feature of music education. The management and particularly the social team, however, discovered negative social processes in the Red as well as positive ones and thus argued that explicit, compensatory social activities were necessary. Some musicians, too, recognized that music education sometimes fostered undesirable social and personal traits and that their training did not prepare them properly for achieving the social objective of the Red; consequently, they saw social action as primarily a job for non-musical professionals. In very simplistic terms, the Red's first decade was dominated by the implicit view, the second by the explicit one.

Both visions have their merits. Implicit social action is a real phenomenon, and there were musicians within the Red who bolstered the implicit argument: who put the human side first, whose practice matched their discourse, whose students seemed positive and empowered, and who carried off SATM successfully with a mixture of musical skills and radiant personality. The problem for a large program is that it is challenging to find hundreds of teachers with these characteristics. Human beings are imperfect, and so SATM based on the implicit philosophy shows the full range of human flaws. The evidence from Medellín and Venezuela suggests that conventional orchestral or band training does not necessarily constitute either a thorough or an entirely positive social education, that an implicit approach to the social can pass on problematic aspects of social and musical cultures, and that music education could have more significant positive social effects if it were tailored and strengthened. A large public program cannot run equitably and effectively on charisma alone; explicit methods and tools for social action are also necessary.[13]

However, if the Red's first decade revealed the flaws in the implicit approach, the second did the same with the explicit, not least because the latter encountered resistance from musical staff. Attempts to add a social ingredient around the music-making had limited success because of the squeeze on time and musical activities that they produced. The social became seen as a distraction or waste of precious rehearsal time. As noted in Chapter 2, one school director described the work of the social team as: "1. A balm that soothes the injustices and tough demands [...] and softens the rigidity of the musical processes. 2. Interventions that make no sense" ("Informe" 2017a, 148). The implicit approach led to problems (injustices, tough demands, rigidity), but the explicit approach soothed those problems only to create others (interventions perceived by musicians as senseless). Adding the social side to the musical—for example, social discussions in the spaces around conventional music education—led to mixed results.

The solution is a combination: implicit *and* explicit, with the social action working *through* music as well as *around* it, in the form of music educational activities shaped by the social objectives. For SATM to work implicitly, musical activities need to be congruous with social goals. It makes no sense for a program to claim that it is striving towards peace, coexistence or solidarity, yet to structure itself in a way that produces competition between individuals, instruments, and ensembles. It makes no sense for a program to claim that it is fostering teamwork, yet to deny students opportunities to negotiate, collaborate, solve problems, and take collective decisions. Research in Medellín, Venezuela, and Buenos Aires has shown that students generally saw SATM as a space of enjoyment and socializing rather than an opportunity to develop social skills (see Chapter 4). The Red's social team pursued the latter goal, but still largely missing were *ways of learning music* designed to foster social skills and exploiting the distinctive features of this art. The implication is that for all the Red's concern over its social objective from 2005 onwards,

---

13   Rimmer (2020) shows that relying on teachers' charisma loomed large in plans for In Harmony Sistema England.

what the program really needed was a musical revolution, not just a social one.

The Red made moves towards such a revolution during my fieldwork. The social team argued that "the pedagogical model should set out which specific values should be fostered in the students and how they may be developed in every action and learning situation" ("Informe" 2017a, 188). The shift to PBL, though, was the biggest step in this direction. The best projects combined implicit and explicit approaches, musical and non-musical activities. They were at heart musical projects, but they often began by identifying a social topic or problem, and their collective construction was a form of social learning. The example of San Javier from Chapter 1 illustrates this advance.

Such questions find echoes in music education research. In their study of an ESI program, Ilari, Fesjian, and Habibi (2018, 8–9) noted that "effects of music education on children's social skills have been found mainly in programs that followed specialized curricula," and

> for music education programs to be effective in developing social skills, perhaps it is necessary to devise curricula that not only break down traditional hierarchies found in collective musical experiences, but also afford children ample opportunities to exercise social skills such as empathy, theory of mind, and prosociality in more direct ways.

In other words, they suggest that for SATM programs to be socially effective, they ought to develop socially focused curricula (such as Sistema Toronto's), rather than relying on a social reading of conventional collective music-making (like El Sistema). Laurence (2008) and Rabinowitch (2012) provide two examples of music education designed specifically for the promotion of empathy, which looks quite different from conventional musical training.

Other researchers point to pedagogy as a focal point for reform. Cobo Dorado's (2015) analysis of group pedagogy shows how more innovative ways of learning music collectively may foster more positive social outcomes. Hess's (2019) vision of music education and social change resolves the implicit/explicit tension: her pedagogies of community, expression, and noticing all have explicit dimensions, yet they also work through, not just around, music-making. But whether the focus is curriculum or pedagogy or both, such work points to the importance of looking beyond the orthodox conception of SATM—as conventional music education with a (theoretically) expanded social constituency—towards the creation of a distinctive SATM method, one that makes the social objective visible in the activities themselves.

In the wider music education field, then, there is increasing critical awareness of the relationship between the social and the musical, and a growing understanding that some kinds of musical activities might be more promising from a social perspective than others. Large, conducted, performing ensembles are an efficient and attractive way to organize large numbers of young musicians, but they may actually be the least effective tool for fostering social skills in students through music education. Govias (2015a), a conductor himself, has called the conventional orchestra "the most anti-social mode of cultural expression."

Orthodox SATM is built on an idealization of large ensembles and an assumption that playing music together with many others generates positive interpersonal dynamics. The flawed nature of this assumption is laid bare in studies of El Sistema and internal documents from the Red. Many of its component elements, such as the supposed generation of teamwork, turn out to be questionable. Orchestras may create various kinds of communal identity, but this is not the same as teamwork; indeed, they may foster cliques and divisions, tensions and rivalries. Competition ran through El Sistema and the Red in their heyday, as it does in the classical music world. It is important to examine collective musical activities in more precise and realistic ways. If "collective" means everybody doing the same thing at the same time with minimal communication between them, directed by a single figure of authority, then the social benefits are likely to be minimal; the political drawbacks are even more obvious, since this is a model of autocracy. With so much research now available on SATM in particular and orchestras and music education in general, there is no excuse for avoiding taking a hard, critical look at the version of SATM popularized by such programs.

The crucial issue is the quality of the interaction between participants. Both research and experience suggest that smaller groupings and activities other than performance (such as composing, improvising, or arranging) may be more productive in this respect.[14] Franco's urge for

---

14 Another logical response is experimenting with or removing the role of the conductor (the focus of Govias's reformist efforts).

more informality and smaller ensembles in the Red was driven primarily by musical considerations, but there is also research to support this shift from social, political, psychological, and cognitive perspectives.

Hess (2021, 63), for example, suggests that if social relations are the priority, "we might consider the types of musicking that facilitate relational engagement," which points to formats such as chamber music or drum circles rather than large conducted ensembles in which musicians are focused mainly on their written music and the conductor. At Boston's CLCS, most ensembles function as chamber music groups. As Barrett (2018, 26) notes: "many ensembles are constructed to promote a more democratic practice than traditional orchestral instruction. Resident artists seek to undermine the authoritarian tendencies of the orchestral construct to give students more voice and control in their musical experience."

Shieh and Allsup (2016) propose an approach that is suggestive for the Red's schools and SATM more broadly: reframing the large ensemble as a collective. This is a flexible, hybrid paradigm in which "multiple projects exist simultaneously and are loosely connected in a community of support" (33). Collectives may coalesce as large ensembles, but also as small groups, individual work, online and offline musicking, composing, making podcasts or radio shows, or any number of other music-related activities. A collective is not large *or* small but rather *both/and*; with groupings and activities shifting according to circumstances, it is a promising model for uncertain times. Shieh and Allsup also imply that frequently breaking down into smaller ensembles is likely to increase student autonomy and independence.

Crooke and McFerran (2014) argue that groups of four to ten students are best for programs focused on psychosocial wellbeing, an assertion backed up by Bolger (2015). After Ilari, Fesjian, and Habibi (2018) found that three years' musical training in an El Sistema-inspired program produced no significant effect on prosociality, confirming the results of the IDB's study of the Venezuelan program, they concluded that "it is probably more difficult to develop and engage in mind reading and prosocial behaviors in large ensembles than in smaller ones" (8). Cobo Dorado (2015) argues that a horizontal learning dynamic (which is easier in smaller groups) produces greater cognitive benefits than a more vertical one (characteristic of large ensembles). Heinemeyer (2018) argues: "To thrive emotionally, young people need their own time and space, that is not explicitly directed at particular outcomes." Good mental health is associated with "exploratory, informal, and pupil directed activity." These are not obvious features of conventional large ensembles. If the priority is the psychosocial wellbeing of students, SATM might well look away from orchestral or band training and toward fields such as music therapy and CM (Crooke et al. 2016).

As for activities, a recent collection of essays makes a strong case for improvisation as a particularly promising tool for social inclusion.[15] It also takes full account of the complexity and risks of the concept of social inclusion—something that has been rare in SATM. Another recent study found evidence to suggest that learning improvisation may have a greater effect on cognitive function than non-improvisatory music instruction (Norgaard, Stambaugh, and McCranie 2019). It supplements Koutsoupidou and Hargreaves's (2009) experimental study, which demonstrated that learning improvisation promotes the development of creative thinking to a greater extent than didactic teaching and may therefore be particularly promising for children's cognitive and emotional development.

A fundamental rethink of SATM's model also makes good sense if we bear in mind the history of the field. El Sistema focused on the orchestra because Abreu was a conductor and he wanted to lead his own orchestra and train young musicians up for this profession. The SATM model is thus driven by Abreu's ambitions, personal preferences, and ideology, not demonstrable advantages with regard to social outcomes. His initial goals were explicitly musical. The social only entered the picture two decades later, as a means of justifying and expanding what El Sistema already did. Nearly fifty years on from El Sistema's beginnings, and with a wealth of research now to draw on, it makes little sense to follow Abreu's route as though it had been designed with social action in mind.[16]

---

15   Special issue of *Contemporary Music Review* (38:5, 2019).
16   It is possible that Abreu might have stumbled accidentally on a perfect formula for social action while pursuing El Sistema's original aim of training orchestral musicians, stated in its founding constitution (see Baker 2014), but, as we have seen, the evidence suggests otherwise.

A SATM program that put social action first would logically start from an analysis of local social problems and build up from there to possible musical solutions. SATM began the other way round: Abreu created an orchestral training scheme, and then two decades later presented (speculative) statements about how it was also an ideal solution to certain social issues. Discipline was his watchword, but it was never clear what societal problem discipline was supposed to solve. No serious social scientist would regard societal poverty, violence, or crime as a consequence of a lack of discipline. As Freire (1974; 2005) argued, transformation starts with critical questioning of norms. Teaching young people to be more ordered and disciplined will only lead to the existing order functioning in a more efficient and pleasant way. The global proliferation of ESI programs has generally been led by the perceived solution (admiration for the Venezuelan model) rather than a mapping and analysis of local social contexts, problems, and opinions (see e.g. Allan et al 2010). Such an approach would be anathema to the development field today, yet it remains quite commonplace in music.

One of Abreu's favourite aphorisms, much quoted by his admirers, was "culture for the poor must never be poor culture." It was used to justify the centrality of classical music in SATM and also the vast expenditure of social funds on El Sistema's headquarters and top-of-the-range instruments for its touring ensembles. A more productive line for the 2020s would be "education for the poor must not be poor education." Rather than perpetuating much-questioned practices, SATM should to strive to provide a socially-focused, research-informed music education.[17]

Recolonizing or Decolonizing the Ear?

An important development that relates to both the social and musical sides of SATM is the growth of decolonial thinking in Latin American

---

17 The charity Aesop (https://ae-sop.org/) provides an example. Its program, Dance to Health, started from identification of a social problem. It consulted with leading researchers about the best ways to address this problem and engaged seriously with academic critiques of commonplace claims about the impacts of arts activities. It recognized that the organization needed to do things differently in order to achieve its desired outcomes: it needed to develop a specialized curriculum.

music education in recent years. Coloniality and decoloniality are major concepts developed in South America specifically for reflecting critically on the transplantation of European knowledge to the continent, so they are eminently suitable for examining a field centred in Latin America and founded on European classical music. Indeed, I would go further and suggest that this is a conversation that SATM needs to have. Decoloniality is a perspective and so it is perfectly legitimate to propose counter-arguments; but simply to ignore or summarily dismiss the questions that it raises over SATM's orthodox model is less justifiable.

Decoloniality was never fully articulated as an approach in the Red, but it informed the thinking of the program's leaders and other key figures during my fieldwork. A fuller expression within SATM can be found in Argentina's Chazarreta program. Outside this field, interest in decolonial approaches to music education has blossomed in recent years and is evident in both practice and research spheres. Guillermo Rosabal-Coto has been an important figure, creating the Observatorio del Musicar at the University of Costa Rica, the Network of Critical and Decolonial Pedagogies in Music and the Arts, and editing journal special issues in Spanish and English.[18] Decolonial thinking has also established itself in North American music education, exemplified by the organization Decolonizing the Music Room, and it moved up the agenda in the wake of the resurgence of Black Lives Matter in 2020.[19]

Shifres and Gonnet (2015) trace the influence of two European models, the mission and the conservatoire, on music education in Latin America, and they imagine alternatives that are more closely aligned with indigenous culture and values. El Sistema has been widely presented as a step forwards from the conservatoire model, but seen through the lens of this article, it looks more like a step backwards towards the mission model (see also Baker 2014). If Denning (2015) encapsulates the connection between new, vernacular popular musics and the decolonial movement of the early to mid-twentieth century as "decolonizing the ear," the efforts of Abreu—a member of Venezuela's white elite—to massify classical music education might be perceived as a subsequent re-colonization. Work by decolonial music education

---

18 *Revista Internacional de Educación Musical* (5:1, 2017) and *Action, Theory, and Criticism for Music Education* (18:3, 2019).
19 https://decolonizingthemusicroom.com/.

scholars encourages us to imagine and explore what a genuine step forwards might look like: a second decolonization of the ear, fully cognizant of the continent's history and cultural richness.

While decolonial approaches can be highly critical of classical music, there are reasons to focus on de-centring and refiguring Eurocentric knowledge production in SATM programs in postcolonial contexts, rather than abandoning classical music education. As Mignolo and Walsh (2018, 3) argue, a decolonial perspective "does not mean a rejection or negation of Western thought"; rather, their target is "blind acceptance" and "surrendering to North Atlantic fictions." Mignolo does not preach avoidance of European culture, which he has studied in depth:

> The choice is not whether to read works by authors who are European, Eurocentric, or critical of Eurocentrism, but how to read them. The question is from where you start. When I read works by European authors of all kind, I do not start from them. I arrive to them. I start from thinkers and events that were disturbed by European invasions. (229)

The classicist Edith Hall (2019) argues: "Classical education need not be intrinsically elitist or reactionary; it has been the curriculum of empire, but it can be the curriculum of liberation. The 'legacy' of Greece and Rome has been instrumental in progressive and enlightened causes." Such sources are a useful starting point for shifting the music education conversation beyond what can sometimes become rather simplistic, sterile, or polarized debates about genre, beyond a dichotomy of devotion and dismissal, and towards the question of rethinking classical music and its pedagogy.

Mignolo's position is suggestive when it comes to reimagining classical music in SATM and Latin American music education more broadly. What if the question became not *whether* to play European classical music but rather *how* to play it (and listen to it, arrange it, discuss it, and so on)? What if young musicians did not *start from* classical music but rather *arrived to* it—if they approached this music after acquiring a grounding in local and national genres and playing styles?

Cobo Dorado (2015), Henley (2018), and Arenas (2020) argue that it is pedagogy rather than repertoire or instruments that is key to social impact. Similarly, a World Bank report underlined how teachers' practices (rather than content) determined whether they had a positive or negative effect on students' socio-emotional development (Villaseñor 2017). The implications of such stances for SATM are profound. If pedagogy is the problem, then neither switching nor mixing genres is the solution in itself.

Nora from the Red's social team made a similar point, as mentioned in Chapter 3. The problem for her was not that the Red focused on classical music; it was that it provided a narrow, technical classical training and contributed to professional saturation in the city, rather than using classical music as a means to provide a rounded humanistic education to young people and as a tool to reflect on their surroundings and their role within it. Her dichotomy was not classical versus popular; it was rounded classical education versus narrow classical training.

One of her colleagues discussed the importance of shifting to PBL. Learning via projects helps students to reason, work in teams, and resolve problems, she said—all important skills for social life. But projects were not genre-specific. In her view, too, it was the method of SATM that was the crucial factor, not the genre.

There may be lessons to be learnt from other contexts. Critical discussions of large ensemble education in North America have led to experiments in promoting democracy and critical reflection (e.g. Scruggs 2009; Davis 2011). In other words, the critical focus has been on the process as well as the music itself. Shieh and Allsup's (2016) reimagining of the large ensemble as a flexible collective has implications for genre, but it does not exclude anything. Govias's orchestral work entails rethinking the roles of the conductor and the musicians, not switching genres. Leech-Wilkinson's recent research on performance suggests that boosting creativity can take place within classical music education.[20] Movements in Canada show that it is possible for symphony orchestras to take the issue of decolonization seriously.[21] With imagination and the right partners, the orchestra can become a critical and educational tool and not just a training ground for performers (Horowitz 2018). While there are good arguments for classical music to cede its dominant role, it could play a valuable part in a rethought SATM.

---

20   Daniel Leech-Wilkinson, "Challenging Performance: Classical Music Performance Norms and How to Escape Them", https://challengingperformance.com/the-book/.

21   Orchestras/Orchestres Canada, "Trust, transparency and truth", https://oc.ca/en/trust-transparency-truth/.

Considering pedagogical reform raises larger questions about classical music itself, ones that go beyond the scope of this book. The main features of orthodox SATM were not dreamt up by Abreu; they reflect norms of the classical music tradition in the twentieth century: for example, the high status accorded to conductors and orchestras, a focus on canonical European repertoire, and an emphasis on arduous training to achieve a high level of technical skill. Classical music pedagogy is bound up with aspirations to musical excellence of a particular kind. Transforming SATM to give more value to small ensembles, musical creation, and rounded education therefore involves more than rethinking the route; it also means reconsidering the destination.

One productive step might be to broaden the definition of "classical music" beyond the Classical, Romantic, and post-Romantic repertoire that dominates SATM programming and include fields such as contemporary music and early music, where a different ethos has sometimes been found. For example, in Holland around 1970, radical musicians critiqued the hidebound practices and ideologies of the classical music sphere, leading to a "flourishing of numerous small groups in the fields of contemporary music, early music, jazz, and improvisation. In conscious opposition to the perceived authoritarianism of the symphony orchestra, new ensembles [...] aspired to a more democratic model of musical practice" (Adlington 2007, 540). Born (2010, 235) takes the example of the Dutch "Movement for the Renewal of Musical Practice" of the 1970s and its "idea of musical practice as a crucible in which could be incubated challenges—and a space of exception—to larger structures of social power." Similar developments were afoot in Germany, where musicians associated with the New Left rebelled against the conventions of classical music culture, particularly the orchestra, and grasped that social change had to go hand in hand with challenges to authoritarian structures and musical practices. There, "[t]he New Leftist spirit manifested itself particularly clearly in the new enthusiasm for improvisation and musical creativity. Both were seen as pedagogical instruments that served to performatively change social behavioral modes in the musical field, and were believed to be transferable to the practices of everyday West German society" (Kutschke 2010, 561). Both avant-garde and early musicians rethought ensemble structures and performance practices in order to minimize hierarchal relationships. What stands out from studies of this period is the variety of the "classical" field, the potential of classical music as a critical culture, even a counter-culture, and the connections made between musical and social change.

Fifty years on, the musicologist and performer David Irving is exploring the connections between early music and decoloniality.[22] Early music has a long history of social activism, with musicians involved in peace, environmental, and social justice movements. This counter-cultural or activist ethos in the field's past makes early music an auspicious site for decolonizing moves, argues Irving. From this perspective, early music appears very suggestive for SATM: it offers a promising model for aligning "classical" music with social change and for squaring the circle—retaining a place for classical music within SATM while also questioning and countering coloniality.

The problem in SATM may not be classical music, then, but rather the limited conception of this music that the most famous programs adopted, focused on European formats and repertoire of the late eighteenth to early twentieth centuries. Bull (2019) suggests that classical music education could be refigured to focus on its critical potential rather than its disciplinary practices. One response might be not only to include other genres and pedagogies, but also to take inspiration from more counter-cultural strands of classical music in order to reimagine the genre within SATM. This approach holds promise as a route beyond stark dichotomies and polarized debates of classical versus popular music.

There are parallels to be found within a recent journal special issue defending the value of classical music education.[23] For example, Varkøy and Rinholm (2020, 173) propose the continued inclusion of classical music as one option within "a genuine pluralist position, an open and tolerant approach," and they draw attention to the value of qualities of slowness and resistance in classical music "that are counter-cultural to modern society characterized by consumerism." Drawing on Adorno's ideas of the critical function of art, and in marked contrast to Abreu's discourses of order and discipline, they reimagine music educators and researchers as figures of resistance and argue that slowness in classical

---

22 David Irving, "Decolonising Historical Performance Practice", Royal Holloway University of London, 2 February 2021.
23 *Philosophy of Music Education Review* Vol. 28, No. 2, Fall 2020.

musical experience may serve as "the stone in the shoe, the pea under the mattress, the break in the rhythm" of consumer society (180).

Whale (2020, 200), meanwhile, offers a caution against reacting too hard against classical music:

> Too often, in educational reform, what should be a dialectical process of growth resembles more a pendulum. The pendulum of enlightened opinion swings from old, outdated practices of teaching and learning, to new, progressive, practices. It then swings back again, apparently unaware that what it now rejects is what it formerly espoused and what it now espouses it had previously rejected. The result is that dogmatic practices are replaced by equally dogmatic reforms; new theories repeat the failings of the original theories until they, too, are countered by a return of the original.

As Whale argues, classical music may stand in a critical relationship to the values of its surrounding society, rather than simply reproducing them, and any music has the potential to provoke (self-)critical reflection—this is not a feature of particular genres. He believes that "Western art music, at its most profound, enables people to question their values and assumptions, in the way that a philosophical or sociological text, a novel, a film, or a piece of journalism can, at its best, challenge people to reflect upon their lives and to grow as they see the world in a new light" (203). In learning to think critically about Bach's music (as opposed to rejecting it), students may also learn "to choose music that will broaden their capacity to meet and to recognize injustice and nurture their ongoing growth and development as human beings" (215).

Whale's words shed further light on SATM. The problem, again, appears to be not classical music itself but rather the culture of classical music education within orthodox SATM, which tends to elide this critical angle and replace it with obedience and reverence. If (self-)criticality, rather than excellence in performance, were to become the central goal of classical music education within SATM, matters would look very different.

A feature of both articles is a focus on attentive listening—a very marginal practice in orthodox SATM. For Whale, listening seems to be key to finding a place for Bach in an age of social justice. Having "the opportunity to attend to his music with empathy" may allow students "to discover, for themselves, that it practices the true reality of their lives, a reality constituted in continual, empathetic, self-evaluation" (215). Varkøy and Rinholm (2020, 169), meanwhile, "argue that how we listen to music is as crucial as what we listen to." These words underline that a combination of adopting a pluralist position and expanding the objects and methods of classical music education may be a productive route for SATM.

Such scholarship provides leads for rethinking social action through classical music, but they also suggest that a conceptually coherent and progressive classical music SATM would look very different from the orthodox version. The challenge for progressive supporters of classical SATM is to bridge the gap between the vision of classical music's most articulate defenders—that it is a critical and potentially emancipatory practice—and the reality of many music classrooms, where it is often no such thing. A model that closed that gap would be worthy of the label SATM.

In short, I point towards rethinking and transforming the role and character of classical music education in SATM, not banishing it—just as the Red's leaders sought a diversification of content, a horizontal relationship between genres, and a new pedagogical approach, not the extirpation of classical music. My question here is not whether young people should have the opportunity to learn classical music, but rather whether, as currently configured, conventional classical training should be the primary model for musical social-action programs; whether it should play such a dominant role in music education in former European colonies, reproducing the cultural hierarchy of the colonial period; and whether it is the best preparation for young musicians in such contexts, who may have more opportunities later in life to play other genres. My concern is not Beethoven; it is the appropriateness of classical music's educational and performance culture to the pursuit of social action; it is when SATM resembles a "visit from the ghost of public-school orchestra rooms past" (Fink 2016, 34); it is the "epistemic totalitarianism" (Mignolo and Walsh 2018, 195) of assuming the superior value of European culture and devaluing other forms of knowledge. The most interesting question for me is not "classical or popular music?" but rather "how can learning music *of any kind* foster reflection, creativity, voice, and freedom rather than social control?"

Inaction is not a justifiable option. The pedagogical conventions of classical music are geared around the performance rather than the performer, around excellence rather than social action. It makes no sense to think that they can be transferred across wholesale to a social program in which the experience of the musicians is supposed to be paramount. Conventional symphonic training works well for acquiring certain skills and habits, but its "pedagogy of correction" (Bull 2019) is a poor fit with goals such as political empowerment, citizenship formation, or the cultivation of autonomy and critical thinking.

Chapter 4 revealed distinct echoes in Latin American SATM of two themes that are prominent in Bull's study of youth classical music in the UK: intensive parenting and boundary-drawing. The classes involved are quite different—in Latin America, it is a fraction of the popular class that is the protagonist rather than the middle class—but the processes are remarkably similar. The common denominators are youth classical music, exclusion, and hierarchization. Unless the educational provision is rethought, SATM risks exacerbating the very problems that it is supposed to solve.

As Peerbaye and Attariwala (2019) make abundantly clear in their study of the Canadian sector, it is symphony orchestras that need to become more like the world around them, rather than society that needs to become more like a symphony orchestra (as El Sistema's leaders have endlessly proclaimed), since "aspects of orchestral music-making are in dissonance with contemporary Canadian social values" (4). They argue:

> the narratives of orchestral leaders, Indigenous artists and artists of colour reveal, time and time again, the colonial characteristics of orchestras that inhibit and even harm relationships—even in the midst of vital initiatives. Orchestras are hierarchical and rigidly structured in terms of creation and production processes and protocols of decision-making, and need to develop flexibility for new and more complex approaches. (ibid.)

In a critique that goes to the heart of orthodox SATM, they state: "'access' and 'inclusion' are insufficient as a context for conversation or a strategy for action for the sector." What is needed, rather, is "engagement with issues of racial equity, Indigenous sovereignty, and the dismantlement of Eurocentricity" (5). They cite the conductor Daniel Bartholomew-Poyser, who argues that despite including more people of colour and Indigenous people, the underlying logic of inclusion is essentially a relic of the nineteenth century. Inclusion is not the same as shifting the balance of power. Similarly, thinking beyond diversity, the authors ask: "Is there a willingness for orchestral culture to be moved, changed by these encounters?" (27).

This report's message is clear: society is changing and orchestras are lagging behind. Its demand for sectoral change is equally relevant to SATM, which has been widely proclaimed by advocates and the media as a vanguard movement but actually lags behind much socio-cultural activism. Many activists have abandoned discourses of inclusion and diversity in favour of those of equity, decolonization, and sovereignty.[24] This is a move that even the more progressive end of SATM has been slow to make. What is needed is not adding repertoire or faces to a model that remains the same underneath, not inclusion into an established system, but rather root and branch reform of the system itself. Until such a time, the much-touted idea that the field is revolutionary will continue to look deeply questionable.

Unless classical music education is substantially rethought, other musics will offer greater advantages to the pursuit of social action. As Denning (2015) argues, social change in the early twentieth century, not least in Latin America, was articulated to the emergence of new, vernacular popular musics, and his study serves to underline the musical and social conservatism of orthodox SATM. While an increased focus on neglected national and regional repertoire is a step in the right direction, a more significant development would be a revamped curriculum and pedagogy that provided heightened social benefits, broader musical skills, and critical engagement with questions of colonization, decolonization, and recolonization.

The Politics of SATM

Also important, if less obvious, is the need to take more seriously the matter of politics. Abreu and Dudamel's denial of this question has seriously impeded a political analysis of SATM; by proclaiming El Sistema

---

24 In the words of Madam Dr. Fleming, diversity and inclusion is the equivalent of "thoughts and prayers" (@alwaystheself, tweet, 5 June 2020, https://twitter.com/alwaystheself/status/1268768893289533441), while for Takeo Rivera, "diverse curriculum isn't justice—it's an alibi" (as reported by Gareth Dylan Smith from a panel on decolonizing the curriculum at Boston University in June 2020).

to be apolitical at every turn, they have thrown many people off the scent and confused the issue. However, such analysis is essential if the field is to act as a catalyst of social change. For social change is political; it rests on critique of the social order. If the field is to speak of social change, let alone social justice, pursuing SATM requires thinking politically as well as socially. Abstracting politics from music education is more likely to lead to social reproduction and control.

The Red, in contrast, has understood that attempting to shape society through music is a political act. Since 2005, leading figures have argued for a political conception of the program. The two heads of the social team since that time have placed empowerment and political subjectivity at the heart of their vision of the Red's potential, and successive general directors have engaged with the political dimensions of SATM in varying ways. There is a world of difference between the politics-denying politician Abreu and the Red's social-team leader Jiménez, for whom the potential of SATM lay in the socio-political processes that it could catalyze. Behind these contrasting examples lies a fundamental dichotomy of correction and empowerment in SATM, which is yet to be properly grasped.

One pending task is to think macro-politically. For example, in order to understand this phenomenon more fully, we need to ask: why has orchestral training been favoured by politicians in contexts like Venezuela, Colombia, or Mexico in comparison to other arts and even other musics? How has SATM served politicians and to what ends? What political agendas does it support, whether explicitly or implicitly? During my year in Medellín, the Red featured prominently in publicity campaigns by the city government. The text focused on the number of participants (an advantage that SATM has over other forms of arts education). However, as a communications employee revealed, the government had also decided that images of the Red conveyed messages that it wished to project: they evoked social concern, inspiring a more emotional connection between the citizenry and the mayor's office than billboards trumpeting infrastructure projects.

For all the utopian rhetoric and the imagery of the poor and vulnerable, El Sistema is a model by and for the powerful, created by a member of Venezuela's social and political elite, and instantly legible to and adopted enthusiastically by politicians, banks, corporations, major cultural institutions, and instrument manufacturers. The creation and persistence of El Sistema's illusory miracle story in the face of years of mounting critiques and counter-evidence illustrates the power of the program and its influential allies to control the public narrative. It is rooted in and seeks to reproduce the culture and ideology of society's dominant actors. It is a world away from a grassroots movement like CM, and it contrasts vividly with the kinds of socially engaged or applied arts practices studied by the likes of Thompson (2009) and Sachs Olsen (2019), which attempt to position themselves in a critical relation to dominant forces. Orchestras are particularly suited to serving as ceremonial and propaganda tools, wheeled out to adorn political events or boost the image of leaders. SATM promises quick and spectacular results—just what politicians concerned with optics and budgets would like to hear; its concerts are a simple way for them to perform their concern with social and cultural issues. It presents an amenable picture of social problems as located among the disadvantaged and therefore susceptible to charity, and as caused by poor people's failings rather than structural factors. It also presents a vision of young people that appeals to the powerful: disciplined, obedient, and productive. As a professional musician and university professor in Medellín put it, politicians like SATM because it enables them to transfer obligations of the state to musicians and look good in the process. We cannot understand SATM without engaging with the ways and reasons that it has been articulated to political parties, programs, and ideologies.

In contrast, there were several orchestral protests as part of social uprisings in Chile and Colombia in late 2019. Orchestral musicians and singers performed a concert entitled "Requiem for Chile," dedicated to the victims of the recent state repression, and a mass open-air rendition of the protest song "El pueblo unido, jamás será vencido!" [The people united will never be defeated] ("Músicos" 2019). In Bogotá, more than 300 orchestral musicians came together to play classical and popular music in support of street protests ("Más de 300" 2019). The contrast with Venezuela was striking: there, social protests had been ongoing for over five years but without any involvement from orchestras. El Sistema had turned Venezuela into the centre of Latin America's orchestral world, yet ironically, despite its slogan of SATM, it had no connection with the grassroots politics that drives social change. On the contrary, it served as a tool of government propaganda. While orchestras in Chile and Colombia took defiant action out on the streets, El Sistema's leaders joined official marches and pressurized employees to vote for the government in elections.

After 400 Russian musicians, led by the pianist Evgeny Kissin, protested publicly against the Putin government's imprisonment of Alexei Navalny in February 2021, Gabriela Montero lamented that Venezuelan musicians had done nothing similar during major demonstrations in 2014 (or any time since), and she contrasted Kissin with Dudamel.[25] Some musicians took part in protests on an individual basis, but the most celebrated, Wuilly Arteaga, criticized El Sistema publicly for trying to force students to support the regime and play at official events.[26] An El Sistema musician who was arrested during the protests of 2017, making himself something of a cause célèbre, made it clear he was not in fact participating but rather was simply on his way to a rehearsal. "I'm a musician, OK!," he shouted at police—as though that ought to identify him immediately as having nothing to do with street politics (Baker 2017b).

Some scholars argue that music or the arts alone may generally have limited influence on society, and that it is in their articulation with social and political movements that their catalytic effect may be most felt—communicating, inspiring, building solidarity, and helping to foster the dispositions for social change (e.g. Henderson 1996; Mouffe 2013). Kuttner (2015, 85) writes: "The arts alone are not enough"; they are most effective "as a form of collective cultural work embedded in larger processes of cultural and political change." The arts and civic education project that he studies "does not see itself as a lone organization with full control over a social change process. Rather, it sees itself as bringing a particular artistic and cultural strength to a larger movement for social justice" (ibid.). Accordingly, if SATM is to play a role in social change in future, rather than serving as an attractive ornament, it needs more connection with political movements: more streets of Colombia, less concert halls of Venezuela.

The Dream Unfinished (mentioned in Chapter 3) provides an example of mixing large-ensemble artistic practice with political activism to forge orchestral "artivism" (Diverlus 2016; Bradley 2018).[27] It points a way forward for SATM programs seeking to prioritize

---

25 "PUTIN POWER: musicians sound their outrage (a statement of support)", Facebook, 11 February 2021.
26 See my blog post "Eric Booth and Wuilly Arteaga, the Sistema icon who isn't", https://geoffbakermusic.wordpress.com/el-sistema-the-system/el-sistema-blog/eric-booth-and-wuilly-arteaga-the-sistema-icon-who-isnt/.
27 http://thedreamunfinished.org/.

democratic citizenship and social change. To return to founder Eun Lee's analogy, orchestral artivism means shifting to Level 3, when the car actually moves: "So that it's not just a concert *about* something, but you can actually *do* the something at the concert."

While SATM's connection to formal politics is an important topic for analysis, so too is its micro-politics. Music education is inherently political, as discussed in Chapter 3. Kanellopoulos (2015) argues for the inseparability of politics and musical creativity. As recent debates over decolonizing music curricula underline, placing classical music at the centre of music education is not a politically neutral act. Privileging the music of European men in a multiracial, postcolonial society is not apolitical, whatever its advocates may claim. Meanwhile, discourses such as social inclusion and social justice have political histories, whether or not those who employ them recognize this. SATM raises political and ideological questions, and they do not go away simply because they are ignored or denied. As Mouffe (2013, 91) notes, "artistic practices play a role in the constitution and maintenance of a given symbolic order, or in its challenging, and this is why they *necessarily* have a political dimension" (emphasis added). The question is not then to be political or apolitical; it is, what *kind* of politics does SATM embody?

It is not just El Sistema's leaders who have sought to marginalize the topic of politics in SATM; much research has contributed to the problem by narrowing its focus towards technocratic questions or disavowing ideology (as though such a thing were possible). Attempting to evaluate the impact of SATM programs is a potentially valuable exercise, even if one more fraught with problems than is generally recognized, but not if it comes at the expense of political (or cultural, ethical, and philosophical) questions. An issue like coloniality cannot be tackled from a technocratic perspective. SATM might be thought of as akin to social mobility or private education in the sense that whether it works or not for individuals does not resolve the question of its value to society as a whole, which is largely a political one.

During my fieldwork in Medellín, it was cultural politics—issues such as identity, diversity, participation, agency, and citizenship—that drove self-critique and change, underlining the importance of qualitative research and debate. In the global North, the public conversation on SATM has been dominated by evaluations and quantitative research, meaning that political, cultural, and philosophical debates have been overshadowed by cognitive, psychological, and health ones. But such research sheds little light on key debates in Medellín and it can easily miss what is most important to arts practitioners—a point driven home by Grayson Perry's ironically entitled vase "This pot will reduce crime by 29%."[28]

Reimagining SATM as a space for empowering students and developing their political subjectivity entails engaging with cultural-political debates and rethinking the orthodox model. It implies changes in organizational dynamics and the music education itself. Students are cast not as passive subjects, waiting to be saved by the power of music, but as active, as actors. SATM then relies on the pedagogical and political choices of leaders and staff, not on music working invisible magic. Students and teachers carry the responsibility for social action; this is not a burden that music can bear. To paraphrase Gaztambide-Fernández (2013), music does not do anything; music is something people do. Similarly, social action is not something that happens to music students but rather something that they make happen. This requires creating spaces for reflection and action within lessons and rehearsals, schools and ensembles, and surrounding society.

Hess (2019)'s model for music education and social change starts from the opposite pole to El Sistema. She recognizes that music is inherently political and therein lies its potential. Her model is built on the experience of activist musicians and examples of protest music. It offers not slogans, magical thinking, and sleights of hand (Fink 2016), but rather a fully articulated and explained program, based in practice and research. Built around contemporary concerns and methods, it contrasts strikingly with the practices and anti-politics of orthodox SATM. As such, it offers considerable food for thought to the field's reformers.

Citizenship

Closely connected with politics is the issue of citizenship, another topic that is ripe for further exploration within SATM. Citizenship might be considered a more ambitious goal than social action or coexistence, but

---

28 https://www.flickr.com/photos/marcwathieu/2722935007.

also a key battleground: carrying both potential and risks, it exemplifies the ambiguity of SATM. It is a word that is often invoked in the field, yet less common is deep consideration of its implications or the question: what kind of citizen?

In orthodox SATM, as discussed in Chapter 3, the ideal is usually close to Westheimer and Kane's (2004) category of the Personally Responsible Citizen. A more progressive route would be to focus on the Participatory Citizen and the Justice Oriented Citizen. At stake here is the very purpose of SATM: whether it is to be a force for social normalization and reproduction, or for political participation and change. It is worth taking the same conceptual step as above and putting citizenship first: starting with some basic tenets and practices of citizenship education and then thinking about how best to realize them through music, rather than taking conventional music education and framing it in a discourse of citizenship. It is hard to imagine this approach leading to the orthodox model.

Orthodox SATM mimics the tendency towards normalization and control in many top-down, state-sponsored citizenship education programs. Yet there are other, more heterodox kinds of citizenship— cultural, creative, critical, reflective, insurgent, subversive—and where better than arts education for such alternative visions to flourish? The arts are a privileged space for exploring issues like the paradox that being a good citizen sometimes requires being a bad citizen. The arts potentially offer much more to citizenship than just correcting behaviour and inculcating norms: for example, imagining alternatives, projecting voices in public, connecting politics and emotions, and reinforcing or transforming identities by imbuing them with affective power. Citizenship, meanwhile, offers a valuable lens to arts education for considering its ideological basis and potential impact on society.

The vision of artistic citizenship presented in Chapter 3 might be proposed as one approach to these various issues. It targets four areas of weakness in orthodox SATM, which was built on principles of playing rather than reflecting, performing rather than creating, following instructions rather than participating in decision-making, and changing unconsciously rather than acting.[29] These four categories of activity might seem unremarkable to some readers, yet they are strikingly absent from El Sistema and from the 2005 evaluation of the Red.

This proposal grew at the interface of the Red's own development and the work of music educators and researchers around the world. It thus seems to hold at least some potential for generalizability. It also dovetails nicely with other educational proposals. For example, there are parallels between a vision of artistic citizenship founded on reflection, creation, participation, and action, and the "4Cs" (critical thinking, creative thinking, collaboration, and communication) that have been proposed as essential skills for learners in the twenty-first century ("Preparing 21st Century Students" n.d.). Indeed, Kim (2017) connects developing the 4Cs, transforming music education, and fostering citizenship. There are also clear similarities with Hess's (2019) model, which proposes a triple pedagogy of community (i.e. participation), expression (i.e. creation), and noticing (i.e. reflection), founded on the experience of activist-musicians (i.e. action). There seems to be a critical mass of similar ideas emerging here.

Taking artistic citizenship seriously holds out promise for SATM. It points a way beyond music education as social control. It moves beyond discredited ideas of deficits and correction and understands societal problems as having predominantly structural rather than individual roots. It potentially overcomes the problems of fostering tribalism and social divisions. Tempering the focus on discipline and technical training, and working more on citizenly capacities and the potential to act on society, would be conducive to playing a larger role in social change. Citizenship, when approached as a political concept and a catalyst for reflection rather than a publicity discourse, offers more clarity and focus than social action or coexistence.

The lens of citizenship also underlines the importance of pedagogical change. Much of the tension over the musical and the social in the Red derived from a poor fit between large-ensemble training and progressive visions of citizenship. Attempts to promote citizenly capacities such as

---

29   There is a large literature on performance as creative practice, but the extent to which it applies to a disciplinary youth orchestral system is questionable.

autonomy and critical thinking bumped up against responses like "we don't have time for that now, we have a big concert coming up and we need to rehearse." Conventional orchestral training is not an obvious vehicle for citizen formation, if what is sought is democratic, critical citizenship. Without changes to symphonic practices and ideologies, SATM will continue to appear deficient in comparison to projects that focus on cultural forms that dovetail more easily with progressive notions of citizenship, such as hip-hop (Acosta Valencia and Garcés Montoya 2013; Ladson-Billings 2015; Kuttner 2015).

Nonetheless, large ensembles still hold potential in imaginative hands. On Black Awareness Day in November 2018, I attended a concert focusing on female black role models, presented by the Liberdade school of NEOJIBA, the SATM program in Salvador, Brazil. Outside the hall were posters about a number of prominent black women, both Brazilian and international, with a photo and short text about their achievements. During the concert, there were frequent references to these figures and positive messages about black women, and relevant images and texts were projected onto the walls. The repertoire was a mixture of Afro-Brazilian, African, and African American music, and the performers (an orchestra, a choir, some percussionists, and an invited female Afro-Brazilian singer) appeared in Afro-diasporic clothing and hairstyles.

Fig. 29. Concert by Liberdade school, NEOJIBA. Photo by the author (2018). CC BY.

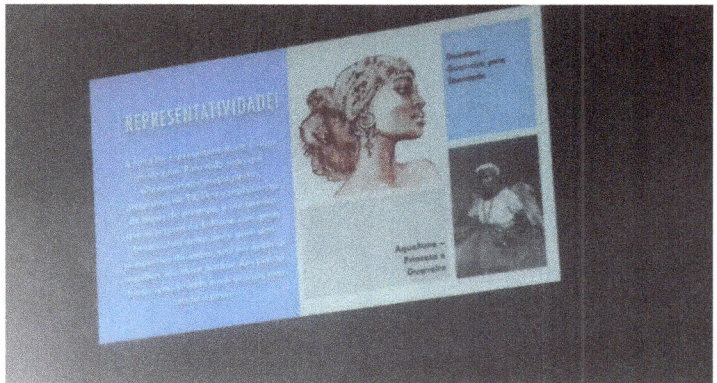

Fig. 30. Projection during the concert. Photo by the author (2018). CC BY.

After the concert, I spoke to a teacher who had been much involved in the project. There was a lot of low self-esteem in Liberdade over the issue of race, she said, and she had experienced this herself: only quite recently had she started to wear her hair in a more natural way, rather than straightening it. As a result, she felt strongly that race was an issue that they needed to work on in the school.

Sitting in the audience, I was struck by the emotional impact of the performance. The audience—many of them black women—cried to some songs and responded enthusiastically to others, singing and swaying along to local carnival hits. There was also a musical, visual, and conceptual coherence that made the concert convincing on a more intellectual level. The messages of black pride and female pride were crystal clear, but the concert felt like a celebration, not a lecture, and its success in connecting with the audience was obvious.

I had already chosen artistic citizenship as the topic of my invited talk to the program later that day, and as I told the audience, they had unexpectedly provided me with an example. The concert illustrated ethical and political action; it connected music education to significant social issues; and it directed a message of hope and social change outwards towards society. It did so in a way that was enjoyable, moving, and informative, creating a strong connection between performers, audience, and message and between politics, identities, and emotions. It exemplified the contribution of the arts to citizenship.

Nevertheless, since citizenship is a concept with its own contradictions, its application to music education requires caution, reflection, and further development. The ambiguity of many of the terms evoked in discussions of artistic citizenship means that we may find a "perverse confluence" (Dagnino 2007) as contrasting political and educational perspectives converge on a shared language. Words can easily become domesticated and lose their potential to catalyze change. Even the most unthinking, repetitive music education is regularly held up in public discourse as an example of creativity; even the most top-down dynamics are proclaimed as fostering teamwork; even the most powerless students are celebrated as an example of participation and citizenship. It is easy to appropriate such terms and pay them lip service; it is vital, therefore, to go beyond the words and engage with what lies beneath them.

The word "participatory" serves as an example. "Participation" can be harnessed to both challenging and reinforcing existing power relations (Brough 2014). As Hart's ladder suggests, there are many forms of participation that entail playing a part but not having a voice. "Participatory music-making" sounds appealing but it may be totally autocratic. A distinction needs to be drawn between musical and political senses of "participatory"—between making music and making decisions. As with politics and citizenship, we must ask: what *kind* of participation?

As argued previously, citizenship discourse has been mobilized in support of both conservative and progressive agendas. It matters considerably whether artistic citizenship is approached from a deficit- or assets-based perspective. If children and young people are regarded as deficient in relation to the various components of artistic citizenship—as faulty or incomplete citizens in need of disciplining and correction—then it does not represent much of an advance. However, if they are regarded as citizens *already*—as reflective and creative individuals with social and cultural assets, capable of and responsible for participating in and acting on society—then matters look very different.

As currently expressed, this proposal for artistic citizenship takes no account of decolonial thinking. There might be tensions between the two; but they might also combine well. Again, the issue of deficits versus assets is crucial. Bringing a decolonial perspective to artistic citizenship might bring greater clarity, supporting efforts to educate a more active, engaged, critical citizenry. In their study of music in Australian indigenous communities, Bartleet and Carfoot (2016) tread carefully, showing critical awareness of the potential pitfalls of artistic citizenship in such contexts, but they ultimately embrace the notion.

Thinking seriously about artistic citizenship is an important first step, but a logical second step would be to ask what a Latin American version might look like, one inflected or transformed by indigenous and/or Afro-diasporic conceptions of culture, coexistence, and citizenship. For example, there has been a resurgence of interest in the 2000s in the ancestral Andean principle of *sumak kawsay* (in Quechua) or *buen vivir* (in Spanish), which might be translated as "living well." Ecuador's 2008 constitution gives a prominent place to this concept. Its preamble states: "We have decided to construct a new form of *citizen coexistence*, in diversity and harmony with nature to reach el buen vivir, el sumak kawsay" (cited in Mignolo and Walsh 2018, 64; emphasis added). Mignolo and Walsh (ibid.) gloss *sumak kawsay/buen vivir* as "the harmonious interrelation or correlation of and among all beings (human and otherwise) and with their surroundings. Included in this relation are water and food, culture and science, education, housing and habitat, health, work, community, nature, territory and land, economy, and individual and collective rights, among other areas of interrelation." This principle thus encapsulates a notion of *coexistence*, that key word in the Red's lexicon, yet one that is quite distinct from, and far broader than, its understanding in Medellín's public programs. In traditional Andean thought, these authors argue, coexistence rests on a cosmology of complementary dualities (and/and) rather than contradictory ones (either/or)—on the acknowledgment that there cannot be A without its opposite B. Coexistence implies seeking harmony and balance and weaving relations with the natural and spiritual as well as human worlds. In other words, coexistence is not a universal and transparent concept; it has a much more holistic connotation in indigenous thought. What might the search for coexistence look like in a SATM program if it embraced a broader conception of the term, closer to traditional South American ones?

There are good reasons to take such a step. The anthropologist Xabier Abo translates *suma qamaña*, the Bolivian equivalent of *sumak kawsay*, as "convivir bien" [living well together], illustrating its pertinence to

SATM (cited in Houtart 2011).[30] Furthermore, it might be argued that colonial logic will struggle to provide the solution to the problems engendered by modernity or coloniality. "The alienation that Western knowledge created by conceptualizing and celebrating competition and individualism (which destroys the social fabric), has to be overcome by visions and conceptions of communal praxis of living that puts love and care as the final destiny of the human species and our relations with the living universe (including planet earth)," argue Mignolo and Walsh (2018, 228). Indigenous philosophy, concepts, and practices may therefore have much to offer the search for coexistence and citizenship through music.

There is potential for artistic citizenship to be brought into dialogue with the fields of Latin American citizenship studies and decolonizing music education to imagine a decolonial Latin American artistic citizenship—for example, one combining concepts of indigeneity and citizenship (giving "indigenship") and based on principles of equality and colonial difference (Rojas 2013), or one built around dignity, "diversality," and epistemological plurality (Taylor 2013). Deep engagement with traditional musics and dances might allow particular kinds of artistic citizenship to become apparent (e.g. Montgomery 2016). The Brazilian program AfroReggae's notion of *batidania*, combining *batida* (beat) and *cidadania* (citizenship), offers one example of a grassroots, Afro-diasporic conception of artistic citizenship (Moehn 2011); Candusso's (2008) exploration of Afro-Brazilian capoeira and citizenship provides another. Keil (n.d.) presents a vision of cultural education and active citizenship based on Afro-Latin dance music: "Paideia Con Salsa."

Galeano and Zapata's (2006) work on citizenship in Colombia points another way forward. These authors argue against a vision of citizenship founded on notions of individual deficits and Western ideals, and propose one stemming from actual practices of civic activism in Colombia, such as social movements and community initiatives to resist and repair the damage wrought by the country's long armed conflict. In this view, citizenship education should be connected to social and political movements if it is to be more than just a symbolic gesture or,

---

30 *Convivir* [to coexist] is the verbal form of *convivencia* [coexistence].

worse, a displacement of real action. It should provide a space for the generation of new, locally derived citizenship knowledge, rather than the imposition of existing theories and values from outside. In short, these authors urge us to stop thinking about ideals of citizenship and measuring students in relation to them, and to start focusing on real-life good citizens, the movements in which they are embedded, and the ways that they have responded to civic problems. Transferred to SATM, this would mean starting and connecting with exemplary (artistic) citizens, not abstract behavioural ideals like discipline and respect. These examples might be national or international—the Santa Fé school of the Red focused on Nina Simone, while the Liberdade school of NEOJIBA chose exemplary black women from both Brazil and overseas—but the best figures to teach young Colombians about citizenship, according to Galeano and Zapata, are Colombian civic activists, some of whom might be living just round the corner. Hess's (2019) vision of music education for social change takes this kind of approach, beginning not with abstract notions but rather with specific activist musicians and building up an educational model from there.

This second step of localizing artistic citizenship and/or combining it with decolonization or indigenization goes beyond the scope of this book, but it is one that I very much hope others will pursue. Such ideas require and deserve much further development. I am limited here to gesturing in this direction.

Demographics and Targeting

Research on an afterschool education program in a Montevideo shantytown found a strong correlation between the program's impact on children and the commitment, aspiration, and cultural capital of their parents (Cid 2014; Bernatzky and Cid 2018). It thus illustrated and explained how the same education program could have varying effects. These findings support the argument in Chapter 4 that afterschool programs may serve as a mechanism of social differentiation, heightening inequality rather than producing inclusion: since the Montevideo program was effective only for children with committed parents, it exacerbated the difference between them and the more disadvantaged students.

This study illustrates the difficulty of providing a single answer to the question of an education program's efficacy, since it depends on the social and cultural characteristics of the beneficiaries' families. This is also a central point of Rimmer's (2018; 2020) studies of In Harmony Sistema England. Having arrived at the same conclusion in relation to SATM in France, Picaud (2018) warns against simplistic accounts of "the effect" of Démos on children. The answer to "does SATM work?" appears to be "for some people," meaning that it is impossible to generalize about its effects. Such research raises questions about the "power of music" literature, since it suggests that the effects of an educational intervention may not be explicable only in psychological or neuroscientific terms. Also, as Ramalingam (2013) argues, attributing social results to any single development intervention is very problematic; impacts are more likely to be achieved by networks or coalitions of actors working in concert. The limited effect on the least advantaged students suggests that we should talk of the impact of music education *in combination with* parental commitment, aspiration, and cultural capital. It underlines the problems of accounts of SATM that homogenize beneficiaries (as "poor," "at-risk," "disadvantaged," and so on), and the need for much more detailed analyses of which segment of a given community participates in a given SATM program and whether benefits vary across participants.

However, it is also possible to see sociological and scientific explanations in a more harmonious relationship. After all, the key question raised here does not concern *whether* music has the capacity to produce benefits in individuals but rather *who* receives those benefits. Orthodox SATM provides a channel for children who initially have a marginal educational advantage to receive an educational boost.[31] Even leaving aside all the political and philosophical questions, then, and taking music's effects as given, SATM may still be ineffective or even counter-productive at a societal level because it does not benefit those

---

31 Similarly, Purves (2019), in a UK study, argues that public extra-curricular music education can potentially bring further advantages to children who already experience more favourable conditions, since such children are more likely to take up opportunities and persist in their engagement over time. Studies of SATM suggest that this argument holds even when economic differences are small or non-existent and more favourable conditions take non-material form, complicating Purves's suggestion that Sistema-style programs are a solution to the problem that he identifies.

most in need but rather serves to widen the divide between haves and have-nots. In this sense, the individual advantages it provides are somewhat irrelevant: if SATM does not work for the most vulnerable or marginalized, then it is not a model of social inclusion. An approach that misses its main target and appeals most to children who enjoy schooling and have supportive families is a poor choice for pursuing educational equity.

At present, SATM's social impact is limited by its design for and monopolization by a self-selecting group with prior advantages that is already largely in tune with the values of the program. This design makes perfect sense from a musical perspective: such students are more likely to arrive with the program's values in place, adapt to its ways of working, and produce good artistic results, and the program can thus depend on them. Appealing to a social fraction with few economic resources but more educational commitment, aspiration, and cultural capital makes perfect sense if the aim is to democratize classical music and secure its future. But social change would require a different approach, one that effectively targeted students from other kinds of families—those with less educational commitment, aspiration, and cultural capital—who tend to fall through the cracks. Indeed, such targeting is precisely what some researchers recommend (e.g. Cid 2014; Bernatzky and Cid 2018; Purves 2019). The challenge, then, is to create a version of SATM that would be more accessible and appealing to those with the fewest advantages—the most excluded rather than the most includible.

Such moves would be a big step towards educational justice and genuine inclusion, but the goal of social transformation also implies targeting a very different group: those who are most likely to grow up to hold the levers of power. Nixon (2019) provides a suggestive example by examining public health through an anti-oppressive lens. She argues that discussions of health inequities and attempts to address them are marred by a near-exclusive focus on effects and those who suffer them (disadvantaged, vulnerable, marginalized, or at-risk groups). Largely absent is half of the picture—the advantaged or privileged—who figure only as supposed experts on social issues and saviours of the first group. Yet ignoring half the picture limits the possibilities for decisive action to disrupt enduring patterns: "If inequity is framed exclusively as a problem facing people who are marginalized, then responses will only attempt to address the needs of these groups, without redressing the social structures causing this disadvantage." Indeed, a presumed equivalence between privilege and expertise can actually strengthen the status quo, reinforcing an unequal relationship between "saviours" and "saved" and encouraging a flow of material resources to privileged people for designing and delivering programs for disadvantaged populations.

Nixon proposes reframing this picture so that the experiences of the under-privileged group are understood as a consequence of the choices of the privileged one; the latter should therefore be considered complicit in the production and maintenance of structural inequities, from which it benefits. If the *causes* of inequities are to be seriously addressed, and not just the *effects* softened, greater attention must focus on the privileged group and on shifting its self-perception from saviours to critical allies. This implies privileged actors unlearning old assumptions and abandoning an urge (however altruistic) to fix others in favour of working in solidarity with disadvantaged groups and taking action on systems of inequality. It also implies acknowledging their complicity with such systems and recognizing that the disadvantaged group is likely to know more about inequities than they do and have more experience and expertise in tackling them. The ultimate goal is not to move people from one place to another within an unfair structure (social mobility); rather, it is to counter the systems that cause these inequities (social change).

The implications of this critique for SATM are profound. It shines a harsh, if indirect, light on the field's orthodox model and philosophy. Nixon dismantles the idea that the best way to address inequities is for social elites to use their "expertise" to help marginalized groups with their problems, and that such problems are caused by individual or group behaviours. She questions the response of privileged actors "going into communities (locally and overseas) to bring their expertise and solutions to needy individuals." Her message is unequivocal: "Stop trying to save or fix people on the bottom of the coin" (her metaphor for the social hierarchy). She proposes that privileged actors reorient their motivation from "I wish to help the less fortunate" or "I use my expertise to reduce inequities for marginalized populations" to the following commitments:

I seek to understand my own role in upholding systems of oppression that create health inequities.

I learn from the expertise of, and work in solidarity with, historically marginalized groups to help me understand and take action on systems of inequality.

This includes working to build insight among others in positions of privilege, and *mobilizing in collective action* under the leadership of people on the bottom on the coin. [emphasis in original]

Providing free music education to poor and disadvantaged children is a noble aim—but it may not sit easily with the goal of social change, at least if that change is to be significant and lasting. As Spruce (2017, 724) notes, the distributive social justice paradigm (widening access to cultural resources) "is now acknowledged within the literature of social justice to be insufficient, both in the understanding of social justice that it offers, and as a framework for identifying and addressing issues of social injustice." An access focus "address[es] only the consequences of the social and power structures which produce inequalities and injustices, whilst leaving those structures untouched and unchallenged." Tackling causes requires a different approach: for example, one that fosters critical allyship between the rich and the poor, the powerful and the powerless. Widening access to music education appeals more—and it may look and feel better—but it is likely to be less effective as a motor of social change.

More disruptively still for SATM, an anti-oppressive approach also implies a shift from seeing the dominant culture and its bearers as a solution to social problems to seeing them as part of the problem: no longer treating them as those who know and have come to save or rescue those who do not, but rather as those who need to listen to and learn from the expertise of historically marginalized groups. It is the latter groups who, drawing on centuries of using music to resist oppression and pursue social healing and cohesion, are the real experts in social action through music; it is their musics, above all, that embody such a concept. As Nixon argues, real change requires privileged actors to de-centre themselves: "to demonstrate humility regarding the assumed rightness of certain ways of doing, communicating, and thinking, and stepping back to make room for alternatives." This picture could not be further from El Sistema's veneration of the all-knowing conductor and its self-imagination as an organization of musical missionaries taking classical music into cultural deserts to rescue disorientated youth (see Baker 2014). Adopting social change as the primary goal and an anti-oppressive approach to achieving it implies turning SATM on its head.

Hess (2018; 2021) provides a pointer, examining music education through an anti-oppression lens. She holds up the example of teachers of predominantly affluent, white students in Canada who not only offer instruction in Afro-diasporic musics but also promote critical conversations about structural issues such as privilege and oppression, illuminating the relationships between music and slavery, colonialism, and resistance. "Facilitating this understanding perhaps opens up a wider conversation about the need for systemic redress. Music then provides the basis for a conversation that historicises present inequality and points to systemic implications" (2021, 66). Here we may see the seeds of an inversion of SATM, in pursuit of the objective of social change: rather than targeting European classical music at poor BIPOC students, aiming Afro-diasporic music at rich white ones.

In short, SATM would logically produce the greatest societal benefits if it focused on the top and bottom of the socio-economic spectrum—those who determine the status quo and those who are most disadvantaged by it. At present, though, its main constituency appears to be somewhere in the middle. A program to widen access to classical music is perfectly legitimate—but it should be recognized for what it is, rather than labelled music for social change. There is nothing wrong with attracting predominantly an aspirational, committed fraction of the popular class interested in free music lessons—but again, it should be recognized for what it is, which is not a social program for the most vulnerable or excluded young people. If the latter aims are real and paramount, then SATM needs to rethink its approach, focusing more attention on other constituencies and the question of how to reach them.

6. Challenges

The third of step of social justice-oriented research is "to understand the obstacles, possibilities and dilemmas of transformation" (cited in Wright 2019, 217). A central theme of this book is complexity, and, indeed, the path of change is not straightforward. If the previous chapter focused on potential areas for growth, here I pay attention to some obstacles to transformation. There are also more conceptual or philosophical dilemmas that complicate an optimistic view of reforming SATM.

Obstacles to Change

2006 saw the release of the influential El Sistema documentary *Tocar y Luchar* and the first of a wave of glowing reports on the Venezuelan program in the UK press (e.g. Higgins 2006). In 2007, the Simón Bolívar Youth Orchestra (SBYO) burst onto the international scene with its Proms debut in London, and in 2008, CBS News broadcast the landmark 60 Minutes film "El Sistema: Changing Lives through Music." This was the watershed period when SATM became a global phenomenon.

Yet in these same years, the Red produced substantial internal reports revealing significant problems with this model. Over the subsequent decade, as influential supporters proclaimed El Sistema to be a miracle and SATM spread across the globe, the Red grappled with the challenge of putting those problems right. The Red thus generated a counter-narrative that might have checked the euphoria sweeping the global North, but it was never made public. As I researched El Sistema in 2010–11 and discovered the gulf between image and reality, I had no idea that such problems had been known about for five years across the border in Colombia and that efforts were already underway to address them. Similarly, I had no idea that Estrada and Frega had produced critical reports on El Sistema as far back as 1997, since this research, too, had remained unpublished (see Baker and Frega 2018). When I began my fieldwork in Medellín in 2017, I did not know that my research had been preceded by a decade of internal reports about the flaws in SATM. My understanding—like that of so many others around the world—was hamstrung because significant information that already existed did not circulate at all. This book is in large part an attempt to bring this history of (self-)critique and change out into the open so that we do not have to keep reinventing the wheel.

Public Debate and the Circulation of Knowledge

Abreu's power over the music sector, zero tolerance for criticism, and vindictive streak meant that frank public discussion of El Sistema's issues was severely constrained in Venezuela (Baker 2014), and his attitude—"we don't have problems"—set the tone for SATM's public face. Furthermore, the predominance of positive narratives about the social impact of the arts today means that external pressure for change is weak. There are few influential voices pushing for critical re-evaluation of the field. Even where changes are afoot, problems are barely mentioned. There is much talk of great new work, much less of what was wrong with the old work. There are increasing signs of distancing from El Sistema's model, as noted in the previous chapter; but the value of the brand to the field, the power of the Venezuelan program internationally, and a sense of allegiance and historical debt are such that there is real reluctance to discuss this process publicly.

Pledging allegiance to the El Sistema brand while shifting to more progressive approaches may be a sensible strategic and educational decision, but it has the downside of sending a public message of continuity rather than change. The framing of such work as "El Sistema-inspired" and the public avoidance of critical issues perpetuate the dominance and reproduction of the old model, even as it is being reformed or replaced in some places. Most ESI websites paint an excessively optimistic picture of El Sistema and some also disseminate inaccurate information about the Venezuelan program, serving in effect to market a problematic model rather than encourage critical reflection about it.

Consequently, those at greater distance who are not already on board with self-critique and change may get little sense that it is an important and necessary process. Whatever moves may have occurred in thinking and practice in some places, the lack of a clear, explicit critique of orthodox SATM means than many others continue down lines that have changed little for decades, even centuries. Public discourse has remained largely the same, and institutional publicity, press reports, and social media commentary on SATM continue much as before. Any changes have not been widely grasped, much less what has been left behind or why. This lack of clarity over continuity and change constrains the development of the field.

The degree of awareness of critical reassessment and change is low in many places. In Colombia, I came across few people who knew in detail what was going on in other SATM programs within the same country, let alone in Buenos Aires, Los Angeles, or Toronto. El Sistema continues to be influential across Latin America in part because its brand name and narrative continue to circulate far more widely than critiques or transformations. To some researchers, critiquing El Sistema in 2021 might seem like flogging a dead horse, but the horse is still alive and kicking in many parts of the world, particularly in the spheres of government, institutions, industry, and the media.

At the heart of the matter is the contrast between private and public debate. I have met a number of SATM leaders and employees around the world who are willing to engage in private critical conversations, but whether as a result of institutional pressure to toe the line or the advantages of adopting SATM's idealistic rhetoric, such critique rarely makes its way into the public realm. The ecosystem of SATM incentivizes public allegiance to the field's orthodoxy rather than open questioning, and this serves as an obstacle to change. More public debate over critical issues therefore is vital. If reformers make more noise about their work and foster more public awareness of shifts that are underway, the pace of change in SATM will inevitably pick up.

Open exchange between SATM and progressive music education research has also been the exception rather than the norm. In recent years, representatives of SATM programs have been thin on the ground at fora such as the International Society for Music Education's (ISME) El Sistema Special Interest Group or the Social Impact of

Making Music (SIMM) conferences, and critical researchers an even rarer sighting at El Sistema advocacy events. The main publication of the ESI field, *The Ensemble*, focuses on music education and social action, but it has ignored most peer-reviewed research on SATM and overlooked swathes of relevant work on CM, social justice in music education, and the sociology and philosophy of music education. Change would be considerably aided by more knowledge of and communication with such fields, where ideas and practices that are central to SATM have been under discussion for many years. André Gomes Felipe, the director of Liberdade school and architect of the NEOJIBA concert described in Chapter 5, is also a researcher who has presented his work at ISME and SIMM conferences; it is no coincidence that a musician who keeps abreast of research in these fields is doing such interesting work within SATM.

Similar problems are also found within the research sphere, however, where a disturbing number of SATM studies fail to take much (if any) account of peer-reviewed critical scholarship. Some qualitative researchers have looked carefully at quantitative studies of El Sistema (e.g. Logan 2015b; Scruggs 2015; Baker 2017a; Baker, Bull, and Taylor 2018), but the reverse has not occurred. Other qualitative scholars, meanwhile, appear barely aware of the field of music education research. This tendency to ignore or dismiss rather than engage critically with existing studies has marred the sub-field of SATM research. Here, too, more open debate is called for: researchers have a professional duty to respond to each other's evidence and arguments, rather than acting as ships passing in the night.

It is not just that information fails to circulate; in some cases, its circulation is actively impeded. Research with ambiguous findings or critical conclusions is systematically ignored. Govias (2015b) has even written about censorship in the ESI sector.[1] In several countries, major stakeholders—institutions, governments, prominent figures in classical music, journalists, and even some researchers—have combined forces to cherry-pick findings, repeat unfounded claims, and overlook counter-evidence (Baker 2018). As such, they have colluded in promoting a

---

1 See also my blog post "Censorship and self-censorship in the Sistema sphere", https://geoffbakermusic.wordpress.com/el-sistema-older-posts/censorship-and-self-censorship-in-the-sistema-sphere/.

deceptive narrative of success. Rimmer (2020) describes In Harmony Sistema England as "too big to fail," and he notes that the national press repeatedly presented the program as a success on the flimsiest of grounds but then ignored an independent, three-year evaluation report that found no positive effects on participating children's attainment, attendance or wider wellbeing. Rimmer suggests that vehement advocacy for In Harmony, particularly by the media, marginalized reasoned reflection on its mixed outcomes.

In short, change and knowledge of change have been constrained by a lack of commitment to the circulation of ideas by the SATM sector and its supporters. Recall a point from Chapter 4: culture is a battleground where ideas come into contact and conflict and play out. If SATM continues to avoid this process, its development will continue to be hampered. Suppression of critique and debate may have provided short-term gains in terms of public image, but over the longer term this is a dangerous game for any organization or field to play, let alone one that proclaims guiding principles such as inclusion, equity, and a spirit of inquiry.

Higher Music Education

Alongside this impediment to transformation lies the problem of musicians' professional training, which was a central issue in Medellín. How were new pedagogies to be put into practice if the training of teachers in universities remained largely the same? How were teachers to impart creative skills when many had been through a conservatoire-style education that Peerbaye and Attariwala (2019, 44) call "training *out* of creativity" (see also Waldron et al. 2018)? How were teachers to promote social justice and avoid perpetuating injustices if they had not been trained to reflect on the social and political aspects of music learning and teaching (Rusinek and Aróstegui 2015)? How were they to take decolonizing steps when they came from a higher education profoundly structured by coloniality (Silva Souza 2019)? This was a huge challenge for the Red. Identifying productive directions was one thing; working out how to pursue them, and who would enact them, was another. It was not just that the program now had an accumulated history, a momentum, and a musical track record; there was also the challenge of finding teachers with more relevant training, capable of implementing new pedagogies. The Red offered professional development activities, but this was a slow route to reform.

Change in SATM cannot progress far as an independent process; it needs to go hand in hand with reforms in higher music education. As Peerbaye and Attariwala (2019, 42) argue in relation to orchestral culture: "Music faculties and conservatories hold a key to change." There is increasing recognition of the importance of a shift in higher music education (e.g. Gaunt and Westerlund 2013), but actual movement has been slower. In Latin America, higher music education has been profoundly shaped by the European conservatoire model, and in many places it remains that way; unless there is a greater shift in emphasis away from preparation for classical performing careers and towards training teachers for musical-social work, efforts to reshape SATM will be hamstrung. In Medellín, if music degrees were more connected to the musical realities of the city, and if local universities introduced a SATM stream (an entirely logical step, given how many of their graduates go on to work in the Red), then music graduates would be better placed to prepare the next generation for social life and musical work.

Countries such as the UK, Canada, and Finland offer undergraduate degrees in community music, but there is no equivalent for SATM. Nevertheless, such degree programs may point to what focused SATM teacher training might look like. Also suggestive is Zamorano Valenzuela's (2020) study of the training of activism-oriented music teachers in a public Chilean university. It depicts the formation of critical, reflexive subjects, with a view to social transformation and not just technical training. Lessons include citizenship education, practices of democratic coexistence, and conflict resolution. Student teachers are encouraged to connect with social movements and mobilizations, which are seen as spaces of learning. In short, the music teacher's role is understood as a political one, and trainee teachers are pushed to question and if necessary invert the norms of their own earlier music education. Graduates of such a program would be well prepared for SATM work.

Resistance

Resistance to change was another significant brake in Medellín. It was linked to the dual spectre of the past and musical excellence. El Sistema and the Red in its Venezuelan phase set the bar high in musical terms: the SBYO became the gold standard for SATM programs, and excellence became equated with high-quality performances of canonic orchestral repertoire. El Sistema also propagated the notion of a "miracle," the musical equivalent of "having it all": that single-minded pursuit of musical excellence also produced astonishing social results. Research has revealed this miracle to be a myth, but it still exerts a significant pull on the field. Many teachers were educated within this ideology, and it is one that suits the keenest and most talented students—the ones who are most likely to remain over the long term. Consequently, these large, Latin American "social programs" are judged primarily according to conventionally-defined standards of musical excellence, and no alternative form of assessment—based on criteria such as inclusivity, creativity, or student voice—has gained wide acceptance.

However, such excellence depended on an extraordinary level of time commitment, a limited vision of social action as widening access, and a militaristic disciplinary regime sometimes characterized as bordering on the abusive, and as such, it set a problematic precedent. Softening those aspects is an obvious step for a program that wishes to take the social side more seriously, but as the Red has discovered over the years, it has musical repercussions. Shifting the balance between the musical and the social means shifting from more to less obvious results—ones that cannot necessarily be presented as a quasi-professional performance on stage. Change might mean improvements in a variety of areas (such as students enjoying better treatment and a more balanced life), but with decreased intensity goes decline in the performance level of the showcase orchestra. A transforming SATM cannot compete with El Sistema on the terrain of conventional measures of excellence. Although there have been some interesting innovations, there is nothing that can be compared with the SBYO in terms of performance level, and considering the peculiarity of that orchestra—its politician-conductor, its huge resources, its unmatched work rhythm—perhaps there never will be.

According to the field's conventional standards, then, change leads to decline. Numerous musicians in the Red, particularly the old guard, believed that more social action meant lower musical standards, as discussed in Chapter 2. It is hardly surprising that a shift towards a more socially-focused SATM might be resisted or at least not embraced by musicians if it came in such a guise. As long as the SBYO and similar orchestras are held up as the gold standard for SATM, it is hard to see the field moving as quickly or comprehensively as it might. As long as barnstorming, high-quality performances of great orchestral works continue to be seen as an exemplar of social action and the principal measure of success, attempts to generate more inclusive, diverse, creative, and participatory music education are liable to be seen by many as failures—or, at least, as less appealing.

In Medellín, I found a number of the first generation caught in limbo between nostalgia for the Red's earlier achievements and recognition that they were gone. They knew that the conditions that supported the first phase no longer existed, but they still lamented a decline in passion, dedication, and sense of belonging. El Sistema was the model of the past for the Red and everyone knew it, whether or not they were happy about it; but romanticization of that past by some staff meant that it still acted as a brake on change. The notion of a "golden age" in the past, of a historical essence tied up with a conventional conception of musical excellence, was one obstacle to envisioning a different future.

Desire for continuity with the orthodoxy of SATM, or resistance to new approaches, may be found at all levels of programs, including students, staff, and management. But there are also systemic and external forces to take into consideration. Institutions have a habit of creating their own momentum or inertia, which goes beyond the interests or desires of individuals within them. In large, longstanding programs, the practical and bureaucratic obstacles to change can be significant, and if a program is *perceived* to have worked—as is the case with many of the large SATM programs mentioned in this book—then the pressure and motivation to innovate may be limited, even when individuals understand that there are issues that ought to be addressed.

It is also important to consider the level above the leadership—the funders, politicians, parent institutions, and so on. The Red's trajectory is closely related to its funding by the city government. If the program embraced critical reflection and change from 2005, it was because the government did the same. During my fieldwork, the culture ministry funded critical, qualitative research in all the city's arts education networks. Also, the Red is not attached to an organization like a symphony orchestra or concert hall, and it does not have a direct publicity or strategic role for the professional music sector. Rather, it is one facet of the cultural policy of Medellín, and the city's cultural plan for 2011–20 focused on democratic cultural citizenship, emphasizing participation, inclusion, diversity, creativity, and critical reflection. There was nothing coming down from the funder about defending classical music or the symphony orchestra; in fact, the policy pointed towards a very different approach to music education than the model that the Red had inherited from El Sistema. Change therefore made sense in Medellín; it was supported by the political and institutional context. But if the funder's top priority is an attractive "success story"—if the program is intended to support a professional symphony orchestra or burnish the image of a powerful figure—then the space to reflect critically and pursue change may be significantly reduced.

Resistance to reform in SATM may therefore take several forms and operate on several levels—individual, institutional, ideological, and systemic. The poor circulation of information is certainly a contributory factor, but stasis and a lack of public critical reflection are not simply a matter of individual choice; they are also structural features of the field. What keeps the wheels of many organizations and of the whole sector turning is an idealistic narrative about the power of music and, more specifically, a mythical tale of its foundational program, El Sistema. Reputations and funding are tied to such stories. How much room for manoeuvre do individuals or even organizations really have, unless those holding the purse strings, like Medellín's culture ministry, grasp the need for change?

El Sistema

Another drag on reform is El Sistema itself, which has always taken an expansionist approach but has also consistently been sought out by other, more recently founded programs. It may have lost its direct influence over the Red, but it has played an important role in the development of the Red's competitor program, Iberacademy. Many SATM programs in Latin America retain close ties with the Venezuelan progenitor, and since El Sistema is a program characterized by continuity, such ties are hardly conducive to self-critique and change. Some SATM programs have grasped the importance of adapting with the times, yet they are tethered to a slow-moving mothership that has barely changed its thinking since the 1970s. The SATM field has thus been caught between the shifting currents of music education and the stasis of its original inspiration and most influential representative, meaning that its movement has been halting and uneven.

Dudamel's YOLA program in Los Angeles is a case in point. Its recent symposia have seen invitees discussing favoured progressive themes such as power, voice, social justice, and race. At the 2020 edition, YOLA invited some speakers from outside SATM to address contemporary topics including equity, culturally responsive programming, and youth development. Lecolion Washington of the Community Music Center of Boston spoke of amplifying youth voice, criticized the approach of teaching as you were taught, and questioned the notion that one could change the system without changing one's own mindset.[2] Echoing a central theme of this book, he stated: "You can't just change your tactics, you need to change your thinking." He also argued for rethinking Eurocentrism, using terms such as "cultural suicide" (what "young BIPOC often feel when entering music learning spaces that have long been dominated by White culture") and a "white saviourist frame." He named systemic exclusion within music education, and suggested that changing only one's tactics may lead to maintaining an exclusive space, just one with more women and people of colour in it. Two other invitees, Eryn Johnson (Community Art Center) and Laurie Jo Wallace (Health Resources in Action), focused on Creative Youth Development and emphasized young people's capacities and strengths and the importance of creativity and criticality in learning.[3] They presented a slide on levels of youth participation that was very similar to Hart's ladder of participation, discussed in Chapter 3.

What was remarkable here was not so much the presenters' arguments (which were excellent but also quite standard for

---

2   "Creating Culturally Responsive Programming", 14 July 2020.
3   "Engaging Youth: Youth Development and Music Education", 20 July 2020.

progressive arts education) as the elephant in the room: El Sistema—the program behind YOLA—embodies all of the problems that the speakers pinpointed and none of the solutions. Creative Youth Development is not simply an interesting addition to the SATM toolkit; it is the polar opposite of El Sistema's vision of "rescuing children and young people from an empty, disorientated, and deviant youth." Washington's focus on equity contrasts starkly with a program that is colour-blind, Eurocentric, and gives pride of place to men.[4] Yet not only were such tensions obviously never mentioned, since this was an El Sistema-inspired event, but the Venezuelan program itself was invited to present its philosophy, an opportunity that it used to replay clips from old documentaries and Abreu's TED-prize talk from 2009.[5] Alongside the progressive sessions addressing contemporary issues, then, YOLA also provided a platform for El Sistema to continue purveying Abreu's conservative vision via old and much repeated footage. Where some speakers urged a change of mindset, this session was devoted entirely to revering the old model. The result was an image of a program with one foot pointing towards the future and the other stuck in a problematic past.

This divided loyalty and hedging of bets led to a lack of cohesion, consistency, and rigour. YOLA continued to hold up El Sistema as an example, yet also invited speakers who flatly contradicted El Sistema's philosophy. Glaring disjunctures between old and new visions begged to be discussed, but they were never mentioned. Speakers talked about change, but there was no critical analysis of the aspects of SATM that needed changing. They held up critical thinking as an important feature of music education, but they did not apply it to SATM itself. El Sistema's continued dominance led to mixed messages about reverence and critique, continuity and change.

El Sistema's top-level influence has been complemented in recent years by the massive exodus of El Sistema's musicians from Venezuela as the country's crisis bit in earnest. Many are now installed as performers

---

4   In addition to the evidence presented in Baker (2014), El Sistema's website in late 2020 included a section entitled "Pioneers", which listed thirteen men and three women—two of the latter being members of Abreu's family (https://elsistema.org.ve/historia/).

5   "The philosophy of El Sistema", 30 July 2020.

and educators across the globe, including in SATM programs. It would take extensive research to determine the influence of these Venezuelan musicians on the development of SATM in other countries, and it should not be taken as given that they would strengthen the orthodoxy as opposed to supporting efforts at change. One of El Sistema's most successful graduates to move to the US, the violinist Luigi Mazzocchi, has argued strongly for the necessity of reform (Scripp 2016a, 2016b). In my research in Venezuela, I encountered similar criticism of El Sistema's methods from its own students, graduates, and teachers, so one should not assume that they would favour reproducing those methods elsewhere. Years earlier, Estrada (1997) made comparable findings: several of her interviewees, all current or former El Sistema members, defined themselves against the program rather than identifying with it. One stated: "now that I teach, I try not to make the same mistakes that they made with us" (25). Another said: "each day I copy less the way that they taught me, I've achieved a relationship with my students in which communication is a real exchange of feelings, emotions, knowledge, concerns, and not a weapon of power for humiliating and dominating them" (17). A third claimed that El Sistema "served me as a model of what not to do pedagogically speaking" (34).[6]

That said, the proliferation of orchestras of former El Sistema musicians across the Americas, and the cachet that the program continues to hold in the classical music and music education worlds, suggests that overt affiliation with the Venezuelan program brings much greater advantages for immigrant musicians than critical distance. It remains a potent calling card. Also, the limited teacher training or spaces for critical reflection offered by El Sistema mean that opportunities to develop alternatives to the program's philosophy of "teach as you were taught" are similarly constrained. In newspaper articles and short films on this topic, immigrant Venezuelan musicians in several countries have talked about El Sistema as a success story that they want to share with the world. In Chile, they have even set up an El Sistema-inspired foundation, Música para la Integración, and with its starter orchestra named after Abreu and support from El Sistema advocacy organizations, it looks to be retaining the Venezuelan recipe.[7] All- or majority-Venezuelan

---

6   See Baker and Frega (2016; 2018).
7   https://musicaparalaintegracion.org/.

programs are less likely to move away from El Sistema's approach than ones where an individual Venezuelan joins a local workforce. After all, unlike the much slower and more limited exodus of earlier years exemplified by Mazzocchi, most of these musicians left out of necessity rather than dissatisfaction with the institution or a search for a better education. On balance, it is reasonable to hypothesize that the recent, rapid El Sistema exodus will have strengthened convention more than innovation in the international SATM field, even if only by reinforcing the El Sistema brand. Nevertheless, there will clearly be exceptions, and such a hypothesis should be tested by future research.

International Support

Thinking again about the level above programs, a number of international and multinational organizations have lined up behind El Sistema and orthodox versions of SATM and have thus acted as a force for continuity rather than change, though there are exceptions, such as Jeunesses Musicales, mentioned in Chapter 5. The Hilti Foundation, for example, supports El Sistema and several ESI programs. In Latin America, its funding is channelled to more conservative orchestral programs—in Medellín, to Iberacademy rather than the Red. The United Nations and the Inter-American Development Bank are also prominent supporters of El Sistema, and they have paid little attention to critical questions arising from research—even their own. In 2018, they participated in an event at the University of Music and Performing Arts in Vienna billed as "El Sistema: A model of social inclusion for the world" (see Baker 2018). Yet the IDB's own evaluation had suggested that El Sistema had a low level of participation by the poor and actually illustrated "the challenges of targeting interventions towards vulnerable groups of children in the context of a voluntary social program." As Clift (2020) concludes about the IDB study: "As poorer children were under-represented, far from addressing social inequalities, the work of the [music] centres served to reinforce them—entirely contrary to the idea of an intervention designed to reduce social and health inequalities." The exclusion of women from positions of authority also makes very obvious El Sistema's failure as a model of social inclusion. Nonetheless, these sponsors not only looked the other way but even claimed the opposite.

Such major organizations have disbursed hundreds of millions of dollars into El Sistema and similar SATM programs. They have played an important role in shaping SATM developments around the world, conferring prestige as well as funds. To date, most of their support has gone into reinforcing the status quo, even if that means repeating unproven and dubious claims and ignoring relevant studies. Change in SATM would undoubtedly be spurred on significantly if major funders took proper account of the problems with the orthodox model revealed by published academic research and gave more support to innovation.

The El Sistema event in Austria took place almost simultaneously with the Guri/Jeunesses Musicales conference in Brazil. The European event saw El Sistema trumpeted as a model for the world; the Latin American one did not even mention the Venezuelan program, focusing instead on new directions in SATM. This dichotomy encapsulates what I perceive as a struggle for the soul of SATM. This struggle is centred in Latin America, though it plays out in countries around the world. Latin America is where the oldest and largest SATM programs are found, where the orthodox model is most persistent, and where El Sistema's direct influence is most notable. In one corner stand the Venezuelan program and others that follow or admire its model. In the other are found the reformers: the Red, Chazarreta, Guri, and so on. Contrasting programs are found in the same countries and even the same cities, like Medellín (the Red and Iberacademy). The battle lines are drawn around educational and cultural ideologies, and also, to a significant extent, musical genres. Most programs in the former camp are aligned with classical music organizations, like symphony orchestras, or led by prominent classical musicians, and they may be seen as extensions of or support acts for the professional orchestral world—El Sistema's original purpose. Programs in the latter camp may have begun that way but shifted their emphasis, like the Red, or been founded along contrasting lines, like Chazarreta.

Like any broad-brush account, this is certainly a simplification. The reality is more of a continuum than a polarity, and the two dynamics may even be found simultaneously at different levels of the same program. The Red is a good example, as is NEOJIBA; in both cases, schools and showcase ensembles lie at different points along the continuum. André Gomes Felipe describes the Liberdade school as a CM initiative within an ESI program.⁸ Nevertheless, the notion of a struggle for the soul reflects rather closely my experience of a year's immersion in the Red, and private communications from reformers in other programs also point towards tensions, conflicts, and ruptures more than polite disagreements and differences of opinion. These are not simply two different approaches; one is a reform—and therefore a critique—of the other. Chazarreta in Argentina directly opposed the Eurocentrism of El Sistema. The Red slowly distanced itself from the kind of elite orchestral training represented by Iberacademy, but the two programs still competed over advanced students and relations were tense. The contrast between the Vienna and São Paulo events was stark; one exalted the old model, the other had no place for it. The announcement of a national ESI program in Mexico in 2019 was met with critical responses by many music education specialists (e.g. Estrada Rodríguez et al. 2019).⁹ However one labels this scenario, currents of continuity and change within SATM in Latin America are in competition, and the dominant forces are largely behind the orthodoxy, making for an unequal struggle. Change is therefore far from assured.

Dilemmas of Transformation

Thus far, the discussion has revolved around efforts at reform and forces that constrain them. At this point, it is also necessary to consider challenges and dilemmas of a more conceptual or philosophical kind that imply a need for a more revolutionary approach. Echoing Ramalingam's call to the aid sector and Lecolion Washington's words to YOLA, new ways of thinking, rather than tinkering with conventional practices, may be required. Some challenges are so profound that they question the very existence of SATM.

There are essentially two categories of critique of SATM: practical and ideological. The former focuses on gaps between theory and practice, the latter on the theory itself. For ideological critics of SATM

---

8 "The Liberdade Nucleo: A Community Music Perspective in a 'El Sistema' Inspired Program", 23 June 2020, https://www.isme-commissions.org/cma-programme.html.

9 This was also a major topic of concern at a music education conference that I attended in Xalapa (Veracruz, Mexico) in January 2020.

and similar enterprises, making programs work better does not resolve the problem, because the problem is the thinking behind them. In this light, reforming practices is not the solution. But practical critiques, too, may raise profound questions.

Is Music Education Really the Answer?

One practical critique is very simple: SATM has existed for more than four decades in Latin America, yet where is the social change? Even after forty-five years of operation on an increasingly massive scale, it is impossible to point to evidence that El Sistema produces the kinds of social transformation claimed by the program's leaders. Venezuela, Colombia, Mexico, and Brazil, which all have large SATM projects, are plagued with violence, and the problem has worsened in Venezuela over SATM's history. In 2018, these four countries accounted for a quarter of all murders on Earth (Erickson 2018). Such high levels of violence do not prove that SATM does not work, of course, but they do suggest that robust evidence is needed if claims such as "orchestras and choirs are incredibly effective instruments against violence" are to be taken seriously. Without such evidence, there must be doubts over justifying music education from this perspective.

John Sloboda (2015) poses a series of questions that is of great relevance to SATM. If social goals are really paramount, Sloboda asks, can it be said for certain that music education is the best way to achieve them? Is it possible that, at least in some cases, significant social change requires a different activity altogether and the most responsible action would be to put aside music and pursue those goals through other means? Does putting music first, making it a non-negotiable part of action, put limits on what can be achieved socially?

At present, there is no research that makes a convincing case that music education is *the most effective and efficient* tool for the kinds of social action that are sought by SATM programs (such as poverty and crime reduction or promoting peaceful coexistence) and therefore the most deserving recipient of funds. This would be less important if social action were a desirable side-effect of music instruction, but in SATM, as the label indicates, it is the primary aim—so then, as Sloboda suggests, a case for "why music?" needs to be made. In fact, as we have seen previously, there are major studies that have concluded that El Sistema has no significant effect on prosociality (Alemán et al. 2017; Ilari, Fesjian, and Habibi 2018). The evidence to support the IDB's theory of change and claims of orchestral training's transformative social effects is decidedly weak, yet the huge investment continues: the cost of El Sistema's new headquarters was originally estimated at $437.5 million USD (CAF 2010). If social action is genuinely the *primary* goal, as the program often states, is building a massive, deluxe classical music centre really the best way to get there? Could those hundreds of millions of dollars of development bank loans not have been spent better in a country that has suffered from severe shortages of food, medicines, and basic medical equipment and has seen an exodus of refugees to rival Syria's?

Sloboda's argument points to an important question mark over the justification for public spending on large, expensive SATM programs. Major investment in an unproven strategy demands serious examination through the lens of opportunity cost. It may be tempting to think that any argument that persuades funders to support music education is one worth making, but considering the social work *not* undertaken as a result may suggest otherwise.

The question of what money should be spent on exercises some socially engaged researchers and artists. For example, Godwin (2020) asks whether SATM budgets might not be better spent on organizations with expertise in social action. Sachs Olsen (2019, 186) writes:

> Wouldn't we better approach change by using our artistic skills and efforts in campaigns, demonstrations, and actions against policies and development schemes that are based on private property and exchange value? Wouldn't it be more effective to set up a community garden or local neighbourhood activity group if we wanted to enhance participation and social relations among urban inhabitants?

Scholarship in economics helps to bring this issue into focus. In her article "Welfare works: redistribution is the way to create less violent, less unequal societies," Justino (2020) argues that economic inequality is the major problem in Latin American society and the principal source of violence, and that government redistributive measures are required to resolve it. Similarly, Veltmeyer and Petras (2011, 1–2) draw on a 2010 report by the UN's Economic Commission for Latin America and the

Caribbean (ECLAC/CEPAL) to argue that when it comes to poverty in the region,

> "exclusion" is not the problem [...] Nor is inclusion the solution. The problem rather is a system which is designed to benefit the few who have the power to advance their own interests at the expense of the many, who have suffered and continue to suffer precisely from their inclusion and participation in this system, under conditions of what CEPAL ... terms "the structure of inequality."

If structural economic inequality is the root of the problem, are arts education programs in the name of social inclusion or coexistence really an effective solution?

There are many doubters. Adorno was blunt: "it is impossible to solve problems that are caused by society's economic situation through the aesthetic power of music" (cited in Kertz-Welzel 2011, 12). Rincón (2015) issues a coruscating critique of Medellín's elites for focusing on cultural and educational charity, which he sees as ineffective and self-serving. Ineffective because it springs from the centre of power, where young people are poorly understood, rather than from the margins and youth's needs and desires; and because "the problem is inequity and inclusion: and that is not resolved by a culture of charity" (133). Maclean (2015, 68) sheds light on the self-serving part of the equation: she suggests that art has been an important part of urban policy in the city because "[f]or the policies in Medellín to be acceptable to and supported by the elites, they had to appeal to elite sensibilities."

Hanauer (2019) makes a similar argument in a different context (the US). He regards "educationism"—a belief in the power of education to fix inequality—as profoundly misguided, confusing a symptom with a cause. Education may help some individuals but it does nothing to shift the fundamental problem. He identifies it as a self-serving narrative of the wealthy and powerful, "because it tells us what we want to hear: that we can help restore shared prosperity without sharing our wealth or power." It also distracts from the true causes of economic inequality and defends an indefensible status quo. Hanauer thus presents educationism as a support act for inequality rather than a solution.

Public art has been the target of similar critical scrutiny. There is no shortage of artists and researchers who have critiqued public art for drawing a veil over the real causes of injustice and decorating the development policies of the neoliberal city. As Vujanović (2016, 116) argues: "socially useful art in support of the advancement of broader civic agendas [...] often serves to heal social antagonisms or give an impression that they are healed, while never dealing seriously with the material bases of antagonisms or disturbing the capitalist system of production and distribution of surplus value." For Merli (2002, 113),

> the concern for addressing social cohesion and inclusion through a "soft" approach, such as the use of cultural projects, might be seen as a convenient means to divert attention from the real causes of today's social problems and the tough solutions that might be needed to solve them. According to this line of reasoning, the whole discourse of social inclusion is a lot more appealing to the political elite than the old fashioned rhetoric of poverty and the call for economic redistribution.

Sachs Olsen (2019, 29) describes participatory art "as a way to provide homeopathic solutions to problems that are systemic," while Anthony Schrag argues that artists should be concerned with asking "deep and probing questions" rather than serving as "the state's cheaper option to proper and appropriate social work" (cited in Deane 2018, 329).

For such artists and writers, not only is public art not an effective solution to major social issues, but it is also frequently part of the problem. Practical and ideological critiques thus merge. For example, Berry Slater and Iles (2009) analyze public art in the UK as a smokescreen and marketing device, funded in place of social infrastructures and welfare: "a cosmetic solution for problems produced by failing infrastructures, at root by other areas of government policy" (Malcolm Miles, cited in ibid.). "Community is killed off only to be 'regenerated' in zombie-like form, a living dead state of social (non)reproduction and officially orchestrated sham spectacles of being together." Public artists are "soft cops working on the front line of social inclusion" and "employed to fabricate totemic symbols of integrated communities." Culture-led regeneration has "now fully developed into a mode of governance—of soft control and increasingly subtle coercion."

Looking through the lens of scholarship on economics and public art, orchestral training under the banner of social inclusion looks like an unlikely candidate for combatting inequality and poverty, however attractive it might appear and sound. SATM misidentifies the root of the problems; it is therefore unsurprising that it has failed to provide demonstrable solutions. A realist perspective might be that promoting music as a way of addressing major social problems is to dance to the tune of, and provide an attractive fig leaf for, governments that are unwilling to devote sufficient resources to effective solutions, above all redistribution. A more critical formulation still would be that music programs and musicians contribute to and collaborate with a false narrative about social problems in order to gain funding for their musical work, distracting from a lack of substantive action to address those problems and, as analysed in Chapter 4, exacerbating social divides. Berry Slater and Iles's analysis of public art is a shoe that fits orthodox SATM: orchestral training, too, extends models of governance, and the ensemble serves as the ultimate symbol or spectacle of community, a simulacrum that conveys a positive message whether the community itself is in rude health, experiencing little material change (as in Medellín), or steadily disintegrating (as in Venezuela). Indeed, this may be precisely the appeal of youth orchestras to governments: an idealized performance of communities that may be neglected or actually under assault by other policies.

SATM may therefore serve, as Logan (2016) suggests, as a "veil of culture," obscuring the real workings of the state, including reductions in social services, and thus help with one hand while harming with the other. It may also cover up reductions in music education provision for the majority of the population, as has happened in the UK. For Logan, programs like El Sistema serve as a support act for educational inequality. He is skeptical of arts programs that promote simplistic ideas about social change at the expense of in-depth discussions about education and society, and that distract from the urgency of transforming the whole education system by focusing instead on social mobility for a few fortunate individuals.

There are good reasons, then, to argue that social change requires political and economic action to reduce inequity and inequality, and that SATM constitutes an attractive but ineffective distraction—a performance of social change that is much more appealing to social elites than the real thing (higher taxes and redistribution). It is one example of a wider phenomenon: artists are portrayed as a solution to social problems, but they often serve instead to shore up the existing system, providing a "veil of culture" that lets governments off the hook. The arts are frequently co-opted to provide an illusion of social action and an alibi for dominant actors, lessening the pressure to provide substantive solutions at a structural level.

As an illuminating contrast, Bregman (2018) argues that giving people money is an effective solution to poverty (see also Orkin 2020). Cash handouts particularly benefit children and are also cheaper than the alternatives. Bregman's argument that "poverty is not a lack of character. It's a lack of cash" (69) raises interesting questions for SATM, since it roundly contradicts Abreu's foundational claims about poverty as a deficit of aspiration, identity, or spiritual resources (see Baker 2016b). Another quotation also hits close to the bone: "Anywhere you find poor people, you also find non-poor people theorizing their cultural inferiority and dysfunction" (cited in Bregman 2018, 92); there are distinct echoes of El Sistema imagining youth as "empty, disorientated, and deviant." Bregman asks: "Why send over expensive white folks in SUVs when we can simply hand over their salaries to the poor?" (31). Why send over musicians, we might also ask, if the aim is to combat poverty?

There are questions of ethics as well as efficacy hanging over SATM. Should musicians serve as "soft cops" for the state? Should they play along with the fantastical story that an orchestra can do the job of welfare? Should they comply with an ideology that puts the values and behaviour of disadvantaged youth under the spotlight rather than the grossly unfair system and the elites who perpetuate it? Is buying into this dubious narrative a price worth paying for funding music education? If SATM is primarily concerned with combatting violence and promoting peace, what does it mean for it to propose activities that make no reference to the principal cause of violence (economic inequality) or the best solution (redistribution)? What does it mean to advocate for public expenditure on a program that has not been proven to reduce inequality (SATM) rather than one that has (welfare)?

Justino is a development economist, but the two photos in her article both depict sonic scenes. Not youth orchestras, though, but the "cacerolazo": the distinctive banging of pots and pans that often accompanies political protests in Latin America. Here, sound is tied to direct political action on inequality. It is mobilized against the real cause of violence rather than in support of conservative myths that blame societal ills on the emptiness and deviancy of youth with too much time on their hands. The images of discordant cacerolazos raise the questions of whether harmonious music-making is really the best way to tackle the biggest social problems of our time, and whether SATM might one day play a role in combating rather than obscuring the causes of poverty and violence.

A Colonialist Conception of Music Education?

If Sloboda encourages us to think harder about the nature of societal problems and the adequacy of music as a response, Guillermo Rosabal-Coto (2019) homes in on the conceptualization of the individual subject. He raises the concern that Eurocentric music education in Latin America is inescapably tainted by its foundation on a colonialist conception of the subject as deficient or flawed and in need of correction and redemption. Rosabal-Coto argues that such music education

> has operated under the rationale to convert individuals into Euro-American, White artists or citizens. For education to succeed in this goal, it is necessary that the music learner is negated in their ways to be in and engage with music, and constructed by family, teachers, peers, and themselves as inferior subalterns. Their traits, memories, sensations, histories, and cognitive make-up are insufficient or in need of accommodation or modification in order to comply with the standards of an ideal individual. (15)

For Rosabal-Coto, the ideological basis of Eurocentric music education is deeply questionable in a Latin American context, since it reproduces the way that, after the Spanish Conquest, "the Indigenous of what became Latin America were instilled with a self-concept of inferior subaltern though conversion to Catholicism and the encomienda" (ibid.). Music education perpetuates colonialist dynamics such as assumptions of the superiority of European culture and those who bear it, and attempts by social elites to reform Others rather than understand and learn from them. If constructing the native population as inferior was fundamental to colonization, then for Latin American elites to take the same ideals and repeat the process is a form of recolonization from within.

El Sistema, with its salvationist vision and its clear echoes of colonial missionary campaigns to "civilize" Latin America's indigenous population through music instruction (Baker 2014), is the epitome of the approach that Rosabal-Coto critiques. It, too, rests on a colonialist notion of young people and their families as socially and culturally deficient, and the path that it prescribes (betterment through absorbing European musical norms) is a colonialist one. As a director of one of El Sistema's largest *núcleos* [music schools] told Shieh (2015, 573), "it is not his *núcleo*'s place to address larger social issues. The system, he says, is about 'reforming individuals.'" The Red is couched in more progressive language, but its goals of inculcating values and transforming individual lives are built on the same ideological foundations. Yet what are the grounds for depicting young people en masse as in need of reform? And what, as Rosabal-Coto asks, would support the concomitant notion that possessing musical skills gives some individuals the moral and social authority to place themselves on a pedestal and attempt to reform others? In his critique of discourses of salvationism in music education, Spruce (2017, 725) notes the frequent absence of "reflection by those occupying 'hegemonic positions' on their right to judge particular lives and communities as requiring transformation" and a failure to ask "why they should be the agents of such transformations."

Decolonial critiques by Latin American educator-researchers like Rosabal-Coto posit the continent's Eurocentric music education as a social problem rather than a solution. As such, they shed doubt on the validity of SATM as a concept.[10] To borrow the terms of decolonial theorists Mignolo and Walsh, they are as concerned with the principles, frame of reference, and logic of coloniality of Eurocentric music education in Latin America as with its practices. As these authors argue: "It is not enough to change the content of the conversation (the domains, the enunciated); on the contrary, it is of the essence to change the terms (regulations, assumptions, principles managed at the level of the enunciation) of the conversation" (2018, 149). Indeed, Rosabal-Coto and other decolonial music scholars go deeper than the surface level of diversifying content and question the very terms and aims of Eurocentric music education. (There are clear parallels here with the discussion of reforming pedagogy in the previous chapter.) Their

---

10 Rosabal-Coto (2016) addresses SATM more directly.

critiques point beyond instruments and repertoire to understandings of what music is, what it does, and what it is for.

The root of the problem is a Eurocentric conception of music and music education as social control or ordering (Gouk 2013). The emblematic institution of European music education, the conservatoire, has its origins in the orphanages (or *conservatorios*) of Renaissance Italy. In Venice, for example, young female orphans were trained in music at the *ospedali grandi*, the primary purpose of which was to regulate the city's social environment (Tonelli 2013). The musical opportunities provided to impoverished girls came with strict control over their day-to-day lives. The young musicians had to submit to an inflexible monastic routine: silence, lots of work, and little leisure time. Musical training was an extension of the orphanages' imposition of social control. This notion of music and music education was transplanted to the Americas in the sixteenth century, and it continues to this day, with SATM as its clearest manifestation.

If SATM is bound up with problematic notions of control, deficit, and development, then what is required is a philosophical revolution—an abandonment of an "ethic of correction," of an urge to "save" others, of a presumption that they lack culture—rather than just practical modifications. *Pace* El Sistema, it is not individuals that need reforming but rather SATM's ideological foundation.

Is SATM Politically Dangerous?

A third existential challenge comes from Alexandra Kertz-Welzel's (2005; 2011) reading of Adorno's writing on music education. Adorno argued that idealistic music education with utilitarian goals and without critical thinking was inherently dangerous, since it was susceptible to appropriation by authoritarian regimes, and it should therefore be avoided. Kertz-Welzel (2011, 12) focuses on Adorno's critique of

> intense musical experiences in joint music making, where being part of community fosters a sense of well-being and escape from the problems of real life. The overemphasis on community nurtures "the liquidation of the individual (which) is the real signature of the new musical situation." The individual disappears and only exists as part of a group. Being part of a community, whether in music or in society, can be dangerous if

individuals completely lose their ability for critical reflection and free will.

Adorno held up music education's assimilation into the Third Reich. At that time, the age-old dream of transforming the world through music education ended up as a support act for Hitler.

This argument is all too relevant to SATM, since El Sistema in the twenty-first century perfectly exemplified Adorno's point. The creation of an archetypical Venezuelan "cultural caudillo" or strongman (Silva-Ferrer 2014), El Sistema revolved around autocratic leadership, unquestioning submission to authority, and a focus on community, and it shunned critical reflection and self-determination. It articulated the kind of pseudo-religious vision of music education—as a mission, as healing and redemption—that was also heard in the Third Reich and provoked such suspicion from Adorno. In Venezuela, the idealistic rhetoric about transforming individuals and building community, and the lack of accompanying criticality, saw young musicians easily reduced to collective political inertia and swept up into de facto support for the government, illustrating Kertz-Welzel's (2011, 16) central point: "Music has the power to transform human beings, but it also has the power to manipulate people." She notes that many German music educators played along because they were granted a more important role in society: "Music education as a means of transforming human beings and society is a compelling and seductive idea for music educators" (Kertz-Welzel 2005, 4–5). In Venezuela, too, many musicians embraced their newfound prominence and prestige and turned a blind eye to the political implications.

The idealistic rhetoric also appealed to the government's ears, and the program became a blatant propaganda tool, providing the soundtrack to the Venezuelan government's self-presentation at home and abroad. Music education and authoritarian politics merged as El Sistema orchestras performed at government ceremonies, accompanied senior politicians on overseas missions, and played a starring role in a government propaganda video.[11] As Gabriela Montero writes, "Venezuelan musicians have cooperated in a state-funded endeavour

---

11   Examples can be found on my blog: https://geoffbakermusic.wordpress.com/el-sistema-the-system/el-sistema-blog/.

to whitewash Venezuela's grave failures with the singular detergent of music. [...] Venezuelan musicians allowed themselves to become the embodiment of Venezuela's state apparatus."[12] Venezuelan politicians have made extensive use of the emotional power of a youth orchestra. When Michelle Bachelet visited Venezuela to research her UN Human Rights report in 2019, she was met by the Simón Bolívar Youth Orchestra "as a sign of fraternity and Bolivarian peaceful diplomacy" ("Canciller" 2019).[13] Given, too, El Sistema's central focus on discipline and obedience, Venezuela illustrates the twin danger that concerned Adorno: music education as propaganda for a specific authoritarian regime, and music education as producing the kinds of subjects desired by authoritarian regimes.

In a similar analysis of the shadow of fascism hanging over idealistic, collective music education, Bradley (2009, 66) notes: "The feelings arising from being included in a collective 'we' are so powerful [...], feel so good and so unconditional, that we seek to replicate those experiences without thought to their potential outcomes." She continues: "The imagined community formed within such moments creates a powerfully seductive sense of oneness that can easily be manipulated with disastrous consequences" (70). El Sistema strove to generate this "powerfully seductive sense of oneness" with its "big family" discourse and monopolization of students' time, and the consequences can be seen in how little resistance there has been to the intensification of the program's politicization from 2007 to the present day. The combination of a powerful ethos of collectivity, strong discipline, the banishment of critical thinking, and magical music-making saw many musicians turn a blind eye to the darker aspects of the program and perform a public propaganda role on behalf of a government that many of them disdained in private.

SATM was thus a compliant and often willing handmaiden in the transition to authoritarianism in Venezuela (Esté 2018; Kozak Rovero 2018). Adorno's concerns over "socially transformative" music

---

12 "PUTIN POWER: musicians sound their outrage (a statement of support)", Facebook, 11 February 2021.
13 This attempt at musical whitewash was unsuccessful, as Bachelet's report was highly critical, underlining "grave violations of economic, social, civil, political and cultural rights" (https://www.ohchr.org/EN/NewsEvents/Pages/DisplayNews.aspx?NewsID=24788&LangID=E).

education were amply borne out. Nor is the Venezuelan program unique. A journalistic investigation of Bruno Campo, the director of an ESI program funded by the municipal government of Guatemala City, alleged that he and his backers exploited his orchestra for political ends:

> In exchange for absolute power in the Municipal Music School and the System of Orchestras, Bruno Campo repaid the Unionist Municipality with concerts by children and young people. And there was an element of exploitation. For the elections of 2007 and 2011, they would do up to three "barrio" concerts a week during months of campaigning. Without compensation. 75 children and young people from impoverished areas of Guatemala City, playing in white and green Municipality sweaters every two or three days. The cellist Rossana Paz, an adolescent at the time, recalls that the concerts took place with the banners of the Unionist Party and fireworks at the end. (Flores 2019)

The reporter concluded: "To the outside world, the Municipality and Unionism shone, thanks to the social project of music for youth." Interestingly, the Unionist Party is conservative, at the opposite end of the political spectrum from Venezuela's socialist government. The appropriation of SATM and music students appears to know no political or ideological boundaries. El Sistema may have become an emblem of the Bolivarian Revolution, but it has also promoted and been promoted by banks, corporations, and other sharp-eyed organizations (Fink 2016). Its largest replica in Latin America, the Mexican program Esperanza Azteca, used public funds to boost the image and business empire of Ricardo Salinas Pliego, the country's third richest man (García Bermejo 2018). Politicians are not the only powerful figures who find SATM to be an attractive accomplice. Indeed, we might extend Adorno's critique and suggest that SATM shows idealistic music education as susceptible to appropriation by commercial as well as political interests, and therefore as doubly ambiguous or risky. El Sistema in its heyday managed the impressive feat of serving as both a tool of soft power for the Venezuelan government and a golden goose for the classical music industry, harnessing the idea of SATM to both political and economic agendas, both socialism and capitalism.

However, it might instead be argued that rather than being appropriated by the Venezuelan government, SATM was actually designed for it. Esté (2018) identifies Abreu's claims of overcoming poverty through musical training as a form of musical populism that was carefully crafted for the "populist ears of Venezuelan presidents" in order to persuade them to fund his project. This is a crucial distinction. It suggests that SATM was not *politicized* in Venezuela so much as *designed as a political strategy* by Abreu, himself a senior politician and economist who knew exactly how the levers of power worked. In 2011, a former top-level figure in El Sistema claimed that the idea of SATM emerged in the mid-1990s when populism was on the rise in Venezuela and Abreu grasped that "there's nothing that a populist politician likes more than the word 'social'" (Baker 2014, 165). Attempts to portray El Sistema's twenty-first-century history in terms of a power grab by the Bolivarian Revolution ignore the various ways in which, "when Chávez came to power, [Abreu] handed El Sistema to him on a silver platter," in the words of Eduardo Casanova.[14] In other words, political ideology is not something that was added to SATM in an act of appropriation; it is foundational and inherent to a concept that was created in order to attract political support.

Adorno, Kertz-Welzel, and the case studies from Germany and Venezuela thus raise a third existential question for SATM. Rather than debating whether it works or not, or how it could be improved, they shed doubt on the very enterprise. SATM was born in 1990s Venezuela as a funding strategy, and this is where it has been an undisputed and dramatic success: in persuading governments and funders to support music education via the argument that it is actually a social program. Yet in an Adornian light, the secret of SATM's success is also its fatal flaw. The social framing appeals to politicians more than an artistic one, but this appeal can lead not only to funding but also to political collaboration or appropriation. El Sistema resolved the funding problem but simultaneously created an ideological one. The question then arises: if this style of music education is inherently dangerous, as Adorno suggests, can it ever be made safe? If SATM's origins are as a political ploy, can it ever be sheltered from political collaboration or

---

14 "La juvenil", Facebook, 24 January 2021. Casanova is a prominent Venezuelan author and former cultural official who worked closely with Abreu. See also my blog post "Writing El Sistema's history", https://geoffbakermusic.wordpress.com/el-sistema-the-system/el-sistema-blog/writing-el-sistemas-history/.

appropriation? Is it possible to reform SATM, or would true reform mean dismantling the very idea of SATM?

Reform or Revolution?

The work of such scholars leads us towards an uncertain, ambiguous conclusion. All, from different perspectives, raise existential questions about SATM. Looking ahead, the main options appear to be: unsatisfactory and indefensible stasis, ignoring all the problems and dilemmas; reform, of the kind that the Red has undertaken, which may at times be painful; or a revolution in the very foundations of the field.

I believe revolutionary thinking to be absolutely necessary: the questions raised by these scholars could not be more important, and a paradigm shift, rather than tweaks and fixes, will ultimately be required if the field is to generate social change. Looking at how the older, larger fields of development and aid have changed in recent decades, it is hard to imagine the 1970s model of orthodox SATM, built on mid-twentieth-century modernist developmentalism, lasting long into the future, at least with any degree of validity. The disjunctures are obvious even today. A Red leader mused privately about the difficulties of reforming a longstanding symphonic program—a process they compared to twisting fingers—and the attraction of tearing it up and starting again. Why go through the painful process of unlearning and relearning with the current staff, they asked? Why not start again with musicians who already get the point and have the tools? This may have been a thought experiment rather than a proposal, but it might be an appropriate course of action in some contexts, particularly where the orthodox model is not yet well established. This kind of revolution had taken place in Medellín's other three arts education networks, so it is not an idle thought.

The example of the Red raises the question of just how reformable SATM may be. Music was the only one of the four municipal networks to resist a revolution during the tenure of Mayor Gaviria (2012–15); progress was tortuous even when the program's funder was behind reform. The city government then proposed to create a parallel, more progressive institution alongside the Red, called Medellín Vive la Música (MVLM), giving young people a choice between the two. But funding was withdrawn with the change of government in 2016. One interpretation of the next phase of the Red was that the new government attempted to merge the two projects by bringing in Giraldo and Franco from MVLM to head up the Red, leading to the struggles between progressive thinking and conventional habits described in these pages. Yet it might also be argued that the last fifteen years (two-thirds of the Red's history) have been spent in various states of disruption, trying to fix one problem only to create another. One possible conclusion is that it might be better to create an alternative to SATM—a new institution with a different philosophy and faculty, along the lines of MVLM—rather than attempt to transform an existing program with a long history, an established image, philosophy, and staff, and a complex array of traditions, routines, and expectations.

Nevertheless, there are many barriers to revolution that make it improbable on a mass scale at present. MVLM's collapse highlights the economic hurdle. A more likely path for SATM in the short term is to attempt reform, bringing the field more in line with progressive social goals and critical thinking in music education.

Still, there is no denying that attempting to bridge this gap has caused pain in Medellín. Introducing progressive educational thinking into a conventional model is not easy, and a challenge for reform of SATM is that this gap can be so large. But given the flaws in the original version of SATM and the necessity of growth, pain is arguably a good sign. Its absence is more worrying: complacent utopianism is the biggest obstacle to SATM's evolution.

The path of reform is not straightforward, then. The IDB's 2017 report on El Sistema revealed a gulf between grandiose claims and barely perceptible effects, implying that either the claims needed toning down or the work needed a serious overhaul. (Neither occurred.) From an educational and intellectual standpoint, less rhetorical grandiosity and more pedagogical ambition would be a big step forward. Sloboda (2019) urges modesty with respect to long-term impacts, which are hard or impossible to measure. But from a pragmatic perspective, it is rhetorical grandiosity, rather than pedagogical innovation, which attracts funding.

Adorno urged music educators to abandon the social ideology and just teach music in a way that fosters critical thinking and self-determination. Accordingly, Kertz-Welzel (2011, 16) rejects idealism in favour of realism: "A teaching philosophy should not be based on pseudo-religious ideals such as healing the world or transforming human beings through music, but rather be more realistic and focused on students' actual needs. Subscribing to abstract ideals can mean refusing to acknowledge the reality and to continue using education as a tranquillizer for students." In words that resonate with SATM, she argues: "Pied Pipers are still playing their tunes in many places and trying to entrance people through the transforming power of music. Perhaps Adorno's most powerful advice is: To resist the myth of the entrancing power of music is to make the world a better place" (2005, 10).

Yet what would SATM be without this entrancing story? Could such an expensive model sustain itself without its idealism?

This looks like a difficult balancing act. Grandiose myths help music education to thrive or at least survive, and so they might be seen as a necessary means to an end that is under funding pressure in many parts of the world. The urge to seize on and amplify every bit of positive evidence, and to ignore or dismiss the negative, is understandable. This may be the price to pay for keeping music education on politicians' radar. But such an approach comes with costs as well: even if it escapes political appropriation, it can work against critical reflection and educational progress, and can lead to questionable policy decisions, construction on shaky foundations, and a pernicious organizational culture.[15] Belfiore (2009, 345) argues that a "consequentialist position"—the argument that any rhetoric is justified by a positive funding outcome—is a form of disregard for truth that undermines the "ethics of accuracy and conscientiousness on which a healthy public sphere thrives." A decade later, in an era of "post-truth" and "alternative facts," this is no minor detail.

Behind the simple and attractive public story, SATM may be destined to be a messy compromise. Boeskov (2019) suggests that ambiguity is inevitable in musical-social work: not something to be overcome but rather understood. Images of Abreu and Dudamel glad-handing with Chávez and Maduro, or Ocampo deep in conversation with Álvaro Uribe, illustrate the kinds of Faustian bargains on which SATM may rely.

---

15   See Spruce (2017) on the drawbacks of music education advocacy.

One of the Red's first generation mused that SATM leaders "selling their soul to the devil" might be an inevitable consequence of running such expensive programs. Perhaps a publicly funded SATM program like the Red is likely to rest on this kind of pact: generous funding (in comparison to other programs), in return for serving as a tool of political publicity and social control. It seems that instrumentalization of students—their use for adult ends—may be part of the deal. Such programs may be destined to promote a vision of social action that is attractive to powerful actors—more social reproduction than transformation—and to remain suspended awkwardly between progressive rhetoric and conservative ideologies.

Turino (2008) argues that music's social benefits lie primarily in its participatory manifestations. Yet in both Medellín and Venezuela, the requirement to serve as an attractive image (of the city, of the Bolivarian Revolution), along with close alignment with the conventions of classical music performance, has pushed SATM programs down a presentational path. They are caught between participatory discourse and presentational expectations, between the pursuit of social goals and the need to demonstrate results through polished musical performances. In socially oriented music programs, student development and the educational process may be compromised by an emphasis on external performances and putting on a good face at all times (Howell 2017).

The performance for the Harvard delegation described in Chapter 4 provides a good example. The Pedregal ensemble arrived in good time and was set up and ready to start at the appointed hour, but at the last minute came an announcement that the delegation would arrive late due to the disturbances in the surrounding area. Without any leading or planning, the students began messing around on their instruments, and soon the messing around had become a fully-fledged, chaotic, but effervescent jam, with the musicians playing, singing, and rapping. It was an entirely spontaneous and joyful eruption of sound, and the Red's leaders watched from the sidelines with broad smiles on their faces. Franco turned to me and said: kids can learn a lot of music very quickly this way. (It was a good example of the kind of spontaneity and creativity in spaces between formal activities that he sought.) When the delegation arrived, there was sudden shushing for the musicians to be quiet and get back to their places. "Why are they stopping?," muttered

Giraldo under his breath. "That's the best part." But being "the new image of Medellín to the world" meant curtailing this creatively and pedagogically rich participatory activity and giving priority to a presentational one.

This kind of compromise is a central theme of Thompson's (2009) exploration of "performance affects" in applied theatre. He recognizes that "the comings and goings of applied theatre will always be embedded in wider discursive, political and cultural processes" (24), that cultural policies may be emblematic and designed primarily to generate political capital, and that applied artists are always, ultimately, part of someone else's show. In one of his case studies he explores how the arts were pressed into service in a problematic rewriting of Rwandan history after the country's genocide, staging visions of the nation that chimed with official policy. His concern is that the arts can be used to clear up or clean up social reality for public consumption. His response is to ask: "is there any potential for the arts to open up history as a problem to be explored rather than a story to be accepted?" (86), and he sets out to look for "ways to disentangle performance practices from the strategies of the powerful" and maintain "the difficultness of the past in the present" (79). He does so by focusing on *affect* rather than *effect*.

Thompson's arguments are relevant to SATM, and the Harvard performance exemplifies some of his points. The Red performed a cleaned-up vision of the city for public consumption while university students were busy messing it up outside. Thompson is wary of simplistic, strategic narratives of effect, shaped by the desires of policy makers, preferring to valorize spontaneous moments of affective movement that escape from such narratives: "It was outside the formal structure of the workshop, was outside the narrative format of the theatre developed up to that point and, instead, it was appreciated as a joyous, small-scale performance" (110). He could have been describing the jam before the Red's presentation. Like Giraldo, Thompson thinks that this spontaneity—rather than idealistic narratives of transformation—is the best part. Rejecting simplistic, utilitarian readings, he "validates the singing of the redemption song as a vital, affective moment, over which meanings are kept deliberately murky" (111). His final anecdote concerns youths doing the "wrong" things at a performance workshop: eating the wrong food in the wrong places, laughing at the wrong moments, using the stage in the wrong way. Yet his point is that there is something tremendously right about this "wrongness." If there are clear echoes of the Harvard performance here, there is also a stark contrast with the official face of SATM, focused on discipline, order, and playing right. Thompson's arguments also mesh well with Kertz-Welzel's: together they point towards a retreat from grand, idealistic narratives towards finding value in the aesthetic, the affective, and the reflective. They imply that SATM's real value may be found not in the illusory order of good intentions and inspirational rhetoric that dominates official narratives, but rather in the messiness that the discipline-obsessed Abreu abhorred.

Shifting the lens from effect to affect may be productive for SATM. There are doubts over whether SATM is *effective*, but much fewer over whether it is *affective*. Those affects are not necessarily positive, as we have seen; SATM can produce negative responses as well—bitter as well as joyful tears—and plenty of ambivalence. But there is real affective work going on, and the affective dimension of SATM is more present than its ambiguous and often imperceptible social effects. The leadership of Abreu and Ocampo was underpinned by their charisma and oratory—their affective power. This power was amplified by the intensity of their approach to music education. They constructed all-encompassing processes that enveloped participants. We might learn more about SATM if we paid less attention to their strategic discourses of effects and more to the ambiguous affective worlds that they created.

Embracing social utility and the language of impact and effect has led to increased funding, but also "to a certain atrophying of the practice" (117)—words that resonate with SATM. Thompson also notes that concentration on utility has had a draining effect on research. Affect tends to be at the centre of artistic work yet the periphery of research, perhaps because affect is complex: it is hard to predict or control what will happen; it is not necessarily reproducible; it does not travel a linear route. Measuring certain kinds of impact is easier, but it can lead to downplaying the complexity of such work. Thompson thus argues for an affective turn for research—one that would sit well with scholarship that engages with complexity in art and development, cited throughout this book. Perhaps the future of SATM research should be to move on from a focus on working or not working—research driven by official, strategic claims—towards exploring the affective dimension, which is much closer to participants' experiences.

I am left with many questions. Is there a version of SATM that is progressive in goals and methods, safe from political appropriation, yet also attractive to funders? Is there a version of SATM that will appeal equally to students, teachers, social workers, researchers, and institutions? The Red's travails in 2017–19 were in part due to the competing demands of different constituencies. Is it possible for one program to keep everyone happy? Is a middle path an acceptable if messy compromise or the worst of both worlds?

From the perspective of music education for social change, it is hard not to be inspired by Vujanović's (2016, 115) vision of "art as a bad public good": "a politically engaged art that criticizes actual society and intelligibly promotes particular, new, and better social orders"; one that "involves chaotic experiments, failures, irrational proposals, alien messes, queer masquerades, and heterotopic cabinets of wonders where there is no illegitimate question and no one is sure of the right answers. The answers here lie only in experiences of artistic situations that temporarily open new possible worlds." Yet as Vujanović notes: "The concept of 'art as a bad public good' implies that art has the potential to be 'bad for' and 'bad from' the perspective of neoliberal capitalist states and their public morals" (118). Artivism, meanwhile, "confronts, interrogates, or even shrugs off the status quo" and "threatens the conventional wisdom" (Artivism network, cited in Diverlus 2016, 191–92). Are such radical visions possible in an expensive field that depends so heavily on political support and the patronage of powerful representatives of conventional wisdom and the status quo?

As Lees and Melhuish (2015, 251) note, in the context of arts-led regeneration, there is "an unspoken expectation for arts and culture to be uncritical or 'minimum risk' and certainly not to question or undermine the motivations of funders and social policy-makers." For Yúdice (2003, 16), the rise of the expediency of culture—of which SATM is a prime example—has greatly reduced the space for critical or playful approaches:

> the "bottom line" is that cultural institutions and funders are increasingly turning to the measurement of utility because there is no other accepted legitimation for social investment. In this context, the idea that the

experience of jouissance, the unconcealment of truth, or deconstructive critique might be admissible criteria for investment in culture comes off as a conceit perhaps worthy of a Kafkaesque performance skit.

SATM exemplifies how the arts have secured their place at the table by becoming a technique of government and thus a vehicle for constrained visions of social action. The implication is a troubling one: that there may be limited room for artistic citizenship or social change when culture is harnessed to utilitarian ends and governmental goals such as social inclusion, peaceful coexistence, or urban renewal.

And yet, Medellín's visual arts program provides a ray of hope, illustrating that institutionalized arts education can allow for pushing boundaries. In SATM, so too do figures such as Andrés Felipe Laverde (the Red) and André Gomes Felipe (NEOJIBA). Progressive individuals can carve out spaces like the San Javier and Liberdade schools within more conventional institutions. More optimistic snapshots may emerge if we zoom in from the institutional picture to observe details. How the two sides weigh up against each other—macro-level limitations versus micro-level possibilities—is a complex and probably unresolvable question.

It is not just practitioners, then, who may be left with ambiguities and messy compromises. I am well aware that I have more questions than answers, and that I have held up concepts or positions that may not sit comfortably together (such as artistic citizenship and decolonizing music education) or appear somewhat contradictory (such as music education for social change and Adorno/Kertz-Welzel's critique). I make no apology for this. I agree with Boeskov that ambiguity is a feature of this field, something to be grappled with and understood better, not overcome and resolved. I hope to stimulate further reflection on these questions, not bring them to a neat conclusion.

7. Possibilities of Transformation

You already know enough. So do I. It is not knowledge we lack. What is missing is the courage to understand what we know and to draw conclusions.

Sven Lindqvist, *Exterminate all the Brutes*

It's the critics who drive improvement. It's the critics who are the true optimists.

Jaron Lanier, in *The Social Dilemma*

Fig. 31. Archive of Red de Escuelas de Música. CC BY.

The conductor Zubin Mehta was asked about music and peace-building. He replied:

> Look, six years ago I went with the Bavarian State Orchestra to Kashmir, where Hindus and Muslims sat down together for the first time to listen to music. And they smiled listening to Beethoven and Tchaikovsky. Just imagine, that was my dream fulfilled. But it's clear that it didn't help resolve the conflict. No, my dream of peace through music has not been realized. (Chavarría 2019)

Daniel Barenboim took a realistic view of the successes and limitations of his West-Eastern Divan Orchestra project. He was proud of its achievements, but he also denied that it was a "utopia" or "an orchestra for peace," stating baldly: "we cannot do that" ("20 Jahre" 2019).

Such a balance of aspiration and realism is less apparent in the field of SATM. The tone is set by El Sistema's head conductor, Gustavo Dudamel, who proclaimed in 2017: "With these instruments and this music, we can change the world, and we are doing it" (Swed 2017). In interviews, too, he eschews the caution that his fellow conductors display, upholding instead a utopian vision of El Sistema and music more broadly.

Yet the gap between rhetoric and reality is glaring. The backdrop to Dudamel's heart-warming statement was his "country on the verge of economic collapse, an increasingly authoritarian government generating a possible constitutional crisis and perpetual demonstrations that could lead to a full-scale revolution" (ibid.). El Sistema is the world's longest and largest SATM experiment, yet far from changing the world, it has seen its home country fall apart around it. In 2019, Dudamel lectured at Princeton University about "music as freedom";[1] back home in Venezuela, El Sistema musicians were obliged to perform at the disputed inauguration of the corrupt, authoritarian President Maduro, the latest in a long line of political subjections and humiliations. Where was their freedom?

The community musician Dave Camlin writes:

> We've had these debates for a long time now in terms of music as a force for introducing social change or all of these things and yet it hasn't

---

[1] "La Música Como Libertad: Gustavo Dudamel en Princeton", 8 January 2019, https://plas.princeton.edu/Dudamel.

necessarily resulted in those changes. I think it's important that all of us working in the cultural sector are able to look really critically at our practices to say are we really making the difference that we think we are? (Camlin et al. 2020, 166).

Looking at Venezuela, the heart of the field, is SATM really making the difference that it thinks it is?

From Grandiosity to Ambivalence: Reframing SATM

The persistence of a utopian narrative in the face of such contradictory evidence points to illusion and rhetorical excess as characteristic features of El Sistema (Fink 2016). Dudamel's public pronouncements exemplify a grandiosity that originated with El Sistema's politician-orator-founder, Abreu, and spread across the field (e.g. Dobson 2016; Rimmer 2020). Here, counterweights such as the realism of Mehta or Barenboim are in short supply. Most programs display the usual ups and downs of music education and large institutions, yet the world has been presented with over-the-top claims about revelations and resurrections. Children from stable, aspirational, educationally committed families have been described as at-risk youths rescued from a life of crime, drugs, or prostitution; playing in a youth orchestra has become "playing for their lives" and "changing the world." As with Medellín's social urbanism, an interesting, attractive, but complex phenomenon with mixed results has been oversold as a miracle. Aspirations have been confused with achievements, and a blurring of institutional propaganda, advocacy, journalism, and even some one-sided research has produced a hyperbolic dominant narrative that is significantly divorced from reality.

Rhetorical excess is not limited to SATM. As Waisman (2004) notes, romanticization and exaggeration of the power of European music in Latin America goes back to the accounts of Spanish missionaries in the sixteenth century, writing about their own supposedly glorious efforts to pacify and convert the indigenous population. Waisman argues that such narratives have been taken too literally by many, rather than being grasped for what they were: publicity for the authors and their religious orders. The parallels with SATM are not hard to spot.

Turning back to the present, Kertz-Welzel (2016) analyses kitsch and romanticization in the field of CM. Mantie and Risk's (2020) recent evaluation of youth folk music camps called Ethno-World recognized that the vast majority of participants enjoyed their experience, but it also underlined that many of the claims about the program were significantly overblown and demonstrated a lack of awareness of the wider field of music education practice and research. The researchers saw Ethno-World's signature approach as "more of a convenient slogan or catch-phrase than an informed approach to the problems of teaching and learning" (10); and its claims of pedagogical innovation point to "a potentially disturbing naiveté about all that is currently known about music teaching, learning, and facilitation" (11). There are close parallels with SATM, in which Abreu's catch-phrases have loomed large, age-old and indeed widely critiqued practices have been presented as novel, and much current knowledge about music education has been overlooked. Music learning can clearly be very enjoyable for the self-selecting group that chooses to pursue it in such voluntary programs; the problem concerns the grandiose claims that accompany it, which frequently do not stand up to scrutiny.

Rhetorical excess appears to be a feature of the wider field of music education and learning, then, but it is nonetheless particularly pronounced in SATM, and it is not just an ornamental feature of this field; it is integral to the model, the fuel on which it runs. Ocampo motivated students by instilling them with the sense that they were on a mission to transform the world through music. Abreu's perorations about music overcoming poverty and violence might have been founded on wishful thinking, but they inspired national and international movements. Grandiose language, big dreams, and extravagant promises kept these programs in motion, generating the commitment to continue, the funds and new participants to expand, and the media attention to build energy.

Major SATM programs usually have a communications officer or team. El Sistema has a very active press office. Much of the information that circulates publicly about SATM starts life as marketing materials produced by communications professionals. Their job is to generate a simple, appealing story and spread it via the mainstream and social media. This process contributes to the general tendency towards exaggerating positives and minimizing negatives in discourse on SATM. Public communications often describe intentions as achievements and over-egg the pudding in ways that may not reflect the views of more thoughtful staff. When a press article about the Red's 2018 tour was presented in a management meeting, the leaders groaned at its talk of the program "rescuing" children—a discourse that they could not abide. Communications may not even reflect the views of the person who wrote them. One communications officer in Medellín told me: I often ask myself if I am a liar. She recognized that her job was to promote an idealized vision of the Red that glossed over less convenient truths.

Not all writing on SATM is so romanticized. As we have seen, critical reports on the Red date back to 2006; in the case of El Sistema, to 1997 (Baker and Frega 2018). In the former, the Red's own musical staff described the program's objective as overly utopian and more of a cliché than a realistic goal. In the latter, most El Sistema interviewees were disillusioned by the contradictions between stated values and actual practices. Not only did they question whether the program even attempted to pursue its social objectives, but they also accused it of fomenting behaviour and attitudes that ran contrary to those aims. The gaps between theory and practice with SATM have thus been known to participants and researchers alike for many years, and they have been put into writing. However, all these reports were internal, so the number of people outside the organizations who knew was minimal. What was missing during these years was not critical analysis but rather its dissemination. Those who produced the critiques were experts in music education in Latin America and social scientists embedded in the Red— in other words, individuals who were highly qualified and knew the realities well. But they had no public platform. In contrast, institutional propaganda, advocacy, and idealistic media commentary had free rein in the public sphere, propagated by program leaders, famous musicians, journalists, and other big players in the classical music sector, most of whom were more distant from the realities but had a story they wanted to tell and a pulpit from which to do so.

Today, there is a mass of critical research in public circulation; there is a major quantitative study of El Sistema that reveals clearly the flimsiness of its theory of change; there is even research that directly analyses the rhetorical excess (e.g. Pedroza 2015; Fink 2016; Dobson 2016). Yet the dominant narrative has hardly changed at all. Only a few music journalists have departed from the official story, and fewer still have delved into the research. Most institutional depictions have not changed one iota. This is not a matter of lack of evidence; it is about a collective refusal to engage with it. By the time critical research began to be published—not discovering unknown problems, but rather rediscovering known ones—it was too late. A global SATM edifice had been constructed by this point, and rhetorical excess was the glue that held it together. As Rimmer (2020) suggests, too many powerful constituencies stood to benefit from the success story for a more realistic account to gain more than a toehold: El Sistema had become "too big to fail."

Rhetorical excess has served not just as a barrier to public discussion and understanding, but also as a brake on progress. El Sistema itself is a crowning example: stuck in a 1970s time-warp, becalmed by its own self-mythologization, and blinkered by hubris thanks to the adulation of outsiders. Idealism has also led to the perpetuation and spread of problems as the field has grown. Thanks to El Sistema, there has been a resurgence of five-hundred-year-old narratives of salvation through music that have been problematized by music education scholars (e.g. Gould 2007; Vaugeois 2007; Spruce 2017). The propagation of an inflated story of its achievements only makes it harder for Venezuela and other postcolonial contexts to put such colonialist conceptions of music education behind them.

Rhetorical excess cannot be put down as simply a bit of innocuous hot air, then. As Easterly (2006, 18) notes, "the new fondness for utopia is not just harmless inspirational rhetoric"; rather, it has pernicious effects on development. Taking SATM's hot air at face value has led many to reproduce problematic practices, shun critical thinking, hold unrealistic expectations, and resist change. The field's exaggerated claims are also shaping policies on music and social action around the globe. In 2018, the UN and IDB promoted El Sistema as "a model of social inclusion for the world," on the shakiest of grounds. In 2019, Mexico announced the creation of a national ESI program, despite the IDB's 2017 study that revealed that El Sistema failed to reach the poor and had negligible social effects, and despite a highly critical journalistic investigation of the Mexican program's ESI predecessor, Esperanza Azteca (García Bermejo 2018). Hot air defeated research and became the foundation of a national program. When rhetorical excess becomes enshrined as national or international policy, there is reason to be concerned.

Many SATM programs now operate within challenging funding contexts in which there are losers as well as winners. Esperanza Azteca, for example, drew funding away from other, existing music programs. Salinas's youth orchestra program received large sums of public money while state culture budgets were slashed. The Mexican investigation reported: "The flourishing of the Esperanza Azteca Children's Orchestras and Choirs [...] has gone hand in hand with the cancellation of theatre, music, dance and film festivals, the disappearance of symphonic orchestras, and the struggle for survival by community culture programs." As its headline put it pithily: "Culture suffocates; the Azteca orchestras flourish." In Harmony El Sistema England received considerable investment at a time when music education funding generally was being cut by nearly a third in England (Bull 2016), and it did so on questionable grounds (Rimmer 2020); Sistema Scotland has flourished against a similarly concerning backdrop (Baker 2017). The excessively optimistic discourse of SATM may therefore have implications for the wider field of music education, potentially diverting resources and/or attention away from other programs, including those that may be more effective, efficient, equitable, or culturally relevant. In Mexico, as in Venezuela, it impacted negatively on other arts as well by monopolizing resources. As Spruce (2017, 723) argues in an article devoted partly to the UK's Sistema programs, "the appropriation of social justice to sustain political agendas or normative discourses within and beyond music education has had the effect of veiling or silencing more radical and potentially disruptive paradigms of music education and social justice."

In short, SATM's rhetorical excess has serious practical consequences. It also raises ethical issues. Is it ethical to claim that a program founded to provide professional training and widen access to classical music is in fact a social program? To advocate for investment of social funds in orchestral training on the grounds that it is socially transformational without good evidence? To ignore significant counter-evidence? To consume funds that could be used for other social programs that are proven to work or other musical programs with a good track record? Is SATM's triumph at the expense of existing music education and cultural programs, as in Mexico, really something to celebrate?

Development experts recognize that major societal issues are often complex, "wicked problems" (Ramalingam 2013, 265). Furthermore, it is "morally objectionable for the planner to treat a wicked problem as though it were a tame one, [...] or to refuse to recognize the inherent wickedness of social problems" (Rittel and Weber, cited in ibid., 269). Yet many of SATM's favourite lines—"from the minute a child is taught how to play an instrument, he is no longer poor"; "a child who takes up an instrument will never take up a weapon"; "orchestras and choirs are incredibly effective instruments against violence"—are the epitome of treating wicked problems as though they were tame ones. A simple, universal formula like creating an orchestra is not only unlikely to be a solution, but it may also impede more realistic efforts at social change; it could even, as some research on development and SATM suggests, make the problems worse. Utopian thinking may "contribute to concealing and naturalizing the power relations upholding the status quo. Disregarding how musicking involves constraining as well as transgressive features may thereby reinforce rather than transform the marginalizing structures that music making supposedly can contest" (Boeskov 2019, 191). The idea of applying a single approach across different places and cultures is widely criticized in scholarship on culture and development (e.g. Thompson 2009). Claiming that orchestras will miraculously resolve complex social problems like poverty and violence is a travesty of musical-social work, and it muddies understanding of music education and social change. Rhetorical excess is not something to be shrugged off as a harmless quirk.

Whether we look at Kashmir, the Middle East or Venezuela, the justification for a highly optimistic view of the social power of orchestras is thin—as even famous conductors like Mehta and Barenboim admitted. The struggles in the first two contexts are no closer to resolution, while Venezuela has declined precipitously. Critical research on SATM mounts by the year, and some of the field's foundational tenets look distinctly problematic in the light of recent scholarship on music education, social justice, and development. In Medellín, the other municipal arts education programs had left behind technical training and magical thinking years earlier.

There is therefore a wealth of reasons to embrace a more ambivalent approach to SATM. Systematic critique may be a hard sell to the music world at large, which has much more use for a "power of music" narrative, but it is necessary step. El Sistema has been one of the most widely reported, promoted, and imitated music education initiatives of the twenty-first century, and it is the cornerstone of a SATM field that now incorporates hundreds of thousands of students in dozens of countries around the world. Gaining a deeper understanding of this field is therefore an important endeavour in its own right. Yet as Erik Olin Wright and Ruth Wright suggest, the importance of critical diagnosis goes beyond the pursuit of knowledge for its own sake: it is the first step in emancipatory or social justice research, which aims to disrupt a problematic status quo and open the door to better alternatives (Wright 2019). Critical research is a foundation stone for the possibilities of transformation.

If the consequences of grandiosity may be quite deleterious, taking a more ambivalent stance may be a source of positive change. It is only through facing up to flaws that they can be seriously addressed. Critiquing the disjuncture between myths and realities has liberatory potential: it may catalyze exploration and experimentation, rather than the reproduction of flawed ideas and methods. It may encourage a search for new approaches to SATM that accord more closely with research in this field. There is now more than enough evidence from studies of SATM and related fields to suggest that there is considerable room for improvement in terms of both music education and social action. The fastest route to such improvement is critical questioning and public debate, not grandiose, idealistic rhetoric.

Ambivalence does not mean disengagement or destruction; it is not a creed of negativity. It can underpin constructive action; the ambivalent researcher may become "a facilitator or a catalyst to change" (Ander-Egg 1990, 36). As Sloboda (2019) notes, "true learning often only follows failure, and understanding why." Ambivalence encourages us to take questions like teamwork and student voice more seriously, rather than assuming that they will take care of themselves. Embracing ambiguity is not about denying music's positive potential—it is about fulfilling that potential.[2]

---

2   Gelb (2004) argues that embracing ambiguity was an essential characteristic of the genius of Leonardo da Vinci and that today, in an era of information overload

The history of the Red illustrates this point. For the first eight years, the program adopted an El Sistema-esque approach of preferring action to reflection. However, reports in 2006 and 2008 revealed that many problems had accumulated as a result. Their findings underline that musical activity needs to be accompanied by critical research and reflection if SATM is to achieve its social goals. Furthermore, this documentation and analysis of problems formed the cornerstone of efforts to transform the program.

Critical research—an ambivalent ethnomusicology or sociology of music education—thus has a vital role to play in rethinking and remaking SATM. All too often in the SATM field, researchers have been asked or happy to play the role of handmaiden, blurring the line between research and advocacy. The reverse of this coin is that critical researchers have been painted as the enemy, to be ignored or dismissed. Some branches of the SATM field have a Manichean, "with us or against us" view of scholarship and critique. However, the Red showed that there is another way. Since 2006, the program has hired social professionals to ask difficult questions, not to pat program leaders and staff on the back and tell them what they want to hear. The social team has sometimes been seen as a thorn in the side, whether by staff or students or even the leaders themselves, yet a dozen years later it is still there. When I arrived at the program, I was treated as a colleague and a potential ally in a process of self-critique and change that the program had already begun. I did not have to pledge loyalty, sign up to any mission, or adulate any leader. With an openness entirely fitting for a public institution, the Red threw open its doors, and we worked together from then on. It was salutary to find that practice and critical research could go hand in hand.

In the light of this experience, and also briefer exchanges with representatives of other programs, I believe that it is eminently possible for SATM and critical scholars to work together productively. This does not mean that the researcher has to curb their critical faculties. On the contrary, I propose that an important role for scholars should be to embrace what Belfiore labels "an anti-bullshit research ethos," and to engage with complexity in SATM in a similar way that Belfiore and

---

and rapid change, "[t]he ability to thrive with ambiguity must become part of our everyday lives" (150).

Ramalingam have done with respect to the social impact of the arts and overseas aid. Such an approach has a deep historical foundation: the social impact of the arts has been a topic for critical interrogation for more than two millennia (Belfiore and Bennett 2008). Scholars are uniquely placed to explore such issues, since higher education institutions can still support work that pursues deeper understanding and not just utilitarian goals.

Music scholars sometimes advocate for a particular topic, perhaps suggesting that the importance of a composer, work, scene, genre, or artist has been insufficiently appreciated. In the case of SATM, however, with support abounding among funders, the music industry, and the media, and general beliefs often excessively optimistic, academics have a role to play in injecting a note of caution and realism. It is not a route to popularity, but it is an important role for music scholars in an age of post-truth. Indeed, the bigger the claims, the more necessary this role. As Reimerink (2018, 194) argues: "Medellín's social urbanism is internationally regarded as a 'success story' in urban transformation, which makes critical research on its accomplishments all the more urgent." Urban researchers have critically scrutinized the Medellín Miracle from many angles; they have banished the promotional bullshit and replaced it with sophisticated critiques. Research on stories of musical miracles should be no different. This "anti-bullshit research ethos" should also have a public element: after all, the general public would expect to be told about the drawbacks and side effects of a public health program or aid project, so why not of musical-social work? Why should music be exempt from serious scrutiny, divorced from advocacy motives? It is in the public interest to debate the pros and cons of existing models and the possibilities for improvement, particularly in contexts where SATM programs are publicly funded.

Taking the goals of SATM seriously and investigating ways to achieve them more effectively is a constructive step. Whether it is seen as such depends on programs and their representatives. If they are firmly wedded to a particular practice, ideology, or music education brand, then a critical researcher may appear as an antagonist. But if they are committed to critical reflection and change, as the Red was, then the same researcher may appear as an ally who might contribute to internal processes, and at that point the possibilities for collaboration between practice and research begin to flower. If their central question is "how could it work better?", then stepping back from a miracle story to a more realistic assessment may be seen not as disparagement but rather a contribution. If arts education is treated as a means of social control and reproduction, then critical scholarship has no place at the table; however, if it is "a vehicle for transformation, reflection, and critique," as Giraldo put it (Vallejo Ramírez 2017), then SATM practitioners and critical scholars may dine happily together.

My views had led to my excommunication by much of the El Sistema field several years earlier, but here, in an emblematic SATM program, they were unremarkable. The Red's social team had little time for "music bullshit." At meetings and in private conversations, I was often on the same page as the Red's senior staff. They treated me as an analyst of SATM's problems and supporter of progressive solutions rather than an enemy. They even offered me a job. In turn, I sent an advanced draft of this book to three senior figures (past and present) and invited them to provide critical feedback before the text was finalized. A few other SATM programs have stretched out a hand, like NEOJIBA, Orquestra nas Escolas (Brazil), and Symphony for Life (Australia). In 2019, I was invited to join the scientific committee of Démos (France). Dialogue and collaboration are possible if program leaders desire it.

My experience in the Red questioned commonplace binaries in SATM such as insider versus outsider, practice versus research, and advocacy versus critique. Many other individuals, too, crossed these imaginary boundaries. The social team were critical researchers who were insiders; and there were music educators who were engaged in research. Franco, the pedagogical coordinator, often insisted that research should be an integral part of music education: a curiosity or exploratory ethos that went hand in hand with music learning. Medellín's visual arts network provides a neighbouring example of critical thinking and practice working well together—indeed, of practice stemming from critical research.

Most importantly, the critical re-evaluation of the Red from 2005 onwards was led by its own employees, and two of the architects of this process from 2017–19 were musicians. A critical ethos became *part of* the Red, not something alien or opposed to it, and debate took place not between insiders and outsiders, advocates and critics, but between supporters of contrasting approaches within the program. The central point of this book has been that if the Red turned out to be more complex in reality than public perceptions of SATM would allow, this was an *internal* diagnosis. The program's management were both advocates *and* critics of the Red, and they showed little interest in the rose-tinted views of observers with little knowledge of the Red's challenges. I hope that uncovering these dynamics will contribute in some way to breaking down some of the barriers and imagined dichotomies that constrained the circulation of knowledge in SATM during the 2010s.

El Sistema's major problems were first unearthed by Latin American researchers in 1997. A growing body of research on related programs reveals that some of these issues have been found elsewhere in the SATM field. Now we can see that the Red displays a comparable picture. How much more evidence is needed? How many times do researchers need to find similar issues in different parts of the field before they are taken seriously? Following the example of the Red, it is time to move beyond the miracle stories and salvation narratives that have dominated public understanding and to pursue more critical discussions and nuanced, innovative visions of socially oriented music education. Both practitioners and researchers are already engaged in this process, but too often apart. When programs recognize the issues and embrace critical reflection and change, researchers can contribute by helping to deconstruct the dominant myth of SATM and to reconstruct something better in its place.

From Access to Action: Rethinking SATM

The final element of the equation of emancipatory research is possibilities of transformation. This chapter has focused so far on the possibilities for transforming the discourse of SATM and renewing the relationship between practice and critical research. Let us turn now to possible transformations in SATM itself and reimagine it from a place of ambivalence and critique.

The primary aim of this book has been descriptive rather than prescriptive—to present and analyse processes of internal criticism, debate, and change that have been underway for many years within the Red, and to compare them to the cornerstone of the field, El Sistema.

As an ethnographer of music education, I see my role as to observe and diagnose rather than prescribe: to try to ask the right questions rather than provide the right answers, as Ramalingam suggests. There is already a large literature on what high-quality socially engaged music education looks or might look like. Also, I heed Ramalingam's warnings about the dangers of blueprints. Answers may be different in every context, so they must be sought by music educators, social workers, policymakers, and other professionals on the ground. In my experience, those who *want* to translate critical thinking into practice are perfectly capable of doing so without being given instructions by researchers. Where there's a will, there's a way.

I will attempt to reconcile these two somewhat contradictory aims—to imagine possibilities of transformation, but without prescribing solutions—by offering a series of questions or prompts. They are an invitation to reflect rather than a recipe; questions for the reader's consideration rather than steps to follow. They point to something deeper than quick fixes or immediate answers: a new mindset, one attuned to an evolving world rather than remaining bound to the prescriptions of the twentieth century. As Lecolion Washington stated in the previous chapter: "You can't just change your tactics, you need to change your thinking."

These questions encourage the reader to imagine a Latin American, socially driven, emancipatory, realist, sustainable SATM. This is not idle dreaming: all its elements are being explored today by music educators, artists, researchers, and thinkers in Latin America and around the globe. What is needed is a broadening and deepening of such efforts *within* SATM, the backing of national and international funders and umbrella bodies, and, above all, the will to put critical questions at the top of the agenda and to reimagine SATM for the 2020s and beyond.

What Might a Latin American SATM Look Like?

The twentieth-century version of SATM was born in 1975, but it looked back to 1875 and even 1575. It is a shining example of what Boaventura de Souza Santos (2018, 1) calls "the imperial South": "the epistemological little Europes that are to be found and are often dominant in Latin America, the Caribbean, Africa, Asia, and Oceania."

Its focus was widening access to classical music, and it was built and revolved largely around European repertoire, methods, and ideologies. Tours to and visits from Europe were the highlight. Despite sporadic efforts at diversity, it had little room for the culture of indigenous or African-descended populations and thus echoed Europe's "musical conquest" of the Americas in the sixteenth century (Turrent 1993). Yet most of Latin America's emblematic musical genres, like tango, samba, cumbia, and son, emerged from the poorest and most marginalized sectors of society, where such populations were concentrated. It is high time to abandon the orthodox SATM view of such sectors as cultural deserts in need of a transfer of European art from their social superiors, and to fully embrace the reality that they have historically been the most powerful source of cultural richness and innovation in the Americas. Some decolonial rethinking and reform is already underway, but it could be developed much more deeply and widely in the SATM field. There is room for much more debate about the limitations as well as the contributions of a European approach to music education in Latin America and the horizons opened up by an epistemological shift of the kind envisaged by Shifres and Gonnet (2015).

Can we imagine a SATM based not on European Jesuit or conservatoire models but on the region's own distinctive contributions? One that drew not on a conception of music education as social ordering and control, but rather on Latin American traditions of communal celebration, familial musicking, or the inseparability of music and dance? One that looked to Salvador or Santiago rather than Salzburg? Fung (2018) proposes a philosophy of music education based on ancient Chinese thought; can we imagine a Latin American equivalent?

Keil's "Paideia Con Salsa" and AfroReggae's *batidania* offer examples of Afro-diasporic approaches to cultural education and artistic citizenship (see Chapter 5). There are many other Latin American cultural forms with similar potential, such as capoeira (Candusso 2008) or *samba de roda*. Their great advantage is that the social aspect is an integral and vital part of the musical culture. Many such forms evolved as ways to strengthen the social fabric within marginalized communities. The social element is neither a discursive layer on top nor a distraction from the music. In this light, it seems more than a little ironic that the orchestra—a European musical organization in which the social experience of participants was historically of minimal concern—should have become the paradigmatic model for SATM in Latin America. The paradox only increases if we consider classical music's historical self-construction as autonomous from the social (Born 2010; Bull 2019). What is the logic for choosing such a genre as the vehicle for social action, rather than one in which the musical and social have always been closely interwoven?

The contrast between SATM and theatre in Latin America is highly revealing. The 1970s saw both the creation of El Sistema, the brainchild of a conservative Venezuelan economist, and the consolidation of the Theatre of the Oppressed, which Augusto Boal based on the ideas of the radical Brazilian educator Paulo Freire. Boal's program, founded on critical analysis of society, revolutionized drama education around the world. Abreu's, founded on disciplining participants, has also been internationally influential, but it has been more of a counter-revolution in music education (Baker 2016b), and its lack of a method leaves significant question marks over what precisely is being transferred to other contexts beyond the name (Frega and Limongi 2019).

More recently, theatre has seen considerable self-critique and experimentation with regard to the figure of the director.[3] SATM, in contrast, remains conductor-centric, and El Sistema has served as both a production line of maestros and a bastion of conventional thinking about musical leadership. One might have expected radical experiments from a youth program in the middle of a political revolution, but the opposite has been the case. It is revealing that the modestly progressive ideas about music education explored by the Red in 2017–19, which will be familiar to many readers with expertise in this field, were contentious within the program and a departure from the norm in Latin American SATM. Strip away the rhetoric and orthodox SATM presents an old and familiar ideology: a musician is someone who plays an orchestral instrument; playing in a large ensemble is the primary goal of music education; the presentation of well-known repertoire in a public concert is both the aim and the measure of the process. SATM has seen the re-transmission of a very old European ideology around the world,

---

3   See, for example, "Re-directing: Directing in the Twenty-first Century", International Conference, Department of Cultural Heritage, University of Salento, Lecce, Italy, 2–4 October 2019; Duška Radosavljević, "The Heterarchical Director", https://podcasts.ox.ac.uk/heterarchical-director-model-authorship-twenty-first-century.

lightly filtered through a Latin American lens. This is one reason why El Sistema has been adopted so easily, quickly, and widely by dominant institutions: it is instantly recognizable and understandable to those steeped in that ideology.

But what might a Music of the Oppressed look like? What sort of contribution might it make to music education around the world? Might it, like Boal's method, upend traditions rather than upholding them? Might it catalyze new ideas and practices rather than reviving or consolidating old ones?

Latin America is the focus of this book and my main area of interest, but readers from other parts of the world, particularly outside Europe, might transpose this question to their context. Is a Eurocentric model the best choice for SATM? What alternatives might there be? Could other forms of SATM based on national or regional philosophies be imagined?[4]

What Might a SATM Look Like That Prioritized the Social?

Can we imagine a SATM that starts not from an established musical practice and takes the social as a means of justifying, funding, reproducing, marketing, and disseminating it, but rather from social goals and looks for the music-making (of whatever kind) that is best suited to achieving them? One that puts music at the service of the social rather than the social at the service of the musical?

Hess (2019) provides a good example of this kind of inversion. Her pedagogical model derives from listening to and reflecting on activist-musicians. She asked what such musicians did and what music for social change looked like, and then considered what kind of music

---

4 I am not simply advocating for a nationalist approach to SATM, though it might be justified in a context where national culture is overshadowed by global and cultural survival or revival is a priority. A national and/or regional focus may make sense in a postcolonial country like Colombia. In a former colonial power in the grip of right-wing nationalism like the UK, however, a contrasting approach might be preferable: for example, focusing on the musics and histories of regions colonized by the British and the variety of cultures that make up the country today as a result. I am not therefore pointing to a one-size-fits-all approach to SATM, but rather to more flexibility and experimentation, and, above all, to greater consideration of cultural-political questions and interrogation of arts education that perpetuates unequal relationships of colonial origin.

education might lead to that goal. The resulting proposal is for a new kind of music education modelled on music for social change, not an old form of music education framed within a social discourse. Starting from the desired social goal, rather than from the training of professional musicians, could revolutionize SATM.

Delivering music education in more "social" ways may be a positive step (if the education is appropriate and high-quality), but more radical moves are eminently possible. For example, a music program that emphasizes a narrow range of genres might promote coexistence, if done well, but largely between likeminded people. A more ambitious approach would be to pursue cultural cohesion by catalyzing musical, cultural, and social exchanges between people with different musical interests and backgrounds. Hess notes: "As we consider what it might mean to teach for connection, introducing musics that allow students to encounter people beyond those with whom they typically interact, we create a mechanism for tangibly humanizing different groups" (78). This is precisely what the San Javier school project in Medellín did. There were other experiments in putting the social first during my fieldwork, such as Intermediaries of Civic Culture, the administrators' away day, and the Afro laboratory, and they looked very different from orthodox SATM.

SATM did not originate as a practice or method; it was a publicity label for widening access to conventional classical music training. As a member of the social team put it in 2018, the Red had spent two decades showing off its students in concerts, festivals, and tours, yet it did not have a distinctive educational model. After nearly half a century of operation, El Sistema has not produced unique, shareable methods or resources. SATM's origins are as a speeded-up, intensified form of orchestral training. Recent adaptations in some places have toned down the intensity and extremes, but then the question becomes how SATM differs from mainstream music education—and the answer appears to be, not much. Although there have been a number of efforts to conceive of El Sistema as a distinctive method or pedagogical approach, research in Venezuela (Baker 2014; Frega and Limongi 2019), the US (Hopkins, Provenzano, and Spencer 2017; Fairbanks 2019), and the UK (Dobson 2016; Baker 2017) suggests that practice is often quite conventional. The challenge today, therefore, is not simply to rein in SATM's excesses but also to construct a new model. An increasing number of progressive music educators understand that the issue of inclusion should revolve not around widening access to existing, exclusive spaces and practices but rather around creating new, inclusive ones.

What, then, might a Latin American SATM *method* look like—a distinctive one, not a familiar one in unfamiliar surroundings, and one that could be explained to and shared with others? Not just group lessons but group pedagogy, carefully thought out and underpinned by research, driven by the distinctive possibilities offered by group learning rather than just an urge to massify (Cobo Dorado 2015)? One that did not simply mimic colonial or European pedagogies and limit diversity to the incorporation of local repertoires but rather constituted a Latin American, mestizo musical pedagogy (Serrati 2017)? One rooted in an epistemological shift and opening up a "meeting of knowledges" (Carvalho et al. 2016)?

If the social objective is genuinely paramount, then SATM's processes and outcomes should reflect this. Rather than modelling itself on the professional symphony orchestra, SATM might look to fields such as CM and music therapy, which offer many examples of putting the social first, or to highly participatory music traditions in which, as Turino (2016, 303) argues, "the success of an event is judged by the degree of participation achieved; the etiquette and quality of sociality is granted priority over the quality of the sound and motion produced." Turino's first specialism was the music of Peru; his vision thus offers another pointer to SATM in Latin America. CM, too, has seen considerable reflection on how artistic quality might be imagined differently in participatory as opposed to presentational arts (e.g. Bartleet and Higgins 2018). Kajikawa (2019, 169) details various musicians and musical projects that "value community as much as if not more than they aspire to aesthetic perfection. [...] The work of these and other individuals and organizations suggests that there are other ways of appreciating the beauty of music that go beyond the technical dimensions of sound." There are plenty of existing examples to which SATM might look in rethinking itself to prioritize the social.

Another suggestive inversion is proposed by Henley and Higgins (2020), who propose redefining the terms excellence and inclusion. Instead of seeing excellence as a product and inclusion as a process, they flip the script. This approach makes good sense for SATM: it implies examining the educational process and the degree of inclusivity (rather than public performances) to determine program quality. It points to a way beyond the endless debates about excellence in older SATM programs like the Red, responding with the question: "excellence *in what*?"

Intermediaries of Civic Culture hosted the program "Improv for life," which explored systematically (and humorously) the lessons from improvised theatre for everyday life. What might "Music for life" look like? Music for living well (*buen vivir* or *eudaimonia*) rather than performing well?[5]

What Might an Emancipatory SATM Look Like?

Since the sixteenth century, European-style music education has been conceptualized as playing a role in pacifying and ordering Latin American society (Baker 2008; 2010). For the Spanish colonists, it was a tool of social control, and in the hands of Abreu, who led the mission model to a comeback in the 1970s, it remained as such to the end of his life. It is time to imagine a SATM that seeks to liberate rather than discipline; that sees youth in terms of potential and creativity rather than emptiness, deviancy, and disorientation; that imagines a different future. One that treats music education not as a tool for bending youth to social norms, but rather for reflecting on and, if necessary, questioning the status quo. One that follows the lead of Medellín's youth researchers (*Jóvenes* 2015), or draws on Mouffe's (2013) agonistic politics, Sachs Olsen's (2019) socially engaged art, or Mould's (2019) urban subversion. One that reimagines SATM not as a harmonizing technique of "the post-political city" but rather as "free spaces": "nodes for experimentation with new urban possibilities [...] where alternative forms of living, working, and expressing are experimented with, where new forms of social and political action are staged, where affective economies are reworked, [...] where proper urban democratic politics emerge" (Swyngedouw 2007). One that sees social mobility as a collective rather than individual endeavour, seeking to improve entire communities rather than principally the lives of successful music students (Folkes 2021). One that embodies not a colonialist mission to save others but

---

5   Salazar 2015; Mignolo and Walsh 2018; Smith and Silverman 2020.

rather a decolonial or anti-oppressive quest to liberate everyone from systemic inequities that increase unhappiness and problems at all levels of society (Wilkinson and Pickett 2010).

The Red's social team dreamt of such a shift. Its 2017 report opened with a quotation by Alfredo Ghiso that concludes: "What is needed then is an education that liberates, not one that adapts, domesticates or subjugates" ("Informe" 2017a, 3). Later on, they quoted Fernando Savater: "Education is the only possibility of bloodless, non-violent, and profound revolution in our culture and our values" (184). They cited these figures in order to urge the program to do more.

Hess (2019, 103) offers a concrete alternative to the individual deficit orientation of orthodox SATM: an activist music education that "creates a space for youth to connect their experiences to others' experiences, challenge dominant narratives, and develop a systemic understanding of the forces that shape their lives." Unlike orthodox SATM, it grants full value to students' own lived experiences, seeks to connect them not just to likeminded individuals but also to others more removed from their realities, and encourages participants to challenge oppressive ideologies rather than discipline themselves. A rethought SATM might well take a non-formal or popular education approach, rather than a colonialist or human capital one (Maclean 2015): this would allow for closer connection with Latin American traditions of music learning and radical education, more space for artistic citizenship, and better psychosocial outcomes. As Ilari, Fesjian, and Habibi (2018, 8) note, "the effects of musical interventions on children's social skills may be [...] more robust in participatory forms of music-making [...] than in formal learning programs, particularly those that tend to be of a hierarchical nature." SATM might seek to transcend the ideology of large ensemble music-making as an expression of harmony, and consider the potential of music to explore and express dissonance.

What Might a Realist SATM Look Like?

The orthodox version of SATM was built on a twentieth-century version of Romantic idealism, shared by its creators and many who have observed, filmed, written about, and advocated for it (Pedroza 2014; Fink 2016). In this book I have presented and argued for realist research.

But what if realism did not stop there but extended to the programs themselves? What if SATM took seriously Adorno's critique of idealism in music education and instead embraced a critical dimension that "consists in making visible what the dominant consensus tends to obscure and obliterate" (Mouffe 2013, 93)? For Adorno, argues Kertz-Welzel (2005, 7), "art has to be true and music should be a mirror for the real conditions of society. [...] Music as social agent has to awaken people, has to raise consciousness concerning the alienation of human beings. Art has to challenge society and human beings in order to break through the power of suppression, alienation, and deification." Accordingly, Kertz-Welzel (2011, 16) rejects idealism in favour of realism, as discussed in Chapter 6: "A teaching philosophy should not be based on pseudo-religious ideals such as healing the world or transforming human beings through music, but rather be more realistic and focused on students' actual needs." Such visions are not so different from that of the Red's social team in 2017–19, which insisted that art should be a tool for naming and engaging with societal issues, not escaping from them.

Research in development studies is often wary of panaceas, magic formulas, and grand, utopian designs (e.g. Scott 1998; Easterly 2006). Ramalingam (2013, 351) proposes:

> in trying to bring about change, development actors need to focus less on attribution of impacts ("we achieved this!"), but on the more modest and realistic goals of contribution to outcomes ("here is how we helped change knowledge, attitudes, relationships and behaviours"), the impacts of which are largely determined by actors and factors outside of any given agency's control.

A realist SATM might eschew ideals of changing the world or vanquishing poverty or violence and focus instead (like Medellín's visual arts network) on concrete, realistic urban and social interventions. Mouffe (2013, 102) holds up the example of a Barcelona museum informed by critical pedagogy that connected artists and artistic practices with social movements and local political struggles: "Several workshops were organized around topics such as precarious labour, borders and migrations, gentrification, new media and emancipatory policies." There are echoes of Barrett's (2018) work at the CLCS. A realist SATM might engage with Stephen Duncombe's notion of an "ethical spectacle," in which music is not an escape or a staging, but rather "members of social movements participate democratically in creating the spectacle" (Silverman and Elliott 2018, 380). It might distance itself from unethical, authoritarian spectacles of order and discipline that reproduce cultural and social hierarchies and put young people on display without giving them a voice.

A realist SATM might eschew simplistic, linear models and draw instead on research on complexity by the likes of Ramalingam: "Complexity thinking can help describe and explain our world, our relationship to it, and to each other far better—*with far greater realism and fidelity*—than the tools we have had handed down to us from nineteenth-century physics" (2013, 362; emphasis added). Ramalingam argues that top-down, hierarchical, blueprint thinking is inadequate and even counter-productive in a world of complex adaptive systems. He upholds the value of bottom-up, self-organized systems, allowing full interaction between actors: "From the perspective of adaptive agents, the edge of chaos is hypothesized as the optimal position for learning [...]. True learning happens when organizations are coupled at the edge, where new ideas come into an environment that is flexible and adaptable" (186). His advice is to "let go and let the positive deviants self-organize in ways that enable them to find their own solutions. This is especially challenging for actors [...] who are imbued with a powerful self-image of being the fixers and the solution providers" (278). He advocates for "minimally invasive education" (328): giving children technologies and letting them get on with learning and sharing ideas, with little intervention from a teacher, in what he calls a "Self-Organized Learning Environment" (330).

This sophisticated but also realist vision of learning at the edge of chaos could hardly be further from orthodox SATM, with its obsession with discipline, order, conductors, and orchestras, which Abreu compared admiringly to a Swiss watch (see Baker 2016a). Recall Peerbaye and Attariwala (2019, 4), who characterized orchestras as "hierarchical and rigidly structured in terms of creation and production processes and protocols of decision-making," and as needing "to develop flexibility for new and more complex approaches." Indeed, Ramalingam holds up jazz improvisation (and rejects classical music) as an answer to his question: "How do we learn to set our knowledge, training and expertise aside and learn to be more adaptive?" (190). He closes his book with a vision:

"Aid in the future would not be an export industry, sclerotic and rigid, shaped by politics of supply and the mental models of early Fordism. Aid would resemble the world of which it is a part: fluid, dynamic, emergent" (363). Replacing "aid" with "SATM" both encapsulates the field's past and points to a possible future.

Although their reforms were only partially achieved in practice, what Giraldo and Franco dreamt of in the Red was something quite similar to Ramalingam's Self-Organized Learning Environment. They too imagined spaces that were more flexible, with adults taking a smaller role and students sharing and seeking solutions among themselves. They tried to bring more of a jazz improvisation ethos into the Red. The moment that I saw them happiest with the Red's music-making was during the jam at the Harvard event—unplanned, self-organized, more than a touch chaotic, yet vibrant and captivating. Ramalingam's educational vision has been realized in non-formal music education; might it be realizable in SATM?

On a more personal note, the Latin American musics that I love most—salsa, for example, or Cuban timba, rumba, and hip-hop—have a realism and ambiguity about them that is lost in SATM's idealism and utopianism. They often speak about life on the street; they have a touch of *badness* about them—a kind of swagger that the Cubans call *guapería*—and roots in Latin American musics of resistance going back to colonial times. Such genres construct community, but their leading musicians are often complex figures; in general, they are not, and do not claim to be, paragons of virtue. This ambiguity gives the musics a particular life force. The will to normalization in SATM—the focus on discipline, order, respect, responsibility—sidelines a lot of what makes Latin American musics special to me. It also minimizes embodiment, which is such a fundamental aspect of these musics.

Is the capacity to instil discipline really what musicians love about music? How could SATM be more than this? What might an aesthetically realist SATM look like, one that reflects the ambiguity of Latin American musics, one that engages with the complexity of real life rather than negating it by removing children into a bubble of idealism and dreams of elsewhere? What might a realist SATM *sound* like? What might it *feel* like?

Is there any place for idealism or utopianism, then? Scholars of culture and development have revealed their dangers. Abreu's supposed utopianism was really an example of what Foucault (1991, 169) called "a military dream of society." Yet a SATM stripped of all utopianism might be a rather dry affair. Ruth Wright offers a way out of this conundrum. She points to "real Utopias" rooted in "Utopian pedagogy": not so much the pursuit of a future societal ideal as "an ethos of experimentation that is oriented toward carving out spaces for resistance and reconstruction here and now" (Coté, Day and dePeuter, cited in Wright 2019, 222). Wright offers a utopianism that is grounded in the realities and achievable goals of music classrooms, in cutting-edge practice and research in music education, rather than in grandiose claims about changing the world or imaginings of a perfectly ordered, harmonious society that runs like a Swiss watch. She describes activist, collaborative, creative pedagogies in pursuit of "new societal Utopias—not in the sense of unattainable perfect futures but in terms of encouraging spaces of social experimentation and resistance, encouraging the collective, reengaging communities with the political" (225). This is a form of pedagogical or educational idealism, focused on providing music students with precisely the kinds of skills that neutralize the dangers of utopianism. This is not Abreu's utopia of disciplined, obedient, apolitical youths singing in unison from his hymn sheet; it is a utopia of autonomous but collaborative, creative, critically reflective, politically engaged musicians, each one with their own voice, pursuing a dialectical harmony that embraces dissonance as well as consonance (Fink 2016).

What Might a Sustainable SATM Look Like?

Some would argue that if there is one area above all in which social action is needed today, it is in combatting the climate crisis. An economic system geared around excessive production and consumption is driving the planet towards the brink. Features of this system such as pollution, overwork, stress, and lack of free time also bring consequences for human beings' physical and mental health and quality of life. An increasing number of social thinkers and activists are pushing back and looking for more sustainable ways of living that relieve the pressure on the planet while bringing additional benefits and pleasures to other areas of human life.

Building on radical economists' questioning of the ideology of growth (e.g. Raworth 2017), Soper's (2020) manifesto for "post-growth living" proposes that what is good for the planet is also good for us. A less work-focused existence and "a less harried and acquisitive way of living" open up the possibilities of "relieving stress both on nature and on ourselves. If the circulation of people, goods and information were to slow down, then the rate of resource attrition and carbon emissions can be cut, and time freed up for the arts of living and personal relating" (53). If a time-scarce, work-dominated society is bad for workers' physical and mental health, play offers an alternative focus: "There is a special pleasure in the concentration of the game and the uncertainty of its outcome, and by 'wasting' more time on the 'pointless' activities of play, rather than 'investing' it in instrumental work activity, this gratification moves against the commodifying logic of our times" (86).

A constellation of "slow" movements has emerged as forms of critique of and resistance to the intensity of modern life (Craig and Parkins 2006), and the cult of work faces increasing scrutiny (e.g. Campagna 2013; Frayne 2015; Suzman 2020). Some writers focus on the environmental angle, others on the political one. Frayne, for example, regards busyness as an enemy of democracy, since people need time to be politically active citizens. He is among a number of thinkers who articulate a politics of (free) time. Such movements are not limited to the global North: *sumak kawsay/buen vivir* is an important example of thinking and action on de-growth, sustainability, and quality of life from the global South (Salazar 2015; Mignolo and Walsh 2018), and similar principles are articulated by indigenous populations across South and Central America (Houtart 2011).

If this historical juncture is generating new philosophies of social action, it also calls for new kinds of social action through music, better aligned with efforts to confront the biggest problems and challenges of our time. Orthodox SATM, however, points the way backwards. El Sistema "produced musicians like sausages," to quote one of its members (Baker and Frega 2018), reflecting Abreu's ideological grounding in mid-twentieth-century industrial capitalism (Baker 2014). In the founder's own words, El Sistema boiled down to hard work. His vision was simple: "we grow, grow, grow." He abhorred *ocio* (free time) and had no interest in grassroots participation or activism. El Sistema was focused on one thing: speeding up and intensifying the process of orchestral training. Its musical claims to fame have always been about more, bigger, louder, faster. It brought together more than 10,000 musicians for a concert in memory of Abreu.

El Sistema emerged on the back of an oil bonanza. The program developed without any conception of ecological limits, flying parties of up to 300 musicians and hangers-on around the world and stimulating massive consumption of tropical hardwoods for instruments (Lafontant Di Niscia 2019). After 2007, the dominant image of SATM was the jet-setting Simón Bolívar Youth Orchestra, continually on tour around the world's great concert halls. In 2019, as I began writing this book, Greta Thunberg led young people in climate protests around the world, but Latin American youth orchestras continued to fly across continents for no reason other than to give concerts. These supposed social programs for youth seemed almost oblivious to the biggest social issue of their time for young people.

Shevock (2021) urges music education for social change to pay greater attention to ecological issues. SATM should recognize that the world today does not need an ethos of discipline and normalization, but rather a new mindset; it is not individuals that need to correct their course but rather economic and political ideologies. The planet does not need "grow, grow, grow"; on the contrary, humans need to rethink our obsession with growth. As Raworth (2017) argues, we have to refocus on thriving instead. Speeding up and intensifying is precisely the wrong approach for our times.

A music education system that reproduces the ethos of the economic and social system that got us into this mess hardly points the way out of it. On the contrary, "the very virtues that defined human progress—our productivity, ambition, energy and hard work—might lead us to perdition" (Suzman 2020, 303). If "we are global warming" (Simms 2011), then hot-house musical training is the wrong model for mass music education in the 2020s, particularly for music education with social objectives.

SATM needs new figureheads—people rooted in the realities of the 2020s, who can inspire new kinds of social action and activism. Or to go further, perhaps it should abandon figureheads altogether, in the light of the field's mixed history of charismatic but authoritarian leaders, cults of personality, and top-down management. Perhaps what are needed are instead principles, concepts, or symbols that may be appropriated and adapted by each community or program, maybe even each individual, and unfold through bottom-up processes of collective construction.

A culture ministry official in Medellín criticized the Red as a system of rapid musical production and argued that it needed to slow down: "Let's stop, take a break, breathe, and have a rethink." This could be a motto for SATM in the 2020s. What might a SATM look like that supported the search for new ways of imagining social life? One connected to the social movements of our time that are responding to climate change and rethinking the social, political, and economic systems that have contributed to it? Recall Mignolo and Walsh's (2018, 64) description of *sumak kawsay/buen vivir* as "the harmonious interrelation or correlation of and among all beings (human and otherwise) and with their surroundings." This is precisely the kind of coexistence that we should be searching for in the 2020s: one that embraces harmony between humankind and the natural world as well as between people.

What might a post-growth model for SATM look like? Varkøy and Rinholm (2020) give one clue, proposing the embrace of slowness and resistance in music education as a way of contesting consumerism, constant action, and economic growth, and thereby contributing to the development of a more sustainable society. Another signpost is provided by Todes (2020), who applies Raworth's model of Doughnut Economics to the classical music sector. Such a thought experiment would be well worth translating to SATM and fleshing out. It offers an example—even if only a brief sketch—of rethinking the conventional model of how a music sector works in the light of radical contemporary thinking about the most urgent social questions.

The classical music sphere is beginning to understand the importance of localism, and it seems increasingly likely that in time it will devote more attention to local community work and less to international touring (Brown et al. 2020). Lebrecht (2021), imagining a revolutionized sector rising from the ashes of COVID-19, proclaims: "Local is the new global." SATM ought to be leading this movement, rather than taking inspiration from a program with a centripetal, export-based model. Music students undertaking ecological projects is a positive step, but rethinking SATM through the lens of ecology and sustainability requires a further one: to reflect on the ways that industry, speed, and growth are woven into the field's orthodoxy at the deepest level, permeating its ideology and practices, and to rethink it in terms of sustainable education (Rustin 2020).

Whichever routes are ultimately taken, the 2020s call for a very different ethos in SATM: one cognizant of systemic problems and attuned to efforts to tackle them; connected to progressive movements that uphold the value of sustainability, quality of life, and free time; committed to play and creation and not just work and performance; and looking beyond the needs of the music profession and industry.

Conclusion

El Sistema re-enacts the same ideology and dynamics of music education that have prevailed in Latin America since the sixteenth century. The parallels between choirs of indigenous musicians performing European music as a symbol of civilization and orchestras of barrio youths performing European music as a symbol of social transformation are hard to overlook. Laid over this substratum is a vision of SATM shaped by mid-twentieth-century industrial capitalism and developmentalism. It is time to think about SATM in a completely different way: without hierarchies of culture and value; without constructing the music student as inferior and in need of correction; without resting on principles of intensity, speed, size, and growth.

Answers to the questions posed in this chapter may come not just from the most progressive voices in SATM but also from smaller grassroots projects. SATM has garnered disproportionate attention and funding because its narrative appeals to politicians and the media, and in some cases it has crowded out other visions, but it has much to learn from smaller programs, which sometimes have a more contemporary ethos and radical agenda.[6] In Colombia, there are many such projects, working in more challenging circumstances, with more disadvantaged

---

6 At the SIMM conference in Bogotá in 2019, some of the most dynamic practices and ideas were presented by small projects in peripheral areas with little media presence.

populations, or in more innovative or holistic ways than orthodox SATM, often with more than one art form at once. SATM may be older, larger, and more famous, and it was novel in some respects when it was created, but it has developed slowly since then and has been overtaken as other forms of socially oriented arts education have advanced, often more attuned to the thinking and practices of social movements. There are also progressive organizations linking practice and research in Latin America, such as FLADEM and Observatorio del Musicar, that receive much less publicity than SATM but serve as incubators of innovative ideas and practices. Beyond the region, CM has generally followed a different path to the large ensemble model, and it has been pursuing creative, participatory, non-hierarchical, small group work for decades, putting into practice many of the ideas proposed in Part II (and more). The fact that such approaches are still somewhat novel in SATM is a testament to the conservative influence of Abreu and El Sistema over this field. More attention to promising alternatives outside the SATM field—smaller, more flexible, more agile music programs, or other arts education projects like Medellín's Dance, Theatre, and Visual Arts networks—could speed up progress within it.

Answers will also have to come from another source: universities and conservatoires. Reform or revolution in SATM will be hamstrung unless it is mirrored in the training of musicians in higher education. Music teachers cannot be expected to implement effectively methods and ideas that have not formed part of their own education. Zamorano Valenzuela's (2020) research on training activist music teachers in a public Chilean university points the way.

In many ways, this invitation to reimagine SATM could extend to many parts of the world. The issue of creating a curriculum and pedagogy that accord more closely with the local context and the social goals arises in many places. This is an area in which more imaginative programs are making progress and it is a path that beckons for others. Pursuing this line will not answer every question raised in this book, but it will be a big step forwards. Adopting an emancipatory, realist approach, focused on assets rather than deficits and critical reflection rather than discipline, might not tie up every loose end, but it too would represent a significant advance. Greater attention to sustainability, meanwhile, would be a positive step anywhere on Earth.

As I have argued repeatedly, the issues in Medellín and Venezuela are not unique to those contexts. In the course of conferences, visits, and conversations with SATM educators and researchers in a number of other countries, I have seen that behind the idealistic public discourse, there are similar challenges, complexities, and limitations, and there are staff willing to provide a realistic account of them (in private). There are other programs that suffer from a lack of suitably trained teachers, or struggle to reach the most disadvantaged, or offer a conservative curriculum and pedagogy, or generate professional desires in contexts where there are few relevant work opportunities. My inquiry may be centred in Colombia and Venezuela but it does not stop there.

Pace Abreu and Dudamel, orchestral music is not going to change the world. Large ensemble music education has been around for centuries; it is not suddenly going to end poverty, violence or crime. More thoughtful conductors such as Mehta and Barenboim do not regard music as a magic solution to intractable problems. Art may of course have social effects, but they are rarely direct or linear, hence Clarke's (2018) preference for the more contingent notion of social *affordances* rather than *impact*. Music may be a source of catharsis, consolation, inspiration, revelation—but the idea that teaching children to play the violin will dissolve "wicked problems" is a fiction, and a pernicious one if it detracts from more serious efforts to tackle such challenges and to understand music's social effects.

So what can SATM do? Can it do more than keep children busy and off the streets? If it looks to develop social skills in a more focused way, grapples with issues such as citizenship and empowerment, conceives of music education as political and ethical action, and learns from the most promising models of music education and social change, it will offer more to participants and engage more directly with society outside its walls. And if the coming years see the emergence of a Latin American, socially driven, emancipatory, realist, sustainable SATM, then the field's promise may be realized.

Afterword

> We are a stubborn species: one that is deeply resistant to making profound changes in our behaviour and habits, even when it is clear that we need to do so. But […] when change is forced upon us we are astonishingly versatile.
>
> James Suzman, *Work*

When I put pen to paper in 2019, I planned to write a book about change in SATM. I felt that this topic deserved more attention. Between the process of reform in Medellín dating back to 2005 and the critical research on SATM since 2014, the case for change was building. Then in 2020, COVID-19 struck. A few months later, George Floyd was murdered, catalysing a resurgence of Black Lives Matter. Issues addressed in this book went from being undercurrents in some parts of the SATM field to major preoccupations in many. As I write these final words at the end of 2020, change is no longer a personal or minority interest: there are few who have not been obliged to confront it over recent months. Consequently, this feels like the right time to focus on change in SATM and pay close attention to a program that has been grappling with it for the last fifteen years.

The tumultuous events of 2020 do not pose new questions for SATM so much as intensify existing ones that have been building slowly across the field for years. Problems in the model had already been identified; change was already called for; but now the need is clearer and more pressing. The crises of 2020 may therefore be seen as a catalyst for a necessary and positive shift. If there was a good case for rethinking SATM when I started writing, that case has only become stronger as I finish.

COVID-19, Black Lives Matter, and Music Education

COVID-19 threw into sharp relief two issues from earlier chapters: the centrality of large ensembles, and SATM as a pipeline into the music profession. Suddenly the issue of large ensembles was everywhere, because COVID-19 turned them into a risk and a liability. Collective music-making became a focal point of concern as stories of choir rehearsals as "super-spreader" events were taken up by the media. Large ensembles were rendered unusable in the short term and question marks lingered over their longer-term future. SATM was thus obliged to rethink its central tool and principal selling-point.

The virus also put stress on the classical music profession, making it appear more challenging than ever. It raised further questions about Abreu's focus on training up large numbers of young people from modest economic circumstances for this career. The idea of orchestral training as route out of poverty has always looked somewhat dubious outside a petrostate classical music bubble economy like Venezuela's, but in 2020, with desperation rising among even quite successful musicians and talk of an exodus from the profession in some countries as work opportunities evaporated, it seemed particularly far-fetched. For SATM programs to continue to focus on the mass production of orchestral musicians therefore looked highly questionable.

Black Lives Matter (BLM), meanwhile, gave much greater prominence and urgency to existing questions of race, Eurocentrism, and decolonization that had been swirling gently around music education, music studies, and the classical music sector for some years. ISME included decolonization as a priority area in its new six-year strategic plan (2020–2026). Its newsletter on 30 June 2020 committed to self-critique and change, referring to "confronting and challenging the colonising practices that have influenced education in the past and that are still present today and often perpetuated through curriculum, power relations, and institutional structures and systems," and aspiring to "encourage critical reflection and actions within the Society." ISME's Decolonising and Indigenising Music Education Special Interest Group was also launched, and the El Sistema SIG was renamed Music Education for Social Change—a symbolic changing of the guard.

As ISME's statement illustrates, George Floyd's killing brought forth a wave of responses and, in some cases, soul-searching from the music education sector, above all in North America. For example, the MayDay Group, like many organizations, made a statement that not only "denounces violence against Black individuals and communities and stands with those who seek justice through political action across the globe," but also centres on a *mea culpa*:

> The state-sponsored murder of George Floyd represents yet another tragedy in a centuries-long history of white-supremacist violence that permeates all sectors of society, including every aspect of the music education profession (e.g., publications, conferences, social media, curricula, pedagogy, hiring practices). Unless and until White music educators are willing to acknowledge their privilege, take responsibility for their past and the impact it has on the present, and commit to creating a future steeped in justice, the list of names to which George Floyd has been added will never end. For too long Black people—along with Indigenous people and People of Color—have been called upon to work against the tide of systems steeped in white privilege. We commit to joining this work, seek to thoughtfully examine the role of white privilege in our history as an organization, and to dismantle the structures that perpetuate this privilege as the MayDay Group moves forward.[1]

El Sistema USA was no exception, putting up a statement on its website, which began: "We mourn with the many families across America who have suffered incredible losses due to over-policing, racial profiling, and systemic oppression."[2] It ended:

> We are inspired again by the call to action from Maestro Jose Antonio Abreu in his 2009 TED Prize speech:
>
> (El Sistema is) "No longer putting society at the service of art, and much less at the services of monopolies of the elite, but instead art at the service of society, at the service of the weakest, at the service of the children, at the service of the sick, at the service of the vulnerable, and *at the service of all those who cry for vindication through the spirit of their human condition and the raising up of their dignity.*" (emphasis in original)

---

1 "Statement of Solidarity and Commitment to Antiracism", 15 June 2020, http://www.maydaygroup.org/2020/06/mayday-group-actions-for-change/.
2 "Statement of Response to the El Sistema-Inspired Community", June 2020, https://elsistemausa.org/2020/06/statement-of-response-to-the-el-sistema-inspired-community/.

Both these organizations responded to current events by expressing empathy and solidarity with those affected, but there is a striking difference between their statements. MayDay's offered an organizational self-critique and commitment to change; El Sistema USA's offered neither. El Sistema USA made no mention of what really preoccupied MayDay: the ways that music education itself has historically participated in structural racism and has thus been part of the problem at the heart of BLM. As music education institutions came forth to accept responsibility and commit to reparative action, El Sistema USA offered a vision of continuity and reaffirmed its allegiance to Abreu's philosophy. Its statement on race ended with the words of a white Europhile, who made no mention of race.

In this sense, Abreu was an inappropriate figure to invoke at the height of BLM. What is more, he and his philosophy are archetypical examples of the problem that MayDay identified. A member of Venezuela's white elite, Abreu privileged the performance of classical music by white European and European-descended composers. In his mouth, the word "music" was synonymous with classical music, above all European (Baker 2014). Abreu told Lubow (2007): "As a musician, I had the ambition to see a poor child play Mozart." In a television interview, he claimed: "El Sistema breaks the vicious cycle [of poverty] because a child with a violin starts to become spiritually rich: [...] when he has three years of musical education behind him, he is playing Mozart, Haydn, he watches an opera: this child no longer accepts his poverty, he aspires to leave it behind and ends up defeating it" (Argimiro Gutiérrez 2010). As Abreu's words illustrate, El Sistema is a colour-blind institution in the sense that it does not "see" or talk about race; yet colour-blindness is very different from a commitment to racial justice (Cheng 2019), and the Eurocentrism of its approach is in fact far from colour-blind (Crenshaw 2019). Abreu and El Sistema argued that classical music could save children around the world (many of them Black, Brown, or Indigenous) "from an empty, disorientated, and deviant youth." In a post-George Floyd world, this looks like not just an organization working within a "white racial frame" (Joe Feagin, cited in Ewell 2020) but also a paradigmatic example of white supremacy and colonialist thinking in music education (Kajikawa 2019).

Iconoclasm

Edward Colston was a British politician and philanthropist of the seventeenth to eighteenth centuries who founded alms-houses, schools, and hospitals in Bristol. For his good deeds, he was commemorated in local place, street, and school names, and in 1895 a statue was erected in his memory. On 7 June 2020, the statue was toppled and pulled into the harbour by BLM protesters, in symbolic retribution for Colston's activities as a slave trader. Years of criticisms and campaigns had had no effect, and eventually protesters took matters into their own hands. The clash between Colston's values and those of contemporary Bristol society had become too much.

We will not have to wait centuries to see the clash between Abreu's values and those of progressive music educators. They were out of sync even before his death. The old-school authoritarianism and domination of students; the extreme working practices; the patriarchal dynamics and systemic exclusion of women from the most prestigious roles; the deficit-based theory of poverty; the salvation rhetoric; the clear hierarchization of musics—these are all unsavoury relics of an earlier age. A mission of transforming the lives of BIPOC youths in postcolonial societies through European orchestral music; converting music students into tools of political propaganda for an autocratic regime; bribing journalists and persecuting critics—we do not need to wait until 2120 to see what is wrong here, particularly if social justice is an aspiration. "Problems? We grow, grow, grow," said Abreu. In a post-George Floyd world, this kind of politician's whitewash (I use the word advisedly) of serious issues is no longer acceptable to many educators and activists pursuing social change.

In 2005, when the Red was redirected, the images of Ocampo were taken down from the program's schools. But El Sistema and its affiliates are still putting up statues to their idol, paying homage to Abreu at every turn. In 2020, when Floyd's murder and BLM led to soul-searching and the figurative tearing down of icons in music education, El Sistema created a Chair of the Thought of Maestro José Antonio Abreu, feeding the cult of personality around its deceased founder and consolidating his conservative vision ("Cátedra" 2020). Programs around the world continued to proclaim that they were seeking social justice or change and also "inspired" by Abreu's approach, either ignoring or oblivious to the contradiction between the two. This sector missed a golden opportunity for self-reflection, to finally see race *within* SATM, and from there to undertake a broader reassessment of its past and its future.

Colston was once considered sufficiently inspiring to be placed on a pedestal. He was an admirable figure according to the values of another age. He no longer is. Eventually a reckoning came. Bristol's city authorities ignored the issue for years. They could have taken the decision to move Colston's statue to a museum: not to erase history but to put it in its place. But they failed to act and the statue ended up in the harbour.

SATM should not wait for others to pull Abreu down and tip him into the harbour. It should act itself, and now, by removing Abreu from his pedestal and putting the man and his philosophy in a metaphorical museum where his achievements and failures may be examined and understood. This is not about disowning history or rewriting it but rather drawing a line under the past and charting a different course for the future.

Reckoning with and learning from history is a mark of a mature and responsible organization. As the chief executive of Oxfam GB wrote recently:

> We can all learn lessons from the past. A key part of Oxfam's journey over the almost 80 years of our history has been a growing understanding of how our attitudes and actions are rooted not just in our desire for a better world, but also our assumptions about it—assumptions that, given our British roots, are inevitably coloured by colonialism. We haven't always got it right—far from it—but as a result we are more aware than ever of the need to ensure we challenge, rather than reinforce, existing imbalances of power. (Sriskandarajah 2020)

After the events of 2020, surely the time has come for such open self-examination in SATM. What are the lessons that this field has learnt from the past?

COVID-19, BLM, and Classical Music

In late July 2020, Marshall Marcus, CEO of the European Union Youth Orchestra, invited another well-known figure in the classical music scene, the journalist Norman Lebrecht, to discuss the future of orchestras in the light of the coronavirus pandemic.[3] Both speakers had no doubt that COVID and BLM meant change for the orchestral world and that innovation—probably radical—was needed. Lebrecht articulated a number of critiques of orchestral culture, focusing on touring, hyper-specialization, and the routine aspects of the work. Speaking about orchestral music as a career, he stated: "what we've created is a boring, two-dimensional life and we have to break free of it." He pointed the finger at music education and professional orchestras for curbing musicians' creativity:

> the system is set up in such a way as to chop their legs off before they start. Everything that they do as they go through the education system is designed to make them fit to the working system rather than to redesign the working system to how they think it ought to be; [...] they are trained to please rather than to challenge.

"We need to change the whole system of education of musicians," declared Lebrecht. "Yes!" replied Marcus.

One joint message was that musicians needed to diversify their skills, rather than taking a unitary approach. Marcus responded to Lebrecht: "it seems to me that one of the things you're saying is that [younger musicians'] future may not be as much in these huge symphony orchestras." He reimagined the orchestra as "an ensemble of possibilities: so you're not just a player, you're a teacher, you're a composer, you make things happen, you're an entrepreneur." Then he directly addressed the topic of change :

> it feels to me as if all of these things you're saying, you've been saying for a long time, and what has happened with Coronavirus is it's like we're in a stretto, suddenly it's all happening, you know, twenty years of change is happening in a few months, and I guess that leads onto the need to change even more fast, so let's get going.

This conversation underlined the obsolescence of SATM's orthodox model in 2020. El Sistema was built around students learning a single skill: to play orchestral parts. Discipline was its watchword. This narrow, unitary training enabled the program to storm the world's concert stages for a decade from 2007. Since The System provided for musicians

---

3   "The Future of Orchestras I: Norman Lebrecht", https://www.youtube.com/watch?v=TAi73WVxt0k.

and occupied all their time, developing complementary skills or being entrepreneurs was low down the agenda. As an El Sistema conductor told Shieh (2015, 572): "The system buys everything and supports everything." Playing orchestral parts excellently was the surest route to success. However, this is the precise opposite of the training that Lebrecht and Marcus proposed for the 2020s: broad, diversified, creative, with space to challenge rather than just to please. As these speakers noted, transformations in the orchestral world mean the training will have to change—and that means a big shake-up for SATM after forty-five years of dominance by El Sistema's model. In future, long hours in the serried ranks of a symphony orchestra will not prepare young people properly even for the music profession, let alone for the wider world. Abreu's twentieth-century symphonic thinking has been left behind by the times.

As Marcus and Lebrecht's conversation illustrated, the winds of change blew through the classical music sector in 2020. Race was a particular focus of attention in the US and the UK. A wave of articles appeared in the mainstream media (e.g. Harrison 2020; Poore 2020; Kelly 2020). *The New York Times* published three articles on racism in classical music on a single day (16 July 2020).

In a widely shared article in *The New Yorker*, Alex Ross (2020) argued that "the field must acknowledge a history of systemic racism." He noted: "The wealthy white Americans who underwrote the country's élite orchestras tended to see their institutions as vehicles of uplift that allowed the lower classes to better themselves through exposure to the sublime airs of the masters," and he went on to explore the contradictions of such paternalism. His concluding paragraph echoes a theme that has underpinned this book:

> The ultimate mistake is to look to music—or to any art form—as a zone of moral improvement, a refuge of sweetness and light. [...] Because all art is the product of our grandiose, predatory species, it reveals the worst in our natures as well as the best. Like every beautiful thing we have created, music can become a weapon of division and destruction.

Ross is hardly a firebrand—more the liberal voice of classical music in the US. Yet the contrast with Abreu could hardly be clearer. Ross directly criticized the ideologies of music that Abreu and his followers espoused. His critique of seeing orchestras as "vehicles of uplift that allowed the lower classes to better themselves" hit painfully close to home. Contradicting Abreu's neo-Romantic idealism, Ross recognized classical music's complicity with systemic problems. Ross's article was just one of many in 2020 that left Abreu's discourse looking distinctly past its sell-by date.

As with music education, critiques did not just come from outside. The League of American Orchestras (LAO) released a statement expressing how it was "coming to grips with its history of racism, reflecting on the impact of racism within the League and the wider community of orchestras, and committing to sustained action."[4] Its president argued that the time had come for permanent structural change, imagining "a future that is richer and far more embracing than where we've come from" (Woods 2020). He critiqued the use of canonic European repertoire of the past as "a recyclable asset, pulled mercilessly off the shelf for marketability and immediate emotional impact." The climate crisis demanded that the sector "finally start an honest discussion about the more carbon-intensive aspects of our work—like touring, [or] the global market for guest artists and attractions." In a ringing self-critique, he looked forward to orchestras redefining themselves from a "legacy art form" to "a sector in permanent evolution, responding to and participating in powerful tides of societal change." The president of the LAO was under no illusions: the orchestral sector had some serious catching up to do.

There is thus increasing recognition from within as well as outside the industry that orchestras have a problem—or even that they *are* a problem. Amid the growing calls for orchestras to transform themselves, to become more diverse and inclusive, Dudamel's claim that they are "a model for an ideal global society" (Lee 2012) appears not just dubious but a complete inversion of reality. As Pentreath (2020) asks, in what field other than the orchestral world would it be acceptable to offer a strong defence of the tyrannical male leader in late 2020, in the full knowledge of the harm that such figures have caused? SATM's foundational idea—that the orchestra provides a model for society to *follow*—is impossible to sustain today.

---

4 "A New Statement on Racial Discrimination", August 2020, https://americanorchestras.org/news-publications/public-statements/racial-discrimination-august-2020.html.

At a time when major upheavals point to the need for radical innovation, the conservative Abreu is no more a figure to turn to for classical music than he is for music education. After forty-five years, the orchestra as an organization looks almost identical in Venezuela as it did before El Sistema. The make-up and quantity of orchestras has changed, though much less than Abreu claimed; behind the discursive gloss about social objectives, though, the ethos and functioning of the ensembles is identical, because Abreu's founding goal was to train young musicians quickly for the profession. Even when he adopted a social discourse, his claim was about changing who got to play the game, not changing the rules.

When the Simón Bolívar orchestra toured Europe for the fortieth anniversary of El Sistema in 2015, it performed Mahler, Beethoven, and Wagner, with the musicians dressed in sober suits. It seemed intent on matching Europe's professional ensembles in terms of repertoire, standard, and appearance. The music critic Richard Morrison (2015) lamented: "The Bolívars shook the world by being irresistibly youthful, iconoclastic and Venezuelan. In the process of 'growing up' they have become just like everyone else." The end product of four decades of effort and investment in Venezuela was an ensemble that was indistinguishable from the European norm. The route to a radical rethink of the orchestra does not lie this way.

In sum, when the upheavals of 2020 arrived, the limitations of Abreu's philosophy were exposed. It provided no answers to pressing questions about large ensembles, Eurocentrism, a shrinking sector, or professional renewal. A model that was conservative in its heyday and had already begun to decline was not the place to look for innovative responses to the crisis. There could hardly be a less appropriate example for the future than the Simón Bolívar orchestra: a huge, expensive, globetrotting ensemble, sitting atop a vast factory of narrowly-trained orchestral musicians.

El Sistema rests on and amplifies an idealization of classical music, so it was seized upon by the international classical music sector and its related media in 2007 and became one of its favourite stories for the following decade. But in the last few years, this idealization has become increasingly hard to sustain, with Venezuela slipping ever deeper in crisis on one side and critiques of classical music culture (particularly around questions of race, gender, and sexual harassment) becoming more public and insistent on the other. Then 2020 saw SATM's signature practices called into question by COVID-19 and BLM. By the end of 2020, the ideological foundations of the field's orthodox model looked shakier than ever, and the need for a rethink clearer than ever.

The Red in 2020

The Red was hit hard by COVID-19; not only did it have to close, but also, since its instruments were housed in the schools, many students were left without. Yet having been on a path of pedagogical reform for some time, it was also well placed to respond. The prior shift to project-based learning (PBL) turned out to have been a felicitous move. The Red's projects were always imagined as going beyond conventional collective instrumental performance. This meant that many interesting projects could be pursued throughout lockdowns and other restrictions in 2020: students made instruments, danced, painted, researched, made radio programs, and so on. Some investigated the musical history of their neighbourhood. The Benjamin Herrera school, for example, produced a series of documentaries about important families of musicians in the surrounding Barrio Antioquia.

In some ways, the Red seemed to be not just coping but actually thriving. For example, the school of Villa Laura made an online show about its 2020 project "Family, literature, and music," presented by the school director, a teacher, and two students. The project theme resulted from a survey of students' families, and the contours of the project (a focus on caring for one's family and oneself, and on collecting community histories and memories) were suggested by the participants. The director described the Red's students as reflexive, critical, political subjects who contributed to the construction of the territory. These words were borne out in the show: the students spoke eloquently about their views and their role in shaping the project. Most interestingly of all, one of them welcomed the new opportunities for narrating their everyday realities through music. As the teacher confirmed, the crisis had opened up possibilities that conventional face-to-face instrumental training tended to limit. Less focus on teaching allowed more opportunities for listening to the voices of students and their families, and for activities normally sidelined due to a lack of time. The crisis appeared to have helped Villa Laura to achieve what the Red's leadership had sought when it introduced PBL in 2018: a reflexive project in which students participated by thinking, talking, and listening, and not only playing or singing.

BLM had much less impact in Colombia than in countries like the US and UK. Also, as with the pedagogical reforms, the Red had started to engage with this issue several years earlier. Giraldo and Franco had placed diversity and identity at the heart of their reforms from 2017, and their commitment was not tokenistic: they championed and performed Colombian musics and instruments (many of them of African and/or indigenous origin). The program had never had a full reckoning with the issue of race, but its leadership was sensitive to the issue and had laid some groundwork.

However, the Red was obliged to face up to another problem that has grown in prominence in SATM and music education more generally in recent years: sexual abuse and harassment. June 2020 saw the publication of a journalistic investigation in Medellín entitled "Sexual abuse in the orchestra" (Ángel 2020). The report identified the city's university music departments—including that of the University of Antioquia, to which the Red was attached—as hotbeds of sexual abuse and stated that at least eight cases had come to light in the Red itself.[5] According to one alleged victim, "the Red is a nest of abuse, the teachers see it as completely normal to flirt with their [female] students from 13 onwards." During my research, I had been given detailed testimony in one interview, but I decided not to write about this issue as it seemed not to be pervasive in the Red. However, the new article implied otherwise, at least in the past.

The Red's response was substantive. A confidential hotline was opened to allow the reporting of incidents. The leadership met with and provided support to victims, and training on combating sexual abuse and violence was organized for staff and students. Other internal activities sought to highlight the problem rather than sweeping it under the carpet. In short, the Red recognized the seriousness of the issue and its responsibility to do something about it.

---

5   Ironically, less than a month earlier the city's arts education networks had been lionized in the media after winning an international prize (Valero 2020).

This is not a new problem for SATM. I have been raising it since 2014. So far, El Sistema has escaped a journalistic investigation like that in Medellín, but it is not through a lack of material to investigate. In 2016, the former El Sistema violinist Luigi Mazzocchi confirmed my concerns, alleging publicly that male teachers having sexual relationships with female students "was the norm. ... Some of the guys, some of the teachers, would actually say it out loud: 'I do this [have sexual relationships] with my students because I think we're actually helping them become better musicians, better violinists'" (Scripp 2016b, 42). He also alleged that at least one known predator (possibly more) continued to work in El Sistema and that sexual abuses were covered up by a code of silence: "People knew that stuff was happening—[...]—everybody talked about it, but nobody reported it" (ibid.).

This issue demands concerted action from the SATM field. "The opposite of racist isn't 'not racist,' it's antiracist," says Ibram X. Kendi.[6] The same might be said about sexism and sexual harassment and abuse. It is not enough for institutions not to support racism, sexism, or abuse; they need to actively oppose such attitudes and actions. This means acknowledging their presence and committing to combating them. It means critically reassessing institutional pasts and presents, practices and ideologies. It means looking seriously at issues of power, hierarchy, and oppression. It means asking whether, by modelling itself on professional classical music, SATM has reproduced the vices of that sector, and therefore whether it is time to look to other models, such as CM or music therapy.

A striking aspect of the scandal that hit the Red in 2020 was that, according to one former general director, at least two of the alleged perpetrators were *hijos de la Red* (sons of the Red): former students who had gone on to become teachers. What does it say about SATM's social education if students who have spent years passing through its ranks can go on to become suspected sexual predators? What were they learning inside the program? What sort of culture were they imbibing? To its credit, the Red's response was serious and appropriate. But the field needs to go deeper, ask why the problem occurs, and tackle the issue at its source. SATM should take pre-emptive action, rather than

---

6   Ibram X. Kendi, "How to Be an Antiracist", https://www.chicagohumanities.org/events/ibram-x-kendi-how-be-antiracist/.

waiting and responding only when cases come to light and the damage is done. This implies, once again, a deep rethink of the field's practices and dynamics, taking fully into account the ways that certain kinds of music education may leave students open to abuse (Pace 2015).

Changing Director, Deepening Reform

The Red has been undertaking critical reassessment since 2005. Nevertheless, as we have seen, this process has not been universally welcomed within the program. Tensions over change reached boiling point in 2019, and a question mark hovered over the Red at the end of that year. It was widely assumed that when Medellín's new mayor took office, he would bring in his own culture team and appoint a new director of the Red. There was much discussion of who might be chosen and in which direction they might point the program. As early as 2018, some of the more disgruntled staff had barely disguised that they were waiting out the remainder of Giraldo's tenure in the hopes that someone more attuned to the Red's traditions would be installed. Would the program continue down the path of self-critique and change or retrench into a more conventional and less controversial approach?

At the start of 2020, the long-expected transition occurred. Giraldo and Franco left, and Vania Abello arrived. Abello is a classical flautist with a background in cultural management, including work with the Colombian Youth Orchestra and Bogotá Philharmonic Orchestra. No sooner had she begun at the Red than COVID-19 struck, and the resulting upheaval made it harder to sense the broader trajectory of the program. But in September 2020, the annual pedagogy symposium, a major event in the program's calendar that was held online and open to the public, revealed that the new leadership was not only continuing but also doubling down on change.

The Red invited a number of speakers from Colombia and overseas to give long, in-depth presentations. There were several striking features. Interdisciplinarity was prominent: a number of the invitees came not only from outside SATM but also from other arts. There was a focus on pedagogical renewal: the Red sought to learn from other programs and forms of arts education with different pedagogical thinking and practices. There was considerable overlap and exchange between research and practice: a number of the invited speakers had one foot in both, and the intellectual level was high. And finally, the criticality of their reflections was pronounced. The five-day event left me with various impressions: a theme of *búsqueda* (a search or quest); a commitment to experimentation, creation, and change; a willingness to listen to and learn from alternative perspectives; an openness to critique and self-critique; and a sense of humility—a feeling that the Red had much still to learn—that underpinned everything else.

The final panel session was hosted by the culture ministry official responsible for the city's four arts education networks, Mábel Herrera. She underlined that it was important that such projects reflected deeply and had a component of research. (Indeed, the ministry funded qualitative research activities in all four networks during my fieldwork.) This meant that Medellín's networks were a changing organism. Alluding to the symposium's title, *Territorios sonoros* (resounding territories), Herrera was open about the Red's failure in the past to connect its schools properly to their communities, something that they were now rectifying. In a rebuke to a salvationist tendency in the field, she declared: "our job isn't to save anyone."

Abello, the Red's new director, not only described the program as engaged in a quest to improve and learn from others, but she also criticized the classical music training that she herself had received and that had historically been the central pillar of the program. "We [classical] musicians are quite rigid in our thinking and in our way of approaching creation," she said, acknowledging that the process of change was difficult for many from such a background. Yet on the topic of coronavirus, her tone was optimistic. She suggested that it provided the Red with an opportunity to push ahead with pedagogical reform. Rather than clinging onto the idea of a return to the old normality as soon as possible, she depicted the disruption as a stimulus to rethink and transform. The staff could not focus on instrumental teaching, so they had to come up with alternatives. This had led to more focus on the students and their questions and desires. Abello even spoke of "a lovely process." By publicly acknowledging some of the problems with SATM's old ways and highlighting the value of new approaches, Abello seemed to be moving reform efforts to a new level.

While it feels unfair to single out one presenter when so many were excellent, the contributions of Eliécer Arenas, a musician, psychologist, and anthropologist with three decades of experience in practice, research, and policy-making in Colombia, were particularly striking.[7] Arenas immediately signalled the ambiguity of music, the gap between utopian discourses and realities, and the complex ethical problems of using music as a tool for social transformation. He thus proposed a more critical, realistic reading of the potential of music for social action. What SATM programs generated above all were questions, he said, but the institutional context rarely allowed for deep, calm, critical analysis: "These programs for social transformation, with their discourse, co-opt the capacity for critique. [...] We start to understand the world through the logic of institutional rhetoric. We begin to think that our obligation is to defend the institution." He expressed sympathy for SATM's employees: they were often victims of institutional dynamics, obliged to inflate results rather than enquire more deeply, and dehumanized by the demand to protect official discourses. Honest critique needs to be incorporated by institutions as a virtue.

Arenas underlined the importance of dialoguing with and valorizing community cultural resources—the "resounding territories" of the symposium's title. Many music projects, he noted, negate the local context, treating it as empty or even dangerous. Consequently, "progress" or a "happy ending" is seen more as students leaving the community behind—advancing their career in the capital or overseas—than giving back. Programs needed to work on persuading students to commit to their territory. He critiqued the export model of spending large sums of money to produce a handful of musicians to go overseas. Why all this focus on the exceptional cases? We need to think more about the vast majority and their everyday lives in the community.

It was important for projects to integrate participants into their territory. Concentrating on foreign musical experiences may lead students to dismiss existing ones, leading to a process of uprooting. There are also implications for sociability. If an institution and its staff transmit the message that the popular culture of the family and community has

---

[7] Some of these ideas are presented in more condensed form in Arenas (2020).

little value, then some social and cultural bonds may deteriorate. If the goal is to improve human relations, this is a problematic outcome.

Arenas criticized the fact that many Latin American musicians end up moving to Europe or North America in order to study Latin American music at a higher level; meanwhile, Latin America remains obsessed with performing central European repertoire of the past. He imagined a Latin American "system," based on Latin American musics. We should aspire to bring people to our region to study our musics, he said, rather than sending our musicians overseas to study, creating a diaspora. There is presently a boom in Afro-Latin musics, which have been a major influence around the world. What are we doing with this patrimonial treasure? It needs to be given equal status in Latin America—not just adding a few Latin American pieces to the repertoire, "not a nice little tune at the end [of the concert], as a populist gesture."

Pedagogy was central to his vision of social transformation through music. Technical training was insufficient to construct critical, creative subjects. Nor was it enough to add psychologists or social workers to standard music education. SATM ought to reinforce the elements of music itself that had potential for social development. There was an urgent need to diversify pedagogies and not just repertoires. Traditional music has much to offer in this respect, he argued. Traditional Latin American pedagogies name and relate to the world through music in different ways—for example, invoking relationships between music and nature. However, his was not simply a traditionalist stance: rather, SATM needed to forge new "mestizo pedagogies" for a heterogeneous world. "We need to construct a new mechanism, one that is more complex and more like us; we need the pedagogies to be more like us, so that the kids feel that we are inviting them to construct a resource that gives more life to life, and not to freeze them in an idealized past."

The problem was not classical music per se, he said, but rather the approach. SATM's current pedagogies have little to do with Latin American social realities. "Classical music is far more beautiful than its pedagogies," he argued. It deserved better. "I think we need to be capable of having a counter-cultural vision of pedagogies."

The world is changing, stated Arenas; if we do not start from this basic premise, we will keep on using the pedagogies of the past rather than pedagogies for the future. In terms of mentality, repertoire, and ways of working, we are training musicians for a world that is disappearing. The sustainability of the symphonic world is ever more uncertain, so producing young people with such a limited profile makes little sense. Pedagogies need to change away from hyper-specialization and towards emphasizing creativity. They also need to slow down: the rapid pace of learning and obsession with preparing repertoire for performance looks more like indoctrination than education, and it leaves little time for thinking or embodying. We should be educating students to imagine and invent the music and the society of the future, one that their teachers do not know; the current system of music schools and conservatoires is a long way from that picture. What they offered, he argued, was normalization, a "pedagogy of fear," and a production line of musicians. Yes, this "works" as a model, it produces results, but at what cost? Is this the kind of world we want to create? He argued that SATM should focus much more on forming amateurs rather than professionals—on the "musicalization of the citizenry" rather than preparing a few participants for conservatoire and the industry.

What form of social development is being pursued in practice, not just discourse, he asked? For a few people to become professional musicians and bring prestige to the program? Arenas critiqued spectacularization in SATM—using huge music ensembles to "demonstrate" social change—and wondered whether the field was more focused on seeking applause than achieving its social objectives. What about social inclusion? Does the program really reach those who most need it? And what sort of inclusion is represented by reproducing a single, closed system of understanding the world? These were uncomfortable questions, he acknowledged, but necessary to deepen the work. Hinting that the time for change was ripe, he argued: "The pandemic has brought a willingness to be more honest. We need policy that is less grandiloquent, but more effective, […] that contains more of the blessed chaos of diversity."

The substance of Arenas's contributions was illuminating, but what was even more remarkable was that this vision of critique and renewal came not in an academic article or at a scholarly conference, but rather from a keynote speaker at a prominent, public SATM event, and that far from sitting awkwardly, it aligned with the central themes of the symposium and the perspectives of other invited presenters. Critical thinking about SATM now had more than a foothold in a major program:

it was seated at the top table. Similarly, the self-critical interventions of Herrera and Abello, the two most senior figures in the Red, were remarkable not because of their content—I had heard such opinions countless times before in meetings and private conversations—but because they were made at a high-profile event, in front of staff, students, the other networks, city government representatives, and hundreds of listeners online. Referring publicly to past errors, present challenges, and a different future felt like a big step.

Arenas was far from the only inspiring speaker. Anthony Trecek-King provided a view from the US, describing his work with the Boston Children's Chorus. Many of his points posed implicit questions for SATM: the issue of race; a critique of a pyramidal program structure; inverting the leadership model; including children with disabilities within the main ensembles rather than creating separate ones; the program as a place of escape for survivors of sexual abuse; incorporating perspectives from critical research; bringing democracy, participation, and politics to the fore; and holding up values such as forgiveness, vulnerability, and empathy as central to the work.

His critique of an access-focused approach to diversity and inclusion went to the heart of orthodox SATM:

> You need to make sure that in every environment and everything that you do you try to create as diverse an environment as possible. In other words, you need to go out and actively seek the type of student that you would like to have in your ensemble, because just opening the doors and saying 'come join me' isn't going to be enough.

He framed diversity and inclusion in terms of repertoire but also pedagogy: "Are we teaching in one specific style that connects to one specific kind of student, or do we have different teaching methods?" He placed great emphasis on learning and practising how to listen and talk: encouraging students to express themselves and their experiences, guiding them through conversations, opening their ears to other people's stories. He would devote time to such conversations, often spending half of a two-hour rehearsal talking and half singing. He would make sure that conversations included difficult topics such as race, gender, and the inequities of the political system. He described a student-led initiative in which participants raised money to buy computers for a school that could not afford them—exemplifying the ideal of action for the benefit of others in artistic citizenship.

As ever, the contrast with SATM's orthodoxy was fascinating. Whereas in 2020 El Sistema turned inwards and backwards to the deceased Abreu and his conservative philosophy of "work and study," the Red treated the crisis as an opportunity for self-critical reflection and extended its search outwards to other arts, innovative pedagogues, and critical researchers to chart a new way forwards. The Red did not focus its attention on classical conductors or performers, who are usually the staple of such events in orthodox SATM. There was nothing here about making a career in music; the focus was on resounding territories and social transformation. Arenas's valorization of "the blessed chaos of diversity" and "the disorder of plurality"—the possibility that every community might want to take its own path—contrasted with Abreu's obsession with order and his recipe of the orchestra as the solution to every problem. Trecek-King highlighted the importance of talking and listening—activities generally seen as a waste of valuable playing time in orthodox SATM. Arenas's call to realism was a challenge to Abreu's politically and economically expedient idealism.

The symposium felt like a turning point. I felt inspired at the end. Still, it did not banish all questions by any means, and I do not see the Red's future as assured. This was a program with many ups and downs across its history. This was not the first time that I had heard excellent ideas in the Red. Would the program manage to translate them into practice? Were enough staff on board this time to enact the reforms? Then there was the issue of COVID. The Red was bravely attempting to see it as an opportunity, but many in the cultural and music education sectors in Colombia were struggling or suffering, so the wider panorama of socially oriented music education was far from encouraging. Undoubtedly such struggles were represented within the ranks of the Red as well. Furthermore, a program like the Red can never be isolated from political developments. A future mayor might decide to reduce the program's budget or be less interested in reflection and adapting processes than in the quick hit of good publicity that the old, spectacular version of SATM provides.

In terms of the international field, there are places where change is afoot, but the biggest players in SATM—Venezuela and Mexico—remain stuck in the old model. SATM is a huge field and any impression is necessarily subjective, but my sense is that pursuing a serious overhaul, as the Red is doing, is still a minority interest. There is also the role of the global North to consider. El Sistema was widely embraced as providing hope for a resurrection of classical music, as Simon Rattle put it, and of classical music education. Are the program's many fans in the global North willing to recognize the deficiencies of El Sistema's model, let go of it, and encourage SATM to move on?

Ambiguity is not something that can be banished from such work, then, as Boeskov argues. It also hovered over a public meeting shortly afterwards, attended by representatives of several Latin American SATM programs.[8] Abello was invited to present the Red to the other participants and the online audience. She began with a description of the program, and I was struck by how conventional it sounded, even after fifteen years of attempted reforms. The program remained organized largely along its original lines, with twenty-six schools whose character was defined by the needs of the program's orchestras and bands rather than the desires or traditions of the surrounding communities. Only one school was devoted to Colombian music.

Then Abello began to speak about the Red's *search*, and words like evolution and transformation started to appear. The Red was created as a response to the particular circumstances of the late 1990s, she said, and since the city has changed since then, the Red ought to evolve as well. It also needs to adapt to the desires of the community, so it has become more open to other musics, moving away from "Eurocentric training." Our imaginary cannot be based on the symphony orchestra alone, she said; we also need other musics that allow participants to recognize themselves and tell the stories of their own lives and communities. It is no longer enough to make music just for the sake of making music. Music is the means; the end is forming reflective, critical, but empathetic citizens, who learn through music how to take decisions in their lives. Behind the search lies pedagogical renewal. COVID-19 has brought opportunities in this respect: above all, greater involvement by families in the projects, rather than just taking their child to the music school and sitting outside waiting for them. Abello's presentation underlined how

---

8   "Educación Musical en América Latina: Arte para la igualdad y los derechos", organized by Constelación Sonora Argentina, 9 October 2020.

far there was still to go in the Red, but also how far it had come. Her determination to press ahead was unmistakable.

A point that caught my attention in both the symposium and the subsequent meeting was the absence of El Sistema, beyond a couple of mentions that the Red and similar programs were initially inspired by the Venezuelan one. On the one hand, there was no adulation; on the other, no mention that the Red broke with the Venezuelan program in 2005 and had spent the last fifteen years seeking a new model. In the global North, we have become accustomed to seeing SATM as a universe that revolves around El Sistema, and public debate has often been reduced to arguments between advocates and critics of the Venezuelan program. But in these Latin American spaces, El Sistema was reduced to a historical footnote—a sign, perhaps, of its decreasing relevance at the progressive end of the field.

However, the final words of the meeting were offered by Claudio Espector, the godfather of SATM in Argentina. There had been brief mentions of El Sistema, he said, but he wanted to underline a critical point: "If a lot was inspired by the Venezuelan model, let's not lose sight of the fact that the Venezuelan model, at the height of its development, took as its transcendental moment not that the Venezuelan orchestras should be present in our Latin American barrios, but rather that they should play at the Salzburg Festival." His point echoed the Red's territorial critique and Arenas's interrogation of SATM's export model; it also came from one of the most senior figures in Latin American SATM. Unusually for a public conversation between SATM programs, the event ended on an ambiguous note.

The symposium and subsequent meeting took place when this book was nearing completion, and I was fascinated to see how the critical perspectives and processes of change that I had witnessed and written about were being consolidated. Many points from the preceding chapters were articulated by multiple voices inside and outside the Red, from Colombia and overseas. After years of slow, incremental change, I had the sensation that the tide was turning. COVID-19 seemed to have served as one catalyst: reducing the program's frenetic pace, making business as usual an impossibility, and thereby creating both time and the requirement for deeper transformation. The symposium itself was another, moving the critical conversation onto a new level—one that left

El Sistema's conservative shibboleths far behind. There was a special energy of rethinking and renewal during the symposium that surpassed anything I had seen within SATM during a decade of research. Listening to voices from different programs, arts, and countries, I sensed that a movement for self-critique and change was gathering steam.

Hope

Despite all the challenges of 2020, then, I end the year with a greater sense of optimism and hope with regard to the Red. Having seen it as neither simply an example to follow nor one to avoid during most of my research, I find my ambivalent feelings shifting as my writing draws to a close. I am increasingly convinced that the Red constitutes a valuable case study of SATM, one deserving of greater attention.

What is distinctive about the Red is not the quality of its musical performances; it is the pedagogical rethinking, the longstanding critical reflection on the social objective, and, above all, the centrality of an ethos of *búsqueda* or search. Arenas argued that SATM programs generated many questions, but the field's institutions and discourses tended to co-opt employees' capacity for critique. This is where the Red differs from the norm. The Red has had leaders who have backed self-critique and change. My meetings with the Red's general directors revolved around critical questions that they themselves raised; they did not "understand the world through the logic of institutional rhetoric," as Arenas put it, in fact they actively queried that logic. Leaders' responses to evaluations of the Red were indicative: rather than seizing hold of and trumpeting any positive report, however flimsy, they tended to accord such studies only limited value. There was a commitment to grappling with the complex issues that SATM raises and trying to do better, not telling the world what great work they were doing. There has been a humility at leadership level that contrasts with the self-congratulation of some of SATM's most famous programs.

In 2020, I wrote to Abello to introduce myself and tell her that I was writing a critical book about the Red. Her response was that she welcomed critical voices as they would help the program to grow. The Red was exploring many fundamental changes, she replied, and my reading would feed into that search. These words were like a breath of fresh air; Abello's openness to critical scrutiny was a welcome change from the extreme defensiveness that I had faced after my previous book.

Consequently, I am inclined to hold up the Red as an example after all: not of "best practice" but of striving towards it; not of inspirational rhetoric but of an openness to critical reflection and dialogue; not of a model program, but of one that shows that change is possible in the SATM field. It is not the achievement of perfection or an ideal that I take away from the Red, but rather the search for improvement: the quest to know more and do better. This is something to celebrate.

Varkøy and Rinholm (2020, 180) offer up hope as an alternative to the extremes of hubris and resignation with regard to music education:

> This hope is neither naïve optimism, nor something similar to religious faith. Hope in our context is not the conviction that something will end well, but a hunch of meaning. Hope allows for more nuanced discussions and actions (or non-actions) than the attitude of belief. Beliefs may lead to an over-confidence in the effects of music that, in our view, does not benefit music education and philosophy of music education over the long-term. The magic of music does not need help from preachers telling us what music can do. Instead, it needs a humbler attitude characterized by hope rather than belief, giving room for wonder instead of over-confidence in music's alleged effects on humans.

Leaving Normality Behind

2020 has been a year of precipitous, forced, and often unwelcome changes. Some pine for a return to normality, but others see the disruption as an opportunity to press a reset button and move away from an unsatisfactory status quo. There have been more than a few cries of "we don't want to go back to normal," recognizing that the old normality was broken. In the US, this conversation was intensified by the election of Joe Biden and defeat of Donald Trump. Robert Reich (2020) argued that returning to normal would be disastrous for the US:

> Normal led to Trump. Normal led to the coronavirus.
>
> Normal is four decades of stagnant wages and widening inequality when almost all economic gains went to the top. Normal is 40 years of shredded safety nets, and the most expensive but least adequate healthcare system in the modern world.

Normal is also growing corruption of politics by big money—an economic system rigged by and for the wealthy.

Normal is worsening police brutality.

Normal is climate change now verging on catastrophe.

Similarly, the Reverend William J. Barber II argued that the US could not afford to go back to normal (Harris 2020), and he recalled that the title of Martin Luther King's "I Have a Dream" speech was in fact "Normalcy—Never Again."

Soon afterwards, a major environmental report for the UK Treasury argued that radical changes to production, consumption, and education were urgently needed around the globe (Elliott and Carrington 2021). Going back to normal simply is not an option if we are to avoid a catastrophic breakdown.

2020 has been a year of rethinking around the world. Critical attention has been directed at inequality and redistribution, work, healthcare, education, and other areas of human life. SATM could go either way: it might return to the orthodox model as soon as COVID-19 allows; or it might use this moment of crisis as a catalyst to engage with longstanding questions.

I would argue that this is the right time not just for the latter but also for more radical action in SATM. Each of the 2020 upheavals in the Red and/or SATM (COVID-19, BLM, and sexual harassment) alone would have been sufficient cause for a rethink, because each is connected to the core practices and ideologies of the field. Taken together, they suggest the need for more: not just to rethink but also to transform SATM for the new decade and beyond.

On the educational front, there is a need to face up to technological shifts and their consequences. As we go deeper into an era of automation and artificial intelligence, breadth of perspective, the ability to make connections across areas of knowledge, and distinctively human skills such creativity and empathy will become ever more important. Routine and highly specialized work will be increasingly taken over by machines. Looking ahead to the future, the narrow, repetitive, hyper-specialized approach of El Sistema—learning orchestral parts and downplaying most other facets of music education, let alone the arts and humanities more broadly—is a poor educational choice if serving as a pipeline into the orchestral profession (El Sistema's original aim) is not the ultimate goal.

On the social front, the rise and then resurgence of BLM has seen a wave of radical critiques of progressive causes like diversity and inclusion. An increasing number of writers argue that these notions are insufficiently self-critical and that genuine change requires something more (e.g. Stewart 2017; Albayrak 2018; Gopal 2020; Wolff 2020). Brigitte Fielder (2020) contends:

> Further racist disgrace will only be prevented by a cultural shift. That shift must be *structural, methodological, pedagogical, generational*. These organizations must be re-envisioned and rebuilt. New methods and organizational structures are necessary because the existing ones have continued (and will continue) to fail us. Organizations will have to think beyond "inclusion" and come to recognize and understand the very real relations of power that have cultural and material effects on our fields. They cannot simply "diversify" themselves only to rely disproportionally on the labor of their BIPOC members. They cannot simply invite more BIPOC colleagues into an unsustainably racist environment.

It is time for SATM to re-evaluate the idea at its core: a discredited conservative notion of social action as individual social mobility through correcting personal deficits. It is time to wrest SATM away from a colonialist salvation narrative and the stigmatization of the young and the poor as "empty, disorientated, and deviant." It is time to decentre a model that was not even designed with social action in mind and forge a new one connected to the needs of our times. SATM's foundational ideas and practices are no longer fit for the purpose of social action—if indeed they ever were. They should be retired, and the field should be re-founded on the best research and practice in social action and arts education.

The problems that beneficiaries face are primarily structural or systemic ones, not personal deficiencies. So rather than pursuing individualized solutions (salvation, social mobility), why not consider how music education could be articulated to organizations or movements that are pursuing systemic change, such as The Democracy Collective or Smart CSOs Lab?[9] How might SATM display "a readiness to participate

---

9   https://democracycollaborative.org/; https://smart-csos.org/.

in actions against particular or local manifestations of larger systemic problems" (Soper 2020, 155)? Global heating is the biggest social problem of the century, yet it is barely on the radar of SATM's largest programs. SATM is not going to solve it, but could it at least play its part? If SATM is supposed to offer a model for society, could it not strive to model a *sustainable* society, focused on quality of life and not quantity of musicians or orchestras?

Transformation does not need to start from scratch. There is an enormous amount of exciting practice and research across music and other arts that ties together culture and development in innovative and productive ways, and I have pointed to a few examples in these pages. In Medellín, the Red took a significant step forwards simply by looking to its neighbour networks of Visual Arts, Theatre, and Dance. The volume *Jóvenes: un fuego vital* (2015) illustrates that programs driven by progressive visions of youth and development surrounded the Red in Medellín; all that was needed was for the program to lift its head from the norms of orthodox SATM. There is a growing literature on music education, ecology, and the environment on which reformers could draw to fashion a sustainable SATM.[10] Traditional Latin American musics and pedagogies often invoke connections between music and nature, as Arenas noted, so they offer an invaluable resource for using music to rethink coexistence and our relationship to the world.

The challenges are great and numerous, and they feel particularly acute at the end of the tumultuous year of 2020. Nonetheless, this is a historical juncture that calls for action. Furthermore, the Red illustrates that such action is possible within SATM. Lebrecht (2021) argues that, for the classical sector, "2021 presents the best chance for change in living memory." To quote Marcus again, "it's like we're in a stretto, [...] twenty years of change is happening in a few months, [...] so let's get going." If ever there were a moment to rethink and transform SATM, it would be now.

---

10   See for example Daniel Shevock's "Literature Review for Eco-Literate Music Pedagogy", http://www.eco-literate.com/relevant-music-education-articles.html.

Bibliography

Primary Sources

Arango, Marta Eugenia. 2006. "Presente y Futuro de la Red: Bases para el Redireccionamiento." Medellín: University of Antioquia.

"Documento de Orientaciones Generales." 2016. Medellín: Red de Escuelas de Música.

Estrada, Eva. 1997. "Diagnóstico y Caracterización de la Situación del Modelo Enseñanza/Aprendizaje del Sistema de Orquestas Juveniles e Infantiles de Venezuela."

"Fundamentos Conceptuales, Metodológicos y Técnicas de Intervención." 2016. Medellín: Red de Escuelas de Música.

"Informe de Actividades: Equipo de Gestión Social (Noviembre-Diciembre)." 2017a. Medellín: Alcaldía de Medellín / Universidad de Antioquia.

"Informe de Actividades: Equipo de Gestión Social (Julio-Octubre)." 2017b. Medellín: Alcaldía de Medellín / Universidad de Antioquia.

"Informe de Actividades: Equipo de Gestión Social. Anexos." 2017c. Medellín: Alcaldía de Medellín / Universidad de Antioquia.

"Informe de Actividades: Equipo de Gestión Social. Seguimiento y Acompañamiento." 2017d. Medellín: Alcaldía de Medellín / Universidad de Antioquia.

"Informe Fase Diagnóstica: Sistematización e Interpretación de Resultados." 2008. Medellín: Red de Escuelas de Música.

"Informe Final 2012. Red de Escuelas de Música de Medellín. Area Psicosocial." 2012. Medellín: Red de Escuelas de Música.

"Intervención Psicosocial. Fase de Proyección y Fortalecimiento. Agrupaciones Integradas. Recuento Histórico. 2009–2013." 2013. Medellín: Red de Escuelas de Música.

"Jornada de Reflexión Diagnóstica: Orquesta Sinfónica Juvenil." 2014. Medellín: Alcaldía de Medellín / Universidad de Antioquia.

"Propuesta de Asesoría y Acompañamiento Psicosocial." 2008. Medellín: Red de Escuelas de Música.

"Propuesta Técnica para la Operación del Programa." 2018.

"Síntesis Talleres con Direcciones, Equipo Coordinador y Secretarias." 2014. Medellín: Alcaldía de Medellín / Universidad de Antioquia.

Secondary Sources

"20 Jahre West-Eastern Divan Orchestra—Daniel Barenboim: 'Keine Utopie.'" 2019. *Nmz—Neue Musikzeitung*, 23 October. https://www.nmz.de/kiz/nachrichten/20-jahre-west-eastern-divan-orchestra-daniel-barenboim-keine-utopie

Acosta Valencia, Gladys Lucía, and Angela Piedad Garcés Montoya. 2013. *Colectivos de Comunicación y Apropiación de Medios*. Medellín: Universidad de Medellín.

Adlington, Robert. 2007. "Organizing Labor: Composers, Performers, and 'the Renewal of Musical Practice' in the Netherlands, 1969–72." *The Musical Quarterly* 90 (3–4): 539–77. https://doi.org/10.1093/musqtl/gdn015

Agrech, Vincent. 2018. *Un orchestre pour sauver le monde*. Stock.

Albayrak, Nihan. 2018. "Diversity Helps but Decolonisation Is the Key to Equality in Higher Education." *Contemporary Issues in Teaching and Learning* (blog), 16 April. https://lsepgcertcitl.wordpress.com/2018/04/16/diversity-helps-but-decolonisation-is-the-key-to-equality-in-higher-education/

Alemán, Xiomara, Suzanne Duryea, Nancy G. Guerra, Patrick J. McEwan, Rodrigo Muñoz, Marco Stampini, and Ariel A. Williamson. 2017. "The Effects of Musical Training on Child Development: A Randomized Trial of El Sistema in Venezuela." *Prevention Science* 18 (7): 865–78. https://doi.org/10.1007/s11121-016-0727-3

Allan, Julie, Nikki Moran, Celia Duffy, and Gica Loening. 2010. "Knowledge Exchange with Sistema Scotland." *Journal of Education Policy* 25 (3): 335–47. https://doi.org/10.1080/02680931003646196

Allsup, Randall Everett. 2016. "Mutual Learning and Democratic Action in Instrumental Music Education." *Journal of Research in Music Education*, August. https://doi.org/10.2307/3345646

Álvarez, Víctor Andrés. 2016. "Los Afro Son Una Población Que Se Hace Sentir en Medellín." *El Colombiano*, 27 January. https://www.elcolombiano.com/antioquia/los-afro-poblacion-que-se-hace-sentir-en-medellin-LI3497490

Ander-Egg, Ezequiel. 1990. *Repensando la Investigación Acción-Participativa*. Buenos Aires: Lumen Humanitas.

Anderson, Sally. 2011. "Civil Sociality and Childhood Education." In *A Companion to the Anthropology of Education*, edited by Bradley A. Levinson and Mica Pollock, 316–32. Chichester: Wiley Blackwell.

Ang, Ien. 2011. "Navigating Complexity: From Cultural Critique to Cultural Intelligence." *Continuum* 25 (6): 779–94. https://doi.org/10.1080/10304312.2011.617873

Ángel, Santiago. 2020. "Acoso sexual en la orquesta: decenas de mujeres denuncian a universidades de Antioquia." *La FM*, 24 June. https://www.lafm.com.co/colombia/acoso-sexual-en-la-orquesta-decenas-de-mujeres-denuncian-universidades-de-antioquia

Ansdell, Gary. 2014. *How Music Helps in Music Therapy and Everyday Life*. Abingdon: Routledge.

Ansdell, Gary, Brit Ågot Brøske, Pauline Black, and Sara Lee. 2020. "Showing the Way, or Getting in the Way? Discussing Power, Influence and Intervention in Contemporary Musical-Social Practices." *International Journal of Community Music* 13 (2): 135–55. https://doi.org/10.1386/ijcm_00016_1

Araujo, Elizabeth. 2017. "Pianista Gabriela Montero: El silencio no es una opción." Actualy.es, 14 March. https://actualy.es/pianista-gabriela-montero-silencio-no-una-opcion/

Arenas, Eliécer. 2020. "La experiencia de la afectividad como dispositivo disruptivo en la pedagogía instrumental." XVI Congreso IASPM-LA, Medellín, 1 November. https://www.youtube.com/watch?v=3rJXTegOrF8&feature=youtu.be

Argimiro Gutiérrez, Freddy. 2010. "San José Antonio Abreu: Maestro de la Codicia, Enemigo de la Diversidad y Patrono del Absolutismo Musical." *Aporrea* (blog), 10 February. https://www.aporrea.org/poderpopular/a94940.html

"ArtsPay 2018." 2019. Arts Professional. https://www.artsprofessional.co.uk/sites/artsprofessional.co.uk/files/artspay_2018_report.pdf

Baines, Donna. 2017. *Doing Anti-oppressive Practice: Social Justice Social Work*, 3rd Edition. Black Point, Nova Scotia: Fernwood Publishing.

Baker, Geoffrey. 2008. *Imposing Harmony: Music and Society in Colonial Cuzco*. Durham, NC: Duke University Press.

———. 2010. "The Resounding City." In *Music and Urban Society in Colonial Latin America*, edited by Geoffrey Baker and Tess Knighton, 1–20. Cambridge: Cambridge University Press.

———. 2011. *Buena Vista in the Club: Rap, Reggaetón, and Revolution in Havana*. Durham, NC: Duke University Press.

———. 2014. *El Sistema: Orchestrating Venezuela's Youth*. Oxford; New York, NY: Oxford University Press.

———. 2015a. "El Sistema: The Future of Classical Music?" In *Déchiffrer Les Publics de la Musique Classique / Unraveling Classical Music Audiences*, edited by Stéphane Dorin. Paris: Éditions des Archives Contemporaines.

———. 2015b. "The Simón Bolívar Orchestra—Why We Should Look Beyond the Music." *The Guardian*, 13 January. http://www.theguardian.com/music/2015/jan/13/the-simon-bolivar-orchestra-why-we-should-look-beyond-the-music-geoff-baker

———. 2016a. "Citizens or Subjects? El Sistema in Critical Perspective." In *Artistic Citizenship: Artistry, Social Responsibility, and Ethical Praxis*, edited by David Elliott, Marissa Silverman, and Wayne D. Bowman, 313–38. New York, NY: Oxford University Press.

———. 2016b. "Editorial Introduction: El Sistema in Critical Perspective." *Action, Criticism, and Theory for Music Education* 15 (1): 10–32. https://act.maydaygroup.org/articles/Baker15_1.pdf

———. 2016c. "Antes de pasar página: conectando los mundos paralelos de El Sistema y la investigación crítica." *Revista Internacional de Educación Musical* 4: 51–60. http://www.revistaeducacionmusical.org/index.php/rem1/article/view/92

———. 2017a. "Big Noise in Raploch?" *Scottish Review*, 21 June. http://www.scottishreview.net/GeoffBaker285a.html

———. 2017b. "No, Venezuela's much-hyped El Sistema music programme is not a hotbed of political resistance." *The Conversation*, 7 July. https://theconversation.com/no-venezuelas-much-hyped-el-sistema-music-programme-is-not-a-hotbed-of-political-resistance-80500

———. 2018. "El Sistema, 'The Venezuelan Musical Miracle': The Construction of a Global Myth." *Latin American Music Review* 39 (2): 160–93. https://muse.jhu.edu/article/717148

Baker, Geoffrey, Anna Bull, and Mark Taylor. 2018. "Who Watches the Watchmen? Evaluating Evaluations of El Sistema." *British Journal of Music Education* 35 (3): 255–69. https://doi.org/10.1017/S0265051718000086

Baker, Geoffrey, and Ana Lucía Frega. 2016. "Los reportes del BID sobre El Sistema: Nuevas perspectivas sobre la historia y la historiografía del Sistema Nacional de Orquestas Juveniles e Infantiles de Venezuela." *Epistemus. Revista de Estudios en Música, Cognición y Cultura* 4 (2): 54–83. https://doi.org/10.21932/epistemus.4.2751.2

———. 2018. "'Producing Musicians like Sausages': New Perspectives on the History and Historiography of Venezuela's El Sistema." *Music Education Research* 20 (4): 502–16. https://doi.org/10.1080/14613808.2018.1433151

Barnes, Marian, and David Prior, eds. 2009. *Subversive Citizens: Power, Agency and Resistance in Public Services*. Bristol; Portland, OR: Policy Press.

Barrett, Brad. 2018. "Cultivating Artistic Citizenship in Urban Schools: Creativity, Critique, and Community at the Conservatory Lab Charter School." DMA, New England Conservatory.

Bartleet, Brydie-Leigh, and Gavin Carfoot. 2016. "Arts-Based Service Learning with Indigenous Communities: Engendering Artistic Citizenship." In *Artistic Citizenship: Artistry, Social Responsibility, and Ethical Praxis*, edited by David Elliott, Marissa Silverman, and Wayne D. Bowman, 339–58. New York, NY: Oxford University Press.

Bartleet, Brydie-Leigh, and Lee Higgins. 2018a. "Introduction: An Overview of Community Music in the Twenty-First Century." In *The Oxford Handbook of Community Music*, edited by Brydie-Leigh Bartleet and Lee Higgins, 1–20. New York, NY: Oxford University Press.

———, eds. 2018b. *The Oxford Handbook of Community Music*. New York, NY: Oxford University Press.

Bates, Vincent C. 2016. "Foreword: How Can Music Educators Address Poverty and Inequality?" *Action, Criticism, and Theory for Music Education* 15 (1): 1–9. https://act.maydaygroup.org/articles/Bates15_1.pdf

Bates, Vincent C. 2018. "Faith, Hope, and Music Education." *Action, Criticism, and Theory for Music Education* 17 (2): 1–21. https://doi.org/10.22176/act17.2.1

Beck, Charlotte Joko. 1995. *Nothing Special: Living Zen*. London: Bravo.

Belfiore, Eleonora. 2002. "Art as a Means of Alleviating Social Exclusion: Does It Really Work? A Critique of Instrumental Cultural Policies and Social Impact Studies in the UK." *International Journal of Cultural Policy* 8 (1): 91–106. https://doi.org/10.1080/102866302900324658

———. 2009. "On Bullshit in Cultural Policy Practice and Research: Notes from the British Case." *International Journal of Cultural Policy* 15 (3): 343–59. https://doi.org/10.1080/10286630902806080

———. 2012. "'Defensive instrumentalism' and the legacy of New Labour's cultural policies." *Cultural Trends* 21 (2): 103–11. https://doi.org/10.1080/09548963.2012.674750

———. 2021. "Who cares? At what price? The hidden costs of socially engaged arts labour and the moral failure of cultural policy." *European Journal of Cultural Studies* (in press). https://doi.org/10.1177/1367549420982863

Belfiore, Eleonora, and Oliver Bennett. 2008. *The Social Impact of the Arts: An Intellectual History*. Basingstoke: Palgrave Macmillan.

———. 2010. "Beyond the 'Toolkit Approach': Arts Impact Evaluation Research and the Realities of Cultural Policy-Making." *Journal for Cultural Research* 14 (2): 121–42. https://doi.org/10.1080/14797580903481280

Bell, Colin, and David Raffe. 1991. "Working Together? Research, Policy and Practice: The Experience of the Scottish Evaluation of TVEI." In *Doing Educational Research*, edited by Geoffrey Walford. London: Routledge.

Benedict, Cathy, Patrick Schmidt, Gary Spruce, and Paul Woodford, eds. 2015. *The Oxford Handbook of Social Justice in Music Education*. New York, NY: Oxford University Press.

Bernatzky, Marianne, and Alejandro Cid. 2018. "Parents' Aspirations and Commitment with Education. Lessons from a Randomized Control Trial in a Shantytown." *Studies in Educational Evaluation* 56 (March): 85–93. https://doi.org/10.1016/j.stueduc.2017.11.004

Berry Slater, Josephine, and Anthony Iles. 2009. "No Room to Move: Radical Art and the Regenerate City." *Mute*, 24 November. https://www.metamute.org/editorial/articles/no-room-to-move-radical-art-and-regenerate-city#

Boeskov, Kim. 2018. "Moving Beyond Orthodoxy: Reconsidering Notions of Music and Social Transformation." *Action, Criticism, and Theory for Music Education* 17 (2): 92–117. https://doi.org/10.22176/act17.1.92

———. 2019. "Music and Social Transformation: Exploring Ambiguous Musical Practice in a Palestinian Refugee Camp." PhD, Oslo: Norwegian Academy of Music.

Boia, Pedro S., and Graça Boal-Palheiros. 2017. "Empowering or Boring? Discipline and Authority in a Portuguese Sistema-Inspired Orchestra Rehearsal." *Action, Criticism, and Theory for Music Education* 16 (2): 144–72. https://doi:10.22176/act16.1.144

Bolger, Lucy. 2015. "Understanding Collaboration in Participatory Music Projects with Communities Supporting Marginalised Young People." *Qualitative Inquiries in Music Therapy* 10 (3): 77–116.

Booth, Eric. 2008. "Thoughts on Seeing El Sistema." http://www.americanorchestras.org/images/stories/lld_pdf/elsistema_Booth.pdf

Borgh, Chris van der, and Alexandra Abello Colak. 2018. "Everyday (In)Security in Contexts of Hybrid Governance: Lessons from Medellin and San Salvador." LSE Latin America and Caribbean Centre / Utrecht University.

Born, Georgina. 2010. "For a Relational Musicology: Music and Interdisciplinarity, Beyond the Practice Turn." *Journal of the Royal Musical Association* 135 (2): 205–43. https://doi.org/10.1080/02690403.2010.506265

Borzacchini, Chefi. 2010. *Venezuela en el Cielo de los Escenarios*. Caracas: Fundación Bancaribe.

Bowman, Wayne D. 2009a. "No One True Way: Music Education Without Redemptive Truth." In *Music Education for Changing Times: Guiding Visions for Practice*, 3–15. Dordrecht: Springer.

———. 2009b. "The Community in Music." *International Journal of Community Music* 2 (2–3): 109–28. https://doi.org/info:doi/10.1386/ijcm.2.2-3.109_1

———. 2016. "Artistry, Ethics, and Citizenship." In *Artistic Citizenship: Artistry, Social Responsibility, and Ethical Praxis*, edited by David Elliott, Marissa

Silverman, and Wayne D. Bowman, 59–80. New York, NY: Oxford University Press.

Bradley, Deborah. 2009. "Oh, That Magic Feeling! Multicultural Human Subjectivity, Community, and Fascism's Footprints." *Philosophy of Music Education Review* 17 (1): 56–74. https://www.jstor.org/stable/40327310

———. 2018. "Artistic Citizenship: Escaping the Violence of the Normative (?)." *Action, Criticism, and Theory for Music Education* 17 (2): 71–91. https://doi.org/10.22176/act17.1.71

Brand, Peter. 2013. "Governing Inequality in the South through the Barcelona Model: 'Social Urbanism' in Medellín, Colombia." https://www.dmu.ac.uk/documents/business-and-law-documents/research/lgru/peterbrand.pdf

Bregman, Rutger. 2018. *Utopia for Realists: And How We Can Get There*. London: Bloomsbury Paperbacks.

Brook, Julia, and Ana Lucía Frega. 2020. "Comparing the Concepts of Sistema in Canada and Argentina to El Sistema Nacional in Venezuela." International Society for Music Education (Research Commission).

Brough, Melissa. 2014. "Participatory Public Culture and Youth Citizenship in the Digital Age: The Medellín Model." PhD, University of Southern California.

Brown, Jeffrey Arlo, Timmy Fisher, and Hartmut Welscher. 2020. "19 COVID Theses." *VAN Magazine*, 2 April. https://van-us.atavist.com/19-covid-theses

Bull, Anna. 2016. "El Sistema as a Bourgeois Social Project: Class, Gender, and Victorian Values." *Action, Criticism, and Theory for Music Education* 15 (1): 120–53. https://act.maydaygroup.org/articles/Bull15_1.pdf

———. 2019. *Class, Control, and Classical Music*. New York, NY: Oxford University Press.

Caldeira, Teresa P. R. 1999. "Fortified Enclaves: The New Urban Segregation." In *Cities and Citizenship*, edited by James Holston, 114–38. Durham, NC: Duke University Press.

Camlin, Dave, Laura Caulfield, and Rosie Perkins. 2020. "Capturing the Magic: A Three-Way Dialogue on the Impact of Music on People and Society." *International Journal of Community Music* 13 (2): 157–72. https://doi.org/10.1386/ijcm_00017_1

"Canciller de Venezuela analiza con Bachelet impacto del bloqueo de EE.UU." 2019. *Venezolana de Televisión* (blog), 19 June. https://www.vtv.gob.ve/canciller-jorge-arreaza-michelle-bachelet-2/

Candusso, Flávia. 2008. "The 'João and Maria, Capoeira Angola, and Citizenship' Project: The Role of Community Music and Civilizing Afro-Brazilian Values in Promoting the Well-Being of Children." In *CMA XI: Projects, Perspectives & Conversations*, 16–24. Rome.

Carabetta, Silvia. 2018. "Reflexiones para la construcción de una educación musical intercultural: Cuando lo pedagógico y lo epistemológico se desencuentran." *Revista Internacional de Educación Musical* 5: 119–27. http://www.revistaeducacionmusical.org/index.php/rem1/article/view/118

Carvalho, José Jorge de, Liliam Barros Cohen, Antenor Ferreira Corrêa, Sonia Chada, and Paula Nakayama. 2016. "The Meeting of Knowledges as a Contribution to Ethnomusicology and Music Education." *The World of Music* 5 (1): 111–33. https://www.jstor.org/stable/44652698

"Cátedra de estudio afianza pensamiento del Maestro Abreu dentro de El Sistema." 2020. El Sistema, Prensa Fundamusical, 20 February. https://elsistema.org.ve/noticias/catedra-de-estudio-afianza-pensamiento-del-maestro-abreu-dentro-de-el-sistema/

Chavarría, Maricel. 2019. "Zubin Mehta: 'Mi sueño de que la música lleve a la paz no se ha hecho realidad.'" *La Vanguardia*, 11 September. https://www.lavanguardia.com/cultura/20190912/47305493265/entrevista-zubin-mehta-director-orquesta-filarmonica-israel-gira-despedida-bcn-classics.html

Cheng, William. 2019. *Loving Music Till It Hurts*. New York, NY: Oxford University Press.

Cid, Alejandro. 2014. "Giving a Second Chance: An After-School Programme in a Shanty Town Interacted with Parent Type: Lessons from a Randomized Trial." *Educational Research and Evaluation* 20 (5): 348–65. https://doi.org/10.1080/13803611.2014.968589

Clarke, Eric. 2018. "Between Scylla and Charybdis: Frameworks for Understanding the Social Affordances of Music." 3rd SIMM-posium on the Social Impact of Making Music, Porto.

Clift, Stephen. 2020. "Fancourt, D. and Finn, S. (2019). What Is the Evidence on the Role of the Arts in Improving Health and Well-Being? A Scoping Review." *Nordic Journal of Arts, Culture and Health* 2 (1). https://www.idunn.no/nordic_journal_of_arts_culture_and_health/2020/01/fancourt_d_and_finn_s_2019_what_is_the_evidence_on_t

Cobo Dorado, Karina. 2015. *La pédagogie de groupe dans les cours d'instruments de musique*. Paris: L'Harmattan.

Cornwall, Andrea, and Deborah Eade, eds. 2010. *Deconstructing Development Discourse: Buzzwords and Fuzzwords*. Rugby: Practical Action Publishing.

Coronil, Fernando. 1997. *The Magical State: Nature, Money, and Modernity in Venezuela*. Chicago, IL: University of Chicago Press.

Creech, Andrea, Patricia González-Moreno, Lisa Lorenzino, Grace Waitman, Elaine Sandoval, and Stephen Fairbanks. 2016. "El Sistema and Sistema-Inspired Programmes: A Literature Review of Research, Evaluation, and Critical Debates." Sistema Global.

Crenshaw, Kimberlé Williams, ed. 2019. *Seeing Race Again: Countering Colorblindness across the Disciplines*. Berkeley, CA: University of California Press.

Crooke, Alexander Hew Dale, and Katrina Skewes McFerran. 2014. "Recommendations for the Investigation and Delivery of Music Programs Aimed at Achieving Psychosocial Well-Being Benefits in Mainstream Schools." *Australian Journal of Music Education* 1: 15–37.

Crooke, Alexander Hew Dale, Paul Smyth, and Katrina Skewes McFerran. 2016. "The Psychosocial Benefits of School Music: Reviewing Policy Claims." *Journal of Music Research Online* 7. http://www.jmro.org.au/index.php/mca2/article/view/157

Crux, Ana Isabel, Graça Mota, and Jorge Alexandre Costa. 2017. "Sociological Portraits: Orchestral Socialization, Paths and Experiences." In *Growing While Playing in Orquestra Geração: Contributions towards Understanding the Relationship between Music and Social Inclusion*, edited by Graça Mota and Teixeira João Lopes, 61–99. Porto: Edições Politema.

Dagnino, Evelina. 2007. "Citizenship: A Perverse Confluence." *Development in Practice* 17 (4/5): 549–56.

Davis, Sharon G. 2011. "Fostering a 'Musical Say': Identity, Expression, and Decision Making in a US School Ensemble." In *Learning, Teaching, and Musical Identity: Voices across Cultures*, edited by Lucy Green, 267–80. Bloomington, IN: Indiana University Press.

Daykin, Norma, Louise Mansfield, Catherine Meads, Karen Gray, Alex Golding, Alan Tomlinson, and Christina Victor. 2020. "The Role of Social Capital in Participatory Arts for Wellbeing: Findings from a Qualitative Systematic Review." *Arts & Health*. https://doi.org/10.1080/17533015.2020.1802605

Deane, Kathryn. 2018. "Community Music in the United Kingdom: Politics or Policies?" In *The Oxford Handbook of Community Music*, edited by Brydie-Leigh Bartleet and Lee Higgins, 177–94. New York, NY: Oxford University Press.

Denning, Michael. 2015. *Noise Uprising: The Audiopolitics of a World Musical Revolution*. London; Brooklyn, NY: Verso Books.

"Denuncian hostigamiento político en Sistema Nacional de Orquestas." 2015. *El Nacional*, 5 December.

Dickenson, James. 2019. "Lives of Orchestral Musicians Hit a Low Note." *Morning Star*, 30 January. https://morningstaronline.co.uk/article/c/impassioned-appeals-support-orchestral-musicians

Diverlus, Rodney. 2016. "Re/Imagining Artivism." In *Artistic Citizenship: Artistry, Social Responsibility, and Ethical Praxis*, edited by David Elliott,

Marissa Silverman, and Wayne D. Bowman, 189–209. New York, NY: Oxford University Press.

Dobson, Nicolas. 2016. "Hatching Plans: Pedagogy and Discourse within an El Sistema-Inspired Music Program." *Action, Criticism, and Theory for Music Education* 15 (1): 89–119. https://act.maydaygroup.org/articles/Dobson15_1.pdf

Drezner, Daniel. 2017. *The Ideas Industry: How Pessimists, Partisans, and Plutocrats Are Transforming the Marketplace of Ideas*. New York, NY: Oxford University Press.

D'Souza, Annalise A., and Melody Wiseheart. 2018. "Cognitive Effects of Music and Dance Training in Children." *Archives of Scientific Psychology* 6 (1): 178–92. http://dx.doi.org/10.1037/arc0000048

Dunphy, Kim. 2018. "Theorizing Arts Participation as a Social Change Mechanism." In *The Oxford Handbook of Community Music*, edited by Brydie-Leigh Bartleet and Lee Higgins, 301–21. New York, NY: Oxford University Press.

Eagleton, Terry. 2004. "The Last Jewish Intellectual." *New Statesman*, 29 March.

Easterly, William. 2006. *The White Man's Burden: Why the West's Efforts to Aid the Rest Have Done So Much Ill and So Little Good*. London: Penguin.

"El BID Revisa Contrato de Bandas Musicales." 2003. *El Tiempo*, 16 July. https://www.eltiempo.com/archivo/documento/MAM-979096

El Libro de la Red: Veinte años de música viva. 2015. Medellín: Alcaldía de Medellín.

Elliott, Larry, and Damian Carrington. 2021. "Economics' failure over destruction of nature presents 'extreme risks.'" *The Guardian*, 2 February. https://www.theguardian.com/environment/2021/feb/02/economics-failure-over-destruction-of-nature-presents-extreme-risks

"El Sistema: Changing Lives Through Music." 2008. 11 April. https://www.cbsnews.com/news/el-sistema-changing-lives-through-music/

Elliott, David, Marissa Silverman, and Wayne D. Bowman, eds. 2016. *Artistic Citizenship: Artistry, Social Responsibility, and Ethical Praxis*. New York: Oxford University Press.

Erickson, Amanda. 2018. "Latin America Is the World's Most Violent Region. A New Report Investigates Why." *Washington Post*, 25 April. https://www.washingtonpost.com/news/worldviews/wp/2018/04/25/latin-america-is-the-worlds-most-violent-region-a-new-report-investigates-why/

Escribal, Federico Luis. 2017. "Orquestas Infanto-Juveniles suramericanas en perspectiva de Derechos Culturales." *Revista foro de educación musical, artes y pedagogía* 2 (2): 107–27. http://www.revistaforo.com.ar/ojs/index.php/rf/article/view/31

"Escuelas de Música: Más Civilidad y Cultura." 1997. *Cambio de Clase*, March.

Esté, Aquiles. 2018. "José Antonio Abreu y los límites del populismo musical." *New York Times*, 6 April. https://www.nytimes.com/es/2018/04/06/espanol/opinion/opinion-abreu-venezuela-sistema.html

Estrada Rodríguez, Luis Alfonso, Cynthia Fragoso Guerrero, Laura Elizabeth Gutiérrez Gallardo, and Federico Sastré Barragan. 2019. "Por una educación musical verdaderamente inclusiva en México." *Este País* (blog), 4 November. https://estepais.com/impreso/por-una-educacion-musical-verdaderamente-inclusiva-en-mexico/

"Evaluación de Impactos." 2011. Sistema Nacional de Orquestas Juveniles e Infantiles. http://idbdocs.iadb.org/wsdocs/getdocument.aspx?docnum=36583351

Ewell, Philip A. 2020. "Music Theory and the White Racial Frame." *Music Theory Online* 26 (2). https://doi.org/10.30535/mto.26.2.4

Fairbanks, Stephen. 2019. "Schooling Habitus: An auto/ethnographic study of music education's entanglements with cultural hegemony." PhD, University of Cambridge.

Fernández-Morante, Basilio. 2018. "Psychological Violence in Current Musical Education at Conservatoires." *Revista Internacional de Educación Musical* 6 (1): 13–24. https://doi.org/10.12967/RIEM-2018-6-p013-024

Ferriday, Zack. 2018. "The Maestro Will See You Now." *VAN Magazine*, 22 March. https://van-us.atavist.com/the-maestro-will-see-you-now

Fielder, Brigitte. 2020. "Your Predominantly White Academic Organization (Yes, Even Yours) Is Exactly One Live-Tweeted Racist Event Away from Public Disgrace." *Avidly* (blog), 22 July. http://avidly.lareviewofbooks.org/2020/07/22/your-predominantly-white-academic-organization-yes-even-yours-is-exactly-one-live-tweeted-racist-event-away-from-public-disgrace/

Fink, Robert. 2016. "Resurrection Symphony: El Sistema as Ideology in Venezuela and Los Angeles." *Action, Criticism, and Theory for Music Education* 15 (1): 33–57. http://act.maydaygroup.org/articles/Fink15_1.pdf

Flores, Pia. 2019. "Muni: Cuatro mujeres narran la historia de abusos sexuales del director protegido." *Nómada, Guatemala* (blog), 6 June. https://nomada.gt/nosotras/somos-todas/muni-cuatro-mujeres-narran-la-historia-de-abusos-sexuales-del-director-protegido/

Folkes, Louise. 2021. "Re-Imagining Social Mobility: The Role of Relationality, Social Class and Place in Qualitative Constructions of Mobility." *Sociological Research Online* (in press). https://doi.org/10.1177/1360780420985127

Fotopoulos, Takis. 2005. "From (Mis)Education to Paideia." *The International Journal of Inclusive Democracy* 2 (1). http://www.inclusivedemocracy.org/journal/vol2/vol2_no1_miseducation_paideia_takis.htm

Foucault, Michel. 1991. *Discipline and Punish: The Birth of the Prison*. London: Penguin.

Fowks, Jacqueline. 2019. "De la filarmónica en Venezuela, a los autobuses de Lima." *El País*, 19 November. https://elpais.com/cultura/2019/11/18/actualidad/1574096922_739738.html

Franz, Tobias. 2017. "Urban Governance and Economic Development in Medellín: An 'Urban Miracle'?" In *Urban Latin America: Inequalities and Neoliberal Reforms*, edited by Tom Angotti, 129-45. Lanham, MD: Rowman & Littlefield.

———. 2018. "Colombia Elections 2018: The Perils of Polarisation for a Precarious Peace." *LSE Latin America and Caribbean Blog*, 9 March. https://blogs.lse.ac.uk/latamcaribbean/2018/03/09/colombia-elections-2018-the-perils-of-polarisation-for-a-precarious-peace/

Frega, Ana Lucía, and Jorge Ramiro Limongi. 2019. "Facts and Counterfacts: A Semantic and Historical Overview of El Sistema for the Sake of Clarification." *International Journal of Music Education* 37 (4): 561–75. https://doi.org/10.1177/0255761419855821

Frei, Marco. 2011. "Wie Viel System Steckt Im System? Venezuela Und Das Soziale Musikprojekt 'El Sistema.'" *Neue Zürcher Zeitung*, 21 November. http://www.nzz.ch/aktuell/feuilleton/uebersicht/wie-viel-system-steckt-im-system-1.13372944

Freire, Paulo. 1974. *Education for Critical Consciousness*. London: Sheed and Ward.

———. 2005. *Pedagogy of the Oppressed*. Translated by Myra Bergman Ramos. 30th anniversary edition. New York, NY: Continuum.

Fukuyama, Francis, and Seth Colby. 2011. "Half a Miracle." *Foreign Policy* (blog), 25 April. https://foreignpolicy.com/2011/04/25/half-a-miracle/

"FundaMusical Simón Bolívar—El Sistema y el PNUD en Venezuela suscriben proyecto para la inclusión social." 2017. El PNUD en Venezuela, 5 December. https://www.ve.undp.org/content/venezuela/es/home/presscenter/articles/2017/12/05/fundamusical-sim-n-bol-var-el-sistema-y-el-pnud-en-venezuela-suscriben-proyecto-para-la-inclusi-n-social.html

Fung, C. Victor. 2018. *A Way of Music Education: Classic Chinese Wisdoms*. New York, NY: Oxford University Press.

Galeano, Deicy Patricia Hurtado, and Didier Álvarez Zapata. 2006. "La formación de ciudadanías en contextos conflictivos." *Estudios Políticos* 29 (December): 81–96. https://revistas.udea.edu.co/index.php/estudiospoliticos/article/view/1297

García Bermejo, Carmen. 2018. "La Falsa Filantropía de Salinas Pliego." Quinto Elemento. Laboratorio de Investigación. https://www.quintoelab.org/falsafilantropia/

———. 2020. "El Gobierno de AMLO Rescata las Orquestas de Salinas Pliego." Quinto Elemento. Laboratorio de Investigación, 22 January. https://quintoelab.org/project/amlo-al-rescate-de-orquesta-de-salinas-pliego

Gaunt, Helena, and Heidi Westerlund, eds. 2013. *Collaborative Learning in Higher Music Education*. Farnham; Burlington, VT: Routledge.

Gaztambide-Fernández, Rubén. 2013. "Why the Arts Don't Do Anything: Toward a New Vision for Cultural Production in Education." *Harvard Educational Review* 83: 211–37.

Gaztambide-Fernández, Rubén, and Leslie Stewart Rose. 2015. "Social Justice and Urban Music Education." In *The Oxford Handbook of Social Justice in Music Education*, edited by Cathy Benedict, Patrick Schmidt, Gary Spruce, and Paul Woodford, 456–72. New York, NY: Oxford University Press.

Gioia, Ted. 2018. "Bach at the Burger King." *LA Review of Books*, May 17. https://lareviewofbooks.org/article/bach-at-the-burger-king/

Godwin, Louise. 2020. "El Sistema in Australia: Risk, Aspiration and Promise." https://www.researchgate.net/publication/343002117_El_Sistema_in_Australia_Risk_aspiration_and_promise

Gómez-Zapata, Jonathan Daniel, Luis César Herrero-Prieto, and Beatriz Rodríguez-Prado. 2020. "Does Music Soothe the Soul? Evaluating the Impact of a Music Education Programme in Medellin, Colombia." *Journal of Cultural Economics*, April. https://doi.org/10.1007/s10824-020-09387-z

Gopal, Priyamvada. 2020. "We Can't Talk about Racism without Understanding Whiteness." *The Guardian*, 4 July. http://www.theguardian.com/commentisfree/2020/jul/04/talk-about-racism-whiteness-racial-hierarchy

Gottfredson, Denise, Amanda Brown Cross, Denise Wilson, Melissa Rorie, and Nadine Connell. 2010. "Effects of Participation in After-School Programs for Middle School Students: A Randomized Trial." *Journal of Research on Educational Effectiveness* 3 (3): 282–313. https://doi.org/10.1080/19345741003686659

Gouk, Penelope. 2013. "Music as a Means of Social Control: Some Examples of Practice and Theory in Early Modern Europe." In *The Emotional Power of Music: Multidisciplinary Perspectives on Musical Arousal, Expression, and Social Control*, edited by Tom Cochrane, Bernardino Fantini, and Klaus R. Scherer, 307–13. New York, NY: Oxford University Press.

Gould, Elizabeth. 2007. "Social Justice in Music Education: The Problematic of Democracy." *Music Education Research* 9 (2): 229–40. https://doi.org/10.1080/14613800701384359

Govias, Jonathan. 2015a. "This Is Where We Flew." 5 April. https://jonathangovias.com/2015/04/05/this-is-where-we-flew/

———. 2015b. "Bonfire of the Inanities—International Censorship in Sistema." 9 May. https://jonathangovias.com/2015/05/09/bonfire-of-the-inanities-international-censorship-in-sistema/

———. 2020. "Reflections on 10 Years in Sistema." 10 February. https://jonathangovias.com/2020/02/10/reflections-on-10-years-in-sistema/

Griffiths, Morwenna. 1998. *Educational Research for Social Justice: Getting off the Fence*. Buckingham: Open University Press.

Hall, Edith. 2019. "Why Working-Class Britons Loved Reading and Debating the Classics." *Aeon*, 13 November. https://aeon.co/essays/why-working-class-britons-loved-reading-and-debating-the-classics

Hallam, Susan. 2010. "The Power of Music: Its Impact on the Intellectual, Social and Personal Development of Children and Young People." *International Journal of Music Education* 28 (3): 269–89. https://doi.org/10.1177/0255761410370658

Hanauer, Nick. 2019. "Better Schools Won't Fix America." *The Atlantic*, 10 June. https://www.theatlantic.com/magazine/archive/2019/07/education-isnt-enough/590611/

Harris, Adam. 2020. "Is American Healing Even Possible?" *The Atlantic*, 29 November. https://www.theatlantic.com/politics/archive/2020/11/william-barber-biden-trump/617235/

Harrison, Phil. 2020. "Black Classical Music: The Forgotten History Review—Challenging Orchestrated Racism." *The Guardian*, 27 September. http://www.theguardian.com/tv-and-radio/2020/sep/27/black-classical-music-the-forgotten-history-review-challenging-orchestrated-racism

Hart, Roger. 1992. "Children's Participation: From Tokenism to Citizenship." UNICEF. https://www.unicef-irc.org/publications/100-childrens-participation-from-tokenism-to-citizenship.html

Hayes, Eileen M. 2020. "In Conversation with President Eileen M. Hayes." College Music Society. https://www.music.org/index.php?option=com_content&view=article&id=1951:in-conversation-with-president-eileen-hayes&catid=139&Itemid=2585

Haywood, Sarah, Julia Griggs, Cheryl Lloyd, Stephen Morris, Zsolt Kiss, and Amy Skipp. 2015. "Creative Futures: Act, Sing, Play. Evaluation Report and Executive Summary." NatCen Social Research. https://e-space.mmu.ac.uk/618917/1/Act__Sing__Play.pdf

Heile, Björn. 2020. "Writing on Living Composers and the Problem of Advocacy: Failure and the Experimental Work of Mauricio Kagel." In *Remixing Music Studies: Essays in Honour of Nicholas Cook*, edited by Ananay Aguilar, Ross Cole, Matthew Pritchard, and Eric Clarke, 164–79. London: Routledge.

Heinemeyer, Catherine. 2018. "Mental Health Crisis in Teens Is Being Magnified by Demise of Creative Subjects in School." *The Conversation*, 3 September. http://theconversation.com/mental-health-crisis-in-teens-is-being-magnified-by-demise-of-creative-subjects-in-school-102383

Henderson, Errol A. 1996. "Black Nationalism and Rap Music." *Journal of Black Studies*. https://doi.org/10.1177/002193479602600305

Henley, Jennie. 2018. "A Challenge to Assumptions of the Transformative Power of Music." 3rd SIMM-posium on the Social Impact of Making Music, Porto.

———. 2019. "Pedagogy & Inclusion: A Critique of Outcomes-Based Research and Evaluation." Research seminar, Guildhall School of Music and Drama.

Henley, Jennie, and Lee Higgins. 2020. "Redefining Excellence and Inclusion." *International Journal of Community Music* 13 (2): 207–16. https://doi.org/10.1386/ijcm_00020_1

Hensbroek, Pieter Boele van. 2010. "Cultural Citizenship as a Normative Notion for Activist Practices." *Citizenship Studies* 14 (3): 317–30. https://doi.org/10.1080/13621021003731880

Hesmondhalgh, David. 2013. *Why Music Matters*. Chichester: Wiley Blackwell.

Hess, Juliet. 2018. "Troubling Whiteness: Music education and the 'messiness' of equity work." *International Journal of Music Education* 36 (2): 128–44. https://doi.org/10.1177/0255761417703781

———. 2019. *Music Education for Social Change: Constructing an Activist Music Education*. London: Routledge.

———. 2021. "Resisting the 'Us' versus 'Them' Dichotomy through Music Education: The Imperative of Living in the 'Anti-.'" In *Difference and Division in Music Education*, edited by Alexis Anja Kallio, 56–75. London: Routledge.

Hewett, Ivan. 2020. "In Defence of the Tyrannical Male Maestro." *The Spectator*, 14 November. https://www.spectator.co.uk/article/in-defence-of-the-tyrannical-male-maestro

Higgins, Charlotte. 2006. "Land of Hope and Glory." *The Guardian*, 24 November. http://www.theguardian.com/music/2006/nov/24/classicalmusicandopera

"HMUK Releases Final CMMYS Report." 2017. Help Musicians, 16 October. https://www.helpmusicians.org.uk/news/latest-news/hmuk-releases-final-cmmys-report

Holston, James. 1999. "Spaces of Insurgent Citizenship." In *Cities and Citizenship*, edited by James Holston, 155–73. Durham, NC: Duke University Press.

Hopkins, Michael, Anthony M. Provenzano, and Michael S. Spencer. 2017. "Benefits, Challenges, Characteristics and Instructional Approaches in an El Sistema Inspired After-School String Program Developed as a University–School Partnership in the United States." *International Journal of Music Education* 35 (2): 239–58. https://doi.org/10.1177/0255761416659509

Horowitz, Joseph. 2018. "Going High (Culture)." *Washington Examiner*, 5 December. https://www.washingtonexaminer.com/weekly-standard/going-high-culture

Houtart, François. 2011. "El concepto de sumak kawsai (buen vivir) y su correspondencia con el bien común de la humanidad." *América Latina en Movimiento*, 1 June. https://www.alainet.org/es/active/47004

Howell, Gillian. 2017. "A World Away from War: Music Interventions in War-Affected Settings." PhD, Brisbane: Griffith University.

Hylton, Forrest. 2007. "Medellín's Makeover." *New Left Review* 44, March–April.

Ilari, Beatriz, Cara Fesjian, and Assal Habibi. 2018. "Entrainment, Theory of Mind, and Prosociality in Child Musicians." *Music & Science*, February. https://doi.org/10.1177/2059204317753153

Irving, David. 2021. "Decolonising Historical Performance Practice." Research seminar, Royal Holloway University of London.

Johnson, Roger. 2009. "Critically Reflective Musicianship." In *Music Education for Changing Times: Guiding Visions for Practice*, edited by Thomas A. Regelski and J. Terry Gates, 17–26. Dordrecht: Springer.

Johnston, Jennifer. 2017. "Yes, Classical Music Has a Harassment Problem—and Now's the Time for Change." *The Guardian*, 8 December. https://www.theguardian.com/music/2017/dec/08/jennifer-johnston-comment-classical-music-cult-of-the-maestro

Jorgensen, Estelle R. 2001. "What Are the Roles of Philosophy in Music Education?" *Research Studies in Music Education* 17: 19–31.

Jóvenes: Un Fuego Vital. Reflexiones y Conocimiento En Juventud. 2015. Medellín: Alcaldía de Medellín.

Justino, Patricia. 2020. "Welfare Works: Redistribution Is the Way to Create Less Violent, Less Unequal Societies." *The Conversation*, 12 March. http://theconversation.com/welfare-works-redistribution-is-the-way-to-create-less-violent-less-unequal-societies-128807

Kajikawa, Loren. 2019. "The Possessive Investment in Classical Music: Confronting Legacies of White Supremacy in U.S. Schools and Departments of Music." In *Seeing Race Again: Countering Colorblindness across the Disciplines*, edited by Kimberlé Williams Crenshaw, 155–74. Berkeley, CA: University of California Press.

Kanellopoulos, Panagiotis A. 2015. "Musical Creativity and 'the Police': Troubling Core Music Education Certainties." In *The Oxford Handbook of Social Justice in Music Education*, edited by Cathy Benedict, Patrick Schmidt, Gary Spruce, and Paul Woodford, 318–39. New York, NY: Oxford University Press.

Kanellopoulos, Panagiotis A., and Niki Barahanou. 2021. "The Neoliberal Colonisation of Creative Music Education in Cultural Institutions: A Hatred of Democracy?" In *Difference and Division in Music Education*, edited by Alexis Anja Kallio, 144–62. London: Routledge.

Keil, Charlie. n.d. "Paideia Con Salsa: Ancient Greek Education for Active Citizenship and the Role of Afro-Latin Dance-Music in Our Schools." MUSE. http://www.musekids.org/consalsa.html

Kelly, Justin. 2020. "Cultural Gumbo." *VAN Magazine*, 14 October. https://van-us.atavist.com/cultural-gumbo

Kelly-McHale, Jacqueline, and Carlos R. Abril. 2015. "The Space Between Worlds: Music Education and Latino Children." In *The Oxford Handbook of Social Justice in Music Education*, edited by Cathy Benedict, Patrick Schmidt, Gary Spruce, and Paul Woodford, 156–72. New York, NY: Oxford University Press.

Kertz-Welzel, Alexandra. 2005. "The Pied Piper of Hamelin: Adorno on Music Education." *Research Studies in Music Education* 25: 1–11.

———. 2011. "Paradise Lost? A Critical Examination of Idealistic Philosophies of Teaching through the Lens of Theodor W. Adorno." *Visions of Research in Music Education* 19: 1–21. https://pdfs.semanticscholar.org/de80/d67bec8d08368b3047631cce61906f95fb47.pdf

———. 2016. "Daring to Question: A Philosophical Critique of Community Music." *Philosophy of Music Education Review* 24 (2): 113–30. https://doi.org/10.2979/philmusieducrevi.24.2.01

Kim, Jinyoung. 2017. "Transforming Music Education for the Next Generation: Planting 'Four Cs' Through Children's Songs." *International Journal of Early Childhood* 49 (2): 181–93. https://doi.org/10.1007/s13158-017-0187-3

Korum, Solveig, and Gillian Howell. 2020. "Competing economies of worth in a multiagency music and reconciliation partnership: The Sri Lanka Norway Music Cooperation (2009–2018)." *International Journal of Cultural Policy*. https://doi.org/10.1080/10286632.2020.1838491

Koutsoupidou, T., and D. J. Hargreaves. 2009. "An Experimental Study of the Effects of Improvisation on the Development of Children's Creative Thinking in Music." *Psychology of Music* 37 (3): 251–78. https://doi.org/10.1177/0305735608097246

Kozak Rovero, Gisela. 2018. "Alabado y Cuestionado: José Antonio Abreu y El Sistema de Orquestas de Venezuela." *Literal Magazine*, 8 April.

Krafeld, Merle. 2017. "Belaestigung-musikhochschulen." *VAN Magazine*, 8 November. https://van.atavist.com/belaestigung-musikhochschulen

Kratus, John. 2015. "The Role of Subversion in Changing Music Education." In *Music Education: Navigating the Future*, edited by Clint Randles, 340–46. New York, NY: Routledge.

Krönig, Franz Kasper. 2019. "Community Music and the Risks of Affirmative Thinking: A Critical Insight into the Semantics of Community Music." *Philosophy of Music Education Review* 27 (1): 21–36. https://10.2979/philmusieducrevi.27.1.03

Kutschke, B. 2011. "The Celebration of Beethoven's Bicentennial in 1970: The Antiauthoritarian Movement and Its Impact on Radical Avant-Garde and Postmodern Music in West Germany." *The Musical Quarterly* 93 (3–4): 560–615. https://doi.org/10.1093/musqtl/gdq021

Kuttner, Paul J. 2015. "Educating for Cultural Citizenship: Reframing the Goals of Arts Education." *Curriculum Inquiry* 45 (1): 69–92. https://doi.org/10.1080/03626784.2014.980940

Kuuse, Anna-Karin, Monica Lindgren, and Eva Skåreus. 2016. "'The Feelings Have Come Home to Me.' Examining Advertising Films on the Swedish Website of El Sistema." *Action, Criticism, and Theory for Music Education* 15 (1): 187–215. http://act.maydaygroup.org/articles/KuuseLindrenSkareus15_1.pdf

La Ciudad: El Laboratorio de Todas. 2017. Medellín: Alcaldía de Medellín.

"La desigualdad en Medellín sigue siendo muy alta." 2020. Medellín Cómo Vamos, 18 February. https://www.medellincomovamos.org/la-desigualdad-en-medellin-sigue-siendo-muy-alta

Ladson-Billings, Gloria. 2015. "You Gotta Fight the Power: The Place of Music in Social Justice Education." In *The Oxford Handbook of Social Justice in Music Education*, edited by Cathy Benedict, Patrick Schmidt, Gary Spruce, and Paul Woodford, 406–19. New York, NY: Oxford University Press.

Lafontant Di Niscia, Attilio. 2019. "Unveiling the Dark Side of Tonewoods: A Case Study about the Musical Instrument Demand for the Venezuelan Youth Orchestra El Sistema." *Action, Criticism, and Theory for Music Education* 18 (3): 259–88. https://doi.org/10.22176/act18.3.259

Lareau, A. 2011. *Unequal Childhoods: Class, Race, and Family Life*. Berkeley, CA: University of California Press.

Laurence, Felicity. 2008. "Music and Empathy." In *Music and Conflict Transformation: Harmonies and Dissonances in Geopolitics*, edited by Olivier Urbain, 13–25. London: I.B Tauris.

Lebrecht, Norman. 2017. "New Research: One in Three Musicians Suffers an Eating Disorder." *Slipped Disc* (blog), 16 July. https://slippedisc.com/2017/07/new-research-one-in-three-musicians-suffers-an-eating-disorder/

———. 2018. "Sex, lies and conductors." *Spectator*, 20 January. https://www.spectator.co.uk/article/sex-lies-and-conductors

———. 2021. "From disaster to opportunity." *The Critic*, January-February. https://thecritic.co.uk/issues/january-february-2021/from-disaster-to-opportunity/

Lee, Chris. 2012. "Bravo, Gustavo! How Maestro Dudamel Is Saving Classical Music." *Newsweek*, 6 February. http://www.thedailybeast.com/newsweek/2012/02/05/bravo-gustavo-how-maestro-dudamel-is-saving-classical-music.html

Lees, Loretta, and Clare Melhuish. 2015. "Arts-Led Regeneration in the UK: The Rhetoric and the Evidence on Urban Social Inclusion." *European Urban and Regional Studies* 22 (3): 242–60. https://doi.org/10.1177/0969776412467474

Levinson, Bradley A. 2011. "Toward an Anthropology of (Democratic) Citizenship Education." In *A Companion to the Anthropology of Education*, edited by Bradley A. Levinson and Mica Pollock, 279–98. Chichester: Wiley Blackwell.

Loar, Josh. 2019. "Overworked Staff and Performing Arts: Let's Not Pretend We're Okay." *TheatreArtLife* (blog), 11 April. https://www.theatreartlife.com/technical/performing-arts-overworked-staff/

Logan, Owen. 2015a. "Doing Well in the Eyes of Capital: Cultural Transformation from Venezuela to Scotland." In *Contested Powers: The Politics of Energy and Development*, edited by John–Andrew McNeish, Axel Borchgrevink, and Owen Logan, 216–53. London: Zed Books.

———. 2015b. "Hand in Glove: El Sistema and Neoliberal Research." https://www.researchgate.net/publication/287202150

———. 2016. "Lifting the Veil: A Realist Critique of Sistema's Upwardly Mobile Path." *Action, Criticism, and Theory for Music Education* 15 (1): 58–88. http://act.maydaygroup.org/articles/Logan15_1.pdf

Lonie, Douglas, and Ben Sandbrook. 2011. "Ingredients for Encouraging the Talent and Potential of Young Musicians." Dartington Hall, Devon: South West Music School. http://www.foundations-for-excellence.org/digi/

Lord, Pippa, Caroline Sharp, Jennie Harland, Palak Mehta, Richard White, and National Foundation for Educational Research in England and Wales. 2016. "Evaluation of In Harmony: Final Report." Slough: National Foundation for Educational Research. https://www.nfer.ac.uk/media/1565/acii04.pdf

Lortie-Forgues, Hugues, and Matthew Inglis. 2019. "Rigorous Large-Scale Educational RCTs Are Often Uninformative: Should We Be Concerned?" *Educational Researcher* 48 (3): 158–66. https://doi.org/10.3102/0013189X19832850

"Los músicos salen a la calle para reivindicar sus derechos: muchas de sus lesiones no son reconocidas como enfermedades laborales." 2019. *LaSexta*, 7 April. https://www.lasexta.com/noticias/sociedad/los-musicos-salen-a-la-calle-para-reivindicar-sus-derechos-muchas-de-sus-lesiones-no-son-reconocidas-como-enfermedades-laborales-video_201904075caa09e60cf2cabe94f17028.html

Lubow, Arthur. 2007. "Conductor of the People." *The New York Times*, 28 October. http://www.nytimes.com/2007/10/28/magazine/28dudamel-t.html?pagewanted=all

Maclean, Kate. 2015. *Social Urbanism and the Politics of Violence: The Medellín Miracle*. Basingstoke: Palgrave Macmillan.

Mamattah, Sophie, Tamsin Cox, David McGillivray, and Gayle McPherson. 2020. "The Role of Arts and Culture in Lifting Communities Out of Poverty: A Review of Evidence." University of the West of Scotland. https://issuu.com/ccse_uws/docs/job_4732_ukri_literature_2020_web

Mantie, Roger. 2012. "Striking Up the Band: Music Education Through a Foucaultian Lens." *Action, Criticism, and Theory for Music Education* 11 (1): 99–123. http://act.maydaygroup.org/articles/Mantie11_1.pdf

———. 2018. "Community Music and Rational Recreation." In *The Oxford Handbook of Community Music*, edited by Brydie-Leigh Bartleet and Lee Higgins, 543–54, New York, NY: Oxford University Press.

Mantie, Roger, and Laura Risk. 2020. "Framing Ethno-World: Intercultural Music Exchange, Tradition, and Globalization (Condensed Report)." University of Toronto, Scarborough.

Martin, Peter J. 1995. *Sounds and Society: Themes in the Sociology of Music*. Manchester: Manchester University Press.

"Más de 300 músicos protagonizan el plantón sinfónico en Bogotá." 2019. *El Espectador*, 27 November. https://www.elespectador.com/noticias/bogota/mas-de-300-musicos-protagonizan-el-planton-sinfonico-en-bogota/

Matthews, Richard. 2015. "Beyond Toleration—Facing the Others." In *The Oxford Handbook of Social Justice in Music Education*, edited by Cathy Benedict, Patrick Schmidt, Gary Spruce, and Paul Woodford, 238–49. New York, NY: Oxford University Press.

McCarthy, Marie. 2015. "Understanding Social Justice from the Perspective of Music Education History." In *The Oxford Handbook of Social Justice in Music Education*, edited by Cathy Benedict, Patrick Schmidt, Gary Spruce, and Paul Woodford, 29–46. New York, NY: Oxford University Press.

"Medellín: Transformación de Una Ciudad." n.d. Medellín: Alcaldía de Medellín / Inter-American Development Bank. https://acimedellin.org/wp-content/uploads/publicaciones/libro-transformacion-de-ciudad.pdf

"Medición de Impactos del Programa de Escuelas y Bandas de Música de Carácter Sinfónico de La Alcaldía de Medellín: Resumen Ejecutivo." 2005. Bogotá: Econometría Consultores.

Mehr, Samuel A. 2014. "Music in the Home: New Evidence for an Intergenerational Link." *Journal of Research in Music Education* 62 (1): 78–88. https://doi.org/10.1177/0022429413520008

———. 2015. "Miscommunication of Science: Music Cognition Research in the Popular Press." *Frontiers in Psychology* 6: 988. https://doi.org/10.3389/fpsyg.2015.00988

Merli, Paola. 2002. "Evaluating the Social Impact of Participation in Arts Activities: A Critical Review of François Matarasso's Use or Ornament?" *International Journal of Cultural Policy* 8 (1): 107–18.

Mignolo, Walter D. and Catherine E. Walsh. 2018. *On Decoloniality: Concepts, Analytics, Praxis*. Durham, NC: Duke University Press.

Miller, Ben. 2017. "Silence, Breaking." *VAN Magazine*, 7 December. https://van-us.atavist.com/silence-breaking

Miller, Toby. 2013. "Culture to Creativity to Environment—and Back Again." In *The Ashgate Research Companion to Planning and Culture*, edited by Greg Young and Deborah Stevenson, 53–67. Aldershot: Ashgate.

Moehn, Frederick A. 2011. "'We Live Daily in Two Countries': Audiotopias of Postdictatorship Brazil." In *Brazilian Popular Music and Citizenship*, edited by Idelber Avelar and Christopher Dunn, 109–30. Durham, NC: Duke University Press.

Montgomery, David T. 2016. "Applied Theater and Citizenship in the Puerto Rican Community: Artistic Citizenship in Practice." In *Artistic Citizenship: Artistry, Social Responsibility, and Ethical Praxis*, edited by David Elliott, Marissa Silverman, and Wayne D. Bowman, 447–68. New York, NY: Oxford University Press.

Montoya, Pablo. 2017. "Medellín: ¿Para Dónde Vamos?" *Arcadia*, 14 November. https://www.revistaarcadia.com/agenda/articulo/pablo-montoya-sobre-medellin-y-el-futuro-de-la-ciudad/66681

Montoya Restrepo, Nataly. 2014. "Urbanismo Social en Medellín: Una Aproximación Desde la Utilización Estratégica de Los Derechos." *Estudios Políticos* 45: 205–22.

Mora-Brito, Daniel. 2011. "Between Social Harmony and Political Dissonance: The Institutional and Policy-Based Intricacies of the Venezuelan System of Children and Youth Orchestras." MA, The University of Texas at Austin.

Morrison, Richard. 2015. "Simón Bolívar Orchestra/Dudamel at Festival Hall." *The Times*, 12 January. https://www.thetimes.co.uk/article/simon-bolivar-orchestradudamel-at-festival-hall-bgl3xnzf67c

Mosse, David. 2004. "Is Good Policy Unimplementable? Reflections on the Ethnography of Aid Policy and Practice." *Development and Change* 35 (4): 639–71.

Mota, Graça, and Teixeira Lopes, João, eds. 2017. *Growing While Playing in Orquestra Geração: Contributions towards Understanding the Relationship between Music and Social Inclusion*. Porto: Edições Politema.

Mouffe, Chantal. 2013. "Agonistic Politics and Artistic Practices." In *Agonistics: Thinking the World Politically*, edited by Chantal Mouffe, 85–105. London: Verso.

Mould, Oli. 2015. *Urban Subversion and the Creative City*. London: Routledge.

Mullin, Diane. 2016. "Working All the Time: Artistic Citizenship in the 21st Century." In *Artistic Citizenship: Artistry, Social Responsibility, and Ethical*

Praxis, edited by David Elliott, Marissa Silverman, and Wayne D. Bowman, 521–48. New York, NY: Oxford University Press.

"Músicos homenajearon a Gustavo Gatica con Réquiem." 2019. *Cooperativa.cl*, 5 December. https://www.cooperativa.cl/noticias/pais/dd-hh/musicos-homenajearon-a-gustavo-gatica-con-requiem/2019-12-05/080601.html

Ndaliko, Chérie Rivers. 2016. *Necessary Noise: Music, Film, and Charitable Imperialism in the East of Congo*. New York, NY: Oxford University Press.

Newey, Laura. 2020. "At Chetham's School of Music." *London Review of Books*, 20 January. https://www.lrb.co.uk/blog/2020/january/at-chetham-s-school-of-music

Nixon, Stephanie A. 2019. "The Coin Model of Privilege and Critical Allyship: Implications for Health." *BMC Public Health* 19. https://doi.org/10.1186/s12889-019-7884-9

Norgaard, Martin, Laura A. Stambaugh, and Heston McCranie. 2019. "The Effect of Jazz Improvisation Instruction on Measures of Executive Function in Middle School Band Students." *Journal of Research in Music Education* 67 (3): 339–54. https://doi.org/10.1177/0022429419863038

Nuijten, Monique. 2013. "The Perversity of the 'Citizenship Game': Slum-Upgrading in the Urban Periphery of Recife, Brazil." *Critique of Anthropology*, February. https://doi.org/10.1177/0308275X12466683

Ochoa Gautier, Ana María. 2001. "Listening to the State: Culture, Power, and Cultural Policy in Colombia." In *A Companion to Cultural Studies*, edited by Toby Miller, 375–90. Oxford: Blackwell.

Odendaal, Albi, Sari Levänen, and Heidi Westerlund. 2019. "Lost in Translation? Neuroscientific Research, Advocacy, and the Claimed Transfer Benefits of Musical Practice." *Music Education Research* 21 (1): 4–19. https://doi.org/10.1080/14613808.2018.1484438

Olcese, Cristiana and Mike Savage. 2015. "Notes towards a 'Social Aesthetic': Guest Editors' Introduction to the Special Section." *The British Journal of Sociology* 66 (4): 720–37. https://doi.org/10.1111/1468-4446.12159

Organismo Vivo y Mutando. 2016. Medellín: Alcaldía de Medellín. https://issuu.com/casatrespatios/docs/libro-rav2016

Orkin, Kate. 2020. "The Evidence behind Putting Money Directly in the Pockets of the Poor." University of Oxford. https://www.research.ox.ac.uk/Article/2020-05-12-the-evidence-behind-putting-money-directly-in-the-pockets-of-the-poor

Pace, Ian. 2015. "Does Elite Music Teaching Leave Pupils Open to Abuse?" *The Telegraph*, 20 February. https://www.telegraph.co.uk/news/uknews/crime/11425241/Philip-Pickett-Does-elite-music-teaching-leave-pupils-open-to-abuse.html

Pedroza, Ludim. 2014. "Music as Life-Saving Project: Venezuela's El Sistema in American Neo-Idealistic Imagination." *College Music Symposium* 54. https://symposium.music.org/index.php/54/item/10545-music-as-life-saving-project-venezuela-s-el-sistema-in-american-neo-idealistic-imagination

———. 2015. "Of Orchestras, Mythos, and the Idealization of Symphonic Practice: The Orquesta Sinfónica de Venezuela in the (Collateral) History of El Sistema." *Latin American Music Review / Revista de Música Latinoamericana* 36 (1): 68–93. https://doi.org/10.7560/LAMR36103

Peerbaye, Soraya, and Parmela Attariwala. 2019. "Re-Sounding the Orchestra: Relationships between Canadian Orchestras, Indigenous Peoples, and People of Colour." https://oc.ca/wp-content/uploads/2019/06/Re-sounding-the-Orchestra-EN-June-5.pdf

Pentreath, Rosie. 2020. "Prominent Critic Has Stood up for the Fragile 'Tyrannical Male Maestro'—Here's Why He's Missing the Point." *Classic FM*, 12 November. https://www.classicfm.com/discover-music/instruments/conductor/prominent-critic-stands-up-for-tyrannical-maestro-figure/

Pérez, Emma, and Yurian Rojas. 2013. "¿Por qué quiero que mi hijo sea músico? Expectativas de las madres, cuyos hijos están en la OSIC." Caracas: Universidad Católica Andrés Bello. http://biblioteca2.ucab.edu.ve/anexos/biblioteca/marc/texto/AAS7348.pdf

Picaud, M. 2018. "Des familles dans l'orchestre: approche sociologique du Projet Démos." Paris: Cité de la Musique Philharmonie de Paris.

"Plan de Desarrollo Cultural de Medellín 2011–2020." 2011. Medellín: Alcaldía de Medellín.

Poore, Benjamin. 2020. "Lived Experience." *VAN Magazine*, 8 October. https://van-us.atavist.com/lived-experience

Powell, Bryan, Gareth Dylan Smith, and Abigail D'Amore. 2017. "Challenging Symbolic Violence and Hegemony in Music Education through Contemporary Pedagogical Approaches." *Education 3–13* 45 (6): 734–43. https://doi.org/10.1080/03004279.2017.1347129

Pratt, Andy C. 2011. "The Cultural Contradictions of the Creative City." *City, Culture and Society* 2 (3): 123–30. https://doi.org/10.1016/j.ccs.2011.08.002

"Preparing 21st Century Students for a Global Society." n.d. National Education Association. https://www.academia.edu/36311252/Preparing_21st_Century_Students_for_a_Global_Society_An_Educators_Guide_to_the_Four_Cs_Great_Public_Schools_for_Every_Student

"Preso En E.U. Apostól de Niños Músicos Paisas." 2005. *El Tiempo*, 21 January. https://www.eltiempo.com/archivo/documento/MAM-1628473

Price, David. 2018. "Foreword." In *The Oxford Handbook of Community Music*, edited by Brydie-Leigh Bartleet and Lee Higgins, ix–xii. New York, NY: Oxford University Press.

Purves, Ross M. 2019. "Local Authority Instrumental Music Tuition as a Form of Neo-liberal Parental Investment: Findings from a Deviant, Idiographic Case Study." *Power and Education* 11 (3): 268–90. https://doi.org/10.1177/1757743819845068

Quadros, André de. 2015. "Rescuing Choral Music from the Realm of the Elite: Models for Twenty-First-Century Music Making—Two Case Illustrations." In *The Oxford Handbook of Social Justice in Music Education*, edited by Cathy Benedict, Patrick Schmidt, Gary Spruce, and Paul Woodford, 501–12. New York, NY: Oxford University Press.

Rabinowitch, Tal-Chen. 2012. "Musical Games and Empathy." *Education and Health* 30 (3): 80–84.

Rahim, Zamira. 2019. "Lecturer Who Called Violinists 'gypos' Awarded £180,000 after Tribunal Finds She Was Wrongly Sacked." *The Independent*, 8 March. https://www.independent.co.uk/news/uk/home-news/francesca-carpos-young-tribunal-royal-academy-music-violin-a8814351.html

Ramalingam, Ben. 2013. *Aid on the Edge of Chaos*. Oxford: Oxford University Press.

Raworth, Kate. 2017. *Doughnut Economics: Seven Ways to Think Like a 21st-Century Economist*. London: Cornerstone Digital.

Reich, Robert. 2020. "Beware going 'back to normal' thoughts—normal gave us Trump." *The Guardian*, 29 November. https://www.theguardian.com/commentisfree/2020/nov/29/beware-going-back-to-normal-thoughts-normal-gave-us-trump

Reimerink, Letty. 2018. "Planners and the Pride Factor: The Case of the Electric Escalator in Medellín." *Bulletin of Latin American Research* 37 (2): 191–205. https://doi.org/10.1111/blar.12665

Rimmer, Mark. 2018. "Harmony or Discord? Understanding Children's Valuations of a Sistema-Inspired Initiative." *British Journal of Music Education* 35 (1): 43–55. https://doi.org/10.1017/S0265051717000146

——. 2020. "Too Big to Fail? The Framing and Interpretation of 'Success'/'Failure' in Cultural Participation Policy: A Case Study." *Conjunctions: Transdisciplinary Journal of Cultural Participation* 7 (1). https://www.conjunctions-tjcp.com//article/view/119747/169504

Rincón, Omar. 2015. "¿Para Qué Se Usan los Jóvenes?" In *Jóvenes: Un Fuego Vital. Reflexiones y Conocimiento En Juventud*, 124–37. Medellín: Alcaldía de Medellín.

Robin, Will. 2020. "How Can Artists Respond to Injustice? Thoughts from Seven Musicians." *NewMusicBox*, 5 June. https://nmbx.newmusicusa.org/how-can-artists-respond-to-injustice/

Rojas, Cristina. 2013. "Acts of Indigenship: Historical Struggles for Equality and Colonial Difference in Bolivia." *Citizenship Studies* 17 (5): 581–95. https://doi.org/10.1080/13621025.2013.818373

Rosabal-Coto, Guillermo. 2016. "Costa Rica's SINEM: A Perspective from Postcolonial Institutional Ethnography." *Action, Criticism, and Theory for Music Education* 15 (1): 154–87. http://act.maydaygroup.org/articles/Rosabal-Coto15_1.pdf

———. 2019. "The Day after Music Education." *Action, Criticism, and Theory for Music Education* 18 (3): 1–24. https://doi.org/10.22176/act18.3.1

Ross, Alex. 2016. "When Music Is Violence." *The New Yorker*, 4 July. https://www.newyorker.com/magazine/2016/07/04/when-music-is-violence

———. 2020. "Black Scholars Confront White Supremacy in Classical Music." *The New Yorker*, 14 September. https://www.newyorker.com/magazine/2020/09/21/black-scholars-confront-white-supremacy-in-classical-music

Rusinek, Gabriel, and José Luis Aróstegui. 2015. "Educational Policy Reforms and the Politics of Music Teacher Education." In *The Oxford Handbook of Social Justice in Music Education*, edited by Cathy Benedict, Patrick Schmidt, Gary Spruce, and Paul Woodford, 78–90. New York, NY: Oxford University Press.

Rustin, Susanna. 2020. "Why We Need to Value Our Low-Carbon Pastimes More." *The Guardian*, 10 February. http://www.theguardian.com/commentisfree/2020/feb/10/everyday-arts-low-carbon-creativity-climate-crisis

Sachs Olsen, Cecilie. 2019. *Socially Engaged Art and the Neoliberal City*. London: Routledge.

Sala, Giovanni, and Fernand Gobet. 2017. "No proof music lessons make children any smarter." *The Conversation*, 9 January. https://theconversation.com/no-proof-music-lessons-make-children-any-smarter-70766

———. 2020. "Cognitive and Academic Benefits of Music Training with Children: A Multilevel Meta-Analysis." *Memory & Cognition* 48 (8): 1429–41. https://doi.org/10.3758/s13421-020-01060-2

Salazar, Alonso. 2018. "Ruinas de Medellín." *Universo Centro*, September. https://www.universocentro.com/NUMERO100/Ruinas-de-Medellin.aspx

Salazar, Juan Francisco. 2015. "Buen Vivir: South America's Rethinking of the Future We Want." *The Conversation*, 24 July. http://theconversation.com/buen-vivir-south-americas-rethinking-of-the-future-we-want-44507

Santos, Boaventura de Sousa. 2018. *The End of the Cognitive Empire: The Coming of Age of Epistemologies of the South*. Durham, NC: Duke University Press.

Sarazin, Marc. 2017. "Can Student Interdependence Be Experienced Negatively in Collective Music Education Programmes? A Contextual Approach."

London Review of Education 15 (3): 488–504. https://doi.org/10.18546/LRE.15.3.11

Sarrouy, Alix Didier. 2018. "Actores de La Continuidad Educativa En Barrios de Venezuela: Madres Del Núcleo Santa Rosa de Agua." *Comparative Cultural Studies—European and Latin American Perspectives* 3 (5): 43–54. https://doi.org/10.13128/ccselap-24323

Scharff, Christina. 2017. *Gender, Subjectivity, and Cultural Work: The Classical Music Profession*. London: Routledge.

Schellenberg, E. Glenn. 2019. "Correlation = Causation? Music Training, Psychology, and Neuroscience." *Psychology of Aesthetics, Creativity, and the Arts*. https://doi.org/10.1037/aca0000263

Schippers, Huib. 2018. "Community Music Contexts, Dynamics, and Sustainability." In *The Oxford Handbook of Community Music*, edited by Brydie-Leigh Bartleet and Lee Higgins, 23–41. New York, NY: Oxford University Press.

Scott, James C. 1998. *Seeing Like a State: How Certain Schemes to Improve the Human Condition Have Failed*. New Haven, CT: Yale University Press.

———. 2012. *Two Cheers for Anarchism: Six Easy Pieces on Autonomy, Dignity, and Meaningful Work and Play*. Princeton, NJ: Princeton University Press.

Scripp, Lawrence. 2016a. "The Need to Testify: A Venezuelan Musician's Critique of El Sistema and His Call for Reform." https://www.researchgate.net/publication/285598399_The_Need_to_Testify_A_Venezuelan_Musician%27s_Critique_of_El_Sistema_and_his_Call_for_Reform_Update

———. 2016b. "All That Matters Is How Good It Sounds." *VAN Magazine*, 21 January. https://van-us.atavist.com/all-that-matters

Scruggs, Bernadette. 2009. "Constructivist Practices to Increase Student Engagement in the Orchestra Classroom." *Music Educators Journal* 95 (4): 53–59. https://doi.org/10.1177/0027432109335468

Scruggs, T.M. 2015. "'The Sistema,' the Euroclassical Tradition, and Education as a Transformative Agent to Supercede Class Status." Society for Ethnomusicology, Austin, TX.

Serrati, Pablo Santiago. 2018. "Cuestionar la colonialidad en la educación musical." *Revista Internacional de Educación Musical* 5: 93–101. http://www.revistaeducacionmusical.org/index.php/rem1/article/view/123

Sharp, Joanne, Venda Pollock, and Ronan Paddison. 2005. "Just Art for a Just City: Public Art and Social Inclusion in Urban Regeneration." *Urban Studies* 42 (5–6): 1001–23. https://doi.org/10.1080/00420980500106963

Shevock, Daniel J. 2021. "Music Education for Social Change: Constructing an Activist Music Education." *Music Education Research*. https://doi.org/10.1080/14613808.2021.1885883

Shieh, Eric. 2015. "Relationship, Rescue, and Culture: How El Sistema Might Work." In *The Oxford Handbook of Social Justice in Music Education*, edited by Cathy Benedict, Patrick Schmidt, Gary Spruce, and Paul Woodford, 567–81. New York, NY: Oxford University Press.

Shieh, Eric, and Randall Everett Allsup. 2016. "Fostering Musical Independence." *Music Educators Journal* 102 (4): 30–35. https://doi.org/10.1177/0027432116645841

Shifres, Favio Demian, and Daniel Gonnet. 2015. "Problematizando la Herencia Colonial en la Educación Musical." *Epistemus. Revista de Estudios En Música, Cognición y Cultura* 3 (2): 51–67. https://doi.org/10.21932/epistemus.3.2971.2

Shifres, Favio, and Guillermo Rosabal-Coto. 2018. "Hacia una educación musical decolonial en y desde Latinoamérica." *Revista Internacional de Educación Musical* 5: 85–91. http://www.revistaeducacionmusical.org/index.php/rem1/article/view/153

Sholette, Gregory, Chloë Bass, and Social Practice Queens, eds. 2018. *Art as Social Action: An Introduction to the Principles and Practices of Teaching Social Practice Art*. New York, NY: Allworth Press.

Silva Souza, Euridiana. 2019. "Higher Music (Educ)ACTION in Southeastern Brazil: Curriculum as a Practice and Possibilities for Action in (de)Colonial Thought." *Action, Criticism, and Theory for Music Education* 18 (3): 85–114. https://doi.org/10.22176/act18.3.85

Silverman, Marissa, and David J. Elliott. 2016. "Arts Education as/for Artistic Citizenship." In *Artistic Citizenship: Artistry, Social Responsibility, and Ethical Praxis*, edited by David J. Elliott, Marissa Silverman, and Wayne D. Bowman, 81–103. New York, NY: Oxford University Press.

Simms, Andrew. 2011. "71 Months and Counting…" *The Guardian*, 1 January. http://www.theguardian.com/commentisfree/cif-green/2011/jan/01/71-months-counting-climate-change

Sloboda, John. 2015. "Can Music Teaching Be a Powerful Tool for Social Justice?" In *The Oxford Handbook of Social Justice in Music Education*, edited by Cathy Benedict, Patrick Schmidt, Gary Spruce, and Paul Woodford, 539–47. New York, NY: Oxford University Press.

———. 2019. "Research into Social Impact of Making Music: Issues and Dilemmas." Keynote lecture at SIMM seminar, Antwerp, 28 November 2019. https://www.youtube.com/watch?v=d82LYl-ICq4

Smith, Gareth Dylan, and Marissa Silverman, eds. 2020. *Eudaimonia: Perspectives for Music Learning*. London: Routledge.

Soper, Kate. 2020. *Post-Growth Living For an Alternative Hedonism*. London: Verso.

Spruce, Gary. 2017. "The Power of Discourse: Reclaiming Social Justice from and for Music Education." *Education 3–13* 45 (6): 720–33. https://doi.org/10.1080/03004279.2017.1347127

Sriskandarajah, Dhananjayan. 2020. "Boris Johnson's Words Show He Still Thinks Aid Is about Africans Wanting Handouts." *The Guardian*, 20 June. http://www.theguardian.com/commentisfree/2020/jun/20/boris-johnson-aid-africans-department-for-international-development

Stauffer, Sandra L. 2009. "Placing Curriculum in Music." In *Music Education for Changing Times: Guiding Visions for Practice*, edited by Thomas A. Regelski and J. Terry Gates, 175–86. Dordrecht: Springer.

Stevenson, Deborah. 2017. *Cities of Culture: A Global Perspective*. London: Routledge.

Stewart, Dafina-Lazarus. 2017. "Language of Appeasement." *Inside Higher Ed*, 30 March. https://www.insidehighered.com/views/2017/03/30/colleges-need-language-shift-not-one-you-think-essay

Stewart, Heather. 2019. "Corbyn to Drop Social Mobility as Labour Goal in Favour of Opportunity for All." *The Guardian*, 8 June. https://www.theguardian.com/politics/2019/jun/08/jeremy-corbyn-to-drop-social-mobility-as-labour-goal

Suzman, James. 2020. *Work: A History of How We Spend Our Time*. London: Bloomsbury Publishing.

Swed, Mark. 2017. "The Pitfalls and Joys of Taking a Stand with Music and with Youngsters." *Los Angeles Times*, 24 July. https://www.latimes.com/entertainment/arts/la-et-cm-laphil-take-a-stand-notebook-20170724-story.html

Swyngedouw, Erik. 2007. "The Post-Political City." In *Urban Politics Now: Re-Imagining Democracy in the Neo-Liberal City*, edited by BAVO, 58–76. Rotterdam: NAI-Publishers.

Taheri, Sema A., and Brandon C. Welsh. 2015. "After-School Programs for Delinquency Prevention: A Systematic Review and Meta-Analysis." *Youth Violence and Juvenile Justice*, January. https://doi.org/10.1177/1541204014567542

Taylor, Lucy. 2013. "Decolonizing Citizenship: Reflections on the Coloniality of Power in Argentina." *Citizenship Studies* 17 (5): 596–610. https://doi.org/10.1080/13621025.2013.818375

Teixeira Lopes, João, Pedro S. Boia, Ana Luísa Veloso, and Matilde Caldas. 2017. "Sociological Portraits: Orchestral Socialization, Paths and Experiences." In *Growing While Playing in Orquestra Geração: Contributions towards Understanding the Relationship between Music and Social Inclusion*, edited by Graça Mota and João Teixeira Lopes, 159–232. Porto: Edições Politema.

Teixeira Lopes, João, and Graça Mota. 2017. "New Points of Departure: The Past, the Present and Possible Future(s) of the Orquestra Geração." In *Growing While Playing in Orquestra Geração: Contributions towards Understanding the Relationship between Music and Social Inclusion*, edited by Graça Mota and João Teixeira Lopes, 235–41. Porto: Edições Politema.

Téllez Oliveros, Verónica. 2013. "Ciudades colombianas: más desiguales." *El Espectador*, 9 October. https://www.elespectador.com/noticias/nacional/ciudades-colombianas-mas-desiguales/

Terauds, John. 2018. "Classical music has always enabled bad behaviour. It's time for that to change." *Toronto Star*, 2 March. https://www.thestar.com/entertainment/music/2018/03/02/classical-music-has-always-enabled-bad-behaviour-its-time-for-that-to-change.html

Thompson, James. 2009. *Performance Affects: Applied Theatre and the End of Effect*. Basingstoke: Palgrave Macmillan.

Todes, Ariane. 2020. "Doughnuts are good for you." *Elbow Music* (blog), 4 December. https://www.elbowmusic.org/post/doughnuts-are-good-for-you

Tonelli, Vanessa M. 2013. "Women and Music in the Venetian Ospedali." Master's, Michigan State University.

Tubb, Daniel. 2013. "Narratives of Citizenship in Medellín, Colombia." *Citizenship Studies* 17 (5): 627–40. https://doi.org/10.1080/13621025.2013.818380

Turino, Thomas. 2008. *Music as Social Life: The Politics of Participation*. Chicago, IL: Chicago University Press.

———. 2016. "Music, Social Change, and Alternative Forms of Citizenship." In *Artistic Citizenship: Artistry, Social Responsibility, and Ethical Praxis*, edited by David Elliott, Marissa Silverman, and Wayne D. Bowman, 297–312. New York, NY: Oxford University Press.

Turrent, Lourdes. 1993. *La Conquista Musical de Mexico*. México: Fondo de Cultura Economica USA.

Valero, Erika. 2020. "Medellín Recibe Reconocimiento Mundial por la Red de Prácticas Artísticas y Culturales." Alcaldía de Medellín, 31 May. https://www.medellin.gov.co/irj/portal/medellin?NavigationTarget=navurl://c16eedc9d81902988c16e401084f5e03

Vallejo Ramírez, Sebastián. 2017. "La Red de Escuelas de Música se renueva en 2018." *Medellín Cuenta*, 15 December [webpage saved but no longer available].

Varkøy, Øivind, and Hanne Rinholm. 2020. "Focusing on Slowness and Resistance: A Contribution to Sustainable Development in Music Education." *Philosophy of Music Education Review* 28 (2): 168–85. https://doi.org/10.2979/philmusieducrevi.28.2.04

Vaugeois, Lise. 2007. "Social Justice and Music Education: Claiming the Space of Music Education as a Site of Postcolonial Contestation." *Action, Criticism, and Theory for Music Education* 6 (4): 163–200. http://act.maydaygroup.org/articles/Vaugeois6_4.pdf

Veloso, Ana Luísa. 2016. "Más allá de la Orquestra Geração: El retrato de Manuela, una joven que soñaba con ser clarinetista profesional." *Revista*

Internacional de Educación Musical 4: 95–103. https://doi.org/10.12967/RIEM-2016-4-p095-103

Veltmeyer, Henry, and James Petras. 2011. "Beyond Pragmatic Neoliberalism: From Social Inclusion and Poverty Reduction to Equality and Social Change." Mexican Ministry of Foreign Affairs, Mexico City. https://www.unesco.org/new/fileadmin/MULTIMEDIA/HQ/SHS/pdf/Mexico_Veltmeyer_Notes.pdf

Villaseñor, Paula. 2017. "How Can Teachers Cultivate (or Hinder) Students' Socio-Emotional Skills?" *Let's Talk Development* (blog), 13 June. https://blogs.worldbank.org/developmenttalk/how-can-teachers-cultivate-or-hinder-students-socio-emotional-skills

Vujanović, Ana. 2016. "Art as a Bad Public Good." In *Artistic Citizenship: Artistry, Social Responsibility, and Ethical Praxis*, edited by David Elliott, Marissa Silverman, and Wayne D. Bowman, 104–22. New York, NY: Oxford University Press.

Waisman, Leonardo J. 2004. "La América Española: Proyecto y Resistencia." In *Políticas y prácticas musicales en el mundo de Felipe II*, edited by John Griffiths and Javier Suárez-Pajares, 503–50. Madrid: Ediciones del ICCMU.

Wakin, Daniel J. 2012. "Venerated High Priest and Humble Servant of Music Education." *The New York Times*, 1 March. http://www.nytimes.com/2012/03/04/arts/music/jose-antonio-abreu-leads-el-sistema-in-venezuela.html

Wald, Gabriela. 2009. "Los Dilemas de la Inclusión a Través del Arte: Tensiones y Ambigüedades Puestas en Escena." *Oficios Terrestres* 24. http://sedici.unlp.edu.ar/handle/10915/44998

———. 2011. "Los Usos de los Programas Sociales y Culturales: El Caso de dos Orquestas Juveniles de la Ciudad de Buenos Aires." *Questión: Revista Especializada En Periodismo y Comunicación* 1 (29): 1–13.

———. 2017. "Orquestas juveniles con fines de inclusión social. De identidades, subjetividades y transformación social." *Revista foro de educación musical, artes y pedagogía* 2 (2): 59–81. http://www.revistaforo.com.ar/ojs/index.php/rf/article/view/27

Waldron, Janice, Roger Mantie, Heidi Partti, and Evan S. Tobias. 2018. "A Brave New World: Theory to Practice in Participatory Culture and Music Learning and Teaching." *Music Education Research* 20 (3): 289–304. https://doi.org/10.1080/14613808.2017.1339027

Westheimer, Joel, and Joseph Kahne. 2004. "What Kind of Citizen? The Politics of Educating for Democracy." *American Educational Research Journal*. https://doi.org/10.3102/00028312041002237

Whale, Mark. 2020. "Talking Bach in an Age of Social Justice." *Philosophy of Music Education Review* 28 (2): 199–219. https://doi.org/10.2979/philmusieducrevi.28.2.06

Wiles, David. 2016. "Art and Citizenship: The History of a Divorce." In *Artistic Citizenship: Artistry, Social Responsibility, and Ethical Praxis*, edited by David Elliott, Marissa Silverman, and Wayne D. Bowman, 22–40. New York, NY: Oxford University Press.

Wilkinson, Richard, and Kate Pickett. 2010. *The Spirit Level: Why Equality Is Better for Everyone*. London: Penguin.

Wolff, Jonathan. 2020. "Rhodes' Statue Is Going. Now Universities Must Ask: What about John Locke, Elizabeth I and Others?" *The Guardian*, 7 July. https://www.theguardian.com/education/2020/jul/07/rhodes-statue-is-going-now-universities-must-ask-what-about-john-locke-elizabeth-i-and-others

Woods, Simon. 2020. "A World More Embracing." 17 November. https://medium.com/@simonwoods_34957/a-world-more-embracing-d14f585c16ba

Wright, Ruth. 2019. "Envisioning Real Utopias in Music Education: Prospects, Possibilities and Impediments." *Music Education Research* 21 (3): 217–27. https://doi.org/10.1080/14613808.2018.1484439

Yúdice, George. 2003. *The Expediency of Culture: Uses of Culture in the Global Era*. Durham, NC: Duke University Press.

Zambrano Benavides, Diego. 2019. "Así son los turistas que visitan Medellín." *El Colombiano*, 28 April. https://www.elcolombiano.com/antioquia/asi-son-los-turistas-que-visitan-medellin-IH10605481

Zamorano Valenzuela, Felipe Javier. 2020. "Moviéndose en los Márgenes: Un Estudio de Caso sobre la Identidad Activista en la Formación del Profesorado de Música en Chile." *Revista Electrónica de LEEME* 46. https://doi.org/10.7203/LEEME.46.16278

List of Figures

Introduction

1	Archive of Red de Escuelas de Música. CC BY.	xvi

Chapter 1

2	Timeline and institutional affiliations of the Red. Diagram by the author. CC BY.	41
3	Corporal expression. Photo by the author (2018). CC BY.	43
4	Archive of Red de Escuelas de Música. CC BY.	68
5	Creating music for the US tour. Photo by the author (2018). CC BY.	69
6	Creating music for the US tour. Photo by the author (2018). CC BY.	69
7	Student-composed lyrics for the US tour. Photo by the author (2018). CC BY.	70
8	Field trip to Salón Málaga tango café. Photo by the author (2018). CC BY.	70
9	Field trip to Latina Stereo salsa recording studio and radio station. Photo by the author (2018). CC BY.	71
10	GC13 Project, Armonía territorial, San Javier (2018). CC BY.	76
11	GC13 Project, Armonía territorial, San Javier (2018). Archive of Red de Escuelas de Música. CC BY.	77
12	Talentodos project, San Javier (2018). CC BY.	78
13	Social cartography exercise. Photo by the author (2018). CC BY.	81
14	Alfonso López school project, outdoor rehearsal. Photo by the author (2018). CC BY.	84

15	Alfonso López school project, outdoor rehearsal. Photo by the author (2018). CC BY.	84
16	Alfonso López school project, "Family is…" Photo by the author (2018). CC BY.	85
17	Alfonso López school project, "Family, pillar of my dreams." Photo by the author (2018). CC BY.	85
18	Santa Fé school project, "Rock, a song of freedom." Photo by the author (2018). CC BY.	86

Chapter 2

19	Virtues of a citizen, Intermediaries of Civic Culture. Photo by the author (2018). CC BY.	100
20	Archive of Red de Escuelas de Música. CC BY.	134
21	Archive of Red de Escuelas de Música. CC BY.	140

Chapter 3

22	Archive of Red de Escuelas de Música. CC BY.	190
23	Constructing theory and pedagogy, Network of Visual Arts. Photo by the author (2018). CC BY.	201
24	Constructing theory and pedagogy, Network of Visual Arts. Photo by the author (2018). CC BY.	201
25	Constructing theory and pedagogy, Network of Visual Arts. Photo by the author (2018). CC BY.	202

Chapter 4

26	Archive of Red de Escuelas de Música. CC BY.	231

Chapter 5

27	Archive of Red de Escuelas de Música. CC BY.	264
28	Archive of Red de Escuelas de Música. CC BY.	278

| 29 | Concert by Liberdade school, NEOJIBA. Photo by the author (2018). CC BY. | 304 |
| 30 | Projection during the concert. Photo by the author (2018). CC BY. | 305 |

Chapter 7

| 31 | Archive of Red de Escuelas de Música. CC BY. | 351 |

Index

4ESkuela 260
12 de Octubre school 54, 82, 218
Abbado, Claudio 16
Abello, Vania 244, 250, 396–397, 401, 403, 405–406
Abreu, José Antonio 7, 15–16, 20–21, 45, 51, 89–92, 95, 119, 132, 161–162, 174–176, 194, 199, 206, 212–213, 215–216, 223, 235, 238, 256, 260, 265–267, 271–272, 275, 277, 280, 286–288, 291–292, 296–297, 316, 325–326, 335, 341–342, 345, 348, 353–354, 366, 370, 373, 375–377, 380–381, 384–388, 390–392, 402
   Abreu Fellows Program 16
activism 17, 129, 171–172, 189, 292, 296, 299, 301, 303, 308–309, 320, 367, 371, 375, 377, 380, 387
Adorno, Theodor W. 292, 332, 338–342, 344–345, 350, 372
affect 57, 62, 103, 169, 237, 302, 347–349, 370
Afghanistan National Institute of Music 191, 228
Africa 88, 134, 166, 234, 304, 364–365, 394
Afro-Brazilian 304, 308
Afro-Colombian 73–74, 88
Afro-diasporic 88, 304, 307–308, 314, 365
Afro laboratory 88, 116, 368
Afro-Latin 308, 399
AfroReggae 308, 365
Agency for Cooperation and Investment (ACI) 209, 246, 253–254, 257

Alfonso López school 83–85
Amadeus Foundation 43–47, 51, 58, 90, 175
ambivalence 6, 9–10, 12, 14, 19, 21, 27, 30, 49, 51, 78, 91, 104, 139, 151, 190, 197, 228, 242, 245–246, 255, 267, 348, 358–360, 363, 405
Andean 68, 79, 307, 354
anti-oppressive 311, 313–314, 371
Antioquia 44–45, 47, 58–59, 82, 101, 118, 153, 191, 204, 234, 393–394
   Antioquia, University of 47, 58–59, 101, 118, 191, 204, 394
Antioquia Symphony (Orchestra) 44–45, 191
Arango, Marta Eugenia 47–52, 54, 58–59, 63, 90, 94, 103–104, 106, 119–120, 128, 131, 136, 141, 143, 156, 173, 211, 270
Arenas, Eliécer 289, 398–402, 404–405, 409
Argentina 177, 271–272, 274, 288, 329, 403–404
Art as Social Action (ASA) 206
Arteaga, Wuilly 299
artistic citizenship 154, 164–167, 170–172, 188, 207, 273, 275, 302–303, 305–309, 350, 365, 371, 402
Artistic Citizenship (book) 97, 161, 165, 171
arts education 65, 115, 121, 156, 164, 169–170, 173, 200, 203, 205–208, 258, 274, 297, 302, 323, 325, 332, 343, 350, 358, 362, 367, 380, 394, 396–397, 408
Asia 364

Australia 218, 277, 307, 362
Austria 328
authoritarianism 7, 13, 169, 195–198, 234–236, 269, 280, 285, 291, 338–340, 352, 373, 378, 387
authority 4, 53, 72, 159, 161, 175, 232, 234, 238, 284, 327, 337, 339
autocracy 53, 173, 175, 284, 306, 339, 387
autonomy 75, 158–159, 162, 165, 170–171, 196, 203, 272, 285, 295, 304, 366, 375

Bach, Johann Sebastian 293
Baltimore 273
Barcelona 253, 372
Barenboim, Daniel 352–353, 358, 381
Barrio Antioquia 82, 393
Bartholomew-Poyser, Daniel 295
Batuta 272
Bavarian State Orchestra 352
Beethoven, Ludwig van 178, 183, 294, 352, 392
Benjamin Herrera school 81, 393
BIPOC (Black, Indigenous and People of Colour) 278, 314, 324, 387, 408
Black Lives Matter (BLM) 24, 288, 383–384, 386–389, 393–394, 407–408
Boal, Augusto 10, 206, 366, 367. See also Theatre of the Oppressed
Bogotá 18, 272, 298, 379, 396
Bolivarian Revolution 237, 341–342, 346
Bolivia 79, 307
Borda, Deborah 276
Boston 165, 285, 296, 324, 401
Botero, Fernando 45
Bourdieu, Pierre 223
Brazil 5, 66, 271–272, 304, 308–309, 328, 330, 366
bubble 71, 178–179, 182, 187, 189, 194, 207, 222, 230, 237, 251, 374, 384
Buenos Aires 125, 177, 181, 217, 219, 222, 224–225, 282, 317
buen vivir 307, 370, 376, 378. See also *sumak kawsay*
Bull, Anna 181–182
bullying 52, 95, 114, 126, 238

cacerolazo 335–336
Campo, Bruno 341
Canada 274, 278, 290, 295, 314, 320
Caracas 5, 119, 194, 214, 225
Caribbean 332, 364
cartography 71, 81, 83, 96, 186, 443
Casanova, Eduardo 342
Catholicism 234, 336
Central America 376
charisma 46, 104, 106, 266, 282, 348
charismatic 51, 89, 103, 199, 234–235, 267, 378
Chávez, Hugo 92, 175, 194, 342, 345
Chile 298, 320, 326, 380
Chocó region 88
choirs 42, 45, 49, 133, 198, 213, 216, 238, 304, 330, 358, 379, 384
citizenship 4, 47–49, 59–62, 73, 99–100, 103, 112, 115, 129, 145, 153–154, 156–172, 187–188, 192, 200, 202, 205–207, 217, 249, 257–258, 261, 268, 273–275, 295, 297, 300–309, 320, 323, 336, 350, 365, 371, 376, 381, 400, 402–403
citizenship education 4, 48, 145, 158, 161–165, 167, 169, 171–172, 187, 302, 308, 320
classical music 2, 5–6, 9–11, 13–14, 35, 43–44, 50, 52–53, 63–64, 66, 82, 89, 94, 96, 104, 118, 121, 123–124, 127–129, 131–136, 139, 142, 148, 150, 155, 157, 168, 174, 176, 181, 184, 192, 194, 198–199, 222, 230, 233–235, 237–238, 245, 247, 256, 259, 270, 273, 276–277, 279, 284, 287–296, 300, 311, 314, 318, 323, 326, 328, 331, 341, 346, 355, 357, 365–366, 368, 373, 378, 384, 386, 388, 390–392, 395, 397, 399, 403
coexistence 2, 48–49, 52, 54, 57, 59, 62, 82, 90–91, 107, 116, 125–126, 145–146, 157, 167, 177, 183–185, 211, 217, 223, 237–238, 241, 244, 254, 282, 301, 303, 307–308, 320, 330, 332, 350, 368, 378, 409
Colombian Youth Orchestra 124, 131, 396

coloniality 64, 97, 171, 173, 259, 287–289, 292, 294–296, 300, 308, 314, 319, 336–337, 356, 367, 369, 374, 387
Colston, Edward 387–388
Communal Creation Laboratories 203
communications 33, 50, 75–76, 198–199, 253, 297, 329, 354–355
Community Music Center of Boston 324
community music (CM) 5, 7–10, 18, 26–27, 35, 97, 175–176, 233, 275, 286, 298, 318, 328, 353, 369, 380, 395
complexity 10–15, 17–19, 27, 29–30, 54, 73, 109, 112, 167, 197, 240, 260, 286, 315, 348, 360, 373–374, 381
composition 78, 81, 83, 86, 123, 140, 143, 195, 257, 272–273, 284–285
Comuna 13 2, 76–77, 250
  Gira Comuna 13 (GC13) 76–77, 80
conductors 2–3, 13, 25, 45, 48, 52–53, 62–63, 78, 88, 119, 124, 129, 132, 143, 145, 159, 182, 195–197, 208, 239–240, 284–286, 290–291, 295, 314, 321, 352, 358, 366, 373, 381, 390, 402
conflict 1, 24, 49, 55, 138, 159, 179–180, 211, 217, 220, 238–240, 254, 308, 319–320, 352
conservatism 63, 93, 176, 205, 234, 236–237, 280, 296
Conservatory Lab Charter School (CLCS) 165, 273, 285, 372
convivencia [coexistence] 2, 167, 308
Costa Rica, University of 288
Cova, Rubén 45, 51
COVID-19 24, 270, 378, 383–384, 388, 393, 396, 403–404, 407
creative city 256–259
creativity 10, 19, 65, 67, 73, 78, 80, 96–97, 121, 123, 131, 137, 142, 145, 148, 157, 159, 170, 212, 256–258, 268–269, 272–273, 290–291, 294, 300, 303, 306, 319, 321, 323–324, 346, 370, 389, 400, 407
Cuban 374
cult of personality 92, 235, 387
cultura ciudadana [civic culture] 115, 167, 169

Cultural Development Plan 58, 66, 73, 157, 168
cultural policy 10, 12, 59, 66, 146, 148, 157–158, 254, 323, 347
cumbia 132, 134, 365
curriculum 42, 48–50, 62, 64, 66–67, 80, 96, 102, 109, 111, 113, 118, 136, 140, 142, 148, 158, 178, 200, 237, 272, 283, 287, 289, 296, 380–381, 384

dance 10, 16, 42, 61, 77, 87–89, 115, 117, 200, 230, 287, 308, 334, 357, 365, 393
Dance Network 88, 204, 380, 409
decoloniality 27, 97, 173–174, 240, 287–290, 292, 296, 300, 306, 308–309, 319, 337, 350, 365, 371, 384, 438
Decolonizing the Music Room 288
deficit 188–189, 215–216, 228, 241, 275, 280, 303, 306, 308, 335, 338, 371, 380, 387, 408
demographics 217, 219, 309
Démos 217, 310, 362
De Vuyst, Frank 50
disabilities 93, 401
diversity 66, 69, 72–73, 80, 88, 97–98, 123, 128, 131, 134, 137, 145, 157, 159, 173–174, 183, 212, 269, 271, 296, 300, 307, 323, 365, 369, 394, 400–402, 408
Domingo, Plácido 16
Dream Unfinished, The 189, 299
dropouts 56, 122, 229
  dropout rate 74, 93, 243, 269
Dudamel, Gustavo 15, 129, 166, 174, 183, 296, 299, 324, 345, 352–353, 381, 391

EAFIT Symphony Orchestra 191
early music 291–292
Early Years Laboratory 87
ecology 80, 83, 136, 377, 379, 409
Ecuador 45, 307
El AKA 79
El Poblado 54, 65
El Sistema 3–8, 10, 13–16, 18–24, 30–33, 45, 47, 49, 51, 73, 89–98, 102, 104–105, 107, 112, 118–119, 127–128, 132, 149–151, 153–154, 161, 165–166,

169, 171, 174–177, 181–183, 188–189, 194, 196–197, 199, 205–208, 212–215, 218–219, 221–226, 228–229, 234–238, 240–244, 247–248, 256, 260, 266–267, 269–270, 272–277, 280, 284–288, 295–301, 303, 314–318, 321–331, 334–342, 344, 352–357, 359–360, 362–363, 366–368, 376–377, 379–380, 384–387, 389–390, 392, 395, 402–405, 407–408
El Sistema-inspired (ESI) 22–24, 33, 272–273, 276–277, 283, 287, 316, 318, 327, 329, 341, 356
El Sistema: Music to Change Life (film, 2009) 16
El Sistema Special Interest Group 208, 274, 317
El Sistema USA 385–386
emancipatory 17, 27, 35, 64, 206, 265, 294, 359, 363–364, 370, 372, 380–381
empowerment 14, 48, 53, 93, 96, 103, 169, 173, 175–176, 211, 229, 273, 295, 297, 301, 381
England 2, 16, 222, 224, 268, 276, 282, 288, 310, 319, 357
Escobar, Pablo 1, 11
Espector, Claudio 404
Esperanza Azteca 341, 356–357
ethnography 25, 29–30, 211
Ethno-World 354
Eurocentrism 67, 88, 97, 121, 176, 240, 272, 289, 295, 324–325, 329, 336–338, 367, 384, 386, 392, 403
Europe 5, 66–68, 79, 88, 123, 131, 133–134, 154, 171, 174, 244, 256, 288–289, 291–292, 294, 300, 314, 320, 328, 336–338, 353, 365–367, 369–370, 379, 386–388, 391–392, 399
European Union Youth Orchestra 388
evaluation 16–18, 25, 56, 92, 94–95, 151, 155, 157, 177, 180, 185, 191, 197, 210–213, 217–218, 222, 229, 238, 240, 276, 294, 300, 303, 316, 319, 327, 354, 362, 405
Evanko, Tony 202

exclusion 10, 49, 54, 58, 90, 93, 126, 170, 183, 185, 211, 222, 225–226, 295, 324, 327, 332, 387

FailSpace 17–19
Fajardo, Sergio 1, 250–251
family values 223–225, 228
Felipe, André Gomes 76–77, 318, 328, 350
feminism 82
Finland 320
FLADEM 66, 380
Floyd, George 383, 385–387
France 217, 310, 362
Franco, Luis Fernando 65–67, 73–74, 136, 140, 142–143, 173, 192, 195, 256, 284, 344, 346, 362, 374, 394, 396
Frega, Ana Lucía 94, 177, 315–316
Freire, Paulo 120, 206, 287, 366
funding 5, 14–18, 20, 44, 89, 92–93, 129, 138, 155, 170, 193, 229, 244, 248, 276–277, 279, 322–323, 327–328, 331, 334–335, 342, 344–346, 348–349, 357, 361, 364, 367, 379

Gaviria, Aníbal 58, 125, 204, 343
gender 49, 52, 82, 93, 198–199, 207, 235–236, 259, 273, 393, 401
 #MeToo 197
Germany 44, 149, 291, 339, 342
Giraldo, Juan Fernando 65–68, 71–73, 88–89, 92, 102, 124, 131, 140–141, 143–144, 148, 156, 173–174, 177, 197, 204, 256, 271–272, 344, 347, 362, 374, 394, 396
government 2, 20, 46–47, 53, 58–61, 65, 68, 83, 115, 120, 129, 137, 154, 162–163, 166, 168, 170, 175–177, 189, 200, 203, 216, 246, 248, 250–251, 253–254, 257, 260, 277, 279–280, 297–299, 317, 322–323, 331, 333, 339–341, 343–344, 350, 352, 401
Govias, Jonathan 19, 196, 277, 284, 290, 318
grandiosity 96, 230, 233, 245, 255–256, 344–345, 353–354, 359, 375, 390
Greece 289

Guatemala 269, 341
Guerrero, Rodrigo 205
Gutiérrez, Federico 157, 254, 386

harmony 15, 64, 67, 77, 91, 101, 144, 152, 183–185, 195, 240, 253, 307, 371, 375, 378
Harvard University 209, 246–248, 252–253, 257, 346–348, 374
Haydn, Joseph 212, 386
Herrera, Mábel 397, 401
hierarchy 7, 53, 92, 123, 197, 234–236, 259, 294–295, 312, 371, 373, 380, 395
higher music education 192, 319–320
Hilti Foundation 127, 280, 327
hip-hop 3, 71, 82, 169, 190, 260, 304, 374
horizontality 48, 67, 89, 143, 162, 173–174, 176, 195, 204, 285, 294
huayno 79

Iberacademy 124, 127–128, 131, 191, 324, 327–329
identity 64, 66, 72, 80–81, 88, 97, 109, 131, 134–135, 137, 145, 173–174, 182–184, 202, 229, 259, 272, 284, 300, 302, 305, 335, 394
improvisaje 77, 186
improvisation 67, 77–78, 81, 86, 117, 124, 133, 139–143, 195, 257, 272, 284, 286, 291, 370, 373–374
inclusion 5–6, 10, 15, 31, 35, 56, 64–65, 73–74, 79, 87, 93, 96, 123, 152, 157, 167, 174, 180–181, 184, 199, 211–213, 222–223, 225–226, 236, 251, 256, 277–280, 286, 292, 295–296, 300, 309, 311, 319, 321–323, 327, 332–333, 350, 356, 369–370, 391, 400–401, 408
Independencias school 82, 218
Indigenous 278, 295, 308, 336, 385–386
inequality 97, 124, 199, 215–217, 223, 241, 249–251, 259, 261, 309, 312–314, 327, 331–335, 406–407
In Harmony Sistema England 224, 276–277, 282, 310, 319, 357
intensity 13, 74–75, 180, 266–269, 321, 348, 368, 376, 379

Inter-American Development Bank (IDB) 5, 46–47, 52, 94–95, 213, 219, 222, 243, 275–276, 285, 327, 331, 344, 356
interculturality 67–68, 79, 87–88, 93, 145, 173–174, 176
Intermediaries of Civic Culture 99, 100, 115, 204, 368, 370. *See also* Mediadores
International Society for Music Education (ISME) 207, 274, 317–318, 384–385
ISME World Conferences 207
Italy 338, 366

jazz 67, 140–141, 143, 291, 373–374
Jesuit 249, 365
Jeunesses Musicales 272, 327–328
Jiménez, Rocío 51–54, 59, 102, 107–108, 155, 173, 176, 297
justice 6–7, 14–15, 27, 35, 163, 166, 176, 189, 199, 206, 215, 236, 265, 279–280, 292–293, 296–297, 299–300, 311, 313, 315, 318–319, 324, 357–359, 385–387
Justice Oriented Citizen 163, 206, 302

Kashmir 352, 358
Kissin, Evgeny 299
Kolacho 260

laboratories 62, 67–68, 73, 87–88, 116, 126, 147, 202–204, 368
Laboratory of Intercultural Creation 87
ladder of participation 161, 248, 324
La Loma school 218
La Milagrosa school 83
Lanz, Igor 94
Laverde, Andrés Felipe 76–80, 186, 350
leadership 2, 15, 20–21, 28, 31, 33, 35, 39–40, 44, 47, 50–52, 56–68, 71, 73–75, 82, 87–90, 99, 101–103, 106, 109–112, 120, 123–124, 126–127, 129–131, 133–136, 139–143, 147–148, 153, 163–164, 171, 173–174, 176–177, 195, 197–199, 203–204, 218, 226, 228, 232, 234–235, 238, 249, 256, 266–267, 274–276, 279–280, 287–288, 291,

294–295, 297–298, 300–302, 313, 317, 322, 330, 339, 343–344, 346, 348, 355, 360, 362, 366, 374, 378, 391, 394, 396, 398, 401, 405
League of American Orchestras (LAO) 391
Lebrecht, Norman 388–390
Liberdade school, NEOJIBA 304–305, 309, 318, 328–329, 350
library parks 2, 43, 251, 268
Locally-Oriented Citizen 164
Logan, Owen 334
London 14, 292, 315
Los Angeles 273, 276, 317, 324
Los Angeles Philharmonic 276

Madrid 45
Maduro, Nicolás 175, 345, 352
Mahler, Gustav 392
management 15, 21, 25, 32–33, 40, 47–48, 59–60, 62–63, 73–75, 80, 87, 90, 92–93, 96–98, 100–101, 108, 110–111, 114–117, 120, 123, 126, 128, 135, 138, 141, 145–146, 148, 152–153, 158, 160, 163–164, 167, 176–177, 186, 189, 192–193, 197–198, 232, 269, 271, 281, 322, 355, 363, 378, 396
Manual for Coexistence 53
Marcus, Marshall 388–390, 409
MayDay Group 385–386
Mazzocchi, Luigi 19, 176, 326–327, 395
Medellín: Creative City 256
Mediadores 115, 116, 117, 118, 204, 205. See also Intermediaries of Civic Culture
Mehta, Zubin 352–353, 358, 381
Metro Culture 168
Mexico 77, 269, 297, 329–330, 341, 356–357, 402
Miami 46
Middle East 358
Ministry of Civic Culture 4, 58, 62, 73, 156, 167, 174
Montalbán 225
Montero, Gabriela 214, 260, 299, 339
Montevideo 309

Montoya, Pablo 249
Moravia school 65
Mozart, Wolfgang Amadeus 11, 212, 386
municipal government 47, 246, 341
musical initiation 67, 74–75, 115, 118, 136

National Youth Orchestra (UK) 123
Navalny, Alexei 299
Nazi 14, 339
NEOJIBA (Núcleos Estaduais de Orquestras Juvenis e Infantis da Bahia) 271, 304, 309, 318, 328, 350, 362
neoliberalism 7–8, 12, 170, 182, 186, 255–258, 276, 333, 349
Network of Artistic and Cultural Practices 115
Network of Critical and Decolonial Pedagogies in Music and the Arts 288
Network of Visual Arts 165, 201, 202. See also Visual Arts Network
New England Conservatory 16
non-formal 8, 65, 136, 141–142, 203, 371, 374
North America 19, 89, 266, 273, 280, 288, 290, 385, 399
Norway 18
nostalgia 39–40, 46, 105, 110, 267–269, 322

Observatorio del Musicar 288, 380
Ocampo, Juan Guillermo 43–47, 50–51, 89–90, 103, 105–107, 109, 132–133, 141, 146, 279, 345, 348, 354, 387
orchestra 2–3, 5–6, 10, 13, 15, 42, 44–45, 49, 53, 58, 64, 66, 68, 73–75, 78–79, 88, 90, 91, 94–95, 105, 108, 114, 118–119, 123–125, 127–133, 138, 143, 151, 156, 159–160, 162, 165, 176–177, 181–185, 189, 191–199, 204–205, 207, 212, 214, 216, 218, 232, 237–239, 242–243, 256, 265, 268, 270–272, 276–278, 281, 284–287, 290–291, 294–300, 303–304, 320–323, 326–331, 333–335, 339–341, 352–353, 357–358, 365–366, 368–369, 373, 377, 379, 381, 384, 387–392, 394,

402–404, 407–409. *See also* symphony orchestra
Orchkids (Baltimore, USA) 273
Orquestra Geração (OG) 10, 93, 149, 181, 224, 241–242

paideia 161, 421
parents 25, 47, 49, 54, 63, 126, 129, 135, 217–218, 220–221, 223, 225–226, 231, 269, 309, 322
Parra, Aníbal 100, 108, 113, 127, 131, 140, 155, 157, 173–174, 176–179, 186, 199–200, 203, 206
participation 5–6, 10, 16, 21, 28, 32, 48–49, 65, 68, 72–73, 75, 80–81, 94, 96–98, 112, 114, 123, 126, 130, 135, 142–143, 146–147, 152, 157, 159–165, 170–173, 177, 181, 183, 195, 211–212, 222, 243, 248, 259, 261, 300, 302–303, 306, 322–324, 327, 331–333, 346–347, 369, 371, 377, 380, 401, 424
Participatory Citizen 163, 302
pedagogy 5, 7, 11, 49–50, 55–57, 60, 64–66, 68, 72, 74, 81, 94–96, 118–123, 126, 128, 135, 142, 145, 149, 156–157, 177–179, 187, 195, 198, 200–204, 207, 230, 237–240, 256, 266, 271–272, 283, 288–291, 294–296, 301, 303, 326, 337, 344, 347, 354, 362, 367–369, 372, 375, 380–381, 385, 393–394, 396–397, 400–401, 403, 405, 408
pedagogy seminar, pedagogy symposium 50, 119, 396–398, 400, 402, 404–405
Pedregal school 42, 82, 174, 209, 236, 346
Perry, Grayson 301
Personally Responsible Citizen 163, 206, 302
Peru 369
pipeline 128, 191, 193, 207, 384, 407
Plato 9
politics 3, 15, 20, 22, 27, 35, 53, 61, 65, 89, 92, 157–158, 160–161, 163, 166, 168–179, 182, 186, 188–190, 194, 200, 204, 206–207, 212, 215–216, 235, 237, 241, 247–248, 251, 253, 255, 257–258, 260, 268, 272, 276–277, 279–280, 284–285, 295–303, 305–306, 308, 310, 319–320, 323, 333–335, 339–342, 345–347, 349, 352, 357, 366–367, 370, 372, 374–378, 381, 385, 387, 393, 401–402, 407
Pope, the 2, 46, 106
popular music 42, 50, 54, 66–67, 77–78, 81, 86, 89, 115, 131–135, 148, 184, 192, 271, 288, 292, 294, 296, 298
popular music ensemble 42, 50, 86, 143, 270
pórtate bien 157, 169
Portugal 10, 93, 149, 181, 224
post-growth 376, 378
poverty 7, 11–13, 45, 48, 54, 57, 63, 92–93, 95, 150, 157, 168, 177, 182, 212–219, 221, 224–226, 230, 249–250, 252, 279, 287, 295, 297–298, 303, 310–311, 313–314, 323, 327, 330, 332–333, 335–336, 342, 354, 356, 358, 372, 381, 384, 386–387, 407–408
professional, professionalism 8, 13–15, 27, 32, 35, 44–45, 56, 60–62, 64, 66, 91–92, 111, 114, 118–119, 124, 127–129, 132, 136, 138, 140, 145, 147, 149–150, 191–195, 197, 200, 203, 207, 243, 245, 270, 272, 286, 290, 298, 318–321, 323, 328, 357, 368–369, 379, 381, 384–385, 389–390, 392, 395, 400, 408
Programa Social Andrés Chazarreta 271–272, 288, 328–329
project-based learning (PBL) 72, 76, 80, 82, 87, 96, 135–137, 139, 141–142, 146, 173, 283, 290, 393–394
Projeto Guri 66, 272, 328
psychology 48, 51–52, 55, 59, 62, 102, 109, 111–112, 125, 154–155, 177, 238–240, 245, 285, 301, 310, 398–399
psychosocial xiv, 48–49, 52, 59–60, 62, 102–104, 107–108, 111, 113, 125, 271–272, 285–286, 371
Putin, Vladimir 299

Quechua 307

race 73, 93, 236, 295, 300, 305, 324, 384, 386, 388, 393–394, 401

racism 249, 305, 385–386, 390–391, 394–395, 401, 408
Rattle, Simon 16, 403
realism 25, 91, 151, 229, 334, 345, 352–353, 361, 364, 371–374, 380–381, 402
Red de Escuelas de Música de Medellín (REMM) Ensemble 87, 126
redistribution 250, 331, 333–335, 407
reflection 18, 20, 24, 34, 39–40, 47–50, 66–67, 72–73, 82–83, 86, 94, 96–97, 107, 112–113, 124, 145, 157–158, 160, 164–167, 171–172, 187, 200, 202–203, 238–239, 247, 290, 293–294, 301, 303, 306, 316, 319, 323, 326, 337, 339, 345, 350, 360–363, 369, 380, 384, 388, 402, 405–406
reggaetón 184
repertoire 5, 45, 63–64, 67–68, 78–79, 81, 83, 86, 90, 95, 105–106, 109, 112, 119, 123–124, 126, 128, 130–132, 134–135, 184, 192, 200, 267, 272, 289, 291–292, 296, 304, 321, 338, 365–366, 391–392, 399–401
resistance 33, 63, 89, 98, 100–101, 108, 110, 112, 117, 124, 129, 136, 140, 142–143, 145, 179, 199, 234, 245, 282, 292, 314, 322, 340, 374–376, 378
Restrepo, Ana Cecilia 61–63, 102, 251, 255–256, 279
rhetorical excess 353–358
rivalry 52, 54, 57, 91, 114, 150, 184, 237, 284
rock 64, 71, 77, 82, 86
Rosabal-Coto, Guillermo 288, 336–337
Rovero, Gisela Kozak 175, 199, 260, 273, 340
rumba 184, 374

Salazar, Alonso 2, 157, 216, 370, 376
salsa 64, 68, 71, 192, 374, 443
Salvador 304, 365
salvation 13, 16, 63, 134, 158, 177, 186, 243–244, 356, 363, 387, 408
salvationism 97, 219, 336–337, 397
Salzburg 365, 404
samba 184, 365

San Javier school 76–78, 80, 186, 283, 350, 368
Santa Fé school 86, 309
São Paulo 272, 329
Scotland 222, 357
self-critique 20–21, 24, 33, 40, 91, 94, 96, 98, 203, 235, 275, 300, 317, 324, 360, 366, 384, 386, 391, 396–397, 405
sexual abuse, sexual harassment 13, 83, 183, 238, 393–395, 401, 407
Simón Bolívar Youth Orchestra (SBYO) 248, 315, 321–322, 340, 377, 392
Simone, Nina 86, 309
Sistema Aotearoa 94
Sistema Scotland 222, 357
Sistema Toronto 273, 283
Sister Cities Girlchoir 273
slowness 292, 378
social change 6, 16, 19, 21–22, 35, 97, 125, 129, 152, 166, 170, 176, 186, 199, 206, 210, 214, 216, 230, 233, 235–237, 242, 252, 277, 280, 283, 291–292, 296–301, 303, 305, 309, 311–314, 330, 334, 343, 349–350, 352, 358, 367–368, 377, 381, 387, 400
social control 168, 205, 234, 294, 303, 338, 346, 362, 370
social development 3–4, 30, 102, 130, 153, 205, 215, 251, 277, 399–400
Social Development Curriculum 273
Social Impact of Making Music (SIMM) 18, 272, 318, 379
socialism 7, 176, 237, 341
social justice 6–7, 14–15, 27, 35, 163, 166, 176, 189, 206, 215, 236, 265, 280, 292–293, 297, 299–300, 313, 315, 318–319, 324, 357–359, 387
social justice in music education (SJME) 6–7, 9, 27
social mobility 129, 216, 280, 300, 312, 334, 370, 408
social reproduction 170, 233–235, 237, 241, 280, 297, 346
social team 31–34, 39–40, 51, 54–55, 57, 66, 68, 71, 73, 90–92, 99–102, 104, 108–109, 111–117, 120–122, 124–126,

129–130, 134–136, 139, 144–146, 151, 153–160, 163–165, 167–168, 170, 172–173, 176, 178–180, 182, 185–186, 190, 192–194, 196, 198–200, 205, 211, 216, 219–220, 222, 227, 230, 232–234, 237, 246, 267, 281–283, 290, 297, 360, 362, 368, 371–372
social urbanism 2, 4, 39, 210, 234, 249–252, 255–256, 260, 279, 353, 361
socio-affective 57, 62, 102, 108, 110–111, 239
South Africa 166
Spain 2, 5, 28, 134, 194, 240, 244, 268, 288, 307, 336, 353, 370
  Spanish Conquest 5, 134, 240, 244, 336
Sri Lanka 18
staff training 118, 185. *See also* teacher training
student agency 158, 165, 173, 175, 198, 203, 274, 300
student voice 29–31, 53, 65, 72, 96–98, 123, 158–161, 165, 173, 177–178, 202, 321, 359, 393
Sub-Ministry of Art and Culture 167
sumak kawsay 307, 376, 378. *See also buen vivir*
survivorship bias 30, 226, 243, 246, 259
sustainability 276, 364, 375–376, 378–381, 400, 409
Suzuki 5, 120
symphonic bands 42, 50, 124, 132
Symphony for Life 362
symphony orchestra 2, 42, 45, 66, 91, 128, 131–133, 183, 185, 195, 256, 291, 295, 323, 369, 390, 403. *See also* orchestra
Syria 331
System of Early Warnings of Medellín (SATMED) 83

tango 42, 51, 68, 70–71, 134, 184, 365, 443
targeting 218, 309, 311, 314, 327
teacher training 119, 121, 148, 200, 320, 326. *See also* staff training
TED (Technology, Entertainment, Design) 15–16, 223, 325, 385
  TED prize 15, 223

TED talk 16, 325
territory 71–72, 76–77, 80–81, 83, 87, 96–97, 102, 108–109, 111–112, 124, 126, 136, 142, 163, 181, 185–186, 279, 307, 393, 398, 404, 443
Theatre Network 204, 366, 380, 409
Tocar y Luchar (film, 2006) 16, 315
Toronto 273, 283, 317
Torres, Eduardo 271
touring 112, 127–128, 287, 378, 389, 391
Trecek-King, Anthony 401–402
tribalism 182–185, 303

UNESCO 209
United Kingdom 7, 15, 17, 29, 74, 123, 181, 183, 216, 259, 279–280, 295, 310, 315, 320, 333–334, 357, 367–368, 390, 394, 407
United Nations (UN) 213, 327, 331, 340, 356
United States of America 14, 16, 46, 48, 68–70, 87, 89, 126, 163, 214, 253, 273, 276, 326, 332, 368, 385–386, 390, 394, 401, 406–407
urban renewal 2, 4, 33, 209, 244, 246, 248, 253, 255, 260, 350
utopia 18, 46, 55–56, 92, 96, 151, 216, 240, 247, 297, 352–353, 355, 372, 375, 398
Utopian pedagogy 375

values education 158–159, 163–164, 169, 241
Vatican, the 2, 46
Venezuela 3–4, 6–7, 13–14, 19–20, 22–23, 29, 33, 45, 51, 90–95, 104–106, 129, 132, 144, 150, 162, 166, 175, 181, 183, 191, 194, 198–199, 207–208, 210, 214–215, 224, 235, 238, 240, 242, 244, 247–248, 256–257, 260, 270, 272–274, 276, 280–282, 285, 287–288, 297–299, 315–316, 321, 324–328, 330, 334, 339–342, 346, 352–353, 356–358, 366, 368, 381, 384, 386, 392, 402, 404
Venice 338
Vienna 327, 329
  University of Music and Performing Arts 327

Villa Laura school 393–394
Villatina school 218
violence 2, 43, 54, 71, 76, 159, 163–164, 169, 179, 185, 187, 209, 213–216, 219, 230, 237–241, 244, 249–250, 254, 260–261, 279, 287, 330–331, 335–336, 354, 358, 372, 381, 385, 394, 417
Visual Arts Network 165, 200, 201, 202, 203, 204, 206, 380, 409. *See also* Network of Visual Arts

Washington, Lecolion 324–325, 329, 364
West-Eastern Divan Orchestra 352
widening access 93, 313, 321, 365, 368–369
World Bank 289

YOLA National Symposium 266, 273, 324–325, 329
Yoo, Scott 48, 60
youth development 97, 189, 272, 324–325

Zuluaga, Shirley 58–62, 175

About the Team

Alessandra Tosi was the managing editor for this book.

Lucy Barnes performed the proofreading and indexing.

Anna Gatti designed the cover. The cover was produced in InDesign using the Fontin font.

Melissa Purkiss typeset the book in InDesign and produced the paperback and hardback editions. The text font is Tex Gyre Pagella; the heading font is Californian FB.

Luca Baffa produced the EPUB, MOBI, PDF, HTML, and XML editions — the conversion is performed with open source software freely available on our GitHub page (https://github.com/OpenBookPublishers).

This book need not end here...

Share

All our books — including the one you have just read — are free to access online so that students, researchers and members of the public who can't afford a printed edition will have access to the same ideas. This title will be accessed online by hundreds of readers each month across the globe: why not share the link so that someone you know is one of them?

This book and additional content is available at:

https://doi.org/10.11647/OBP.0243

Customise

Personalise your copy of this book or design new books using OBP and third-party material. Take chapters or whole books from our published list and make a special edition, a new anthology or an illuminating coursepack. Each customised edition will be produced as a paperback and a downloadable PDF.

Find out more at:

https://www.openbookpublishers.com/section/59/1

Like Open Book Publishers

Follow @OpenBookPublish

Read more at the Open Book Publishers BLOG

You may also be interested in:

Classical Music
Contemporary Perpsectives and Challenges
Michael Beckerman and Paul Boghossian

https://doi.org/10.11647/OBP.0242

Annunciations
Sacred Music for the Twenty-First Century
George Corbett

https://doi.org/10.11647/OBP.0172

A Musicology of Performance
Theory and Method Based on Bach's Solos for Violin
Dorottya Fabian

https://doi.org/10.11647/OBP.0064

www.ingramcontent.com/pod-product-compliance
Lightning Source LLC
Chambersburg PA
CBHW062025290426
44108CB00025B/2779